ELITES AND THE POLITICS OF ACCOUNTABILITY IN AFRICA

AFRICAN PERSPECTIVES
Kelly Askew and Anne Pitcher
Series Editors

Unsettled History: Making South African Public Pasts,
by Leslie Witz, Gary Minkley, and Ciraj Rassool

Seven Plays of Koffi Kwahulé: In and Out of Africa,
translated by Chantal Bilodeau and Judith G. Miller
edited with Introductions by Judith G. Miller

The Rise of the African Novel:
Politics of Language, Identity, and Ownership,
by Mukoma Wa Ngugi

Black Cultural Life in South Africa:
Reception, Apartheid, and Ethics,
by Lily Saint

Nimrod: Selected Writings,
edited by Frieda Ekotto

Developing States, Shaping Citizenship:
Service Delivery and Political Participation in Zambia
Erin Accampo Hern

The Postcolonial Animal: African Literature and Posthuman Ethics
Evan Maina Mwangi

Gender, Separatist Politics, and Embodied Nationalism in Cameroon
Jacqueline-Bethel Tchouta Mougoué

Textile Ascendancies: Aesthetics, Production, and Trade in Northern Nigeria
edited by Elisha P. Renne and Salihu Maiwada

The Black and White Rainbow: Reconciliation, Opposition,
and Nation-Building in Democratic South Africa
Carolyn E. Holmes

Elites and the Politics of Accountability in Africa
edited by Wale Adebanwi and Rogers Orock

Elites and the Politics of Accountability in Africa

Wale Adebanwi and
Rogers Orock, Editors

University of Michigan Press
Ann Arbor

Copyright © 2021 by Wale Adebanwi and Rogers Orock
All rights reserved

For questions or permissions, please contact um.press.perms@umich.edu

Published in the United States of America by
the University of Michigan Press
Manufactured in the United States of America
Printed on acid-free paper

First published May 2021

A CIP catalog record for this book is available from the British Library.

ISBN 978-0-472-07481-5 (hardcover : alk. paper)
ISBN 978-0-472-05481-7 (paper : alk. paper)
ISBN 978-0-472-12873-0 (ebook)

For the late Sir Olaniwun Ajayi, KJW, who exemplified some of the finest virtues of what it means to be *enlightened*

For Peter Geschiere, an excellent example of kindness, generosity, and mentorship

CONTENTS

Acknowledgments   xi

Introduction:
The Logic of Elite Accountability in Africa   1
Rogers Orock and Wale Adebanwi

PART 1: ELITES AND DEMOCRATIC ACCOUNTABILITY IN STATE AND CIVIL SOCIETY

CHAPTER 1
The Ocular President:
Political Aesthetics of an Upstart Campaign in Sierra Leone   31
Danny Hoffman

CHAPTER 2
The Renewal of Local Elites in Times of "Participation" in Morocco   60
Yasmine Berriane

CHAPTER 3
Elites and Political Representation in Africa:
Members of Parliament in Ghana and Togo   85
Anja Osei

CHAPTER 4
Elite Conflict and Consensus in Ghana's Fourth Republic   112
Alex K. D. Frempong and Emmanuel K. Siaw

CHAPTER 5
Is the African University a Site of Elite Reproduction or Disruption?
What the Senegalese Experience Tells Us   137
Michael C. Lambert

PART 2: ELITES, RACE, AND CLASS

CHAPTER 6
Who Holds the Power?
Elites and Accountability in Democratic South Africa — 159
Roger Southall

CHAPTER 7
Land, Freedom, and Legal Elites:
Rights Debates in South Africa — 188
Timothy Gibbs

CHAPTER 8
Elites and the Practice of (Non)accountability in Mauritius — 218
Ramola Ramtohul and Roukaya Kasenally

PART 3: ELITES, ETHNOREGIONAL COMPETITION, AND (COUNTER)HEGEMONIC POLITICS

CHAPTER 9
Elite Associations in Cameroon:
SWELA, Development, and the Cultural Politics of Redistribution — 249
Rogers Orock

CHAPTER 10
Elite Incorporation in Nigeria: The Case of Ohanaeze Ndi-Igbo — 280
Godwin Onuoha

CHAPTER 11
Beyond Afro-Pessimism:
Party-Monialism, Registers of Accountability, and the
Politics of Corruption — 308
Wale Adebanwi

PART 4: ELITES AND COMPETITIVE LEVERAGE IN VIOLENT CONTEXTS

CHAPTER 12
    Commanders, Classrooms, Cows, and Churches: Accountability and the Construction of a South Sudanese Elite   339
      Naomi Pendle

CHAPTER 13
    Sudanese Elites: Riverain Arabs, Political Dominance, and the Sudanese State   365
      Jennifer Pekkinen

Contributors   387

Index   391

Digital materials related to this title can be found on the Fulcrum platform via the following citable URL: https://doi.org/10.3998/mpub.11628987

ACKNOWLEDGMENTS

The seed for this book was planted when we submitted a panel proposal, "Elites and Political Leadership in Africa: Ethnographic and Theoretical Issues," for the Biannual Conference of the African Studies Association, United Kingdom, held at the University of Sussex in September 2014. Unfortunately, none of the panelists could make it to the conference. Undeterred, we returned to the project three years later and invited more people to contribute to an edited volume in 2017. This time, we refocused the theme of our collaboration around elites and accountability more broadly—rather than "political leadership" specifically. We encouraged our contributors to explore the different means or methods—political, social, cultural, economic, and so on—through which elites are rendered "accountable" by others, and/or how they render themselves "accountable." We recognized that what "accountability" or the process of "accounting" entails can be contextual—as well as potentially conflictual. Therefore, we wanted context-specific analyses that will not only illuminate the challenges and dynamics of the politics of accountability in Africa, but can also provide the bases for comparative analysis.

We thank our contributors for their patience as we went through the long and demanding process of arriving at our common goal. We thank the African Perspectives series editors, Anne Pitcher and Kelly Askew, who supported the project from the point that we made our initial contact with the publishers. Anne was particularly generous with her time as she met with the editors of the volume at conferences in Europe and the North America in the course of the preparation of the manuscript. Our editor at the University of Michigan Press, Ellen Bauerle, was very helpful throughout the process. We are very grateful to her.

The Africa-Oxford Initiative (AfOx) at Oxford gave us the AfOx Travel Grant to enable Rogers spend a few weeks in Oxford in late 2018 so we could finalize the introductory chapter. For this we are grateful to AfOx, the director of AfOx, Kevin Marsh, and the program coordinator, Anne Makena. A research grant from the Oxford School of Area and Global Studies (OSGA),

University of Oxford, helped in paying for some of the images used in the book. Wale is grateful to the school's head of administration and finance, Erin Gordon, the administrative staff of OSGA, and his colleagues at the African Studies Centre for their support. He is also grateful to the Warden of St Antony's College, Roger Goodman, the former head of OSGA, Rachel Murphy, and the former administrator of the African Studies Centre, Marta Mas i Serra. During the period of this project, Wale was the director of the Oxford African Studies Centre. In this context, Marta was the most efficient, effective, hardworking, and self-sacrificing administrator that the director of any unit could have hoped to work with.

Rogers thanks his colleagues at the University of the Witwatersrand in Johannesburg who have supported his work, including colleagues in the Department of Anthropology who have offered generous comments during presentations in the Wits Anthropology Seminar Series in 2017 and 2018. He is particularly grateful to Hylton White, Julia Hornberger, Kelly Gillespie, Nosipho Mngomezulu, George Mahashe, David Copland, Robert Thornton, and Caroline Taylor. Rogers's colleagues at the Wits Institute of Social and Economic Research, including Sarah Nuttall, Achille Mbembe, Keith Breckenridge, and Joshua Walker, were also very supportive during the development of this project.

We will also like to thank Temitope (Wale's wife) and Solange (Rogers's wife) and our children, who bore our long absences from home with such loving calmness and grace.

We have dedicated this volume to two very *good* men—who also happen to be members of different elites. The late Sir Olaniwun Ajayi (Knight of John Wesley), lawyer and politician—to whom Wale dedicates the book—was a member of a politico-cultural elite in Nigeria. Professor Peter Geschiere, an anthropologist and historian—to whom Rogers dedicates the book—is a member of the global academic elite. Both men have, in different ways, not only helped in advancing our individual careers, but also taught us how *privilege* can be deployed toward redeeming ends. We thank them immensely.

Introduction

The Logic of Elite Accountability in Africa

ROGERS OROCK AND WALE ADEBANWI

EXPECTATIONS OF ACCOUNTABILITY

This book is about elites and the politics of accountability in contemporary Africa. We examine the ways by which accountability offers an effective interpretive lens to the social, cultural, and institutional struggles by both the elites and ordinary citizens in Africa in the negotiation of the complexities of social life.

A dominant trend in the return of plural democratic governance in most of the countries in Africa since the late 1980s is an emphasis on accountability. The notion has acquired various interpretations, manifestations, practices, guises, and even disguises. Even in systems that are democratic only in name or semi-democratic, the emphasis on *accounting* for power and governance and its privileges, whether by those in power or by those who are subjects of, or subjected to, power, has become ascendant. The interpretations, manifestations, practices, guises, and disguises of accountability have particular manifestations in the transformations of the post–Cold War era. But they build on or respond to the late colonial and immediate postindependence eras. The multiple forms of authoritarianisms and their unaccountable modes of rule in these earlier periods led in different ways to the collapse of collective aspirations for [multiparty] democracy, inclusivity, and social justice in most African countries. Therefore, this historical backdrop to the immediate postcolonial era, constitutes an important context for the contemporary politics of accountability.

Two recent citizens' campaigns against official corruption and lack of democratic accountability in South Africa and Nigeria mirror the contemporary struggle to challenge the power/ruling elite in the continent and ensure accountability. The first is the 2017 protests in Johannesburg, South Africa, under the banner of "Zuma Must Fall." Citizens bearing the placards reading "#Not my president" and "Zuma not my president" accused the South African president, Jacob Zuma, of presiding over "state capture" and massive corruption. The protesters called for his resignation. Partly as a result of these pressures, Zuma resigned from office in February 2018. Since then, Zuma and the Gupta brothers (three India-born businessmen linked to Zuma), infamously dubbed the "Zuptas," have been embroiled in legal battles at the hands of South Africa's National Prosecuting Authority (see Southall in this volume).

In Nigeria, "#OurMumudondo"[1] protests in Lagos and Abuja were organized in 2016 and 2017 against the ineptitude of President Mohammadu Buhari, who came to power in 2015. The protesters described themselves as "A Coalition of All Angry, Vexed and Frustrated Nigerians." They wanted an end to "business as usual," particularly in the context of President Buhari's lethargic leadership and his long absences in the United Kingdom while attending to his failing health. Twice in 2017, Buhari was in the United Kingdom due to undisclosed illness, first for two months (January–March) and later for three months (May–August).[2]

Both examples illustrate citizens' collective political aspirations and struggles for accountability from political (and occasionally, economic) elites in Africa. These examples do not invert the logic of elite power as pithily articulated by Higley and Burton (2006: 6), who argue that "elites are persons and groups who have the *organized capacity* to make real and continuing political trouble." Nevertheless, the protests show that, in the context of seeking accountability, the masses (although sometimes led by rival or protesting elites) can mobilize an *organizing capacity* to make real, even if occasional, trouble for the ruling elite.

The two examples also point to one aspect of our approach to elite accountability. We believe that an elites-masses dichotomy is not always useful in understanding social processes. Rather we see the elites and the masses (and the many social formations between these poles) as connected. Articulating this connection, we believe, is necessary for understanding the politics of accountability. As evident in this book (see Adebanwi's, Hoffman's, and Orock's chapters), the capture and retention of power and privilege, among other effects, force elites into specific forms of interaction with the masses. Such interactions provoke particular forms of the politics of accountability. In fact, the dichotomy between the two categories is sometimes thrown into crisis by the forms of interaction that are often predicated on elites' responses (real or imagined) to the pressures from below to demonstrate accountability, both formal and informal.

Even though the outcomes of the protests in South Africa and Nigeria are significantly different owing to their different institutional and political cultures, it is important in both contexts to take note of the social and political pressures on the elite to be more accountable. To these collective aspirations for accountability must be added the more particular, personal expectations of social responsiveness (and readiness to redistribute) that less successful kinsmen, friends, colleagues, supporters, and so on have on their more successful relations, friends, patrons, and even acquaintances. Nigeria and South Africa are hardly exceptional in this regard. Rather, across the continent this demand for elite accountability is strong, despite the limited success of campaigns for public accountability in many countries. Given these differences, what does the notion of accountability even mean for political interactions and claims across African settings? Furthermore, considering these variegated expectations for political recognition, responsiveness, and practices of claim-making, how do Africans—both ordinary citizens and elites alike—negotiate these expectations for accountability in different contexts? What would it mean to take this demand for elite accountability seriously, as a category of contemporary social and political analyses in Africa? And to the extent that we do so, to what objects of scholarly enquiry can or should we direct our attention?

We suggest that mobilizing accountability as an analytic lens in relation to current political processes and developments affords an opportunity to re-engage with contemporary interests in Africanist scholarship. These include, but are not limited to, how Africans (re)negotiate political concerns with redistribution, leadership, citizenship, social justice, and even the very definition of the state as a political community that is constantly in the making, subject to interrogations and redefinitions under changing social and political conditions (cf. Ekeh 1975; Chabal 1986, 2009; Bayart 1993; Ihonvbere 1994a; Ake 1996; Olukoshi and Laakso 1996; Mamdani 1996; Werbner 1996, 2004; Chabal and Daloz 1999; Mkandawire 2001; Comaroff and Comaroff 1999; Mbembe 2001; Konings and Nyamnjoh 2003; Englund and Nyamnjoh 2004; Tonda 2005; Dorman, Hammett, and Nugent 2007; Geschiere 2009;

Adebanwi and Obadare 2016). The chapters in this book illustrate that the study of elites through the framework of accountability opens up potentially rich examinations of questions of power and its public deliberation and negotiation in Africa. These include matters relating to debates about political subjectivity and agency, especially as these arise from ongoing struggles around identities and belonging as well as representation and legitimacy. Who speaks to whom? And on whose behalf do they speak?

Contributions to this volume offer careful analyses of how such concerns are embedded in wider forms of cultural, social, and institutional discussions about transparency, collective responsibility, community, and public decision-making processes. These concerns affect prospects for democratic oversight, as well as questions of alienation, exclusivity, privilege, and democratic deficit. It is therefore appropriate that we begin by situating our understanding of the emergence, meaning, and conceptual relevance of elite accountability, each in turn, for the purposes of studying political practices in Africa. We will then specify this contextualization of accountability in relation to our thematic concern with the practices of African elites. This, we think, is a necessary, if neglected, dimension in the return of elites as an object of scholarly engagement in African studies.

STUDYING ELITES IN AFRICA: OLD AND NEW TRAJECTORIES

The study of African elites became a scholarly tradition in the late decolonization era of the 1950s and the 1960s (Adebanwi 2014: 13). This is partly due to the fact that the first crop of African leaders had only recently and formally taken the reins of power from colonial administrators. Driven by the "modernization" thinking of the time, these early studies of elites in Africa considered a number of themes and questions. Initially, a major line of inquiry was the extent to which the cultural realities of status, hierarchies, leadership roles, and so on that might be involved in the analysis of social conflicts and political struggles in Africa could be explained by conventional categories of Western social theories of power and social differentiation, such as, for example, class, race, and education (see, e.g., Miller 1974).

Unsurprisingly, the African elite at this time was simultaneously described as "new," "colonial," "modern," and or "educated" (see, e.g., Tardits 1958; Clignet and Foster 1964, 1966; Foster 1965; Lloyd 1966a, 1966b; Kuper 1965; Grohs 1967; followed later by Ronen 1974; Cole 1975; Cohen 1981; Zartman et al.

1982).³ Crucially, there was an unmistakably paternalistic reading of the African elite. They were assessed, more than in any other sense, in terms of how much they had suitably adapted to and had been socialized in Western cultural norms. Access to and accommodation of Western education through schools established by missionaries and colonial governments were considered the most important "social basis" for the power of the "new elite" (Lloyd 1966a). It was assumed that education gave the new elite access to and control of the "modern" institutions of colonial power and the resources it commandeered (Wallerstein 1965).

Furthermore, the overriding focus of these early studies of African elites appears to be on the nomenclature of the elite groups, whether they fit the definition of what an elite anywhere might be. Accordingly, between the late 1960s and early 1970s a major debate centered on whether African elites were a class or whether classes even existed in early postindependence Africa. Several African leaders of the time insisted that African societies were defined by communalism, thus denying social conflict as a prominent feature of political life. This was framed as a thesis of "classlessness," which scholars such as Robin Cohen (1972: 231–32) maintained was only a quest for "traditional legitimation" by African leaders, a "distortion" of a romanticized, precolonial African past (for a similar critique, see also Kopytoff 1964). Instead, adopting what he termed "foreign-induced forms of stratification," Cohen argued that the longue durée of material exchanges between African and European traders (to which Arabs might also be added) in both precolonial and colonial times, especially in the coastal areas, must be considered an important element in social stratification. This material basis for foreign exchange provided a strong-enough ground for the emergence of indigenous class formations within which ruling groups and intermediary figures of trade assumed major roles (Cohen 1972: 234–35; see also Miller 9174). For this reason, Cohen chose to describe these ruling groups as the "political class" (1972: 248). Eventually, this Marxist emphasis on class as the dominant category of elite studies came under scrutiny and critique (see Graf 1983: 1989–90), calling greater attention to other parameters of social inequality in Africa, such as generation (age), tribalism, or ethnicity (see, e.g., Le Vine 1975). Put simply, African elites in the late colonial and early postcolonial periods were approached, studied, and evaluated mainly as transformational actors, agents of positive social change. By their labor, it was often written, Africa would be brought closer to the teleological promises of Western modernity.

These expectations were suddenly shelved in the face of the manifest deterioration of the conditions of social, political, and cultural life between the late 1980s and the late 1990s. During these years Africa was mainly defined by multilayered economic (debt-induced structural adjustments), political (struggles for democratization), and social (HIV/AIDS pandemic) crises. During this time also, African elites remained prominent in scholarly discussions about the continent. However, in contrast to the past, the focus shifted from the nomenclatural debate on whether African elites are a ruling class or not to a more moral debate. This time, the emphasis was placed on the responsibility of Africa's elite for the continent's failure to successfully "take off" on the path of development and modernization. Indeed, the critical Marxist scholarship of the preceding decades largely represented African elites, following Frantz Fanon, Amilcar Cabral, Samir Amin, and others, as merely constituting a "comprador elite" serving as postcolonial intermediaries for foreign (essentially Western) interests (see Amin 1974, 1976, 1977; Ihonvbere 1994b). As Samba Diop (2012: 223) writes, the tragedy of African postcolonial elites is that "for the most part—they willingly allow themselves to succumb to the temptations and blandishments of neoliberal capitalism."

In this later postcolonial context, then, discussion of these elites was mainly framed along two lines of enquiry. The first concern during this period was to understand how African elite groups were redefining themselves in the wake of the political and economic transformations of that time (e.g., Lentz 1994; Nyamnjoh and Rowlands 1998; Eyoh 1998). A second area of scholarly attention essentially linked these concerns about transformations in elite identities and their roles to the discussions of state failure, rampant corruption, and the desire for good governance (see, e.g., Hope and Chikulo 1999; Tangri and Mwenda 2013; Blundo and Olivier de Sardan 2006; Booth 2009; Adebanwi and Obadare 2011; Adebanwi 2012). Thus in the broader social analyses of the multiple crises hobbling the continent between the late 1980s and the early 2000s, the disillusionment of postcolonial promises and hope has meant that elites have been studied generically as part of Africa's problems rather than as a positive social force (see, e.g., Mbeki 2009; cf. Mkandawire 2015). Inevitably, African elites were increasingly discussed in relation to questions of social and material inequalities (see Bayart 1993: 60–85)—with an assortment of dark metaphors invented to totalize and trivialize this social category (see, e.g., Chabal and Daloz 1999).

More recently, however, there has been a return to an explicit focus on elites as a distinct category of social and political analyses in Africa. Doubtless, attention to their "social basis" remains an important point of departure. But rather than looking to education or income as the main attribute of social differentiation or distinction, scholars have been focusing on a diverse set of considerations, including but not limited to kinship and ethnicity (e.g., Adebanwi 2014; Gibbs 2014; Ignatowski 2005; Orock 2014), race (Salverda 2015), democracy (Osei 2015), nationalist past (MacDonald 2011), and concern for the public good and involvement in philanthropy (Werbner 2004; Orock 2015, among others). For instance, whereas Adebanwi (2014) writes that since the late colonial moment in Nigeria the "cultural agency" of the Yoruba elite under the leadership of Obafemi Awolowo has been grounded in ethnic politics to advance specifically Yoruban, and generally progressive, political and socioeconomic interests, Tijo Salverda (2015) demonstrates that, in the context of Mauritius, whiteness is the important factor around which income and social inequality is constructed. In a departure from the framing of the elites in the work of the latter authors, Swidler and Watkins (2017), in their study of "the ferment of AIDS altruism" in Africa, call attention to elites as "brokers."

In this context, the brokers are "educated or unusually entrepreneurial Africans who mediate between foreign altruists [international NGO actors] and local people who are trying to survive the epidemic and care for those who are ill" (vii). While Watkins and Swidler (2017: 80–82) alert us to the "mutual dependence" that is produced by the unique role of these brokers, the distinctions they identify among the different kinds of elites (cosmopolitan, national, district—and interstitial) are useful for our purposes here in that they point to different levels and foci of accountability. While the district elites are formally the closest to the beneficiaries, as brokers they have complicated processes of accountability to the donors through national and cosmopolitan elites—as well as to the beneficiaries (sometime through interstitial elites). Yet, as Watkins and Swidler (2017) show in their study of rural Malawi, the reality of the process of accountability by the district elites is often not only blurred but also messy. (The complicated role of brokers or "intermediaries" is further explored in Berriane's chapter on local elites in Morocco in this volume.)

Despite what has now emerged as a *tradition* of elite studies in sub-Saharan Africa since the 1960s, Jean-Pascal Daloz (2017: 241) still finds extant literature in this area inadequate, as he concludes recently that "elite perspectives have *never* been given a priority in African studies." Though elite perspectives have not received the same priority as other perspectives, such as ethnicity, corruption/clientelism/neopatrimonialism, party/electoral democracy, to cite a few examples, Daloz appears to ignore (1) the ways in which elite perspectives are imbricated in other perspectives that have received "high priority," such as those mentioned above, and (2) the growing and robust contemporary scholarship in and on African elites that is neither "stigmatizing" nor "hagiographic," to use his words (2017: 241).

Indeed, common to most of the recent studies is their explicit attention to understanding the elites in their own terms, by eschewing a demonization and "Machiavellian suspicion of elites," which, as Richard Werbner (2004: 8) has argued, is unproductive for social science enquiry on power and politics in Africa.[4] However, important also is the need to stress that some of the registers within which the social bases of African elites are defined remain unexplored. This is the case, for instance, with the appeal to law and ethics. Also important to underline is the extent to which the registers that constitute the social bases of African elites might be working collectively or differently to define the ways that African elites represent themselves, their interests, and their social actions in relation to the politics of accountability broadly defined.

ACCOUNTABILITY AS POLITICAL CONCEPT

Accountability defines a specific set of interests, intentions, and responsibilities that bind one set of actors to another. Though its meanings are far from uncontested (see, e.g., Ebrahim and Weisband 2007: 3), accountability is a critical concept in political theory and analysis of political institutions. Less contested is the idea of accountability as a social fact, constituted in the cultural dynamics of both interpersonal and collective relationships and institutions of everyday life. Judith Butler (2005: 10–11) invokes Nietzsche's *On the Genealogy of Morals* to suggest that *we give an account of ourselves* only because we are *interpellated* by a system of justice and punishment. In other words, any notion or practice of accountability is simultaneously constituted by and constitutive of (social) relationships and the moral fabric within which the human community survives. As Butler (2005: 15) writes, "By giving account of myself I am implicated in a relation to the other before whom and to whom I speak." In this sense, accountability is a speech act. Beyond querying Nietzsche's starting point in morality and law as the foundations of accountability, Butler also recognizes that attention to the dynamics of accountability is also shorthand for, an opening into the dynamics of, power that prevails in a given society or organization. This is precisely the argument advanced by Grant and Keohane (2004: 3, cited in Ebrahim and Weisband 2007: 7) who write that "accountability presupposes a relationship between power-wielders and those holding them accountable."

Coinciding with the ascent of neoliberalism since the late 1980s, accountability and its associated concept of transparency have thus become new buzzwords for governments, businesses, and civil society organizations (Sanders and West 2003). As Giorgio Blundo and Jean-Pierre Olivier de Sardan (2006: 6) write in their study, *Everyday Corruption and the State*, "Efficiency, accountability, transparency and the rule of law have become the keywords of this new form of aid conditionality which is inspired in particular by the neoliberal movement." The rise of an "audit society" (Power 1997) has facilitated the triumphant ascent of neoliberal capitalism as the ideological linchpin of the global order, especially following the fall of the Berlin Wall (cf. Fukuyama 1989). This, argue scholars, is manifested in the proliferation of "audit cultures" across different countries and domains of human activity that nonetheless share a fixation with managerial "performance," institutional "efficiency," and workers' "productivity." It is also applied to areas of social life previously considered exempt from or immune to such politics of calculability (Strathern 2000; Merry 2009, 2016). This is especially so in the case of education, especially higher education (Strathern 2000; Hall and Sanders 2015; Shore and Wright 2015a, 2015b; Pritchett 2015; Wright and Shore 2017), as well as in health care and related social service provision (Walker 2002).[5]

Unsurprisingly, accountability, like transparency, has been popularized in large part by the work of international financial and development institutions over the last three decades or so. The World Bank, the International Monetary Fund (IMF), and the United Nations (UN) have all championed a policy-driven focus on accountability that has largely been framed in a depoliticized discourse yet anchored in the politically contested project of new public management (NPM) reform. This depoliticized, neoliberal project is anchored in the view that civil society organizations will put significant pressures on state bureaucratic apparatuses and international development management organizations. This kind of accountability is called "social accountability" (see, e.g., World Bank 2004; Ackerman 2005). It aims at a neoliberally orientated technocratic transformation of state-society relations, particularly in regards to a quest for "good governance" in the provision of public services (Fox and Brown 1998). However, as Jean and John Comaroff (2001: 31) point out, although "neoliberal capitalism, in its millennial moment, portends the death of politics by hiding its own ideological underpinnings in the dictates of economic efficiency, in the fetishism of the free market," this dissimulation does not hide what is only too manifest for those living with accountability's effects.

If accountability appears to be invading new areas of human activity, it is already familiar in the case of organized politics as a specific area. Indeed, particularly in relation to discussions of democratic or multiparty politics, accountability has long been argued as a defining feature. Liberal political imagination in particular envisages accountability as a concrete outcome of representative government, with the promise of control over the conduct of elites or leaders (Dahl and Lindblom 1953; Olsen 2017).

This, it seems, is the fitting "context" from which to begin any discussion of elites and the sociocultural fabric within which the politics of accountability in Africa might be studied. In saying so, we do not just refer to the so-called third wave of political liberalizations in Africa that occurred mostly in the 1990s (cf. Huntington 1991)—or even the more recent "fourth wave" of democratization (McFaul 2002; Drezner 2005; Abushouk 2016). Rather, we also intend attention to the role of elites in the broader experimentations—in the longue dureé—with both modernity and/or liberal democratic as well as authoritarian forms of government (colonial and postcolonial) in Africa. In the colonial period, as Olufemi Taiwo (2010) has argued persuasively, the emergent African elites who embraced missionary Christianity in late nineteenth- and early twentieth-century Africa helped spread Enlightenment ideals in their societies, in order to ensure that Africans benefited from the "distinctive markers" of modernity, that is *subjectivity*, *reason*, and *progress*. These agents of "the introduction and implementation of modernity" or "graduates of the missionary school of modernity" (Taiwo 2010: 6, 12) were, however, subverted, or in Taiwo's word, "preempted," by colonial administrators who worked hard to disable African agency (cf. Masilela 2010).

Several African states briefly experienced multiparty politics in the late decolonization era and the early years of postcolonial self-rule. But many of these states quickly embraced either one-party rule (either as an ideological and practical expression of their nascent nationalist political visions or as the consequence of the struggle for monopoly of power by the ascendant leader) or military rule (as an excuse in saving the state from collapse under the weight of corruption, ethnic fractionalization, economic crisis, etc.). Yet in many of these states where the one-party rule was the norm, elites and non-elites were not only bound together within the structures of the state and the "national" party (or parties) tied to it, but also through formal or informal social (e.g., local, ethnic, professional), cultural (e.g., ceremonial rituals/practices), or religious (e.g., churches, mosques) institutions. As "those who occupy the most influential positions or roles in the important spheres of social life" (Shore 2002: 4), members of the elite at various levels were therefore subject to multiple registers of accountability—in relation to the non-elite and the mass of the people—according to the different rationalities that informed each of these contexts. Even in states where multiparty politics persisted or where military interventions occurred intermittently but with lasting effects, politically active elites remained embedded within the social and cultural logics framing cultural, socioeconomic, and political action in these early postcolonial moments (see, for instance, Ekeh 1975) and beyond.

Following the painful years of economic crisis beginning in the 1980s, including the structural adjustment programs imposed by the World Bank, IMF, and other donors in the 1990s, economic and political liberalizations led to the emergence of actors or social formations that continue to affect and are, in turn, affected by elite politics. Some of these important new or renewed actors and terrains of mobilization include political parties (where these had not been banned), (neo-)Pentecostal churches, mosques and militant Islamist groups, civil society organizations (including local and transnational NGOs), foreign investors/transnational corporations, alliances and networks of gender identities and sexual orientations, emergent corporations (such as those selling mobile telephony), and social media (Facebook, Twitter).

Whether politically active or not, these actors, social formations, and terrains of mobilization have added to the older social registers within and through which elites in contemporary Africa construct themselves culturally, socially, and politically, and through which they might seek to legitimate their political, economic, and social actions as well as lend themselves to scrutiny and critique. Whatever the claim any elite group may have regarding power, prominence, and distinction, to be able to affirm or confirm their leverage in practical terms, they often need to constitute themselves as a *cultural formation*—with substantial investment in, and dependence on, symbolic legitimation. And because they constitute a cultural formation, elites need to *present* and *represent* themselves to other elites, the non-elite, and society at large. Such (re)presentation necessarily involves specific forms of accountability. Since, as Marcus (1983: 10) suggests, elites "represent a way of conceiving power in society and attributing responsibility to persons rather than to impersonal processes," a careful study of the social construction of elite accountability in different societies and states in Africa is critical in understanding these societies and states. As Pritchett (2018) points out, this process of "attributing responsibility" is one that must be *account based*. Thus, accountability must constitute an *account*, that is, narratives that involve "justifications" about why specific agents think that what they do is "the right thing to do (or not) in the circumstances to advance the shared objectives within the accepted norms."[6]

In this volume, we approach *elite accountability* as a specific form of accounting that involves "complex performative representational practices" (Joseph 2014: x) manifesting in social (including economic and political) relationships and narratives; these representational practices or forms of symbolic legitimation and the attendant narratives constitute ways in which those at the apex of any society attempt to reconcile power, influence, opportunities, distinction, leverage, and prominence with personal or collective responsibility. However, we recognize that a "plethora of intervening variables" (Dekmejian 1984: 442) affect the means and ways in which such processes of social accountability occur or are made manifest.

These means and ways are some of the concerns that animate the chapters in this volume. We seek to analyze what a focus on the different constituencies of the elites and the actually existing modes and practices of accountability tells us about African elites.

The contributors explore these concerns empirically (including ethnographically) and/or theoretically from different disciplinary traditions and with different methodologies in ways that engage critically with this key *analytic* frame—elites and accountability. In focusing on these questions in a way that enriches current theorizations of elites and accountability as techniques of constituting and attributing agency in Africa and beyond, the challenge is to offer contextualized explications of sociocultural, economic, and political dynamics, including the "varying nature of those who stand at the apex of society" (Daloz 2010: xii) in different African settings. We hope that such analyses will highlight common and also divergent threads, within and beyond periods of both authoritarianism and democratization in Africa. Through cross-cultural interrogation and comparative insights, the contributors build on existing scholarship on elites in Africa. From different disciplinary perspectives, the contributors go beyond the "moralistic tones" of most immediate postindependence studies of the African elites (Lentz 1994: 150). Similarly, the contributors reflect on, yet eschew, what Patrick Chabal (2008: 605) identifies as "academic snobbishness against the study of African elites" that dismisses them as self-interested political agents with little redeeming value.

Furthermore, the contributors examine accountability from three intersecting angles. First is elites' *(self-)constitutive* conception and elaboration of their ideals, ideas, and practices of accounting, as individuals and/or as corporate group(s) in relation to the non-elite. Second is elites' *legitimating* conception, elaboration, assumption, and contestation of the ideals, ideas, and practices of competing elites—as individuals and/or as corporate groups. Third is the non-elite conception, elaboration of, and contestation regarding the ideals, ideas, and practices of accounting adopted by elites—as individuals and/or corporate groups. These three angles for examining elite accountability singly and jointly provide illuminating nodal points for the examination of social, political, and economic life in Africa.

WHY STUDY ELITE ACCOUNTABILITY IN AFRICA?

For this volume, a stimulating point of departure is how to engage with the *elite in Africa*[7] as a sociopolitical, cultural, and economic category with a specific relationship to the most important resources in society. Related to that is *elite accountability* approached in historically specific narratives and representational forms that can be studied ethnographically. We do not seek to make assumptions, whether negative or positive, about elites. Such assumptions either overstate and dramatize their damaging effects on the social process (Bayart 1993; Bayart, Ellis, and Hibou 1999) or understate their constructive contributions to society (see Werbner 2004: 3), including their conscious work of building developmental states (Mkandawire 2001, 2015). Rather, the chapters offer fresh, dynamic, and multifarious accounts of elites and their practices of accountability and locally plausible self-legitimation (cf. Greenhouse 1996: 12). In the end, these chapters offer illuminating accounts of contemporary African elites in relation to their socially and historically situated outcomes of contingency, composition, negotiation, and compromise.

Much of the existing literature on African elites and the ruling classes, as Mkandawire (2015: 602) states, renders "monochromatic the many colorful and varied characters who have taken the African political stage over the last half century." Therefore, in planning this volume, we encouraged contributors to explore the range of possibilities, diversity, and options evident in the public lives and activities of the elites in Africa. This helps in avoiding the flattening of the inherent complexities and normativities that define the moral universes in which African elites live.

Accordingly, whether under the one-party states of old or the multi-party contexts of contemporary era, how significant agents in Africa attain recognition as elites and render themselves accountable or seek to produce accountability from other social actors or institutions within or beyond the bureaucratic apparatuses of the state is important. It raises ethnographically interesting possibilities and analytically and theoretically challenging questions. Therefore, the following chapters critically explore the diversity of social practices of political auditing that elites and their different constituencies draw upon to elicit different forms of accountability based on different rationalities. By focusing on different sites of accountability within and beyond the state, we expect to reinvigorate debates on alternative sites of agency, representation, and political action in contemporary Africa. To do so effectively, we think, requires taking into account the very fact that elite accountability is not pursued in a vacuum. Rather, it is pursued through the everyday, lived, social and political realities of citizens in their encounters with elites and the bureaucratic power of the state. Grappling with practices of elite accountability therefore requires awareness of the nature of state-society relations in African contexts. This, it seems to us, is an important starting point that bears returning to.

Without returning to the elaborate debate about the state, particularly in Africa (see Lefort 1986; Hyden 1980; O'Brien and Rathbone 1989; Zartman 1995; Rotberg 2003; Bates 2008), it is important to note that in the Afro-pessimist reading of the state, representations were trapped in a "swinging" view of the state as either "feeble" or "total" (Otayek 1989). Between these dynamic poles of excess capacity for violence and predation, on the one hand, and the manifest insufficiencies of most states to deliver public welfare, on the other, the African state was almost cast as a black box. In these efforts, the defining effort became that of explicating the social, economic, legal, and political conditions under which African elites and peoples negotiate over, compromise with, and live through power and domination. In the late 1980s the neoliberal project to streamline the state in Africa gave rise to scholarly efforts to theorize "civil society" as the alternative, countervailing force to a state that might be too strong and to be "resisted" or too weak and to be "supported" by complementary development initiatives beyond those available to the state.[8]

A major development against this current of thinking is *Political Domination in Africa: Reflections on the Limits of Power*, a collection of essays edited by Patrick Chabal (1986). Contributors to *Political Domination in Africa* were among the first to call for attention to the role of accountability in the articulation of this relation between state and civil society in Africa from the standpoints of both historically grounded and anthropologically informed analyses. In other words, the volume set out to take political representation and accountability as the starting point for the study of African politics. As Chabal writes, in the early years of independence in Africa, "Most independent countries, but by no means all, started life with representative political systems in which accountability was secured, as in the West, by elections," although these governments subsequently jettisoned electoral representation for other models of rule (1989: 6). We are persuaded by Chabal's observation that it is by paying attention to practices of accountability, rather than those explicitly enacted in the name of democracy, that we make sense of political life in contemporary Africa (1989: 12). The social complexity of "more developed societies, whether pre-colonial kingdoms or modern countries," he argues, means that accountability is "more diffuse" and "more difficult to apprehend conceptually and in reality" (12). We must look beyond "the constitutional and institutional devices which formally hold rulers to account for their deeds," by also examining "the social fabric of society," including the relation between state and civil society (12).

Although Chabal's oeuvre is not sanguine about the constructive role of elites in Africa, his position on the value of approaching political analysis from the perspective of the politics of accountability is manifestly productive. As Peter Geschiere (1988) has suggested, Chabal's position appears to have been inspired by the call in the late 1970s among French political scientists, including Jean-François Bayart, to eschew an approach to African politics that dwells on authoritarianism and domination. Rather, as "ambiguities of the relation between the state and society became a central issue in debates on state formation in Africa, this group of French Africanists promoted a focus on 'popular modes of political action' around and beyond the institutional context of the states themselves" (Geschiere 1988: 36). Bayart, Comi Toulabor, Achille Mbembe, and others developed this focus, even pioneering a theoretically innovative approach that they framed as "politics from below" (see, e.g., Bayart, Mbembe, and Toulabor 1992). As Geschiere notes, the crucial point in this approach lies in specifying how people in any given African context understand power and politics, as well as the issues in contention and the popular modes of political action adopted in relation to these issues. This can only be done through detailed study of specific contexts.

In the 1990s, Chabal returned to the subject, essentially reiterating the need to recognize that there are different models and visions of accountability animating political life and order in Africa but also cautioning against researching "the 'manifest politics' of political accountability" in a manner that is "ahistorical" and separate from attention to related concepts such as political community and legitimacy (1992: 31, see also 54–68). Subsequently, a controversial book cowritten with a French Africanist, Jean-Pascal Daloz, suggested that the "informalization" of politics in Africa, in contrast to Western settings, has implications for African forms of accountability (Chabal and Daloz 1999: 51). Beyond the national institutional state, Chabal insisted, communities of belonging within the wider society (ethnic groups, rural villages, urban neighborhoods, religious communities, etc.) are, even more than the bureaucratic state, "at the heart of the everyday realities of morality, accountability and representation" (Chabal 2009: 5; see also Chazan et al. 1992: 207).

Strikingly, Chabal's views reflect an earlier argument made by Nigerian sociologist Peter Ekeh (1975). The latter had warned against an uncritical transposition to Africa of notions of the "public" and the "private," especially in relation to concepts such as the public sphere and civil society in the West. According to Ekeh, an important legacy of colonial rule in Africa was the creation of "two publics": a civic public associated with the state and its bureaucracy, on the one hand, and the more primordial public of ethnic or subnational sentiment, on the other (see also Osaghae 1995, 2006; Onuoha 2014; Adebanwi 2017). This distinction is important for some of the chapters in this volume (see, e.g., Orock's and Onuoha's chapters on Cameroon and Nigeria). If the civil public is deemed amoral and can therefore be plundered or disengaged from by social actors (both elites and ordinary people alike) without remorse or a sense of accountability, the primordial public is deemed the repository of moral responsibilities. In West Africa "bad" patrons are not those who are corrupt but those who fail to redistribute their gains to their kin and friends (Olivier de Sardan 1999; Chabal and Daloz 1999: 99–101). Similarly, obedience to traditional rulers (chiefs) remains an important register for the performance of social responsiveness in villages where such figures still exert a meaningful moral authority, such as in the Cameroonian grassfields or in Uganda (Geschiere 2018; Nyamnjoh 2003; see also Karlström 1996, 1999). It is important to note, however, that the rich literature emphasizing the interpenetration of modernity and traditional forms of life and governance in Africa, or what Daloz (2003: 277) describes as the existence of "African elites . . . in a universe which combines both the realms of the 'modern' and the 'traditional'—in congruence with the beliefs of the rest of the population," has been criticized for overlooking the fact that this bifurcation was largely the product of the philosophical anthropology that produced indirect rule in Africa as a political project of domination that ensured the defenestration of the emerging, modern, educated elites in early twentieth-century colonial Africa (Taiwo 2010) in the project of self-rule.[9]

In expanding the analysis of social accountability, anthropologist Tim Kelsall writes that "while holding, or attempting to hold, people to account is a feature of all societies, the process of accounting, as well as the ends of accountability, can take a variety of different forms" (2003: 174). Hence, Kelsall focuses on "breaking the pot," a form of cursing that serves as "ritual of verification" or social audit in the Mount Meru area of northern Tanzania. As he shows, this ritual parallels the institutionally anchored bureaucratic forms of accountability. Positing pot-breaking as one among different kinds of "indigenous accountability" in African societies, Kelsall argues that these get suppressed by an imagination that insists on the universalist vision of "imported," bureaucratic accountability promoted by state and international development institutions. Under these conditions we must contend with "plural accountabilities," given the moral efficacy of indigenous forms and the fixation on "imported" forms (Kelsall 2003: 198; see also Kelsall 2011).

In the same vein, anthropologists Charles Gore and David Pratten explain that understanding the claims of different marginalized groups in southern Nigeria through idioms of community necessitates an attention to "repertoires of accountability" enacted at the interface of state and society (2003: 214). These, they argue, reveal the complexities of statehood, redistribution, and citizenship in Nigeria more generally. More recently, a French anthropologist, Giorgio Blundo, has also directed his attention to the "multiple accountabilities" that characterize the postcolonial state in Africa. Inspired by Kelsall's approach, Blundo (2015) outlines a variety of accountabilities that range from the personal and private (e.g., in patron-client or big man / small boy relations; old-boys solidarities) to corporate or collective forms (local-quarter heads, chiefs, elected and appointed public officials, colleagues at the workplace, etc.) and that all impinge on social actors (Blundo 2015: 67–76).

OVERVIEW OF THE CHAPTERS

The chapters in this book are divided into four parts so as to make those that address similar strands speak to one another. However, the chapters address issues beyond the key themes in each part. What unites them is the different ways in which accountability and the vectors of power and privilege (and the deprivation of both) manifest in different contexts in Africa. We draw on case studies from ten countries in Central, East, North, Southern, and West Africa and the Indian Ocean. The inclusion of the latter is critical, given that the volume engage with *elites in Africa*, including elites of groups not indigenous to Africa—that is, members of diasporas. The chapter on North Africa (Morocco) is particularly important because oftentimes that region of the continent is *surrendered* to the Middle East and therefore obscured from analysis of continental patterns in social dynamics.

Southall's, Gibbs's, and Ramtohul and Kasenally's chapters examine the elites of *nonindigenous* groups in Africa (white South Africans, Indian South Africans, Franco-Mauritians, and Indo-Mauritians) in their often racially inflected relations with one another and with members of groups indigenous to Africa. In both South Africa and Mauritius, "belongingness" is further thrown into crisis, as evident in the politics of "non-belongingness" of the Indian-born South African businessmen, the Guptas, in their controversial relationship with President Jacob Zuma (Southall's chapter) and the complicated belongingness of Afro-Creoles of Mauritius, who, though indigenous to Africa, are not indigenous to the Indian Ocean island (Ramtohul and Kasenally's chapter). In the cases examined by Southall and Ramtohul and Kasenally, while race is latent or manifest in the discourses of accountability, class is often evident in actually existing processes of accessing power and privilege.

The cases from different regions of the continent provide opportunities for cross-country as well as cross-regional comparisons. Most of the chapters reflect the fact that the most dominant elite formation in most regions of the continent is the political elite. The chapters also reflect the dominance of men in elite formations in Africa as well as what Berriane (in this volume) describes as the "long absence" of women and gendered analysis in the literature, even while emphasizing the "growing number [of women] within the body of elected representatives" in Morocco—which "has led to a rise in the publication of studies dealing with this process." In her chapter, Berriane shows that "newly established norms have contributed to providing local associative actors (both men and women) with new 'lines of argumentation,'" thus alerting us to a blind spot in Africanist analysis of elites—that is, gendered and feminist analysis of elite formations. (In her chapter, Osei raises the question—in the context of Ghana and Togo—of whether the "growing number of female parliamentarians" has contributed to more gender equality.)

The contributors also examine how political elites (Hoffman, Berriane,

Osei, Frempong and Siaw, Lambert, Southall, Gibbs, Ramtohul and Roukaya, Onuoha, Adebanwi, Pendle, and Pekkinen)—interact with business elites (Southall, Ramtohul and Roukaya, and Adebanwi), the intellectual/professional elites (Gibbs and Onuoha), cultural elites (Gibbs, Orock, and Onuoha) civil society elites (Berriane), and military elites (Pendle and Pekkinen). In these chapters, the evident forms of accountability are relations not only between the elite and masses and among the political elites, but also across different elite formations.

Since the end of the Cold War and the so-called third and fourth waves of democratization in Africa (Huntington 1991; Lynch and Crawford 2011), democratic accountability has become a critical means of evaluating the role of political elites in the continent. In Part 1, the studies examine the processes of democratic accountability within state and society through concepts of "political aesthetics," "participation," "representation," "conflict and consensus," and "reproduction and disruption." In Part 2, the chapters reflect on how elite accountability is challenged (or leveraged) through ethnoracial politics, even if racialization is challenged by class interests in some cases, as in "state capture" in South Africa (Southall), or where racialization provokes professional activism in the service of liberation, as in the "complex relationships between elite lawyers/land activists and the rural communities they sought to represent" in rural South Africa (Gibbs).

In Part 3, ethnoregional competition for power, influence, and privilege among the elites who mobilize cultural resources to fight for private or collective public good is examined in two Nigerian (Onuoha and Adebanwi) and one Cameroonian (Orock) cases. The struggles for power among the political elites, in relation to the struggle for accountability by the mass of the people in Africa, not infrequently lead to violence, including low-intensity conflicts and outright wars.

Part 4 focuses on colonial and postcolonial settings. Pendle's and Pekkinen's chapters examine how violence can be deployed as a means of either guaranteeing or disregarding accountability among the (South) Sudanese elites.

Although most of the chapters deal with contemporary elite formations, many of the contributors provide a short historical context for contemporary politics (Frempong and Siaw, Lambert, Southall, Ramtohul and Roukaya, Onuoha, and Pekkinen), and others deal with the late colonial and early postcolonial periods (Gibbs and Adebanwi).

In a sense, accountability can be deployed as a cultural currency of power. Perhaps the images of members of the elite on currency notes (King Mohammed VI, Kwame Nkrumah, Ghana's "Big Six," Seewoosagur Ramgoolam, Azikiwe, al-Nimeiry, and Garang) is a salute to a peculiar form of accountability (see figures 2.1 and 10.1). Indeed, there is hardly any stronger, public means of accounting for the flow of power than the distribution of fiscal resources symbolized by currency. The monumentalization of the elite is one way by which we can map the contours of accountability in Africa. While the chapters in this book do not dwell on this, these images provoke a reflection on the *aesthetics of accountability*.

In the end, it is in this nexus of state-society relations that the social, cultural, and moral grammar (cf. Honneth 1995) of accountability is most manifest and meaningful. This nexus underpins the fields of accountabilities in which elites navigate and negotiate their political projects. That is, practices of accountability make manifest the public role of the state and the private intimacies that leaders and ordinary people forge within and around the state. Focusing on the practices of accountability by both elites and ordinary people tells us concrete things about the social, material, and discursive meanings of the state, society, citizenship, participation, inclusion and exclusion, development, and good governance, among other topics.

NOTES

1. "#Our apathy is over."
2. See https://uk.reuters.com/article/uk-nigeria-buhari/nigerias-buhari-returns-home-after-three-month-sick-leave-in-britain-idUKKCN1AZ06O
3. See also a volume (Dülffer and Frey 2011) that reconsiders the elites in the era of decolonization by focusing on elites, leaders, and social groups who changed the course of history.
4. For a useful response to Werbner's critique of the demonization of Africa in the literature, see Chabal 2008.
5. For instance, in the field of education, Pritchett (2015) has developed "four design elements of accountability," that is, delegation, financing, information, and motivation.
6. Pritchett (2018) makes a distinction between "account based" and "accounting based" accountability. The first involves narratives of justification, while the other involves "hard numbers, data."
7. These include not just members of the elite who are Africans, but also non-Africans or non*indigenous* Africans, the diasporas who are members of the elite in the continent—including Indian, Chinese, Syrian, Lebanese, Jewish, American, European, etc. Some have become citizens, while others remain only residents but have significant leverage where they live and work. See Southall's and Gibb's chapters in this volume for the historical consequences of the domination of the European diaspora in South

Africa, and Southall for the dominance of the Guptas under President Zuma. Elizabeth Tonkins (2002) has examined "settler elites"—including Arabs, Lebanese, Indians, and Europeans—in Kenya and Liberia, while Tijo Salverda and Iain Hay (2014) examine the Franco-Mauritian elite in Mauritius. See also Gijsbert Oonk's book *Settled Strangers* (2013), on the Asian business elite in East Africa, and Tijo Salverda's *The Franco-Mauritian Elite* (2015) on the white French elite in Mauritius.

8. This tendency to think in terms of binaries, resistance versus passivity or state versus civil society, is the object of Achille Mbembe's (2001: 103) productive critique of postcolonial political analyses.

9. Taiwo (2014) makes this point more stridently.

REFERENCES

Abushouk, Ahmed Ibrahim. 2016. "The Arab Spring: A Fourth Wave of Democratization?" *Digest of Middle East Studies* 25, no. 1: 52–69.

Ackerman, John C. 2005. "Social Accountability in the Public Sector: A Conceptual Discussion." Social Development Papers: Participation and Civic Engagement Paper no. 82, March. Washington, DC: World Bank.

Adebanwi, Wale. 2012. *Authority Stealing: Anti-corruption, War and Democratic Politics in Post-military Nigeria*. Durham, NC: Carolina Academic Press.

Adebanwi, Wale. 2014. *Yoruba Elites and Ethnic Politics in Nigeria: Obafemi Awolowo and Corporate Agency*. New York: Cambridge University Press.

Adebanwi, Wale, and Ebenezer Obadare. 2011. "When Corruption Fights Back: Democracy and Elite Interests in Nigeria's Anti-corruption War." *Journal of Modern African Studies* 49, no. 2: 185–213.

Adebanwi, Wale, and Ebenezer Obadare. 2016. "Governance and the Unending Search for Leadership in African Politics." In Ebenezer Obadare and Wale Adebanwi, eds., *Governance and the Crisis of Rule in Contemporary Africa: Leadership in Transformation*, 1–22. New York: Palgrave.

Ake, Claude. 1996. *Democracy and Development in Africa*. Washington, DC: Brookings Institution.

Amin, Samir. 1974. "Accumulation and Development: A Theoretical Model." *Review of African Political Economy* 1, no. 1: 9–26.

Amin, Samir. 1976. *Unequal Development: An Essay on the Social Formations of Peripheral Capitalism*. Translated by Brian Pearce. Sussex, England: Harvester Press.

Amin, Samir. 1977. *Imperialism and Unequal Development*. New York: Monthly Review Press.

Bates, Robert H. 2008. *When Things Fell Apart: State Failure in Late-Century Africa*. Cambridge: Cambridge University Press.

Bayart, Jean-François. 1993. *The State in Africa: The Politics of the Belly*. London: James Currey.

Bayart, Jean-François, Stephen Ellis, and Béatrice Hibou. 1999. *The Criminalization of the State in Africa*. Oxford: James Currey.

Bayart, Jean-François, Achille Mbembe, and Comi Toulabor. 1992. *Le politique par le bas en Afrique noire: Contributions à une problématique de la démocratie*. Paris: Karthala.

Blundo, Giorgio. 2015. "Le roi n'est pas un parent: Les multiples redevabilités au sein de l'état postcolonial en Afrique." In Pascale Haag and Cyril Lemieux, eds., *Faire des sciences sociales: Critiquer*, 59–85. Paris: Éditions de l'École des hautes études en sciences sociales.

Blundo, Giorgio, and Jean Pierre Olivier de Sardan, with Bako N. Arifako and Tidjani M. Alou. 2006. *Everyday Corruption and the State: Citizens and Public Officials in Africa*. Translated by Susan Cox. Cape Town: David Philip; New York: Zed Books.

Booth, David. 2009. "Elites, Governance and the Public Interest in Africa: Working with the Grain?" Africa Power and Politics Discussion Paper no. 6. London: Overseas Development Institute.

Butler, Judith. 2005. *Giving An Account of Oneself*. New York: Fordham University Press.

Chabal, Patrick, ed. 1986. *Political Domination in Africa: Reflections on the Limits of Power*. Cambridge: Cambridge University Press.

Chabal, Patrick. 2008. "On Reason and Afro-Pessimism" (review article). *Africa* 78, no. 4: 603–10.

Chabal, Patrick. 2009. *Africa: The Politics of Suffering and Smiling*. London: Zed Books.

Chabal, Patrick, and Jean-Pascal Daloz. 1999. *Africa Works: Disorder as Political Instrument*. London: James Currey.

Chazan, Naomi, Robert Mortimer, John Ravenhill, and Donald Rothchild. 1992. *Politics and Society in Contemporary Africa*. 2nd ed. Boulder, CO: Lynne Rienner.

Clignet, Remi P., and Philip Foster. 1964. "Potential Elites in Ghana and the Ivory Coast: A Preliminary Comparison." *American Journal of Sociology* 70, no. 3: 349–62.

Clignet, Remi P., and Philip Foster. 1966. *The Fortunate Few: A Study of Secondary Schools and Students in the Ivory Coast*. Evanston, IL: Northwestern University Press.

Cohen, Abner. 1981. *The Politics of Elite Culture: Explorations in the Dramaturgy of Power in a Modern Africa Society*. Berkeley: University of California Press.

Cohen, Robin. 1972. "Class in Africa: Analytical Problems and Perspectives." *Socialist Register* 9: 231–55.

Cole, Patrick. 1975. *Modern and Traditional Elites in the Politics of Lagos*. Cambridge: Cambridge University Press.

Comaroff, Jean, and John L. Comaroff, eds. 1999. *Civil Society and the Political Imagination in Africa*. Chicago: University of Chicago Press.

Comaroff, Jean, and John L. Comaroff. 2001. "Millennial Capitalism: First Thoughts on a Second Coming." In Jean Comaroff and John L. Comaroff, eds., *Millennial Capitalism and the Culture of Neoliberalism*, 1–56. Durham, NC: Duke University Press.

Dahl, Robert A., and Charles E. Lindblom. 1953. *Politics, Economics, and Welfare*. Chicago: University of Chicago Press.

Daloz, Jean-Pascal. 2003. "'Big-Men' in Sub-Saharan Africa: How Elites Accumulate Positions and Resources." *Comparative Sociology* 2: 271–85.

Daloz, Jean-Pascal. 2010. *The Sociology of Elite Distinction: From Theoretical to Comparative Perspectives*. New York: Palgrave Macmillan.

Daloz, Jean-Pascal. 2017. "Political Elites in Sub-Saharan Africa." In Heinrich Best and John Higley, eds., *The Palgrave Handbook of Political Elites*, 241–53. New York: Palgrave Macmillan.

Dekmejian, Richard H. 1984. "Review of *Political Elites in Arab North Africa* by William Zartman." *International Journal of Middle East Studies* 16, no. 3: 442–44.

Diop, Samba. 2012. "African Elites and Their Post-colonial Legacy: Cultural, Political and Economic Discontent—by Way of Literature." *Africa Development* 37, no. 4: 221–35.

Dorman, Sara, Daniel Hammett, and Paul Nugent. 2007. *Making Nations, Creating Strangers: States and Citizenship in Africa*. Leiden: Brill.

Drezner, Daniel W. 2005. "The Fourth Wave of Democratization?" *Foreign Policy*, March 24. https://foreignpolicy.com/2005/03/24/the-fourth-wave-of-democratization/

Dülffer, Jost, and Marc Frey. 2011. "Introduction." In Jost Dülffer and Marc Frey, eds., *Elites and Decolonization in the Twentieth Century*, 1–10. New York: Palgrave Macmillan.

Ebrahim, Alnoor and Edward Weisband, eds., 2007. *Global Accountabilities: Participation, Pluralism, and Public Ethics*. Cambridge: Cambridge University Press.

Eckert, Andreas. 2011. "Julius Nyerere, Tanzanian Elites, and the Project of African Nationalism." In Jost Dülffer and Marc Frey, eds., *Elites and Decolonization in the Twentieth Century*, 216–40. New York: Palgrave Macmillan.

Ekeh, Peter P. 1975. "Colonialism and the Two Publics in Africa: A Theoretical Statement." *Comparative Studies in Society and History* 17, no. 1: 91–112.

Englund, Harri, and Francis B. Nyamnjoh, eds. 2004. *Rights and the Politics of Recognition in Africa*. London: Zed Books.

Eyoh, Dickson. 1998. "Through the Prism of a Local Tragedy: Political Liberalisation, Regionalism and Elite Struggles for Power in Cameroon." *Africa* 68: 338–59.

Ferguson, James. 2007. *Global Shadows: Africa in the Neo-liberal World Order*. Durham, NC: Duke University Press.

Foster, Philip. 1965. *Education and Social Change in Ghana*. Chicago: University of Chicago Press.

Fox, Jonathan A., and David L. Brown, eds. 1998. *The Struggle for Accountability: The World Bank, NGOs, and Grassroots Movements*. Cambridge, MA: MIT Press.

Fukuyama, Francis. 1989. "The End of History?" *National Interest* 16 (Summer): 3–18.

Geschiere, Peter. 1988. "Sorcery and the State: Popular Modes of Action among the Maka of Southeast Cameroon." *Critique of Anthropology* 8, no. 1: 35–63.

Geschiere, Peter. 2009. *The Politics of Belonging: Autochthony, Citizenship and Exclusion in Africa and Europe*. Chicago: University of Chicago Press.

Geschiere, Peter. 2018. "African Chiefs and the Post–Cold War Moment: Millennial Capitalism and the Struggle over Moral Authority." In Jean Comaroff and John L. Comaroff, eds., *The Politics of Custom: Chiefship, Capital, and the State in Contemporary Africa*, 49–79. Chicago: University of Chicago Press.

Gibbs, Timothy. 2014. *Mandela's Kinsmen: Nationalist Elites and Apartheid's First Bantustan*. Oxford: James Currey.

Gore, Charles and David Pratten. 2003. "The Politics of Plunder: The Rhetorics of Order and Disorder in Southern Nigeria." *African Affairs* 102, no. 407: 211–40.

Graf, William D. 1983. "African Elite Theories and Nigerian Elite Consolidation: A Political Economy Analysis." In Yolamu R. Barongo, ed., *Political Science in Africa: A Critical Review*, 189–209. London: Zed Press.

Greenhouse, Carol J. 1996. *A Moment's Notice: Time Politics across Cultures*. Ithaca, NY: Cornell University Press.

Grohs, Gerhard. 1967. *Stufen afrikanischer Emanzipation: Studie zur Selbstverständnis westafrikanischer Eliten*. Stuttgart: Kohlhammer.

Hall, Elizabeth T., and Todd Sanders. 2015. "Accountability and the Academy: Producing Knowledge about the Human Dimensions of Climate Change." *Journal of the Royal Anthropological Institute*, n.s. 21: 438–61.

Higley, John, and Michael Burton. 2006. *Elite Foundations of Liberal Democracy*. Lanham, MD: Rowman & Littlefield.

Honneth, Axel. 1995. *The Struggle for Recognition: The Moral Grammar of Social Conflicts*. Cambridge, MA: MIT Press.

Hope, Kempe R., and Bornwell C. Chikulo, eds. 1999. *Corruption and Development in Africa: Lessons from Country Case Studies*. London: Palgrave Macmillan.

Huntington, Samuel P. 1991. *The Third Wave: Democratization in the Late Twentieth Century*. Norman: University of Oklahoma Press.

Huntington, Samuel P. (1968) 2006. *Political Order in Changing Societies*. New Haven: Yale University Press.

Hyden, Goran. 1980. *Beyond Ujamaa in Tanzania: Underdevelopment and an Uncaptured Peasantry*. Berkeley: University of California. Press,

Ignatowski, Clare A. 2005. "Making Ethnic Elites: Ritual Poetics in a Cameroonian Lycée." *Africa* 74, no. 3: 411–32.

Ihonvbere, Julius O. 1994a. "The 'Irrelevant' State, Ethnicity, and the Quest for Nationhood in Africa." *Ethnic and Racial Studies* 17, no. 1: 42–60.

Ihonvbere, Julius O. 1994b. *Nigeria: The Politics of Adjustment and Democracy*. New Brunswick, NJ: Transaction Publishers.

Joseph, Miranda. 2014. *Debt to Society: Accounting for Life under Capitalism*. Minneapolis: University of Minnesota Press.

Karlström, Mikael. 1996. "Imagining Democracy: Political Culture and Democratisation in Buganda." *Africa* 66, no. 4: 485–506.

Karlström, Mikael. 1999. "Civil Society and Its Presuppositions: Lessons from Uganda." In John L. Comaroff and Jean Comaroff, eds., *Civil Society and the Political Imagination in Africa: Critical Perspectives*, 104–23. Chicago: University of Chicago Press.

Kelsall, Tim. 2003. "Rituals of Verification: Indigenous and Imported Accountability in Northern Tanzania." *Africa* 73, no. 2: 174–201.

Kelsall, Tim. 2011. "Going with the Grain in African Development?" *Development Policy Review* 29, no. 1: 223–51.

Konings, Piet, and Francis B. Nyamnjoh. 2003. *Negotiating an Anglophone Identity: A Study of the Politics of Recognition and Representation in Cameroon*. Leiden: Brill.

Kopytoff, Igor. 1964. "Socialism and Traditional African Societies." In William H. Friedland and Carl G. Rosberg Jr., eds., *African Socialism*, 53–62. Stanford, CA: Stanford University Press.

Kuper, Leo. 1965. *An African Bourgeoisie: Race, Class and Politics in South Africa*. New Haven: Yale University Press.

Lefort, Claude. 1986. *The Political Forms of Modern Society*. Cambridge, MA: MIT Press.

Lentz, Carola. 1994. "Home, Death and Leadership: Discourses of an Educated Elite from Northwestern Ghana." *Social Anthropology* 2: 149–69.

Levine, Donald N. 1965. *Wax and Gold: Tradition and Innovation in Ethiopian Culture*. Chicago: University of Chicago Press.

Le Vine, Victor T. 1975. "Leadership Transition in Black Africa: Elite Generations and Political Succession." In *Munger Africana Library Notes*, no. 30, May. Pasadena: California Institute of Technology.

Lloyd, P. C., ed. 1966a. *The New Elites of Tropical Africa*. London: Oxford University Press.

Lloyd, P. C. 1966b. "Class Consciousness among the Yoruba." In P. C. Lloyd, ed., *The New Elites of Tropical Africa*, 328–41. London: Oxford University Press.

Lumumba-Kasongo, Tukumbi, ed. 2005. *Liberal Democracy and Its Critics in Africa: Political Dysfunctions and the Struggle for Social Progress*. Dakar: CODESRIA.

Lynch, Gabrielle, and Gordon Crawford. 2011. "Democratization in Africa 1990–2010: An Assessment." *Democratization* 18, no. 2: 275–310.

MacDonald, Mairi S. 2011. "A 'Frontal Attack on Irrational Elements': Sekou Toure and the Management of Elites in Guinea." In Jost Dülffer and Marc Frey, eds., *Elites and Decolonization in the Twentieth Century*. New York: Palgrave Macmillan.

Mamdani, Mahmood. 1996. *Citizen and Subject: Contemporary Africa and the Legacy of Late Colonialism*. Princeton, NJ: Princeton University Press.

Marcus, George. 983. "'Elite' as a Concept, Theory and Research Tradition." In George Marcus, ed., *Elites: Ethnographic Issues*, 7–27. Albuquerque, NM: University of New Mexico Press.

Masilela, Ntongela. 2010. "African Intellectual and Literary Responses to Colonial Modernity in South Africa." In Peter Limb, Norman Etherington, and Peter Lidgley, eds., *Grappling with the Beast: Indigenous Southern African Responses to Colonialism, 1840–1930*, 245–75. Leiden: Brill.

Mbeki, Moeletsi. 2009. *Architects of Poverty: Why African Capitalism Needs Changing*. Johannesburg: Picador Africa.

Mbembe, Achille. 2001. *On the Postcolony*. Berkeley: University of California Press.

McFaul, Michael. 2002. "The Fourth Wave of Democracy and Dictatorship: Noncooperative Transitions in the Postcommunist World." *World Politics* 54, no. 2: 212–44.

Merry, Sally Engle. 2009. "Measuring the World: Indicators, Human Rights, and Global Governance." *Current Anthropology* 103: 239–43.

Merry, Sally Engle. 2016. *The Seductions of Quantification: Measuring Human Rights, Gender Violence, and Sex Trafficking*. Chicago: University of Chicago Press.

Miller, Robert A. 1974. "Elite Formation in Africa: Class, Culture, and Coherence." *Journal of Modern African Studies* 12, no. 4: 521–42.

Mkandawire, Thandika. 2001. "Thinking about Developmental States in Africa." *Cambridge Journal of Economics* 25, no. 3: 289–314.

Mkandawire, Thandika. 2015. "Neopatrimonialism and the Political Economy of Economic Performance in Africa: Critical Reflections." *World Politics* 67, no. 3: 563–612.

Nyamnjoh, Francis B. 2001. "Delusions of Development and the Enrichment of Witchcraft Discourses in Cameroon." In Henrietta L. Moore and Todd Sanders, eds., *Magical Interpretations, Material Realities: Modernity, Witchcraft and the Occult in Postcolonial Africa*, 28–49. London: Routledge.

Nyamnjoh, Francis B., and Michael Rowlands. 1998. "Elite Associations and the Politics of Belonging in Cameroon." *Africa* 68, no. 3: 320–37.

O'Brien, Donald C., and Richard Rathbone. 1989. "Introduction." In Donald B. Cruise O'Brien, Richard Rathbone, and John Dunn, eds., *Contemporary West African States*, 1–12. Cambridge: Cambridge University Press.

Olivier de Sardan, Jean-Pierre. 1999. "A Moral Economy of Corruption in Africa." *Journal of Modern African Studies*, 37, no. 1: 25–52.

Olsen, John P. 2017. *Democratic Accountability, Political Order, and Change: Exploring Accountability Processes in an Era of European Transformation*. Oxford: Oxford University Press.

Olukoshi, Adebayo O. and Laakso, Liisa, eds. 1996. *Challenges to the nation-state in Africa*. Uppsala: Nordiska Afrikainstitutet, in cooperation with the Institute of Development Studies, University of Helsinki.

Onuoha, Browne. 2014. "Publishing Postcolonial Africa: Nigeria and Ekeh's Two Publics a Generation After." *Social Dynamics* 40, no. 2: 322–37.

Oonk, Gijsbert. 2013. *Settled Strangers: Asian Business Elites in East Africa, 1980–2000*. New Delhi: Sage.

Orock, Rogers T. E. 2014. "SWELA, ethnicity, and democracy in Cameroon's patrimonial state: An anthropological critique." *Critique of Anthropology* 34, no. 2: 204–33.

Orock, Rogers T. E. 2015. "Elites, Culture, and Power: The Moral Politics of "Development" in Cameroon." *Anthropological Quarterly* 88, no 2: 533–68.

Osaghae, Eghosa. 1995. "Amoral Politics and Democratic Instability in Africa: A Theoretical Exploration." *Nordic Journal of African Studies* 4, no. 1: 62–78.

Osaghae, Eghosa. 2006. "Colonialism and Civil Society in Africa: The Perspective of Ekeh's Two Publics." *Voluntas* 17, no. 3: 233–45.

Osei, Anja. 2015. "Elites and Democracy in Ghana." *African Affairs* 114, no. 457: 529–54.

Otayek, René. 1989. "Burkina Faso: Between Feeble State and Total State, the Swing Continues." In Donald B. Cruise O'Brien, Richard Rathbone, and John Dunn, eds., *Contemporary West African States*, 13–30. Cambridge: Cambridge University Press.

Piot, Charles. 2010. *Nostalgia for the Future: West Africa after the Cold War*. Chicago: University of Chicago Press.
Porter, Arthur T. 1963. *Creoledom: A Study in the Development of Freetown Society*. London: Oxford University Press.
Power, Michael. 1997. *The Audit Society: Rituals of Verification*. Oxford: Oxford University Press.
Pritchett, Lant. 2015. "Creating Education Systems Coherent for Learning Outcomes: Making the Transition from Schooling to Learning." Working paper, Research on Improving Systems of Education (RISE). Cambridge, MA: Harvard Kennedy School and Center for International Development.
Pritchett, Lant. 2018. "Account-Based Accountability and Aid Effectiveness." *Building State Capacity Blog*. Center for International Development, Harvard University. https://buildingstatecapability.com/2018/06/28/account-based-accountability-and-aid-effectiveness/
Ronen, Dov. 1974. "The Colonial Elite in Dahomey." *African Studies Review* 17, no. 1: 55–76.
Rotberg, Robert I., ed. 2003. *State Failure and State Weakness in a Time of Terror*. Washington, DC: Brookings Institution Press.
Salverda, Tijo. 2015. *The Franco-Mauritian Elite: Power and Anxiety in the Face of Change*. New York: Berghahn Books.
Salverda, Tijo, and Iain Hay. 2014. "Change, Anxiety and Exclusion in the Post-colonial Reconfiguration of Franco-Mauritian Elite Geographies." *Geographical Journal* 180, no. 3: 236–45.
Sanders, Todd and West, Harry G. 2003. "Power Revealed and Concealed in the New World Order." In Harry G. West and Todd Sanders, eds., *Transparency and Conspiracy: Ethnographies of Suspicion in the New World Order*, 1–37. Durham: Duke University Press.
Shore, Cris. 2002. "Introduction: Towards an Anthropology of Elites." In Cris Shore and Stephen Nugent, eds., *Elite Cultures: Anthropological Perspectives*, 1–21. New York: Routledge.
Shore, Cris, and Susan Wright. 2015a. "Audit Culture Revisited: Rankings, Ratings, and the Reassembling of Society." *Current Anthropology* 56, no. 3: 421–44.
Shore, Cris, and Susan Wright. 2015b. "Governing by Numbers: Audit Culture, Rankings and the New World order." *Social Anthropology* 23, no. 1: 22–28.
Smythe, Hugh H., and Mabel M. Smythe. 1960. *The New Nigerian Elite*. Stanford, CA: Stanford University Press.
Strathern, Marilyn, ed. 2000. *Audit Cultures: Anthropological Studies in Accountability, Ethics and the Academy*. London: Routledge.
Swidler, Annand, Watkins, Susan C. 2017. *A Fraught Embrace: The Romance and Reality of AIDS Altruism in Africa*. Princeton: Princeton University Press.
Taiwo, Olufemi. 2010. *How Colonialism Preempted Modernity in Africa*. Bloomington: Indiana University Press.
Taiwo, Olufemi. 2014. *Africa Must Be Modern: A Manifesto*. Bloomington: Indiana University Press.

Tangri, Roger, and Andrew M. Mwenda. 2013. *The Politics of Elite Corruption in Africa: Uganda in Comparative Perspective*. London: Routledge.

Tardits, Claude. 1958. *Porto-Novo: Les nouvelles générations africaines entre leurs traditions et l'occident*. Paris: Mouton & Cie; La Haye.

Tonda, Joseph. 2005. *Le souverain moderne: Le corps du pouvoir en Afrique centrale (Congo, Gabon)*. Paris: Karthala.

Tonkin, Elizabeth. 2002. "Settlers and Their Elites in Kenya and Liberia." In Cris Chore and Stephen Nugent, eds., *Elites Cultures: Anthropological Perspectives*, 129–44. New York: Routledge.

Walker, Peter. 2002. "Understanding Accountability: Theoretical Models and Their Implications for Social Service Organizations." *Social Policy and Administration* 36, no. 1: 62–75.

Wallerstein, Immanuel. 1965. "Elites in French-Speaking West Africa: The Social Basis of Ideas." *Journal of Modern African Studies* 3, no. 1: 1–33.

Werbner, Richard P., ed. 1996. *Postcolonial Subjectivities in Africa*. London: Zed Books.

Werbner, Richard P. 2004. *Reasonable Radicals and Citizenship in Botswana: The Public Anthropology of Kalanga Elites*. Bloomington: Indiana University Press.

World Bank. 2004. "State-Society Synergy for Accountability: Lessons for the World Bank." World Bank Working Paper no. 30. Washington, DC: World Bank.

Wright, Susan, and Cris Shore, eds. 2017. *Death of the Public University? Uncertain Futures for Higher Education in the Knowledge Economy*. New York: Berghahn Books.

Zartman, I. William, ed. 1995. *Collapsed States: The Disintegration and Restoration of Legitimate Authority*. Boulder, CO: Lynne Rienner.

Zartman, I. William, Mark A. Tessler, John P. Entelis, Russell A. Stone, Raymond A. Hinnebusch, and Shahrough Akhavi. 1982. *Political Elites in Arab North Africa: Morocco, Algeria, Tunisia, Libya, and Egypt*. New York: Longman.

PART 1

Elites and Democratic Accountability
in State and Civil Society

CHAPTER 1

The Ocular President

Political Aesthetics of an Upstart Campaign in Sierra Leone

DANNY HOFFMAN

Mohammed Tarawalley Jr. (MT) is running for president. His is an upstart campaign. Four months before the election, the Popular Patriotic Reformation Movement, or PPRM, has yet to officially register as a national political organization in Sierra Leone. The PPRM has an eight-page charter but is still looking for appropriate clip art for its party crest. There is a PPRM media team, but the campaign suffers a temporary setback when MT's phone and computer are stolen, and with them the party's entire database of contacts.

But MT is not worried. Funds are coming in. Support is building. By the time balloting begins in early March 2018, MT believes, the PPRM will have emerged as a strong alternative to the entrenched parties and personalities that have dominated Sierra Leone's politics for decades. It will be the champion of urban youth and the rural poor. "The Movement," according to its charter, "shall focus on post-independence generation of selfless and corrupt-free patriotic younger people, with radical and nationalistic mindset, to take up leadership." MT plans for the PPRM to be a "third force" that will "remove from our body politics the corrupt establishments." As voting day gets closer, he and the other founding members are plotting a populist mobilization against the traditional Freetown elite.

In this chapter I trace the aesthetics of MT's nascent political career. I do so primarily by drawing on a series of extended conversations with MT as he shaped his plans to enter the difficult world of national politics in

Fig. 1.1: Mohammed Tarawalley Jr. (MT). Photo by John D. Hoffman.

Sierra Leone. A forty-five-year-old veteran of the wars in both Sierra Leone and Liberia, largely unemployed, and living a precarious existence moving between households across both countries, MT followed an unusual route to national candidacy. Still, he was a legitimate pretender to political office, even if an unconventional one. As such he was by necessity a thoughtful student and commentator on a world in which he was both insider and outsider. Approaching the dynamics of elite accommodation and accountability from an oblique angle required considerable critical reflection on his part.[1]

Given his position, MT was forced to both master and subvert the complex operations of political culture in this region. The "vulgar aesthetics" that Achille Mbembe (1992) once identified as characteristic of postcolonial governance have grown more nuanced in the decades since the end of the

Cold War.[2] Many of the basic institutions of governance in African states have changed dramatically in recent years, rewiring the connections between elites as well as the nature of relations between elites and their publics. New communications technologies have proliferated across the continent, vastly expanding the field of political signs. The spectacular performances of state power that enabled neopatrimonial regimes in the first decades of independence can now be harder to orchestrate and more subject to internal and external critique. And the expectations that many Sierra Leoneans have for their national politics and for their political leaders are changing.

There are, of course, any number of entry points into this complex aesthetic economy. MT's campaign, like those of other candidates contesting for power at all levels, illustrates the ever-growing importance of social media, of transnational and diasporic networks, of nongovernmental organizations in the orchestration of power, and the expanding footprint of both new and old players in resource extraction economies across the continent. Each of these factors and many more have shifted the nature and conduct of political campaigns, and by extension the nature and conduct of elite practice.

Here, however, I step back and focus more broadly on what Crispin Sartwell has called "political aesthetics" (2010). Every political form, Sartwell argues, has an aesthetic. Or, more accurately, every political form *is* an aesthetic: "A politics," he writes, "is an aesthetic environment, whatever else it may be" (2010: 2). The strategies through which elite actors are made legitimate in the political field and held accountable by their publics are therefore aesthetic practices. They are often visual practices, and always performative ones. Taken together and understood in context, these political aesthetics throw into sharp relief the workings of power in the contemporary African postcolony. But they also underscore how tenuous and experimental those strategies can be.

As I trace here, MT's political aesthetic was one of distinctly postmodern bricolage. Though unique in the field of candidates, his peculiarities were instructive and, I would suggest, predictive. Sierra Leone's political class has long drawn on symbols from across cultural fields to legitimize themselves. MT did so as well, but made his claim to legitimacy as a presidential candidate through fabulations that do not necessarily cohere into a comprehensive political vision and were often unmoored from traditional political practice. They were "ocular" performances, to use Filip de Boeck's (2011) term for the fantastical visions of a future in which no one entirely believes, but in which the mastery of the performance is itself a legitimizing claim. In MT's case,

Fig. 1.2: Sierra Leone People's Party presidential candidate Julius Maada Bio campaigns during his party's final rally day in Bo, Sierra Leone's second largest city. Photo by Danny Hoffman.

that performance was one of a commitment to subvert, even destroy, the state apparatus that he hoped eventually to sit atop.

Therein lay MT's challenge to the historical practices of elite legitimacy and accountability. Rather than rendering him unacceptable or unappealing as a candidate, and therefore as a claimant on elite power, his magical realism seemed to be what his constituents wanted and for which they would hold him accountable. The run-up to the Sierra Leone elections, especially when set against the backdrop of contemporaneous elections in Liberia and Kenya, and populist, outsider electoral victories in the United States and France, offered a particularly stark case study in a modern political aesthetics that seemed increasingly millenarian. The moment was a dangerous one in Sierra Leone, as it was across much of Africa. That danger lay in large part in the fact that the "practices of accountability and locally plausible self-legitimation" (introduction, this volume) were, at that moment, especially improvisational and uncertain. The future they suggested was one that called into question not simply the mechanics of elite cultures but the functioning of the African state.

In what follows I begin by tracing MT's alternative pathways, his various "bush paths," toward Sierra Leone's presidency. I then consider the generational gap that is so important in Sierra Leone's recent history of warfare, and which creates the conditions of possibility for a youthful aspiration to elite status that simultaneously promises to annihilate elite culture. In the final two sections of the chapter, I consider how performing the subversion of the state, historically the vehicle for elite accommodation in Africa, has come to appear as a precondition for access to wealth and power in Sierra Leone; first by exploring the utopian fantasy of "development" as wealth without state interference, and then by exploring the discourses of violence and security that undergird this utopian vision.

THE BUSH PATH TO POWER

MT's run for national office began along a route that seemed challenging but plausible. A charismatic and intelligent man, he had long maintained that it was his destiny to play leadership roles. Then, in 2015, MT began to speak openly of his desire to bid for the Sierra Leonean parliament seat representing the eastern district that includes his ancestral chiefdom of Malema. A seat in parliament, he argued at the time, would allow him to funnel "development" resources to his rural constituents and solidify his relationship with power brokers in the capital, Freetown. Because he was not part of the Freetown establishment, MT would need strong support from the decentralized, rural power structures that play an important role in Sierra Leone's political life. MT felt a single term in parliament as a member of the Sierra Leone People's Party (the SLPP, one of the country's two major parties) would be enough opportunity for him to garner the support to then contest for the presidency.

In the end, MT elected to skip this first step in his political ascent and directly compete for the presidential vote under the banner of his own party. But his initial parliamentary intentions highlight an important component of MT's claims to legitimacy and the way he intended to cultivate a supportive public: MT recognized the need to establish himself as a son of the soil with a hereditary claim on authority. By itself this is a rather conventional political calculus for a rural politician. And yet the particularities of MT's biography and the recent history of Sierra Leone rendered this a complex, even contradictory proposition.

Malema Chiefdom, MT's ancestral homeland, lies in Sierra Leone's far east, hard against the border with Liberia and dominated by the Gola Forest. It is in many respects closer to Monrovia (the Liberian capital) than to

Freetown, a not insignificant fact both to MT's personal trajectory and to the logics of elite power in Sierra Leone. Dominated by ethnic Mendes and historically associated with the SLPP, the region was deliberately marginalized and underdeveloped by longtime ruler Siaka Stevens (1967–85) and his All People's Congress (APC), the party aligned more closely with the country's north. (In fact, the physical and political distance of the east and southeast of the country from the capital are often cited as reasons that the Revolutionary United Front [RUF] invasion of Sierra Leone in the early 1990s gained so much traction before registering as a problem in the nation's capital [see Gberie 2005 and Richards 1996 for more on this history]).

The result is that in Sierra Leone's south and east there is a rural elite whose authority is exercised largely through chieftaincy and local social institutions, an elite with complicated and at times overtly hostile relationships to the patronage networks through which power flows in the capital (see Fanthorpe 2001, 2005; Jackson 2005, 2007; as well as Ferme 1999). Yet with access to the resources of Sierra Leone's dense eastern forests—including timber, gold, and diamonds—as well as the backing of key figures in socially powerful Mende sociopolitical institutions, an ambitious person could reasonably chart a political path from Malema to Freetown.

As the eldest son of an important chiefdom figure, MT could lay legitimate claim to this rural hereditary authority. "I hail from a royal family," he told me. "My family is the founding family of that chiefdom, and we have been ruling that land for over nine generations before the British came." That history, MT maintained, was critical to MT's father becoming the current Malema *lavalie*, or chiefdom speaker.[3] "There is succession, just like you obtain in the British monarchy. My dad is the head of that family, and I am the crown prince, to put it in the monarchy's terms." MT therefore perceived a certain inherited right to contest for political office, if not to accede to it automatically.

For MT, however, this laying claim to the ancestral pathway toward political office was enacted despite, and sometimes through, a complex dynamics of place. Though extended members of his family continue to reside in their ancestral village, and though his father now lives in the chiefdom seat of Jojoima, MT himself grew up in Monrovia, where his father worked for years in the offices of foreign automobile and mining companies. Remittances from the family in Monrovia to an extended network of kin in Malema were an important source of support for decades. Funds sent from across the border underwrote important community celebrations and the construction of cement block housing, regarded across southern Sierra Leone (as elsewhere) as important visual markers of a continued connection between urban and rural kin (see Piot 1999: 105–30).

This is not in itself unusual. Positions of authority in the chiefdom system are often held by individuals with long, and sometimes ongoing, histories of residence outside the chiefdom itself—even, increasingly, outside of Sierra Leone. Symbolic demonstrations of connection to the village, through attendance or subsidizing ritual events or the public sponsorship of infrastructure projects, can often supplant physical residence in situ as a signifier of care and commitment to the chiefdom and its residents.

But MT's absenteeism was made especially complex by the dynamics of Sierra Leone's war history. Fighting in Monrovia and then eastern Sierra Leone in the early 1990s pushed MT's extended family, along with thousands of others, out of both Monrovia and Malema and into southern Sierra Leone. MT's family used their own funds to establish a provisional internally displaced person (IDP) camp until much of the population was settled into the larger camps set up around the region. There MT befriended a mixed ethnic group of young men, most of them urban youth and many of them veterans of the Liberia fighting whose units had been forced across the border. These youth later formed the core of a fighting unit affiliated first with the progovernment Civil Defense Forces in Sierra Leone and then the antigovernment Liberians United for Reconciliation and Democracy in the Liberia front of the war (see Hoffman 2011). As the war continued, MT used those friendships to create for himself an unusual position: he spent the last years of the war in Sierra Leone and the entirety of the second round of fighting in Liberia as a major recruiter and broker of mercenary labor on both sides of the border.

MT, like many fighters, drew little distinction between fighting as an economic and as a political activity, and claimed to be fighting for democracy when he was both a pro- and an antigovernment partisan. It was a position that did not make him rich. But it allowed him to carry on the family's visible symbolics of caring for the chiefdom through material remittances—but with funds and commodities secured through "pay yourself" military operations (zinc roofing, automobiles, and domestic appliances, as well as cash) and through wartime agreements with profiteers seeking to exploit Malema's forest resources in an unregulated and uncertain market. As MT put it, the people of Malema looked up to him as someone who had always sent them "development" and "project proposals," and as a "mentor, advising and guiding them and directing them towards what we call self-reliance and how to create wealth for yourself."

MT's wartime activity therefore opened a second, alternative "bush path" toward Freetown that was in some ways in tension with the first.[4] As a broker of violence, MT was among the best-known, and arguably most trusted, figures in the large population of young fighting men across the region. This gave him access to high political circles in both Sierra Leone and Liberia and among both country's diasporas. MT had a close (though fraught) relationship to Sierra Leone's deputy minister of defense, Hinga Norman, and to Army Chief of Staff Maxwell Khobe, a Nigerian national working officially in the Sierra Leonean government. He circulated in the orbit of figures in the diaspora who served as a conduit to financial backers in the United States and Europe. Through these assiduously cultivated relationships, MT became a relatively successful middleman in a network of actors united by the conflict, but whose interests and points of intersection were simultaneously political, economic, and social. For these individuals, it was MT's links to a population perceived as largely unmoored from rural networks and associations that legitimized him. He was the agent who could navigate a population immersed in urban youth culture, a marginal population of young men willing and able to do the labors of war.

MT's personal history provided him, in sum, with a set of identity claims that sometimes complemented, and sometimes competed with, one another: an urban youth in Liberia; the favorite son of a prominent Monrovia businessman; scion of a ruling family in rural Sierra Leone; a refugee on both sides of the Sierra Leone / Liberia border; a progovernment partisan and antigovernment rebel; a coldly calculating recruiter of mercenaries; a political revolutionary; a committed democrat; a shadow operator brokering violence on behalf of more powerful men. MT could, and did, use each of these identities throughout the war and the postwar periods. He deployed his multiple identities strategically, navigating the crises of Sierra Leone in the 1990s and 2000s by shifting his claims to legitimacy with the shifting circumstances of the war.

Whereas in the early 1990s Mbembe and Roitman (1995) could trace a subject in crisis because of the nature of power in the postcolonial state (in other words, because of the ways elite political actors deployed crisis as a governing strategy that "fractured" those subject to their authority), here I want to suggest that it is precisely this fractured subjectivity that MT deployed as a way to legitimize himself as a pretender to elite authority. MT needed no coherent personal story or singular identity claim to deploy as part of his claim to power. The same creative but contradictory positioning, the same fracturing of identities that allowed him to navigate the crisis state of the war and its disorderly aftermath, allowed him to pursue multiple, sometimes contradictory forms of legitimacy depending on his audience. It was a breadth that allowed a canny operator to gain at least some traction with very different kinds of constituents with very different ideas of what constitutes political legitimacy. And it allowed him to claim a unique capacity to navigate postcolonial political realities. But basing his claim to political legitimacy on the fact that he had mastered the crisis state of authoritarian governance, that he perfectly embodied the fragmentary subjectivity of the postcolony, had its political cost: it meant that MT's vision of governance was nakedly millenarian and destructive. That became increasingly apparent when MT began to articulate his appeal to the nation's youth.

THE POLITICAL ONTOLOGY OF A CRISIS OF YOUTH

In a lengthy email from August 2016, MT relayed the news of his plans for the presidency. "On the political front," he wrote, after a brief update on friends and family,

> there is a very big U-Turn. Because of the lackadaisical actions of the main SLPP in opposition, coupled with the infighting and brutal exchanges among different factions that have emerged within the ranks of the party, it is sounding clear that the party is no longer a viable alternative to the failed ruling APC party. Based on this hypothesis or rather these facts, my comrades from within the ranks of the VETERANS have petitioned me to start a new political movement that will seek to displace both the ruling party and the main political opposition from the body politics of the country, and to position ourselves to take state power. It's a carrion [sic] call that I have answered to.[5]

The war in Sierra Leone (1992–2002) is widely characterized as a crisis of youth. Different observers have understood that crisis somewhat differently. For scholars like Paul Richards (1996), Krijn Peters (2011), Abu Bakkar Bah (2011), Marc Sommers (2015), and David Keen (2005), the origins of the conflict lie in the way that Sierra Leone's "gerontocracy" largely excluded a generation of young men. The patronage systems that previously allowed young people to accumulate resources (resources of material wealth and social prestige) had largely collapsed, and with them a predictable life course. The known pathways to joining the ranks of adults with local or even national prestige had been thrown into doubt or were wholly unattainable for many.[6] Young men therefore joined in a war that they viewed as an assault on the forces confining them to the margins. Other scholars attributed the nature of the conflict, and to some degree its cause, to an inherently "lumpen" youth culture (see, for example, Abdullah 1998, 2002; Abdullah and Muana 1998). These lumpen youth blended casual violence and largely undirected revolutionary discourse, producing a cohort that reveled in destroying establishment institutions (both physical and social) but did not in itself offer any counterprograms or attempt much in the way of self-legitimation.

Despite their differences, both positions point to a highly destructive, and at times millenarian, logic of targeting those perceived as elders and the institutions through which they were thought to be illegitimately withholding wealth and progress from the next generation.[7] After a war that is widely seen to have produced no real structural change, and in the face of a floundering postwar economy, that generational split remains profoundly important in Sierra Leone today. MT belonged squarely in this youth demographic throughout the war, and remained strongly identified with it in his campaign for the presidency.

MT also therefore belonged to a generation of Sierra Leoneans with no direct lived experience of European colonialism, a fact that further complicated his ability to make the familiar performative claims that made eliteness legible for decades after independence. As it did in many other sub-Saharan African countries, both service in colonial institutions and participation in anticolonial and independence movements functioned in Sierra Leone as legitimating claims to elite status after independence in 1961 (see Cartwright 1970, 1978; Kilson 1966). "Fathers" of the nation such as Milton Margai, Siaka Stevens, and John Karefa-Smart deployed their overseas education, experiences of travel or military deployment, the early and relatively peaceful negotiation of sovereignty, and their competence in navigating both European and indigenous Sierra Leonean cultural institutions to legitimize their status and rule. In the 1970s it was possible for Abner Cohen (1981) to trace a relatively predictable path through which Freetown's ruling class cultivated its future generations of leaders: the school infrastructure, social clubs, and church and mosque networks that all worked to incorporate young people, especially young men, in the practices of privilege and power (see also Reno 1995). Well into the first decades of independence, competent cosmopolitanism was a prerequisite of Freetown political life.

The upshot is that while Sierra Leone's crisis of youth might be felt most acutely by the urban and rural poor, it has also confounded those who might once have been brought into the fold of political parties or positioned as junior, loyal functionaries of state institutions.[8] What Jean-François Bayart referred to as the "reciprocal assimilation of elites" (1993) does not fluidly cross the generational divide in Sierra Leone today. In fact, it is precisely that fact—the exclusion of a younger generation of politicians from the former pathways of elite accommodation—that constituted the foundation of MT's and other youth political aspirants' claims.

Lamine Tarawalley, (a distant relative of MT's) is a young man from Kenema who campaigned for parliament with the SLPP. He summarized the generational divide this way in an interview just prior to the election:

> That's the good thing about this moment right now. One side of African politics I appreciate right now, we are looking toward the younger generation. It was always the grandpas, the fat men, that were the politicians. We're past that. There has not been any dividends on the ground. People have embraced the young people who have shown that they have the country at heart. That grandpa stuff, the experience stuff—most of the time as far as we Africans are concerned, politicians should be seventy-five or eighty years old. But now people are seeing that some of us . . . were on board with the development of the country, and we should be given our chance.

MT's own rhetoric on this point was even more strident when I asked him whether Sierra Leoneans were truly prepared to accept a young person as head of state, especially someone so clearly associated with the youth violence of Sierra Leone's war:

> We want to tell the people of Sierra Leone that it is time to stop the recycling of politicians in this country. We are not going to bring into the political arena a big buffoon, an old fat man. We are bringing positive radicalism in this country. That is the image we are bringing, of positive radicalism and militancy. So the type of picture we are going to bring is of a young generation. We are bringing in a generation that is younger than Sierra Leone [i.e., that was not part of the colonial or early postcolonial apparatus]. This is a complete youth face, a generational push to change the order, a true postcolonial leadership.

The PPRM charter is equally direct: "Notwithstanding the valuable contributions of [the] pre-independence generation of elders," it reads, the members of that generation "shall only qualify for leadership roles" if they eschew corruption and follow the lead of "radical and nationalistic patriotic young people."

In sum, MT's campaign is based on a significant schism across generations, a schism that MT is employing to legitimize his own "rightful" claim on power. It was a discursive framing with its roots in Sierra Leone's war, a framing that pulls in much of the rhetoric of illegitimate exclusion and antidemocratic gerontocracy. And as happened in the framing of the war itself, it is the illegitimacy of existing elite structures rather than a specific program or vision that MT used to legitimize his own claims. As Richards has written of the RUF rebels, the "theory of accession to state power" promoted by the rebels "was based on an understanding that . . . it is not revolution that succeeds but weak government and civil society that fail" (2005: 121). Having established a complex and somewhat contradictory claim on legitimacy as a candidate, MT similarly sought to build a campaign around defeating the forces that seemingly frustrated his and his cohort's paths toward power. The result was a political project with little coherence as a program. What it offered instead was a bricolage of spectacular images and a utopian promise that the mechanisms of exclusion—including the state itself—would inevitably be destroyed.

TO SWEEP THE WORLD AWAY

In a conference call with university students in the United States, MT responded immediately to a question about the long odds against the PPRM in a field dominated by two major parties and many smaller ones. "We believe," he said, "that the PPRM is going to institute the Emmanuel Macron style in Sierra Leone," referring to the recently elected young president of France. Macron, in MT's analysis, came from nowhere and seized the highest office because the French voting public had lost all respect for France's traditional political vehicles. "I'm going to be the Macron of Africa. Definitely, we will be France in this place."

Macron was one of a number of telling global touchstones for MT. Asked which African leader he would emulate in office, MT named Rwandan president Paul Kagame. More surprisingly, MT also frequently made admiring reference to the man who once imprisoned him and against whom he fought a protracted war: Liberia's warlord president Charles Taylor. And both before and after the 2016 presidential elections in the United States, MT compared himself to the candidate who had never held political office but rode a populist wave to victory. "We," he told me, "are going to be the Trump of this place. You can call me Donald Trump. We are going to take the world by surprise.... The system has failed this country. Men have to stand up and make sure we take this country back."

The constellation of reference figures with which MT oriented himself in the global political universe make a certain sense. Both Macron and Trump were long-shot candidates with little initial support from the governing elite of their respective nations. Kagame and Taylor had each ascended to power from outside the official apparatus of the state, then quickly consolidated their authority over national institutions of governance and over the formal and informal networks of power. What the portraits assembled in MT's hall of presidential fame pointed to was, however, more than simply the possibility of unexpected victory from outside the traditional or legitimate pathways. Each figure represented a vision of sovereign authority exercised primarily as the power to make capital flow effectively around, rather than through, the traditional institutions of governance. MT's vision was, however, more millenarian than neoliberal. He seemed to find in these world leaders a set of signifiers for the strength to subvert, or even destroy, the state at those moments in which it might pose a threat to his and his constituents' utopian visions. And it was on this basis that he saw himself accountable to his (future) publics.

Elaborating on his enthusiasm for a Rwanda-style presidency, MT pointed first to the "massive development" of Rwanda after the violent period of the mid-1990s. "Rwanda," he said, "is one of the fastest developing countries in Africa. That is the kind of pace we want to use to move this country, to catapult this nation to prosperity." "Development" in MT's telling was not, however, measured in social services or infrastructure projects, but in individual wealth. "I will not bring promises" to the people of Sierra Leone, he said.

> I will not tell you if you vote for me I will bring you roads and electricity. I will bring them a platform that will bring them wealth—wealth management and wealth distribution. And they will see this can work. It's a platform of action. All the other platforms I see are donor driven. They draw from the IMF [International Monetary Fund]. They draw from the UN [United Nations]. I will be showing them a way to become independent.... Politics is business. If

you run a country on a business basis you succeed. If you run it on a project basis you fail. The great United States is a business. It is succeeding because it is a business. The United States believes in investment. It is capitalism. You have investment, and only out of that can you do development. If you sit and wait for charity, you will fail. So we will deploy a business model you will see succeed. That is very appealing to the youth. Every youth, every human bring aspires. You want to improve on your condition. You want to lift yourself out of poverty. You want to own vehicles. You want to own houses. The only way you can do that is to own businesses. That's the only way. We have to release the funds from out there.

MT's formulation of a state of radical capitalism was decidedly utopian, a term he himself used repeatedly in describing his plans for the nation. We will, he said, make Sierra Leone "a paradise for all" and a nation in which there will be "wealth to all, poverty for none."

The greatest threat to that utopian vision, according to MT, is the state itself. "Most young people do not know the history of the country," he told me. "How the state started to decay, what was here in the 1960s and '70s. So we will bring them that history. We will show them who and what is responsible for the current situation." Time and again MT returned to this theme. A generation of Sierra Leone's elite political leaders had wrecked the nation. But in his framing there was a good deal of slippage between the holders of office and the offices they held. As often as not, both forms of "decay" were in need of eradication.

MT's was a more radical, even millenarian, vision than the one that underpinned the cynical warlordism of both Sierra Leone and Liberia in the 1990s. As William Reno has argued, both West African nations have long been weak states. Political control was exercised in each case by cultivating partnerships with external actors, partnerships that generated private wealth for an elite that could thereby maintain their grip on power without being accountable to their citizenry via the calculus of effectively providing state services. "Strongmen," Reno writes, "rule through control of commerce rather than by mobilizing a bureaucracy. They do not seek to infuse their political rule with universal claims to sponsor 'development' or to defend any broad based popular interest" (Reno 1998: 79–80). Africa's "warlord politics," in this framework, did not simply emerge from conditions of state collapse and weak bureaucracies. Rather, coalitions of indigenous elites, external financial backers, and the capacity for violence of mobilized youth allowed for an alternative to a functioning bureaucracy as a means of securing, holding, and exercising state power (cf. the essays in Themnér 2017 and Utas 2012).

However, even as he adopted many of the classic warlord's rhetorical devices (especially those of Charles Taylor), MT in effect inverted the warlord political logic. There was, in his vision of Sierra Leone's political future, a strong developmentalist narrative and an explicit promise that Sierra Leoneans, simply by dint of their membership in the national body, were legitimate claimants to the resources of the republic. But unlike those leaders who perpetuated the weakness of state institutions under the false promise of "rebuilding" the state through structural adjustment and neoliberal austerity or reform, MT simply named the state as the biggest obstacle to true independence for Sierra Leoneans—and then all but promised to do away with it. "Politics to me," as he put it,

> is supposed to be a social contract between the politician and the people. You honor your own part by electing me to go and represent you. My own part of the bargain is to bring development to you. I should create opportunities for you. Those who are willing to work hard will make it. Those that are lazy remain down there. The transformation of any nation begins from its manpower development, before you come to infrastructure. If the manpower is not developed, no amount of infrastructure can make it.

MT's was, in short, a vision of national development absent state processes. And in what he said next, he seemed prepared to accept the consequences of such a regime: "If you honor your part by electing me, and I renege on my part to bring back [wealth], you can riot. You can take me out if I don't deliver."

Writing about South Africa in the late 1990s and early 2000s, Patrick Bond (2006) portrayed a population eager for a functional state with strong institutions. In Sierra Leone in the late 2010s, MT perceived a population eager for someone to publicly declare the state to be "empty" (Piot 2010)—and to move its ruins out of the way. With varying degrees of explicitness, MT promised a poststate future for a public that had largely lost faith in the pledges not only of the ruling elite, but of the institutions of governance themselves. To legitimize himself before his (potential) publics, in other words, MT undertook a performative project of demonstrating that he could master, and if necessary destroy, a state apparatus that many Sierra Leoneans experienced as a burden and a threat.

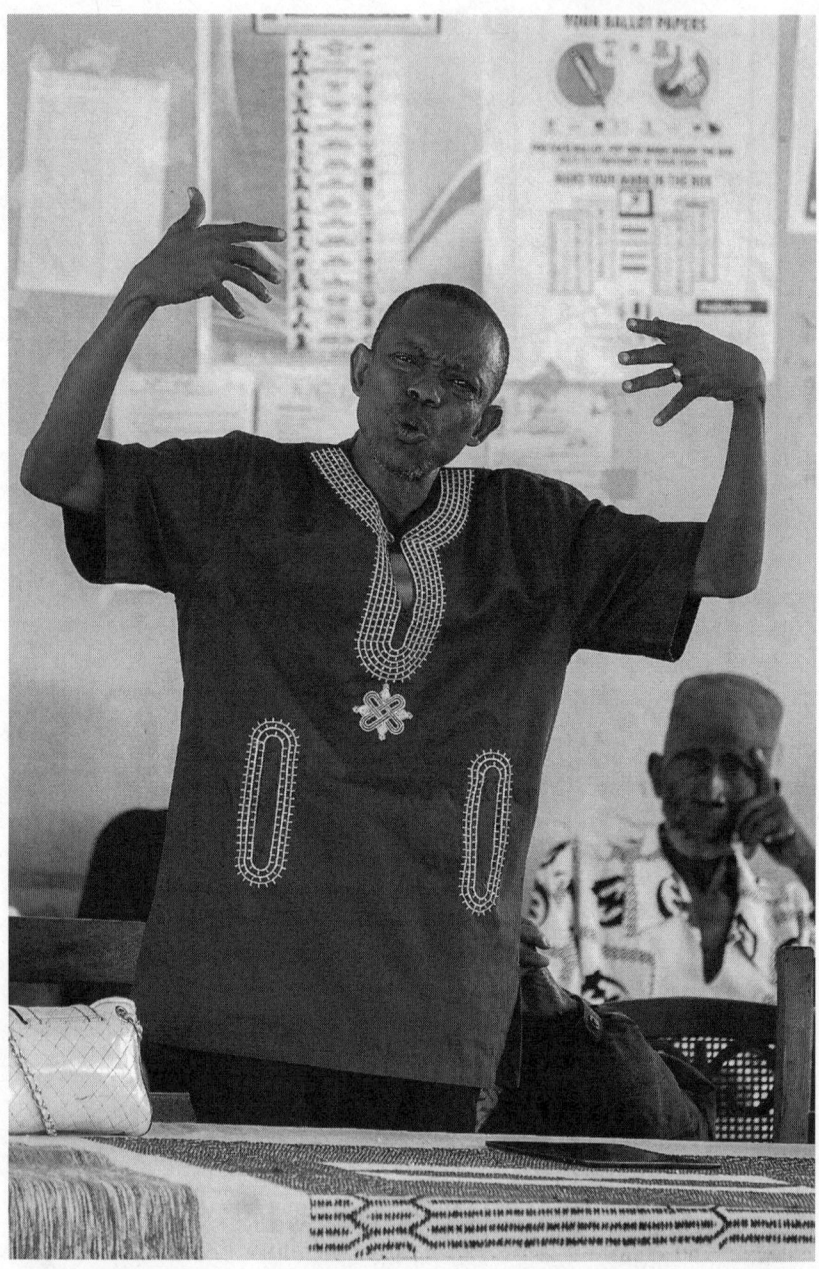

Fig. 1.3: Campaigning in the small town of Jojoima, the political seat of the eastern Malema chiefdom, MT addresses community leaders at the central meeting hall, or court barri. Photo by John D. Hoffman.

It was a promise with resonance, at least for young Sierra Leoneans with little or no memory of the country prior to the sustained state of crisis that began in the 1980s.[9] Ibrahim, for example, is a teacher from a small town in the Pujehun District. A self-proclaimed Mende nationalist, he has historically supported the SLPP. "Politics here," he put it, somewhat facetiously, "is hereditary." Months after the APC won the election, Ibrahim lost his job as a middle school teacher in Bo. The superintendent of schools was an APC man. He stopped paying Ibrahim's salary and those of other SLPP-affiliated teachers, and then failed to renew their contracts. By default, Ibrahim says, he will vote for the SLPP again. But Ibrahim doesn't think an SLPP victory will bring his job back. There is no reason to expect that it would, since Ibrahim is not himself well connected within the party. Even an SLPP-aligned superintendent would have his own clients and dependents to look out for and to reward. But, Ibrahim told me, "We are hoping that at least the opposition will take the power so there will be some changes in life generally; the conditions here are excessively bad." Those changes to "life generally" went unspecified, even when I pushed him for particulars. The majority of the population, Ibrahim said, simply hope that "the situation will be fixed."

That unspecific future in which change is ideally a seismic shift, but which has no political program, object, or goal, is a common refrain among young Sierra Leonean voters. Patrick Kapuwa, a political scientist who took leave from a university teaching position after his salary went unpaid, described it succinctly in an interview before the vote:

> They [the people of Sierra Leone] are ready for change. But change from where to where? Everybody wants a change of government. But is it a change of political ideology? Of public policy? If you talk to university students, the changes they want are changes to fees, a regular calendar, better facilities. So if you talk to them, that's the type of change they want to see. We [university faculty] have gone for four months without salary. If you talk to me, I will say I want that to change. That's a change in my situation as an individual. But that is not a change of policy.

There are striking echoes here of the way many young Africans regard and navigate the contemporary urban environment in cities across the continent. Filip de Boeck, for example, has described how Kinois (residents of Kinshasa) have largely lost faith in master plans and the master narratives of city leaders. Few if any of Kinshasa's residents imagine that the grand plans and promises of urban elites will ever come to pass or even produce modest improvements in the practices of everyday life; the detritus and ruins of past grand central plans are everywhere, daily reminders of the failed promises of top-down transformations. The majority of urban residents have long since given up on the idea of city governance as anything other than a policing mechanism meant to foil or complicate the creative strategies they have developed in order to get by (see also Hoffman 2017; Melly 2017; Simone 2009; and Wainaina 2005).

What many urbanites therefore hope is that these master plans and urnarratives will fail in generative ways—that they will, in other words, clear away obstacles to the individual, improvised strategies through which residents attempt to satisfy their own needs without creating unnecessary new challenges. In Kinshasa, as de Boeck describes it, this paradoxically accounts for the universal popularity of the most fantastic or outrageous urban plans (the most "heterotopian" and unrealizable) that circulate through rumors, billboards, and other spectacular images. "It is," de Boeck writes, "precisely in the specular qualities of the image of the new city, the very process of mirroring, realized in all those spaces where the interplay between real and unreal, or visible and invisible is realized, that this new heterotopology for Kinshasa is generated, allowing Kinois to overcome, even if only for a moment, the fragmentedness, the contradictions, and the ruptures that have scarred the face of the city's existence for so long now" (2011: 278). A wholesale, almost apocalyptic erasure of the present in favor of a phantasmatic vision of the future would allow the city's residents to maneuver more effectively on their own, opening the space of possibility for them to accumulate the wealth and resources that the city of the present makes so difficult to achieve.

MT's campaign is predicated on the idea that many of Sierra Leone's youth (urban youth in particular), have adopted a similar stance toward the national vote—and the established political class contesting it. Cleansing the scene of the ruins caused by the machinations of the political elite, without replacing them, would allow for a good deal more room to maneuver and even, perversely, a good deal more certainty and security. It is not a completely apolitical vision. But it is a vision tethered to an ideal without physical or institutional form—an ocular politics, to extend de Boeck's framing. Much as the various armed factions in both Sierra Leone and Liberia during the war years adopted a rhetoric of being the true defenders of democracy even against two democratically elected governments, many young Sierra Leoneans saw the normative mechanisms of democratic practice as impediments to, rather than the vehicles for, true accountability on the part of their ruling class.[10] After a brokered government of national unity in Côte d'Ivoire, a postponed election in Liberia, and repeated violence and uncertainty around each of Kenya's last few election cycles, there is little faith in the idea of the vote as a mechanism for creating either stability or accountability. "We need," as Kapuwa put it, "to find democracy with African dimensions. Why our overt reliance on elections and electioneering for democracy in Africa, when in Kenya thousands of people died [in 2007 and 2017]? Really, are elections the answers to our problems?"

For MT and his cohort, this creates a strange kind of accountability mechanism. MT needed no credible plan to make his utopian claims to "wealth for all and poverty for none" believable. What was required of him, at least as he interpreted the mood of the young Sierra Leoneans on whom he depended, was that he be willing and able to perform the single state effect that demonstrably curtailed the capacity of the state itself to perpetuate crisis: the performance of violence in the name of security. It is to this last dynamic of MT's political aesthetic that I turn next.

THE POST-WARLORD POLITICIAN

Among the telling moments in Barbet Schroeder's 1974 documentary film *General Idi Amin Dada: A Self-Portrait* is a scene of the title subject standing in swimming trunks at the edge of a pool. To each side is a line of younger, fitter men looking decidedly scared. Along with the others, the president of Uganda flings himself into the pool, and then flails his way diagonally through the water. Amin pummels at least one other swimmer and, not surprisingly, wins the race. His competitors laugh and applaud, but above all they look relieved at not having accidentally defeated the man who must always finish first.

The aesthetic of power in the big-man era of African governance was, according to Achille Mbembe (1992), an aesthetics of vulgarity. Neopatrimonialism was characterized by excessive appetites and outlandish spectacles, many of them prominently featuring the bodies (and often the sexual prowess) of the ruling elite. These ostentatious displays were inevitably drawn from multiple repertoires of signs. In Schroeder's film, Amin demonstrates his sharpshooting while in full military uniform, boasting (against the visible evidence to the contrary) that he has hit the heart of the target every time. He improbably extols his prowess as a national champion rugby player and wrestler, the latter a sport with credence both as a staple of modern Olympics and as a village contest associated with the passage to manhood. Amin dances animatedly with spear and shield and in coat and tie. He delivers a nonsensical lecture to student doctors from the head of a classroom and threatens his cabinet ministers seated at the head of the table in his general's uniform.

Material flows of wealth and the opportunity for its accumulation were critical to big-man rulers like Amin. Excessive performances of state authority expressed in the physical form of the neopatrimonial ruler indexed a capacity to use state coffers and state bureaucracies to cultivate and maintain networks of clients. Yet when the end of the Cold War and the maturation of structural adjustment loan conditions made such extensive patronage systems vastly harder to maintain, the immediate effect in many states was counterintuitive: the spectacles of political legitimacy grew more extravagant even as the actual institutions of state (and thereby the mechanisms by which national elites remained accountable to their publics) grew weaker (see Joseph 1997: 368–69). The political form that belonged to this aesthetic environment of increasingly vulgar performance is one in which being seen to perform gross caricatures of state functions (highly stage-managed elections not least among them) became the operational logic of sovereignty, even as the actual exercise of rule was increasingly informalized and outsourced (see Mbembe 2000).

This is what Charles Piot (2010), in his analysis of Gnassingbe Eyadema's Togo, has labeled the performance of state effects even as the state itself is increasingly empty. What MT promises is a parallel, but qualitatively different: the staging of market effects. Rather than the vulgar aesthetics of neopatrimonial power or its late manifestation as hollow state-like exaggerations, MT promised the hyperperformance of smoothly flowing capital. It is an outlandish claim, built on the fantastical possibility of making Sierra Leone a financial utopia that leaves no citizen behind. But its veracity is not the issue. What matters is a shared participation in the performance, a capacity of both the elite (who would be included) and the poor (who would be excluded) to equally "revel as much in this dream" of wealth and inclusion (de Boeck 2011: 278; see also Piot 2010: 166).

In Liberia under Charles Taylor, the performance of state effects was primarily to establish legitimacy on the world stage—with, in other words, a non-Liberian coterie of elites at the African Union and the United Nations. Domestically, Taylor embraced the emptiness of the Liberian state, hastening the informalization and outsourcing of state effects to private or nongovernmental agencies from which he could profit directly and indirectly, or in which he had some other personal stake (see Reno 1998). Crucially, as Mary Moran has argued, Taylor made himself accountable to the Liberian populace primarily by arguing, implicitly and through spectacularly violent performances, that only he possessed the strength to make them safe (Moran 2008). Taylor's claim on legitimacy was that he could tame the upheaval that had plagued Liberia since the 1989 invasion, much of which came from Taylor's own forces.

Taylor and his ability to "control" Liberia was a recurrent theme in my conversations with MT over the years, as it was in conversations I had with many Liberians (see, for example, Hoffman 2017: 154–55). But where Taylor promised to use violence to protect against the violence of others, MT promised to use it against the vicissitudes of the state itself. His somewhat surprising opposition to Liberian presidential candidate George Weah in the 2017 Liberian vote is instructive. Much like MT himself, Weah, he argued, could mobilize and inspire the youth. (Weah, though a political neophyte, is one of Africa's best-known professional footballers.) But Weah, according to MT, was "soft":

> For any country in Africa you need a very decisive leader. You need a leader that can think for himself and deploy those thoughts and make sure they are acted on. But any leader who lets people dictate what happens and lead him, then he will have a problem. He won't know which direction to go. If one person tells him, "Mr. President, you should nationalize the schools" and he follows him, and then the next minister of education comes in and says, "You must privatize the schools," that's chaos. That's a disaster. And that's my concern with Weah. The educated elite are stronger than he is. Since he's not able to control his own men, you have a lot of corruption and there is a risk that disintegration will come to Liberia.

MT was even more disparaging of the outgoing Liberian president, Ellen Johnson-Sirleaf. In highly gendered terms, MT argued that "as a woman" Johnson-Sirleaf would have been an effective leader for a peaceful and stable country. Liberia was neither in MT's mind, despite the decade and a half that had passed since the official end of Liberia's war.

> This female president is not able to stand up to the tensions. She is not able to use the security apparatus in this land to quell down the perceived tensions.

> If it was a male candidate that was running this land, he would have been able to stand up to any tension that is coming. The female president has a motherly heart, motherly passion. There are certain things they don't stand up to. There are certain risks that comes to them, and they are cold right away, they are cowed.

By contrast, MT went on, "Charles Taylor is and was one of the leaders of this country that could stand up to any tension, to beat back any threat."

MT was, in essence, promising a Taylor-like mastery of violence. As he described it, violence was the sine qua non that could vanquish one's political opponents absolutely and could also settle the uncertainties and insecurities that came with postwar life. Indeed, the two collapsed as MT described how he would bring both stability and victory to Sierra Leone:

> This isn't about fun. You don't mess with this guy. That is the strength we are bringing to the political table. All other political institutions in this country can be intimidated. But you cannot do that with us. They [the established political class] don't believe that my party will come up in this short period of time. But I am telling them we will wait and see. I am the guy who will come up and shoot the SLPP in the head.

But unlike Amin, for whom the institutions of state mattered for the dispensation of his largesse, or for Taylor, whose warlord brand of politics depended on at least the fiction of functioning governance, MT proffered only the spectacle of violence as a governing mechanism. He seemed intent on waging what Deleuze and Guattari once referred to as "total war": employing all available resources toward the goal of securing peace through the endless reproduction of violence (1987: 421). It was through the endless reproduction of force—the force that could tame and conquer the state itself—that MT would be accountable to the people of Sierra Leone.

CONCLUSION

"The curriculum vitae of leaders," writes Richard Joseph, "can offer little guidance as to whether once in power they will follow the ideals they championed in opposition or just reinstate personalist and patrimonial systems" (2011: 327). MT was unlikely to win Sierra Leone's presidency. And were he to do so, it was by no means clear that he would actualize his millenarian revolution, his antistate political aesthetics. But the way he articulated his political vision, the means by which he entered and maneuvered through the world of signifying practices and political signs, paint a vivid picture of elite political aesthetics in the contemporary postcolony. As someone whose chances were slim and who straddled diverse worlds and identities as a would-be politician, MT occupied a precarious political position but a privileged vantage point on how eliteness in political life is constituted.

What MT's insider/outsider campaign suggests is the continued evolution of postcolonial governance and elite roles within it. If the early decades of political life in many African states were characterized by Mbembe's "vulgar aesthetics" of the big man, an aesthetics followed by the rise of neoliberal discourse after the Cold War, the present is a moment of emergence. What is emerging is an ocular politics with a decidedly violent, millenarian, and postmodern cast. Figures like MT are playing for elite status through a creative sampling of the aesthetic strategies that once led to and secured elite status, strategies that are no longer effective if adhered to with fealty; the promises of "big manity" (Utas 2012) and the market ring hollow across the continent today. So MT performed a mastery of both neopatrimonial politics and modern capital selectively and spectacularly, all the while demonstrating to his intended audience that he could simultaneously liberate Sierra Leone by violently doing away with both. It was a schizophrenic political game, built on a fractured and fracturing political landscape.

With this in mind, it bears mentioning that MT may have at the same time been playing a complex bluff with his PPRM and his presidential bid. While he vehemently denied it, it is certainly possible that his ambitions were not actually so grand; his intention may not have been the presidency, but rather a canny long game of positioning himself once again as the broker who could deliver young men to do the violent labor of campaigning. This has, after all, been the cycle in each of Sierra Leone's postwar presidential campaigns, with former commanders achieving a certain power for themselves by orchestrating violence on behalf of other political aspirants (see Christensen and Utas 2008; Utas and Christensen 2016). If so, it will be tempting to read the outcome of the presidential contest as more of the same: the perpetuation of an elite culture that employs Sierra Leone's marginal male youth for the work of violence, a work that continues to lock them out of the processes of elite accommodation even as it enables it for an older generation of political figures. While not incorrect, such a reading of the vote risks missing the dangerous appeal that a candidate like MT holds for a growing percentage of Sierra Leone's population, especially its youth. No longer content to simply ply the fiction of sovereignty while sitting atop an empty state, MT represents the possibility of a thoroughly ocular president, the leader who manipulates a postmodern pastiche of signifiers in a utopian promise to sweep the ruins of the state away.

POSTELECTION POSTSCRIPT

The weeks prior to the March 7 vote proved to be tumultuous ones for MT and the PPRM. By mid-January it had become clear that the PPRM did not have the resources to open a party office in each region, a prerequisite for legally contesting the national campaign. The PPRM leadership therefore took the decision to align with the Unity Party, which had (barely) managed to meet all the basic criteria to qualify for the national vote. After protracted negotiations, MT was announced as the vice presidential running mate to UP leader Dr. Femi Claudius Cole.

The PPRM/UP alliance was an uneasy but instructive one. MT, who had long maintained that no woman could exert the control necessary to tame the state apparatus and guarantee security in Sierra Leone, found himself as the running mate to one of only two women on the presidential roster of sixteen candidates. As he campaigned in Freetown and around the southeast of the country, MT developed a stump speech that reversed his gender analysis while still maintaining, and indeed underscoring, his fundamentally millenarian message. Sierra Leone, he told potential UP voters, had been destroyed by men. It was time to bring a woman to power to clean up the mess. "If you try a woman," he told voters at a house-to-house campaign in the J-Matta informal settlement in Freetown, "there is a chance we will change this country. You know how women are very strict with spending? The men who have ruled this country? You know I'm a man, we're extravagant! If I turn president tomorrow, I've got ten girlfriends, twenty girlfriends. I've got to support them all!" A female president, he repeated over and over, represented the possibility of a different, though undefined, political landscape that would replace Sierra Leone's corrupt patriarchy.

MT also began to describe himself as "the most radical running mate" in the campaign. His radicalism, too, was largely undefined. When I pressed him on what "radical" meant in this context, he defined it as both the will and

Fig. 1.4: MT, left, and his principal adviser, Abubakar Juana, unfurl the banner that announces him as running mate to Dr. Femi Claudius Cole of the Unity Party. Photo by John D. Hoffman.

the power for change. The content of that change was less important to MT than the fact of its existence and its totality. Not unlike the RUF worldview that a revolution in Sierra Leone would occur not because of the RUF's own positive message but because of the rottenness of its enemies (Richards 2005: 121), for MT "change" was platform enough. A vote for the UP/PPRM coalition, he argued, was an endorsement of the view that the destruction of the existing political order was the best way to participate in it.

Though it took a number of days to verify the vote tallies and declare the need for a second-round runoff, the UP/PPRM's fortunes were clear by early afternoon the day after the vote. The party had not finished last. In the final analysis, the UP received just under 4,000 votes of 2.7 million cast—enough to rank thirteenth of the sixteen parties. For MT, it was a resounding success. Most of those votes, he argued, came from supporters of the original PPRM. Many more voters told him that their votes were locked up by the time they were aware of his campaign. Had he started earlier, he surely would have done better. For MT it was enough. Claiming he had no interest in the results of the second round of balloting, MT set out planning ways to raise the money needed to get the PPRM on the ballot for the presidential context five years down the line.

NOTES

1. The methodological approach I adopt here is one with a long history in Africanist anthropology. As Victor Turner once wrote of Muchona the Hornet, certain "marginal" figures frequently possess "a great ability to compare and generalize" (1967: 134) precisely because their marginality requires constant critical analysis. In addition to Turner, see also Griaule (1965) and, more recently, Ashforth (2000) and Chernoff (2003, 2005). Although not exactly a "marginal" figure, Michael Jackson's (2004) semibiographical work with the Sierra Leonean politician S. B. Marah is also a useful reference point for thinking political cultures through the combined experiences of an ethnographer and a principal, engaged collaborator.

2. On the importance of the end of the Cold War for understanding the shifting political landscape in West Africa, see Piot 2010.

3. The *lavalie* is essentially the second position in the hierarchy of Mende chieftaincy. For a description of the historical role and importance of the *lavalie* see Little 1967: 196–97.

4. I use this term in reference to both the physical routes through which rural Sierra Leoneans navigate the countryside and to two key texts for understanding Sierra Leonean politics: the Revolutionary United Front's political manifesto "Footpaths to Democracy" and Ibrahim Abdullah's (1998) analysis of the RUF, "Bushpaths to Destruction."

5. I have no doubt that MT meant to write "clarion call" in the final sentence of his note, but have left the original misspelling; the unintended meaning is every bit as telling as the intended one.

6. For more on this as a problem across sub-Saharan Africa, see Sommers 2015; Vigh 2006; and the essays collected in Christiansen, Utas, and Vigh 2006.

7. For an examination of the long-term impacts of how the targeting of elder "elites" has impacted rural communities in Liberia, see Mitman 2016. It is important to note that this age-based schism was not a universal sentiment among Sierra Leonean or Liberian youth, as Mary Moran (2008) has documented in the Liberian case.

8. For more on the fragility and uncertainty of patronage networks in the context of postwar electoral politics, see Utas 2012; Bolten 2016; Utas and Christensen 2016.

9. As Paul Richards has argued, many young Sierra Leoneans experienced the financial crises of the 1980s most poignantly through the collapse of the education system—a fact that contributed greatly to the frustrations that eventually led to war. See Richards 1996, 2005.

10. For work examining earlier iterations of the popular notion that "true" democracy in Sierra Leone is better served by subverting, rather than supporting, the norma-

tive institutions of democratic governance, see Bolten 2016 and Ferme 1999. For a more thorough analysis of how the Sierra Leone Civil Defense Forces eventually adopted the logic of normative party politics at the expense of its earlier, more revolutionary vision of democracy in Sierra Leone, see Hoffman 2011.

REFERENCES

Abdullah, Ibrahim. 1998. "Bush Path to Destruction: Origin and Character of the Revolutionary United Front (RUF/SL)." *African Development* 22, nos. 3–4: 45–76.

Abdullah, Ibrahim. 2002. "Youth Culture and Rebellion: Understanding Sierra Leone's Wasted Decade." *Critical Arts* 16, no. 2: 19–37.

Abdullah, Ibrahim, and Patrick Muana. 1998. "The Revolutionary United Front of Sierra Leone: A Revolt of the Lumpenproletariat." In Christopher Clapham, ed., *African Guerrillas*, 172–94. Bloomington: Indiana University Press.

Ashforth, Adam. 2000. *Madumo: A Man Bewitched*. Chicago: University of Chicago Press.

Bah, Abu Bakkar. 2011. "State Decay and Civil War: A Discourse on Power in Sierra Leone." *Critical Sociology* 37, no. 2: 199–216.

Bayart, Jean-François. 1993. *The State in Africa: The Politics of the Belly*. Longman: London.

Bolten, Catherine. 2016. "'I Will Vote What Is in My Heart': Sierra Leone's 2012 Elections and the Pliability of 'Normative' Democracy." *Anthropological Quarterly* 89, no. 4: 1019–47.

Bond, Patrick. 2006. *Looting Africa: The Economics of Exploitation*. London: Zed Books.

Cartwright, John. 1970. *Politics of Sierra Leone, 1947–67*. Toronto: University of Toronto Press.

Cartwright, John. 1978. *Political Leadership in Sierra Leone*. London: Croom Helm.

Chernoff, John. 2003. *Hustling Is Not Stealing: Stories of an African Bar Girl*. Chicago: University of Chicago Press.

Chernoff, John. 2005. *Exchange Is Not Robbery: More Stories of an African Bar Girl*. Chicago: University of Chicago Press.

Christiansen, Catrine, Mats Utas, and Henrik Vigh, eds. 2006. *Navigating Youth, Generating Adulthood: Social Becoming in an African Context*. Uppsala: Nordic Africa Institute.

Christensen, Maya M., and Mats Utas. 2008. "Mercenaries of Democracy: The 'Politricks' of Remobilized Combatants in the 2007 General Elections, Sierra Leone." *African Affairs* 107: 515–39.

Cohen, Abner. 1981. *The Politics of Elite Culture: Explorations in the Dramaturgy of Power in a Modern West African Society*. Berkeley: University of California Press.

Cooper, Frederick. 2002. *Africa since 1940: The Past of the Present*. Cambridge: Cambridge University Press.

de Boeck, Filip. 2011. "Inhabiting Ocular Ground: Kinshasa's Future in the Light of Congo's Spectral Urban Politics." *Cultural Anthropology* 26, no. 2: 263–86.
Deleuze, Gilles, and Félix Guattari. 1987. *A Thousand Plateaus: Capitalism and Schizophrenia*. Translated by Brian Massumi. Vol. 2. Minneapolis: University of Minnesota Press.
Fanthorpe, Richard. 2001. "Neither Citizen Nor Subject? 'Lumpen' Agency and the Legacy of Native Administration in Sierra Leone." *African Affairs* 100: 363–86.
Fanthorpe, Richard. 2005. "On the Limits of Liberal Peace: Chiefs and Democratic Decentralisation in Post-war Sierra Leone." *African Affairs* 105: 27–49.
Ferme, Mariane. 1999. "Staging *Politisi*: The Dialogics of Publicity and Secrecy in Sierra Leone." In John L. Comaroff and Jean Comaroff, eds., *Civil Society and the Political Imagination in Africa: Critical Perspectives*, 160–91. Chicago: University of Chicago Press.
Gberie, Lansana. 2005. *A Dirty War in West Africa: The RUF and the Destruction of Sierra Leone*. Bloomington: Indiana University Press.
Griaule, Marcel. 1965. *Conversations with Ogotemmêli*. Oxford: Oxford University Press.
Hoffman, Danny. 2011. *The War Machines: Young Men and Violence in Sierra Leone and Liberia*. Durham, NC: Duke University Press.
Hoffman, Danny. 2017. *Monrovia Modern: Urban Form and Political Imagination in Liberia*. Durham, NC: Duke University Press.
Jackson, Michael. 2004. *In Sierra Leone*. Durham, NC: Duke University Press.
Jackson, Paul. 2005. "Chiefs, Money and Politicians: Rebuilding Local Government in Sierra Leone." *Public Administration and Development* 25: 49–58.
Jackson, Paul. 2007. "Reshuffling the Deck? The Politics of Decentralisation in Sierra Leone." *African Affairs* 106: 95–111.
Joseph, Richard. 1997. "Democratization in Africa after 1989: Comparative and Theoretical Perspectives." *Comparative Politics* 29, no. 3: 363–82.
Joseph, Richard. 2011. "Democracy and Reconfigured Power in Africa." *Current History* (November): 324–30.
Keen, David. 2005. *Conflict and Collusion in Sierra Leone*. New York: Palgrave.
Kilson, Martin. 1966. *Political Change in a West African State: A Study of the Modernization Process*. New York: Atheneum.
Little, Kenneth. 1967. *The Mende of Sierra Leone: A West African People in Transition*. New York: Routledge.
Mbembe, Achille. 1992. "Provisional Notes on the Postcolony." *Africa* 62, no. 1: 3–37.
Mbembe, Achille. 2000. "At the Edge of the World: Boundaries, Territoriality, and Sovereignty in Africa." *Public Culture* 12, no. 1: 259–84.
Mbembe, Achille, and Janet Roitman. 1995. "Figures of the Subject in Times of Crisis." *Public Culture* 7: 323–52.
Melly, Caroline. 2017. *Bottleneck: Moving, Building and Belonging in an African City*. Chicago: University of Chicago Press.
Mitman, Gregg. 2016. *The Land beneath Our Feet*. London: Alchemy Films. DVD.

Moran, Mary. 2008. *Liberia: The Violence of Democracy.* Philadelphia: University of Pennsylvania Press.
Peters, Krijn. 2011. *War and the Crisis of Youth in Sierra Leone.* Cambridge: Cambridge University Press.
Piot, Charles. 1999. *Remotely Global: Village Modernity in West Africa.* Chicago: University of Chicago Press.
Piot, Charles. 2010. *Nostalgia for the Future: Africa after the Cold War.* Chicago: University of Chicago Press.
Reno, William. 1995. *Corruption and State Politics in Sierra Leone.* New York: Cambridge University Press.
Reno, William. 1998. *Warlord Politics and African States.* Boulder, CO: Lynne Rienner.
Richards, Paul. 1996. *Fighting for the Rainforest: War, Youth and Resources in Sierra Leone.* Portsmouth, NH: Heinemann and James Currey.
Richards, Paul. 2005. "Green Book Millenarians? The Sierra Leone War from the Perspective of an Anthropology of Religion." In Niels Kastfelt, ed., *Religion and Civil War in Africa,* 119–46. London: C. Hurst.
Sartwell, Crispin. 2010. *Political Aesthetics.* Ithaca, NY: Cornell University Press.
Schroeder, Barbet. 1974. *General Idi Amin Dada: A Self-Portrait.* New York: Criterion Collection. DVD.
Simone, AbdouMaliq. 2009. *City Life from Jakarta to Dakar: Movements at the Crossroads.* New York: Routledge.
Sommers, Marc. 2015. *The Outcast Majority: War, Development, and Youth in Africa.* Athens: University of Georgia Press.
Themnér, Anders, ed. 2017. *Warlord Democrats in Africa: Ex-Military Leaders and Electoral Politics.* London: Zed Books.
Turner, Victor. 1967. *The Forest of Symbols: Aspects of Ndembu Ritual.* Ithaca, NY: Cornell University Press.
Utas, Mats, ed. 2012. *African Conflicts and Informal Power: Big Men and Networks.* London: Zed Books.
Utas, Mats, and Maya M. Christensen. 2016. "The Gift of Violence: Ex-Militias and Ambiguous Debt Relations during Post-war Elections in Sierra Leone." *African Conflict and Peacebuilding Review* 6, no. 2: 23–47.
Vigh, Henrik. 2006. *Navigating Terrains of War: Youth and Soldiering in Guinea-Bissau.* Oxford: Berghahn Books.
Wainaina, Binyavanga. 2005. "My City." Video interview, *National Geographic.* http://ngm.nationalgeographic.com/ngm/0509/feature2/multimedia2.html

CHAPTER 2

The Renewal of Local Elites in Times of "Participation" in Morocco

YASMINE BERRIANE

INTRODUCTION

This chapter contributes to the literature on the making of elites in Africa by analyzing recent transformations that have led, in Morocco, to the emergence of a new kind of local elite whose legitimacy rests upon its participation in the associational sphere. This sphere has expanded rapidly since the end of the 1990. In this analysis, my aim is to go beyond interpretations that focus merely on the instrumentalization of such actors through upgraded authoritarian regimes. I will rather focus on the way new local elites come to legitimize and account for their role as key intermediaries within an expanding associational sphere by drawing upon diverse registers and norms that refer to the two main forms of government that constitute Morocco's hybrid political system: participatory governance and monarchical rule. Building on Michael Bratton's critique of views that limit "associational life to activity that is at odds with the state" (1989: 418), this chapter shows, more generally, how associational life may also contribute to the renewal of local elites.

Research on Morocco's political elites has been dominated by three main strands. The first and main focus of this literature lies on the monarch and his entourage, also known as the *makhzen*,[1] and on the foundations of this particular type of political system built upon an understanding of power that sees the king as the sole supplier of symbols of authority and the main architect of the dominant political culture (Tozy 1999; Hammoudi 1997; Leveau 1985; Waterbury 1970). Several authors have further studied the making and (un)making of the state bourgeoisie that is connected to the palace and represented by powerful individuals and families who are legitimized by their descent from the Prophet (*shorfa* families), their religious knowledge and expertise (the ulama), their mercantile activities, or, since the mid-1970s, their background as highly educated nonpartisan technocrats (Benhaddou 1997; Vermeren 2002; Tessler 1982). The transformation of this state bourgeoisie is intimately linked to global and national economic and political developments, to the growing monopoly of the palace over the economic sector, and—more recently—to the emergence of a new group of entrepreneurs who gained political power against the backdrop of economic liberalization and privatization (Bogaert 2018: 95–122; Oubenal and Zeroual 2017; Catusse 2008).

As a constitutional monarchy, Morocco is also ruled by an elected parliament and government led by a head of government who is appointed by the monarch following legislative elections. The relationship between the monarchy and the representatives of the political parties rests upon an implicit political pact and a political culture of compromise and negotiation that has evolved over time (Tozy 2010, 2008). A second strand of the literature on elites has therefore explored elected elites by studying the role of political parties in the making of the Moroccan state postindependence (Burke 1971), followed by studies either analyzing the contribution of elected elites to the development of democracy (Storm 2007) or their role in maintaining the monarchical system (Barwig 2012; Zerhouni 2002). More recently, Mounia Bennani-Chraïbi (2013) has conducted an extensive study highlighting the differences between "parties of activists" and "parties of notables" and identifying the sociopolitical, ideological, and socioprofessional characteristics of the leading members of these parties. While women have long remained absent from this literature, their growing number within the body of elected representatives has led to a rise in the publication of studies dealing with this process (Berriane 2016b; Darhour and Krit 2012).

The third strand of the literature on elites in Morocco focuses on the local arena and, more particularly, on the role played by various forms of local (urban and rural) elites in the making of the political order. Since Morocco's independence in 1956, local elites have known many transformations that have been summarized by Tozy (2003) in three main phases. During the "time of rural notables," representatives of the traditional rural elite acted as allies of the monarch and contributed to neutralizing oppositional elites that were developing in the cities (Leveau 1985). The "time of civil servants" started in the second half of the 1970s when public servants entered local politics through their election in communal districts. With the 1990s started the "time of a relative fragmentation of the elite," characterized by technocrats', entrepreneurs', and civil society activists' emergence as local political players (El Maoula Iraki 2003).

Building upon this periodization, I will argue in this chapter that local elites have further fragmented and diversified during the last two decades, opening up to new social categories. Through their participation in the associational sphere, actors with limited social capital, often unemployed and belonging to the working class or the lower middle class, have been able not only to climb the social ladder but also to become part of the local decision-making apparatus as political actors. These transformations reflect changes that have become apparent in today's Morocco: the increasing number of local associations, the introduction of new resources into the local associational sphere, and the inclusion of civil society actors into the decision-making process. Similar trends have been noticed in other parts of Africa, north and south of the Sahara, where associations have become spaces in which social and political notabilities are being constructed (Ben Néfissa 2002; Woods 1994; Lucas 1994).

In her analysis of this "participative phenomenon" in Morocco, Irene Bono (2010) first identifies a renewal of the "art of making civil society," an expansion of the category of what is, in Morocco, defined as "civil society" and a transformation of the nature of the actors that make it up. She shows that these transformations come from a top-down renewal of the regulatory norms that govern participation in associations dedicated to the development of the country. This analysis concurs with interpretations that read current transformations of elites in North Africa and the Middle East as a result of the instrumentalization of such actors through upgraded authoritarian regimes (Heydemann 2007). For my part, I wish to concentrate on the role that these new norms played in the life trajectories of local association[2] leaders by emphasizing how they reappropriate these new values to establish themselves locally and account for their role by simultaneously differentiating themselves from the local population and highlighting their social and territorial belonging to this same population. More particularly, I will show that these newly established norms have contributed to providing local associative actors (both men and women) with new "lines of argumentation" (based upon the ideas of "autochthony," "professionalism," and "nonpartisanship") that they combine with older sources of elite legitimacy (notably their symbolic "closeness to the king").

In the first part, I will present my case study, describe the emergence of these local associational leaders, and justify the use of "associational elite" to qualify them. I will then focus more particularly on the different modes of accountability used by associational leaders in working-class neighborhoods of the city of Casablanca to legitimize their newly attained role as representatives of the local population. The conclusion will open up to some more general reflections on the transformation of local elites in times of participation.

THE EMERGENCE OF LOCAL "ASSOCIATIONAL ELITES" IN MOROCCO

Concepts such as "elite" are not "fixed or tangible social science categories." Therefore, in order to distinguish between different kinds of elites, "qualifying adjectives" are often used (Shore 2002: 4). It may, however, seem odd to qualify an elite as "associational" in light of the opposition commonly made between state and civil society actors (Bratton 1989). The aim of this chapter is precisely to question this dichotomy by showing that associational life is an avenue not only for grassroots participation, but also for the recruitment, integration, and renewal of local elites. The term "associational elites," therefore, refers in this chapter to a category of individuals who assume a leadership role within a grassroots association, whether as president, vice president, secretary-general, or other executive function. As I will show below, their leadership position and their mediating functions between the grassroots and the state provides them with privileged access to resources allocated to state officials, bureaucracies, and services for the implementation of local development programs. This privileged access enhances their social status and popularity at the level of their neighborhood, city district, or village. They gain authority and social prestige and are able to build clientelist relationships that represent their power base. This position enables them further to play a critical political role as privileged interlocutors of local state officials, to be elected in the municipal district, and to participate actively in local decision-making. This is how women and men from very modest economic and social backgrounds were recently able to become part of the local decision-making apparatus and to be viewed as key leaders within their community of origin. In this context of participatory governance, elites may therefore be associational. I will illustrate this in more detail below.

The first increase in the number of associations is noticeable in the 1980s, when structural adjustment programs were introduced in Morocco, leading to the state's withdrawal from the social policy sector. This is the period when associations working in the fields of social, economic, and cultural development and human rights organizations appeared. This trend increased in the late 1990s coinciding with the enthronization of Mohammed VI in 1999 after his father passed away. The new king came to power with a whole reform package, stressing the importance of human rights and freedom of speech and using terms such as "participation," "decentralization," and "good governance" in his public rhetoric and in the reforms to be implemented. These new norms are clearly linked to global contemporary development discourses and neoliberal governance agendas that stress the importance of decentralizing power and of including citizens in policymaking. More particularly, in 2002, a reform of the code of public liberties regulating associational life enabled associations to receive funding from public and private institutions. While associations already existed, their number increased substantially during this period.

A turning point came after 2005, when the National Initiative for Human Development (INDH) was launched by the king with the support of the European Union and the World Bank as well as private donors such as the king of Saudi Arabia. This initiative was presented as one of the new king's long-term projects to fight poverty, illiteracy, and social exclusion in certain rural and urban areas considered the most deprived parts of the country (Bergh 2012; Bono 2010; Berriane 2010). The INDH included local associations as key organizations representing the interests of local populations and participating in designing and implementing local development projects. Projects that could generate revenues at the local level and that included underrepresented social categories (such as women) were particularly encouraged. Having a registered association became a condition to get access to this funding.

The implementation of programs such as the INDH led to an increase in the numbers of a particular type of association within poor neighborhoods and villages: small, locally based, and formally apolitical organizations specializing in social, developmental, and educational issues and targeting mainly women and young people.[3] These organizations offer a broad range of services, ranging from various forms of training (such as literacy,[4] sewing, IT, and catering) to sport activities, providing legal advice, distributing clothes and food supplies, supporting unemployed youngsters, and organizing community clean-ups, vacation camps, and medical campaigns that include treatment at a nominal fee. As highlighted by Driss Khrouz, "Requests for help are so many and varied that learning to do 'a bit of everything' comes with the territory" (2008: 48).

At the national level, less than thirty thousand associations existed in the late 1990s, while today an estimated fifty thousand are registered, most of them having been created since the end of the 1990s. This process has been coupled with the development of an infrastructure aimed at giving associations spaces to organize their activities. A whole range of public centers aimed at offering social services and cultural activities through associations have since appeared throughout the country. While these centers are supervised by the state, they are managed by local associations that not only offer activities within these centers but are also responsible for finding the necessary funds to finance them (Berriane 2016a). The reformed constitution of 2011 includes articles reinforcing the role of civil society organizations (and more particularly associations) in public life and the implementation of concrete measures such as broadening the prerogatives of the deputy minister in charge of relations with the parliament, who is now also in charge of relations with civil society organizations.

While opening up spaces of negotiation and social action, associations function also as spaces of social promotion and political inclusion (Berriane 2010). This is particularly true for local and social development associations active in poor and formerly deprived regions. The top-down promotion of this kind of organization has contributed to the emergence of new elites to which the necessary means of becoming locally influential were given. This is particularly striking in regions that used to receive little attention from authorities, such as the working-class neighborhoods of Casablanca in which I conducted my research. Actors who did not belong to the traditional local notabilities or to the intellectual and economic elite and actors belonging to underrepresented social categories (such as women) have been able not only to climb the social ladder but also to become part of the local decision-making apparatus. They were included within local commissions working on the implementation of the INDH or are acting as key intermediaries between representatives of the state and local populations.

Their status rests upon their ability to redistribute public resources to the neighborhood by channeling funding and public assistance downward. The local population receives these funds indirectly through the activities proposed by the association. Wage earners and those receiving even minimal financial compensation in exchange for their monitoring or teaching activities within the association must also be counted among the beneficiaries of associational work. In areas where unemployment is rampant, such income sources are of an importance that should not be underestimated. At the same time, association leaders are also spokespeople for the local population (and especially for the beneficiaries of their association) in dealings with the local authorities. They fulfil this role, for example, by lobbying the authorities to facilitate access to certain administrative documents (like national identity cards or birth certificates). Their newly acquired status of key development actors allows them to draw the authorities' attention to problems the local population is experiencing or to organize meetings between the latter and public officials. The number of members or beneficiaries of their association gives the main representatives of the association an ability to mobilize that they can capitalize on with the local authorities in exchange for privileged access to public resources and support for their community work, or even their own personal projects. The activities organized by these leaders—both male and female—are therefore ways of showing their mobilization abilities and popularity, as measured by the number of individuals in attendance.

In all, the leaders interviewed could be considered, according to the language of current development policies, "local development courtiers" since they "serve as intermediaries to drain . . . external resources relevant to what is commonly referred to as development assistance" (de Sardan 1995: 160, trans. by author). But insofar as how they contribute, as mediators, to disseminate technological and scientific knowledge (literacy, training, questions related to health, etc.) at the local level, they are also "agents of development" (de Sardan 1995: 155–56). Jean-Pierre Olivier de Sardan draws a distinction between these two types of interventions, but my interlocutors are equally comfortable with both. This double function provides them with a certain social prestige and quickly contributes to establishing their notoriety in the neighborhood, sometimes at the district level. Their intermediary role, the privileged connections they maintain between the local representatives, and the ability to attract and redistribute material resources underlie the affirmation of social notability. The INDH reinforced this role by allowing community organization leaders to drain a portion of the proceeds from this initiative toward associations and their beneficiaries. By creating new spaces for interaction between local elected officials, public authorities, and association leaders, the INDH has also consolidated the latter's relational capital.

At the same time, this intermediary capacity also allows for the affirmation of an "associational clientelism" (Bennani-Chraïbi 2004: 42–43). Links of patronage tie these association leaders to their "clientele" of beneficiaries:

in exchange for services provided to the local population, they earn their support and loyalty. It is therefore interesting to see that this clientelism can also sustain the ties that exist between association leaders and certain government agents (the administration's civil servants, low-level state clerks, etc.). In exchange for exclusive access to the services proposed by the organizations, the latter guarantee them their support by facilitating, for example, certain administrative processes or by providing them with insider information on subjects such as funding or provisions made for local residents. The role of this associational clientelism fully expands during electoral campaigns, which some association leaders participate in as local relays or candidates.

Indeed, the symbolic and material resources gained through this process have led to an increase in the number of association representatives who campaign as candidates during municipal elections (Royaume du Maroc and USAID 2010). Both their newly gained local popularity and their alleged capacity to mobilize and communicate with people make them privileged local candidates who attract the attention of political parties. This process is particularly striking when looking at female trajectories. While most studies on women's access to political offices in Morocco used to highlight the importance of family connections in empowering women to participate in political parties, public affairs, and electoral campaigns (Sater 2007: 736), their participation in an association represents today a new gateway to local political positions (Berriane 2015).

Thus, recent transformations illustrate how state programs aimed at reinforcing the associational sphere have led to a renewal of the local elite, through the emergence of an "associational notability." But—paraphrasing Chris Shore (2002: 2)—how does this new elite legitimize its role and maintain its hegemony in the current period of social and economic change that Moroccan society (like other North African societies) is undergoing? I will tackle this question in the following section by drawing on extensive fieldwork conducted between 2006 and 2010 and between 2012 and 2014 among local association leaders living in suburban working-class neighborhoods of the city of Casablanca, situated in the districts of Sidi Moumen, Hay Mohammadi, and Sidi Bernoussi.[5] Over this period, I interviewed and observed the work of more than fifty association leaders (both women and men, the youngest being in her late twenties and the oldest in her mid-sixties), using different techniques—in situ observations as well as biographical and semi-open interviews.

As both an industrial and an economic capital, and as the largest city in the country, Casablanca has been the subject of special government attention over the years. This applies in particular to the implementation of development programs set up in several target neighborhoods identified as "underequipped," "poor," and "marginalized." This trend gained in importance after the terrorist attacks of May 2003, whose main protagonists came from slums situated on the outskirts of the city, and intensified even more after the INDH was launched. While the case of Casablanca is certainly specific, this city is also a living laboratory (Rabinow 1995) where we can observe the effects of demographic, social, and political mutations induced by such factors as urbanization, the reconfiguration of political action, and the dissemination of new norms of participation affecting, albeit in varying ways, the whole country.

PROXIMITY AND LOCAL EXPERTISE: "AUTOCHTHONY" AS CAPITAL

In order to legitimize their roles as associational leaders and as representatives of the local inhabitants, these local association representatives emphasize their rootedness in the neighborhood in which they are active and in which all of them also live. They highlight their social and territorial belonging to the local community by picturing themselves as "daughters" or "sons" of the neighborhood in which they grew up and into which their parents moved as part of the first waves of migration that brought rural populations from the countryside to Casablanca. They further insist on their working-class and rural roots, assigning great importance to their relatives' rural origins, the tribes to which they belong, and the difficult circumstances surrounding their adjustment to city life.

The neighborhoods in which I have conducted my research appeared in times of the French Protectorate in the context of the rapid expansion and industrialization of Casablanca. At that time, the city attracted consecutive waves of rural populations migrating from different parts of the country to find work in Morocco's industrial capital. They settled down in the outskirts of the city, where the biggest slums of the country developed. Today, the districts of Sidi Moumen, Hay Mohammadi, and Sidi Bernoussi have developed into socially mixed urban spaces in which one finds slums and social housing but also modest residential areas. The association leaders I interviewed were all heading local organizations and were either born in the districts into which their parents migrated from the countryside in the 1940s or 1950s or, at a very young age, accompanied their parents in their rural exodus.

It is interesting to note that the emphasis placed on these aspects of their life trajectories often reappears when they interact with their associations' beneficiaries, local authorities, or potential funders. Their rural origins and working-class background, the story of their parent's migration to the city, their belonging to the local community, and their attachment to the neighborhood represent a weighty resource that the current context allows them to convert into associative capital. Yet this "rhetoric of autochthony" (Hilgers 2011) takes different shapes, depending on the interlocutor the association leaders are facing.

When they speak with the members of their associations or with neighborhood inhabitants (especially those who moved to the city after the 1980s, with the more recent waves of migration), the language they use tends to change. It is sprinkled with words that are more common in the countryside than in the city and with allusions to rural practices and habits. When mentioning their associations, they tend, for instance, to use the word *jmâ'a*, which refers to traditional village councils. When they face local authorities or potential funders, they emphasize instead their intimate (firsthand) knowledge of the needs of the population who lives there. They insist on the fact that they were not only born in the neighborhood but also that they have, for the most part, lived there all their lives. Consequently, they have directly confronted the problems that the current inhabitants are experiencing, which not only allows them to better identify their needs but provides them with the tools to better communicate with this population. In so doing, they avail themselves of a legitimacy that rests on their role as experts whose expertise is based on "autochthonous" knowledge of the terrain and of local specificities.

If these new local elites can transform their social origins into resources, it is notably because they are valued in the current context. The insistence on local expertise is a part of a discourse on the importance of community outreach, which is undertaken as close to the ground as possible. Proximity, as a "label" and "norm" in current public policies, manifests itself at the local level through certain tools, such as a participatory approach or participatory diagnosis, which stipulate that the populations concerned must participate in the identification of their needs and the problems they need solved. These work methods and the vocabulary that refers to them have been transmitted to the association representatives through the intermediary of training undertaken either within the framework of the INDH, or through training proposed by other national or international organizations and bodies.

Both male and female association leaders refer to their social origin and to their belonging to the neighborhood to account for their specific capacity to implement participatory approaches based on the idea of "proximity." Women, however, tend to valorize their own role even more by insisting on their specific contributions to outreach work, reproducing certain gender stereotypes. The competencies that outreach work demands are often connected to characteristics that are generally tied to representations of femininity and especially to women's "domestic" competencies such as providing a listening ear to one's entourage, and caring about having a clean and healthy living environment. In addition, the easier access that women have to homes allows them—so the argumentation put forward—to better communicate with the population, allowing certain messages to more easily circulate in the neighborhood, over a cup of tea or around a sewing circle.

By insisting on their local expertise, the leaders not only legitimize their actions vis-à-vis the local population but also establish themselves in an increasingly competitive field where a multitude of associations—who are more or less well established—try to create a space for themselves on the local associative stage and to access the resources necessary to ensure the continuance of their association. In this context, the "proximity" and "autochthony" argument takes on greater importance in the power struggle between local association actors (who are often newcomers) and long-established civil society actors who head national development organizations that started appearing in the early 1990s, who have access to much more consequential social capital, but who are not natives of the neighborhood. In numerous interviews, the local association leaders tended to discredit the monopoly and experience that national associations pride themselves on, by emphasizing their own "well-founded" and "firsthand" knowledge of the problems plaguing the community. It is—so the argumentation put forward—the local expertise of the leaders that allows them to identify the real needs of the neighborhood's men and women and to act as their representatives.

PROFESSIONALIZATION: GUARANTEEING QUALITY, LEGITIMIZING WAGES

The emergence of association leaders as key political actors also results from the current valorization—through development policies—of training, qualification, and professionalism. Moreover, the importance given to associations as vectors of development and the scope of the projects implemented, are less and less compatible with volunteer work done by temporary and undertrained community organizers. This trend toward professionalization and qualification within the community organization field is also a result of the new model of associational work promoted by state programs and international organizations: management, durability, and continuity. In 2007, for instance, the Ministry of Social Development, Family and Solidarity launched a qualification program to distribute quality labels to associations that have signed an "ethical charter" and that have accepted monitoring by the ministry.

Yet in order to reach the expected levels of "quality," specific skills are necessary: notably the ability to conceive of, implement, and manage a project. In this new context, the fact that all association leaders have been to school and that some of them have studied a few years at university adds to their legitimacy as local associational elites. Their academic capital notably allows them to more easily access the trainings proposed by different government-financed national or international organizations. The INDH has put special emphasis on the importance of training by even proposing a university program lasting several months that would prepare associative and administrative executives for the management of the INDH projects. These trainings target all of the association leaders implicated in the INDH process: workshops on local development and participative work, communication techniques, project implementation modules, accounting techniques, and so on.

Most interviewed actors have relatively mild opinions regarding the effectiveness of these trainings, but they emphasize their symbolic meaning, since the fact of having been chosen by local officials and trained by well-known representatives of Morocco's "civil society" adds to their important status as agents of development and as legitimate spokespersons of the local population. These trainings are also an opportunity to get in contact with local officials and civil servants, who take part in the same trainings. The status of an "educated and trained woman or man" facilitates their access to the public sphere, puts them in a position apart, and confers upon them more respectability. They are instructors, guides, and experts on what goes on behind the scenes both at an administrative level and within bureaucratic hierarchies. They know how to "talk to the ones in charge" and are in contact with those who are needed to help neighborhood residents who do not have access to the same networks and knowledge.

The reliance on academic programs and training has a threefold function. It is first a way to highlight one's role as a community organization representative and to be noticed by the authorities. It is also a way to distinguish oneself from other association leaders: the distinction between those who are "educated" and those who are "basically illiterate" is very common. It notably allows the association leaders in question to differentiate themselves from those they consider to be amateurs—both men and women—who do not really know what they are doing. The men and women I interviewed emphasized their training as a mark of quality, the guarantee of a serious and professional engagement with the community that is based on knowledge acquired though a state-recognized education. In this context, the curriculum vitae gains a primordial importance. Refining and maintaining one's curriculum vitae is accomplished by means of many different trainings, which can at times appear excessive. By extension, training becomes institutionalized more and more as a necessary condition for all associational engagement.

The importance given to education and training is also apparent through the emphasis certain local association representatives place on what it is that differentiates them from other neighborhood residents, more specifically from the associations' beneficiaries. Paradoxically, while their proximity to the local population and their belonging to the neighborhood contributes to establishing their role as "autochthonous experts" and legitimate representatives of the population's interests, their status as educated women and men comes from distancing themselves from that same local population. In order to highlight their own educational background, they emphasize the fact that the majority of the inhabitants of their district are "illiterate," "uneducated," or even "ignorant." Therefore, the problems that they encounter in their work are often identified as being caused by "the mentality of the people around here," by their "conservativism" and their lack of "openness to changes taking place." This last point highlights the inherent paradox of their status as intermediaries, which both implies a proximity to the population they represent and a distance from them, due to the competencies they pride themselves on having as association leaders.

The importance given to the professionalization of local association actors is accompanied by a tendency toward paid employment within the associational sphere. Professionalization and the provision of salaries are quite common in the big and well-established associations that work at the national level, as they have access to much more funding on a regular basis; whereas funds are still limited in the case of neighborhood associations. However, the phenomenon is gaining ground within grassroots associations as well, and expanded after the launch of the INDH. The funds allocated within the framework of this program not only allow for the funding of projects, but also offer chances for employment as instructors or project coordinators.

The world of associational work is becoming more and more like a labor market, an alternative to the precariousness of daily professional existence. This evolution echoes the arrival of new funding initiatives in the field of community outreach but it also comes from the deployment of community action within social strata that are less privileged than those that benefited from it historically. More than a motivating factor, the possibility of transforming community action into remunerated work serves to secure its sustainability. The costs of all active engagement within the association (means of transportation, telephone, etc.) are such that they cannot be borne, in the long run, by association representatives who have limited material resources. The ability to generate revenue is even more important in the case of women, as most of them depend on their families for financial support. The appearance of these women in the associative field remains a marginal phenomenon, in large part due to the restrictions imposed by those closest to them on their public activities. In such a context, a salary also serves as an essential alibi that justifies and legitimizes associational work outside of the home.

Talking about compensation raises the question of volunteer work, which represents a powerful symbolic resource on which most association leaders have to rely to legitimize their work: "The symbolic arm of volunteer work provides dignity (as opposed to politics) and respectability (defence of the general interest)" (Barthélémy 2000: 199, trans. by author). According to this thinking, only the desire to serve the general interest and to help one's fellowman should motivate the associative actor. Any form of personal compensation, whether it be material or symbolic, is seen as contrary to the values that are supposed to govern the associative sphere. Yet the transition between volunteerism (which is central to the image used by association representatives to legitimize their role) and paid employment can be fluid, and the preservation of the image of volunteer, completely disinterested work bears the risk of rapidly falling apart as soon as financial compensation becomes more important within an association.

The paradox posed by this split between volunteering and professionalization obliges those interviewed to juggle different forms of legitimization. When speaking about volunteering, the association leaders tend to emphasize the sacrifices that they themselves do not hesitate to make for the good of the association and by extension for the neighborhood residents. In other words, since the value of the price paid (in sacrifices) largely exceeds that of any compensation received, such compensation can be considered minimal and not as the source of any personal enrichment. The most established association leaders—those who receive regular remuneration in exchange for their work within the association—justify their access to revenue by emphasizing their professionalism. If they receive pay for their work it is above all because the services that they provide are of a quality superior to those provided by most other associative actors (both men and women) classified as amateurs. In this context, remuneration becomes a symbol of quality. Moreover, when they discuss the question of wages (which rarely happens), they almost never use the term remuneration (*khlâs*), but rather use the term "compensation" (*taʿwîd*) or "punctual assistance" (*musâʿada muʾaqqata*), which allows them to euphemize the material benefits they gain from their activities.

This euphemizing of their compensation has become even more important now that certain representations transmitted about associations tend to describe them as means of personal enrichment that attract shady individuals. This image has gained prominence with the implementation of an increased number of local development programs financed by the state or by national and international donors. It became even stronger once the first evaluations of the implemented INDH projects showed that funds were misappropriated and that funded projects failed to be implemented. To counterbalance this image and legitimize their role vis-à-vis the local population, those affiliated with associations have to make more effort to highlight the virtuous character of associational life.

VIRTUOUS ASSOCIATIONS AND CORRUPT POLITICAL PARTIES: APOLITICISM AS A VIRTUE

Among the sources of legitimization that those interviewed have access to, one can count their distance from "politics." Between the 1960s and the early 1990s, during the so-called years of lead, when the repression against political opponents was at its highest, politics were associated with risks that implicated the closed-off context of the time, whereas today they have become "an expression of the opportunism" of elected officials and political leaders (Tozy 2007: 199). It is above all from the latter that the association leaders try to distance themselves.

By distancing themselves from parties and political representatives, the association leaders I studied emphasize their own integrity. Weakened by several decades of restrictions, transformed into synonyms of corruption and cronyism, the political parties have, essentially, lost their credibility. By putting distance between themselves and political parties, association representatives valorize an alternative path to political legitimacy. All while denigrating the parties' actions, they highlight the "useful" contributions of associations to the invention of a "different kind of politics" (Catusse 2002: 308), founded on social action, closer to the population and more aware of its needs. They highlight in this way their alternative role as effective and efficient intermediaries for the local population, a role that local elected officials, according to them, have ceased to fill. The public discourse provides them with the references needed to accentuate the distinction that they make between associations and parties, a distinction that provides them with yet another way of accounting for their legitimacy. To add weight to their statements, they notably allude to the way in which the king values and supports associations, while he tends to devalue the role played by political parties.[6]

A first expression of their public distancing from political parties is tied to the way in which some association leaders construct the narratives of their career paths. Political experiences play a very minor, or sometimes even nonexistent, role in the narratives of those who have recently joined the associative sphere. Even when they have had such experiences (notably as members of a party, or even as local candidates during past municipal elections), this part of their history disappears from the narratives that they share today. The relationship with the political past is different in the case of association leaders who have participated in protests during the 1970s or 1980s. Instead of hiding this experience, they emphasize it and use it to legitimize their current engagement. Unlike the experiences they had within political parties, participation in left- and far-left-leaning movements during the 1970s and 1980s is perceived by these association representatives as valuable because it allows them not only to secure a place for themselves within the history of a certain kind of political activism but also to situate themselves in the continuation of mobilizations that have increased in importance today. The reference group here is that of former political opponents who, after having been victims of repression during the 1970s and 1980s, became a part of the associative sphere during the 1990s and have achieved a certain status or even a certain level of prestige (Fillieule and Bennani-Chraïbi 2003: 82). They are recognized within today's associational sphere as being "true" or even "great" activists.

In other words, not just anyone can claim to be an activist: there are "real" and "fake" ones, "great" and "small" ones. The example of former political opponents is held up as a model, and the designation of "activist" has a positive connotation today. Moreover, the distinction is clear—with regards to both men and women—between the associative actor (*al-fâ‘il al-jam‘âwi*) and the associative activist (*al-munâdil al-jam ͨ âwi*), the second designation having a higher symbolic value than the first. By emphasizing their past participation in leftist movements or far-left movements, association leaders claim both titles. This allows them to distinguish themselves from the majority of associative representatives who can only claim the first title, that of associative actor. But all while claiming their past as engaged protestors, these association leaders clearly differentiate between their work and that of political parties.

This distancing is accompanied by a nearly systematic contrast between associations that are described as being "virtuous," "active," "transparent," "aware of the people's true needs," on the one hand, and political parties that are "corrupt," "disconnected from the population's reality," and "motivated by their own interests," on the other. The differentiation between parties and associations also takes place through the emphasis that the associative sphere puts on freedom, as opposed to the ideological restrictions that allegiance to a political party entails. The conflictual dimension of politics and the obligation to "take a position" are considered to be signs of ideological confinement and loss of liberty. In order to clearly mark the difference between themselves and political parties but also to emphasize their own integrity, they work to denigrate associations with close political ties. Any rapprochement between associations and political parties is decried because it is a sign both that the association in question is being manipulated by a political party and that its directors are not solely motivated by the best interests of the residents of the neighborhood, but are above all concerned with their own political interests.

This vision is also maintained through contrasting "active" associations, which offer concrete and efficient action, and political parties that no longer fulfill their representative role, take no interest in what is happening locally, and work only to advance their own interests. Association leaders highlight the difference between "the social," which is understood to mean a large domain that is disconnected from partisan politics, and power struggles between and within political parties. Interestingly these same distinctions are reproduced during electoral campaigns when local association leaders run as political candidates. They base most of their campaigns on their specific capacity as representatives of an association to renew and enhance the political sphere, and a distinction is made throughout the campaigns between "good" associations and "bad" political parties (Berriane 2015). References to their association enable the candidates to illustrate their privileged relationship with the state through their access to resources that it makes available, holding out the prospect of offering, through their association, special help and services for all supporters who agree to vote for them. In a context such as Morocco, where "voters . . . primarily seek to reap patronage benefits" and therefore "support candidates whom they believe they will deliver advantages to them" (Gandhi and Lust-Okar 2009: 409), associations become new concrete avenues through which patronage and access to state resources can be promised to voters.

LEGITIMIZED BY THE KING: THE MONARCH'S ACTIONS AS A KEY REFERENCE POINT

While most of the interviewed local association leaders distance themselves from politics, several of them use the king as a primary frame of reference to whom they attribute the characteristics of an accomplished associative actor, indirectly drawing parallels between him and themselves. They further highlight various moments that link them to the king, emphasizing their role in implementing one of the monarch's main sites of initiative: social and communal action. As already mentioned in the introduction, highlighting one's connection to the king and his family or, more generally, to the palace has been one of the main sources of legitimacy for elites throughout Morocco's history postindependence (Benhaddou 1997). In the era of participative governance, grassroots associations use the same kind of argument by building connections to the king through their associative experience.

During the first interview conducted with Siham, this fifty-year-old head of a local association for disabled women and children failed to indicate that she had taken part in the 2002 legislative campaign as a political candidate. However, she chose to frame the official narrative of her trajectory as a social actor around another significant moment: her meeting with King Mohammed VI when he was still crown prince.

> While we were talking, he told me, "Siham, do you have an association?" I told him, "No, Your Majesty (*mulây*), I do not." "And you haven't thought about creating one?" I told him, "No, Your Majesty, I have never thought of it." . . . He said to me, "Think about creating an association and call it the Solidarity Association." The name came from him, not me. . . . He told me, "Create this association and you will have my full support." . . . I asked him, "But how will I see you, Your Majesty?" He said, "The same way as this time.

Fig. 2.1. King Mohammed VI on Moroccan one-hundred-dirham note.

You made your way to me; you will do the same next time." . . . And then, since that time, I've wanted to create an association. . . . The next time I'll go to see him in the name of the Solidarity Association!

Born in the early 1960s in Casablanca with a leg deformity, Siham moves with the help of crutches and today presides over an association that was created in 2004 and that helps the disabled. After having stopped her education early on, she trained as a seamstress before opening her own workshop on the ground floor of her family home. During the 1990s, she decided to follow the example of a friend who managed, a few months earlier, to have an audience with the crown prince, who was known for his actions in favor of those in need, which had earned him the nickname "prince of the poor." Siham spent six months at Rabat, waiting every day near the prince's palace, before being received. Upon meeting her, the prince granted her a concession to operate a taxi and a sum of money, before suggesting that she create an association.

As indicated by the above excerpt, Siham situates the premises of the creation of her grassroots association within that meeting. Through this story that has become famous throughout the neighborhood, she confers a royal genealogy on the organization that she presides over: the crown prince is at the origin not only of the concept of this organization but also of its name. The manner of presenting her association as being the direct materialization of a royal will to see it created fits into the narrative shared among most of the association leaders interviewed: the king as the direct initiator of the dynamic that goes through the associative sphere. The "social," as a national project initiated and carried out by the king, takes the place of the "political" in its partisan and competitive dimension. These representations rely on an official discourse that supports—notably since the advent of the INDH—development as a "national cause." It has demonstrated that this cause distinguishes itself not only through its "consensual character," which generates the "demobilization of forces which could destroy it," but also "at a symbolic level, through the insertion of the Initiative into the patriotic imagination of the country" (Bono 2010: 21–22, trans. by author).

While seeming to play on this convention, Siham's statement has the advantage of illustrating to what extent the king and his "long-term projects" are situated at the center of the frames of reference of most of the association leaders interviewed. In a number of interviews, the description of the king contrasted greatly with that of political actors. The latter were described as corrupt, inefficient, and disconnected from the real needs of the population, whereas the majority of the local association leaders attributed qualities such as intimate knowledge of the population's needs (notably of the poor), dynamism, and rigor to the monarch. One cannot help but note the numerous parallels between the figure of the associative actor and that of the monarch, who represents the most accomplished example of an associative actor: a peerless champion and supporter of the social question.

On the ground, this perception is seen in the conviction that many people have that the association represents a sure pathway to become closer to the monarch. This concept is evidently maintained through numerous examples of local association leaders who have had the opportunity, by means of their associative activities, to meet the king—for a kiss on the hand, a photo, or some words exchanged—during the inauguration of a social center or during some official ceremony organized within the palace. Whenever one can approach the monarch, it is generally thought to be an opportunity to ask for his help, but these types of meetings also contribute to the valorization of the individual, who gains social prestige.

The emergence of the INDH has contributed to establishing the image of the monarch as a frame of reference for many of the association leaders interviewed. This program is generally seen as emanating directly from the king, the initiator, architect, and guarantor of a large-scale project. He has contributed to raising associations to the rank of institutions that are known and recognized by the state. Thus, certain association representatives believe not only that they have a particular status but also that they benefit—through the governor, the king's local representative—from a direct connection to the palace. Such a perception is not based only on the recent valorization that local associations have achieved in the eyes of public authorities. It also comes from the lived experiences in their daily lives as association representatives as they have become privileged interlocutors, the most established ones with a direct contact to the governor. By adapting their strategies to this redistribution of resources and power, association leaders manage to legitimize and maintain their hegemony as local associational elites. At the same time, they indirectly contribute to the redeployment and reaffirmation of the power of the *makhzen* and the weakening of the role played by local elected officials.

CONCLUSION

It is apparent that the pro-participation policies established by the state over the past fifteen years have contributed to the renewal of local associative elites. Through their participation in the associational sphere, actors with limited social capital, often unemployed and belonging to the working class or the lower middle class, have been able not only to climb the social ladder but also to become part of the local decision-making apparatus as political actors. The emergence of new means of legitimization has played a decisive role in this. It has allowed the newcomers that I have studied to transform their social origins and competencies into ways to account for their role. In order to account for their role as association leaders and as local decision-makers and to assert their social notability, they combine various lines of argumentation. They highlight their own social and territorial belonging while simultaneously differentiating themselves from the local population through references to their educational capital and their professionalism. They further distance themselves from political parties as a way to prove their integrity. Paradoxically, these new lines of argumentation are combined with narratives that highlight their "closeness to the king," an older source of elite legitimacy, which is reproduced, today, in a new "participative" form.

These trends reveal two things. On the one hand, they show that the associational sphere is not only a space that can be used by elites to reinforce their position and get access to more privileged elites (Woods 1994) or pursue novel strategies of class formation (Lucas 1994). In the current context, in which the implementation of participatory means of governance has become a norm, the associational sphere can also contribute to the emergence of new types of elites, even among populations that used to lack the necessary social, material, and symbolic capital to become an elite. This process of elite formation is made possible by the emergence of new frames of legitimacy that can be used as means of accountability. Within these new frameworks, autochthony becomes a guarantee for proximity and firsthand knowledge, instruction and remuneration an indicator of professionalism and better quality, and distance from political parties a proof of integrity.

On the other hand, this process of elite formation enables us also to question the often-assumed separation between the sphere of the state and that of associational life, which some authors portray as a "political space beyond the state's purview" (Bratton 1989: 411). Recent developments of the associational sphere in Morocco illustrate the interconnectedness of both spheres. The increasing number of associations does not reflect a decline in the state but rather a redeployment of the state apparatus via associations. Local development associations such as those described in the current chapter make it possible for the state to redeploy itself indirectly at a lower cost by including many new actors in the government of the social sphere, renewing and diversifying the composition of its local elite (see also Berriane 2016a). The state—symbolized by its main representative, which is the person of the king—plays a central role in the frames of reference used by association leaders to account for their role and position. This example shows that the monarch remains a principal determinant behind elite circulation and upward mobility in Morocco.

NOTES

1. The notion of *makhzen* has a very broad meaning. It "is closely associated with monarchy's inner circles of power. The notion has changed over time to mean coercive state apparatus, as well as the education, health care, administration and economic services the state provides" (Maghraoui 2011: 698).

2. I prefer using the word "association" rather than "NGO" here since there is no clear line separating these organizations from state institutions. This will become clear throughout the chapter. In addition, the term "association" is a better translation of the Arabic term *jam'iyya* used to name this kind of civic organizations in Morocco.

3. These associations are similar to what is referred to, in other African countries, as "local development associations" or, in some cases, "home town associations" (Woods 1994).

4. According to official estimates of the high commissioner for the plan based on the census of 2014, the illiteracy rate in Morocco is declining: it moved from 87 percent in 1960 to 32 percent in 2014. Yet illiteracy still represents a striking feature of Morocco's population, especially of the categories of women (41.9 percent illiteracy), rural population (47.7 percent illiteracy), and people older than fifty (61 percent illiteracy).

5. The research conducted between 2006 and 2010 was part of my doctoral dissertation (see Berriane 2013). During the following years I have continued my research as postdoctoral research fellow within the associational sphere of working-class neigh-

borhoods in Casablanca, concentrating more particularly on the making of spaces of participation (see Berriane 2016a).

6. The condemnation of political parties by the king reached a new level in his "Throne Day" speech of July 2017, in which he highlighted the deficiencies of the political class. As shown by Mounia Bennani-Chraïbi (2017), this has been a recurrent official narrative based on the myth that "the king is good, the political class is bad"—a tool used by the palace to legitimize itself and discredit political parties.

REFERENCES

Barthélémy, Martine. 2000. *Associations un nouvel âge de la participation?* Paris: Presses de Sciences Po.

Barwig, Andrew. 2012. "The 'New Palace Guards': Elections and Elites in Morocco and Jordan." *Middle East Journal* 66, no. 3: 425–39.

Benhaddou, Ali. 1997. *Maroc: Les élites du royaume. Essai sur l'organisation du pouvoir au Maroc.* Paris: L'Harmattan.

Bennani-Chraïbi, Mounia. 2004. "Représenter et mobiliser dans l'élection législative au Maroc." In Mounia Bennani-Chraïbi, Myriam Catusse, and Jean-Claude Santucci, eds., *Scènes et coulisses de l'élection au Maroc: Les législatives 2002*, 15–53. Paris: Karthala.

Bennani-Chraïbi, Mounia. 2013. "L'espace partisan marocain: Un microcosme polarisé?" *Revue française de science politique* 6, no. 63: 1163–92.

Bennani-Chraïbi, Mounia. 2017. "The King Is Good, the Political Class Is Bad: A Tired Myth." *Jadaliyya*, September 5. http://www.jadaliyya.com/Details/34540/%60The-King-Is-Good,-the-Political-Class-Is-Bad%60-A-Tired-Myth

Ben Néfissa, Sarah, 2002. "Associations et ONG dans le monde arabe: Vers la mise en place d'une problématique." In Ben Néfissa Sarah, ed., *Pouvoirs et associations dans le monde arabe*, 7–26. Paris: CNRS.

Bergh, Sylvia I. 2012. "'Inclusive' Neoliberalism, Local Governance Reforms and the Redeployment of State Power: The Case of the National Initiative for Human Development (INDH) in Morocco." *Mediterranean Politics* 17, no. 3: 410–26.

Berriane, Yasmine. 2010. "The Complexities of Inclusive Participatory Governance: The Case of Moroccan Associational Life in the Context of the INDH." *Journal of Economic and Social Research* 12, no. 1: 89–111.

Berriane, Yasmine. 2013. *Femmes, associations et politique à Casablanca*. Rabat: Centre Jacques Berque.

Berriane, Yasmine. 2015. "The Micropolitics of Reform: Gender Quota, Grassroots Associations and the Renewal of Local Elites in Morocco." *Journal of North African Studies* 20, no. 3: 432–49.

Berriane, Yasmine. 2016a. "Construire l'espace du social: Les multiples figures de l'intermédiation dans les maisons de jeunes à Casablanca." In Irene Bono and Béatrice

Hibou, eds., *Le gouvernement du social au Maroc*, 45–82. Paris: Karthala Collection "Recherches internationales."

Berriane, Yasmine. 2016b. "Political Parties and Participation: Morocco." *Encyclopedia of Women & Islamic Cultures*, Online Supplement 13.

Bogaert, Koenraad. 2018. *Globalized Authoritarianism: Megaprojects, Slums, and Class Relations in Urban Morocco*. Minneapolis: University of Minnesota Press.

Bono, Irene. 2010. *Le phénomène participatif au Maroc à travers ses styles d'action et ses norms*. Les Etudes du CERI, n°166. Paris : Centre d'études et de recherches internationales (IEP Paris).

Bratton, Michael. 1989. "Beyond the State: Civil Society and Associational Sphere in Africa." *World Politics* 41, no. 3: 407–30.

Burke, Edmund. 1971. "Parties and Elites in North Africa: Algeria and Morocco." *Africa Today* 18, no. 4: 50–59.

Catusse, Myriam. 2002. "Le charme discret de la société civile: Ressorts politiques de la formation d'un groupe dans le Maroc 'ajusté.'" *Revue internationale de politique comparée*, no. 2: 297–318.

Catusse, Myriam. 2008. *Le temps des entrepreneurs? Politique et transformations du capitalisme au Maroc*. Paris: Maisonneuve & Larose.

Darhour, Hanane, and Salah-Ddine Krit. 2012. "Empowered or Not? Moroccan Women MP's Strategies to Empowerment." *European Journal of Scientific Research* 77, no. 2: 174–86.

de Sardan, Jeanne-Pierre Olivier. 1995. *Anthropologie et développement: Essai en socio-anthropologie du changement social*. Paris: Karthala.

El Maoula Iraki, Aziz. 2003. *Des notables du Makhzen à l'épreuve de la "gouvernance": Elites locales, territoires, gestion urbaine et développement au Maroc (cas de trois villes moyennes de la Région Nord-Ouest)*. Paris: L'Harmattan.

Fillieule, Olivier, and Mounia Bennani-Chraïbi. 2003. "Exit, voice, loyalty et bien d'autres choses encore. . . ." In Mounia Bennani-Chraïbi and Olivier Fillieule, eds., *Résistances et protestations dans les sociétés musulmanes*, 43–126. Paris: Presses de Sciences Po.

Gandhi, Jennifer, and Ellen Lust-Okar. 2009. "Elections under Authoritarianism." *Annual Review of Political Science* 12: 403–22.

Hammoudi, Abdellah. 1997. *Master and Disciple: The Cultural Foundations of Moroccan Authoritarianism*. Chicago: University of Chicago Press.

Heydemann, Steven. 2007. "Upgrading Authoritarianism in the Arab World." Saban Center Analysis Paper no. 13. Washington, DC: Saban Center.

Hilgers, Mathieu. 2011. "Autochthony as Capital in a Global Age." *Theory, Culture & Society* 28, no. 1: 34–54.

Khrouz, Driss. 2008. "A Dynamic Civil Society." *Journal of Democracy* 19, no. 1: 42–49.

Leveau, Rémy. 1985. *Le fellah marocain défenseur du trône*. Paris: Presses de la Fondation nationale des sciences politiques.

Lucas, John. 1994. "The State, Civil Society and Regional Elites: A Study of Three Associations in Kano, Nigeria." *African Affairs* 93, no. 370: 21–38.

Maghraoui, Driss. 2011. "Constitutional Reforms in Morocco: Between Consensus and Subaltern Politics." *Journal of North African Studies* 16, no. 4: 679–99.

Oubenal, Mohamed, and Abdellatif Zeroual. 2017. "Gouverner par la gouvernance: Les nouvelles modalités de contrôle politique des élites économiques au Maroc." *Critique internationale*, no. 74: 9–32.

Rabinow, Paul. 1995. *French Modern: Norms and Forms of the Social Environment*. Chicago: University of Chicago Press.

Royaume du Maroc and USAID. 2010. "Rapport relatif aux résultats du diagnostic participatif sur l'état de l'exercice de la fonction d'élue et de la participation des femmes à la gouvernance locale." Unpublished report. Rabat.

Sater, James N. 2007. "Changing Politics from Below? Women Parliamentarians in Morocco." *Democratization* 14, no. 4: 723–42.

Shore, Cris. 2002. "Introduction: Towards an Anthropology of Elites." In Cris Shore and Stephen Nugent, eds., *Elite Cultures: Anthropological Perspectives*, 1–21. New York: Routledge.

Storm, Lise. 2007. *Democratization in Morocco: The Political Elite and Struggles for Power in the Post-independence State*. London: Routledge.

Tessler, Mark A. 1982. "Morocco: Institutional Pluralism and Monarchical Dominance." In I. William Zartman et al., eds., *Political Elites in Arab North Africa: Morocco, Algeria, Tunisia, Libya, and Egypt*, 35–91. New York: Longman.

Tozy, Mohamed. 1999. *Monarchie et Islam politique au Maroc*. Paris: Presses de Sciences Po.

Tozy, Mohamed. 2003. "Préface." In A. El Maoula El Iraki, *Des notables du Makhzen à l'épreuve de la "gouvernance": Elites locales, gestion urbaine et développement au Maroc*, 7–9. Paris: L'Harmattan.

Tozy, Mohamed. 2007. "Religiosité au féminin." In M. El Ayadi, H. Rachik Hassan, and M. Tozy, eds., *L'islam au quotidien: Enquête sur les valeurs et les pratiques religieuses au Maroc*, 177–223. Casablanca: Prologues.

Tozy, Mohamed. 2008. "Islamists, Technocrats and the Palace." *Journal of Democracy* 19, no. 1: 34–41.

Tozy, Mohamed. 2010. "Introduction." In M. Tozy, ed., *Elections au Maroc: Entre partis et notables (2007–2009)*, 11–25. Casablanca: CM2S / Konrad Adenauer Foundation.

Vermeren, Pierre. 2002. *La formation des élites marocaines et tunisiennes: Des nationalistes aux islamistes (1920–2000)*. Paris: La Découverte.

Waterbury, John. 1970. *The Commander of the Faithful: The Moroccan Elite. A Study in Segmented Politics*. London: Weidenfeld & Nicolson.

Woods, Dwayne. 1994. "Elites, Ethnicity, and 'Home Town' Associations in the Côte d'Ivoire: An Historical Analysis of State Society Links." *Africa* 64, no. 4: 465–83.

Zerhouni, Saloua. 2002. "Morocco: Reconciling Continuity and Change." In Volker Perthes, ed., *Arab Elites: Negotiating the Politics of Change*, 61–85. Boulder, CO: Lynne Rienner.

CHAPTER 3

Elites and Political Representation in Africa
Members of Parliament in Ghana and Togo

ANJA OSEI

INTRODUCTION

As the central institution of democracy, [parliaments] embody the will of the people in government, and carry all their expectations that democracy will be truly responsive to their needs and help solve the most pressing problems that confront them in their daily lives. (Beetham 2006: 1)

This quotation powerfully demonstrates how important elected legislatures are for modern political systems. Parliaments fulfill a number of core functions, such as lawmaking, oversight, accountability, and representation. Among these, representation is a key issue that connects citizens to the political process by making their views present in the arena of decision-making. While there is an abundance of literature on parliaments in Western countries (see, for example, Best and Cotta 2000), African legislatures are among the least-studied subjects in the contemporary democratization literature (Barkan 2009; Azevedo-Harman 2012). Since the 1990s, African political regimes have undergone profound changes: parliamentary democracy has taken root on the continent, and the regular holding of elections has become a norm. As the growing body of literature on electoral authoritarianism[1] suggests, however, it would be wrong to equate the existence of parties, parliaments, and elections with the existence of liberal democracy (see Levitsky and Way 2010; Schedler 2006): a number of regimes in Africa and elsewhere hold regular elections but violate liberal-democratic principles at the same time (Schedler

2006: 3). Intuitively, one would expect that the type of political regime also exerts a considerable influence on the quality of parliamentary representation, but research in this area is rare and the results are at best mixed (see Golosov 2014: 52). Moreover, the Africanist literature suggests that the nature of political representation is largely similar across the continent. In their book *Africa Works* Chabal and Daloz (1999: 37) argue that the "relation between the rulers and the ruled [continues to] rest on links between big men, patrons, and their communities." The work of Lindberg (2010) and (van Vliet 2014) supports this view by showing how the behavior of members of parliament (MPs) is shaped by clientelistic demands.

This raises at least two important questions that will be addressed in this chapter: How representative are parliaments in African countries? Are there differences between parliaments in democratic and less democratic countries?

Following Pitkin (1967), two core dimensions of representation will be analyzed. The first one is *descriptive representation*: Does the parliament reflect the composition of society, and is there a spokesperson for each socially relevant group? The second dimension is *substantive representation*, which is concerned with the question how responsive parliamentarians are toward their constituents.

To answer these questions, this chapter will use a comparative case studies design. This is a rare approach in the field of representation, which is so far dominated by quantitative studies dealing with issues such as the representation of women or ethnic groups either on a worldwide basis (see, for example, Ruedin 2013), or with a focus on the African continent (Yoon 2004). Systematic cross-country research is largely absent due to the shortage of available data (see also Randall 2007: 86; Joshi 2013: 2). This is exactly the contribution that this chapter will make. It uses data from standardized surveys in the parliament of Ghana in 2013, and the parliament of Togo in 2014–15. Data collection included biographical characteristics as well as attitudes and self-perceptions of MPs. The high response rates (92 percent in Ghana and 79 percent in Togo) allow deeper comparative insights into political representation. In addition, the two countries vary in their degree of democracy: while Ghana is considered as one of Africa's most democratic countries, Togo is an electoral authoritarian regime.[2] The comparative design is rather explorative and hypotheses-generating than strictly hypothesis-testing. Although the findings cannot be easily generalized, they can inspire future research on African parliaments.

The next two sections review the most important theoretical debates regarding the topic of representation. Next, I explain the research design and provide some details about the data collection process. Following this is empirical analysis, while the last section draws conclusions from the findings.

THE THEORY OF REPRESENTATION: A SHORT OVERVIEW

Definitions of democracy differ markedly in their conceptualization of the relationship between rulers and ruled. This chapter does not provide a discussion of the theoretical varieties and practical consequences of these conceptions. Instead it starts from the empirical reality that most modern democracies are representative systems in which elections are the primary mechanism to hold leaders accountable. Or, as Best and Cotta (2000: 492) express it, "Modern democracy has at its centre the idea of representation: those who govern are the representatives of the people."

In its simplest form, representation can be understood as "the making present of something which is nevertheless not literally present" (Pitkin 1967: 144). While authors like Mansbridge (2003) and Dryzek and Niemeyer (2008) have refined and redefined the concept, Pitkin's work still remains a key to understanding and analyzing representation.[3] She distinguishes between four dimensions of representation: formal, descriptive, symbolic, and substantive. *Formal representation* is focused on the rules and procedures by which representatives are chosen. *Descriptive representation* requires the legislature to be a "mirror" of the nation (Pitkin 1967: 61). In other words, the composition of the parliament shall be demographically representative to guarantee "the presence in it of spokesmen for all groups in proportion to their number in the electorate" (63). *Symbolic representation* is concerned with how the representatives are perceived and evaluated by those they represent (Schwindt-Bayer and Mishler 2005: 409). Both descriptive and symbolic representation are concepts in which representing means "standing for" someone (Pitkin 1967: 113). In contrast to that, *substantive representation* requires the representative to be "acting for" his constituents (Pitkin 1967: 145). Here, representing means to act in the interest of the represented and to be responsive to them (145).

A great amount of the literature on descriptive representation deals with the representation of women in national assemblies or cabinets around the world. Authors like Yoon (2001, 2004) have explicitly focused on women in African politics. To a much lesser extent there are studies devoted to the representation of ethnic or religious minorities (Arriola and Johnson 2014; Ruedin 2009) or age groups (Joshi 2013). It is important to note that "representation by resemblance" is also a matter of which characteristics are seen as socially relevant enough to be politically represented (Pitkin 1967: 87; Mansbridge 1999: 634). One argument why descriptive representation is important is that certain views can only be articulated by people who are directly affected (Ruedin 2013: 13; Phillips 1995). Descriptive representation can also have an important symbolic effect and therefore work to reduce political alienation (Ruedin 2013: 14). In addition, the quality of political debates on the problems of minority groups is greatly enhanced if representatives from these groups are included (14). In short, descriptive representation can help to reduce social conflict and contribute to greater political stability (14).

Research on substantive representation is generally scarcer than research on descriptive representation (for an overview see Wängnerud 2009). Very often, substantive representation is understood as ideological congruence between voters and representatives (Achen 1978). Many studies thus operationalize responsiveness as "the translation of constituent policy demands into the policy responsiveness of legislators" (Carman 2007: 3) and focus on the link between voter preferences and party platforms (Miller and Stokes 1963; Luna and Zechmeister 2005). While the debate about the actual meaning of "substantive" representation goes on (Celis 2009), it is widely acknowledged that the underrepresentation of certain groups in decision-making and political institutions is a "democratic problem of justice, legitimacy, responsiveness and effectiveness" (Celis 2009: 95–96; Phillips 1995). It cannot, however, be taken for granted that elected deputies act in the interest of the group with which they share descriptive characteristics (for an overview of the arguments see Mansbridge 1999: 630). Studies on the representation of women have found that not all women necessarily share the same interest, and that women in high political positions do not by default defend women's rights (see Wägnerud 2009; Schwindt-Bayer and Mishler 2005). The same can be said for ethnic, religious, or other minority groups (Ruedin 2013). Nevertheless, many scholars claim that there is a causal link between descriptive and substantive representation (Mansbridge 1999; Wängnerud 2009: 52; Beckwith 2007).

Another important question that is raised in this context is that of the relationship between democracy and representation. Elite theory argues that there are two dimensions to the relationship between elites and regimes: horizontal integration and vertical integration (Putnam 1976: 107). Horizontal integration describes the interrelations between elites and the extent of cooperation between them, while vertical integration is concerned with the relations between elites and the masses. In an ideal setting, elites should hold democratic values themselves, act in accordance with the preferences of the electorate, and be demographically representative (Hoffmann-Lange 1986). Reality often falls short of these high expectations, but for empirical research on regime types it is reasonable to assume that elites in democracies come closer to these ideals than elites in nondemocratic systems. If democracy is understood as a system in which governments are accountable and responsive to their citizens, we would expect that parliaments in democratic countries will be more representative than their counterparts in less democratic states. Democracies are often assumed to create a favorable environment for groups to organize themselves and voice their concerns (Yoon 2001: 173; Goetz 1998). In addition, parties in competitive settings must compete for the votes of these groups, which in turn makes them more representative over time. There is some evidence that democratization has created more space especially for the representation of women (Yoon 2001; Arriola and Johnson 2014), but the empirical findings are inconclusive. While some studies argue that there is a positive link between the level of democracy and descriptive representation, others find the opposite. The proportion of females in African legislatures has risen from 7 percent in 1990 to 18 percent in 2008 (Stockemer 2011: 694), but, as Yoon (2001, 2004) has demonstrated, democracies have fewer female deputies than autocracies. Ruedin (2013) finds no impact of the regime type on women's representation. Democracy does therefore not automatically increase the representation of women. There is significantly less work on the representation of ethnic groups or age groups. Joshi (2013) argues that younger people are generally underrepresented in young democracies, but Ruedin (2009) finds no evidence that older democracies are ethnically more representative than younger democracies. More recently authors have begun to explore the effects of political clientelism on representation in greater detail. As Bjarnegard (2013) and Arriola and Johnson (2014) have shown, clientelistic party politics have a negative impact on women's representation because women often lack the social status and network to be regarded as patrons. The same argument could also be made in the case of underrepresented younger age groups.

To sum up, all these findings—most of them published in political science journals—add valuable insights into the determinants of descriptive or substantive representation. The Africanist literature, on the other hand, has approached the problem of representation from a different point of view, focusing more on the mechanisms that connect big men to their communities. This strand of literature makes interesting arguments especially with regard to ethnic groups and will be reviewed in the next section.

REPRESENTATION IN AFRICA: ISSUES AND DEBATES

There are relatively few scholarly works that directly deal with African parliaments. There is, however, a larger body of literature that deals with the elite-citizen linkages in a broader sense. Three interrelated themes appear in this strand of literature: (1) the pervasive role of clientelism in African party politics, (2) the view that representation in Africa takes the form of the representation of ethnic groups, and (3) the low salience of ideological issues in electoral politics.

The first problem is articulated by Chabal and Daloz (1999). In Africa, the authors argue, votes are "not primarily a token of individual choice but part of a calculus of patrimonial reciprocity" (1999: 31). As a consequence, multiparty elections have not fundamentally altered the structures of political loyalty, which continue to "rest on links between big men, patrons, and their communities" (1999: 37). Similarly, van de Walle (2003: 314) notes that "parties do not really serve to aggregate interests—rather they serve a representation function in a context of clientelistic politics." Mkandawire (2015) has rightly criticized the fact that this literature has given rise to an uncritical use of terms like "neopatrimonialism" that depict Africa as a place of endemic clientelism and failure in governance. While, according to him (2015), this analytical lens has not proven to be useful to depict the variety of African realities, deeper knowledge can be gained from more concrete depictions of elites' behavior. Some empirical studies have argued that MPs engage in private matters of their voters, such as the paying of funeral costs, school fees, or other bills; finding someone a job; or giving out "chop money" (Lindberg 2003: 124). While the general salience of clientelism is beyond doubt, its impact on voting behavior is contested. Young (2009) argues that personalized relations between MPs and voters are only of a limited importance for voting behavior. Lindberg and Morrison (2008) find that in Ghana only one in ten voters is decisively influenced by clientelism or ethnic and family ties, while 85–90 percent behave as "mature" citizens.

A second line of argument concerns the relationship between ethnicity, voting behavior, and political accountability. Some authors see voting in multiethnic countries as little more than an ethnic census (Horowitz 1985). Most parties in Africa are, however, multiethnic, and the political salience of ethnicity varies significantly across countries (Basedau et al. 2011). Ethnicity "does not explain party preference as a whole" (Basedau et al. 2011: 462). It is mostly a combination with clientelism that makes ethnicity a resource for political mobilization, because, as Posner (2005: 91) holds, ethnicity is assumed to convey information about the likely patterns of patronage distribution. Similarly, Chabal and Daloz (1999: 39) quote a Zambian minister with the words, "If I don't appoint people from my region, who else will?" Thus, ethnicity may be seen as a source of strategic coordination among voters and parties (Mozaffar and Scarritt 2005: 400) that provides a certain predictability in Africa's young and often fluid multiparty systems.

In part as a consequence of the combined effect of ethnicity and clientelism, ideological competition is underrepresented in African elections. Although African parties readily use labels such as "liberal" and "social-democratic," elections rarely include debates over macroeconomic policy or the role of the state in the economy (Bleck and van de Walle 2011: 1127). African elites often have an instrumental understanding of democracy and see multiparty politics as little more than a way to power (Aké 2000: 133). As a result, political competition was (and still is) often reduced to leadership alternation.

From the discussion above it becomes evident that whatever the relationship between ethnicity, clientelism, and voting might be, descriptive representation remains an important issue. If, as Posner (2005) suggests, ethnicity conveys information about patronage distribution, then the underrepresentation of ethnic groups in parliament would result in the exclusion of these groups from access to state resources or development programs. The same logic could in principle also apply to other social groups, for example religious minorities. This does, however, not mean that the communities necessarily directly benefit from descriptive representation. As has been frequently noted, clientelism does not necessarily result in redistributive politics, and most of the material gains are limited to a small elite (van de Walle 2003: 313). Yet it could also be argued that the fact that a member of one's own group has made it to parliament indicates better chances of upward social mobility for all group members (Randall 2007: 91; Chabal and Daloz 1999: 42). Randall (2007: 91) suggests that, under such circumstances, "descriptive representation becomes a pledge or sign of responsive representation." Randall's remark is illuminative because it also shows that substantive representation, at least in the African context, is tightly connected to the allocation of material benefits. In party systems largely devoid of ideological competition, it is problematic to think of substantive representation in terms of policy congruencies between voters and legislators. The existing evidence suggests that African voters are indeed primarily interested in the delivery of material benefits. Afrobarometer Round 4[4] included a question on the most important responsibilities of MPs. The aggregated results for all countries are shown in table 3.1.

As the table shows, one-third of the respondents believe that an MP should deliver material benefits, such as jobs and—on a more general level—development. Voters in established Western democracies also expect material benefits—this is nothing peculiar to Africa. In countries with a strong ideological competition, however, parties are often expected to be policy responsive: voters of social democratic parties, for example, would support the expansion of the welfare state, while voters of conservative parties have different preferences. In Africa, this type of ideological competition is mostly absent. MPs are much frequently evaluated by the development benefits they bring to their constituencies—public goods such as water supply, educational facilities, and health care—*and* by their personal generosity. The quotations from interviewed MPs in the empirical section give a taste of how they themselves perceive their roles. This pattern fits well into the findings of van Vliet (2014: 57), who studied the Malian legislature and concludes that African legislatures "are best understood as hybrid institutions that perform the de facto informal task of responding to clientelistic demands as well as their formal core responsibilities." Working on Ghana, Lindberg (2010) comes to similar conclusions about the accountability pressures that are faced by legislators. Other authors have shown that clientelistic practices continue to exist in African democracies or have even intensified (Pitcher, Moran, and

Table 3.1: Afrobarometer Round 4: Most important responsibility of MP (percent)

Listen to constituents and represent their needs	43.7
Deliver jobs or development	30.5
Make laws for the good of the country	16.0
Monitor the president and his government	5.4
None of these	4.3
N	27,713

Source: Afrobarometer data, compiled by the author.

Johnston 2009; Beck 2008). However, clientelism may exist in all political regimes (Kitschelt 2000). In his work on Eastern Europe, Kitschelt (2000: 851) argues that clientelist politics are not to be viewed negatively, as they can establish "tight bonds of accountability and responsiveness." These findings are interesting because they shed doubt on the often assumed incompatibility of clientelism and democracy (for a good summary of the arguments see Erdmann and Engel 2007; Gazibo 2012; van de Walle 2012). For a better assessment of the role that clientelism plays in the relationship between parliaments and citizens, we would, however, need more comparative data from African countries.

AIMS AND SCOPE OF THE EMPIRICAL STUDY

The discussion in the last two sections shows that much more empirical work on the relationship between voters and their representatives in Africa is needed. This is true for the relationship between descriptive representation of social groups and substantive policy effects, but also for the relationship between democratization, clientelism, and representation. The many different meanings and usages of the concept of political clientelism will not be discussed here. The ambition of this chapter is more moderate: it contributes to theory-building by presenting new insights on the basis of comprehensive survey data. To achieve this aim, a comparative approach is preferable to a single-case approach (Sartori 1991; Landman 2008; Lijphart 1971; George and Bennett 2005). Dogan and Pélassy have rightly pointed out that the observation of single cases could lead to serious misinterpretations, because the observer "who studies just one country could interpret as normal what in fact appears to the comparativist as abnormal" (1990: 7). Although the chapter is rather explorative than strictly hypotheses-testing, the countries that are chosen for this chapter differ in an important aspect: their degree of democracy. Ghana is one of the most democratic countries in Africa, and Togo is an electoral authoritarian regime. This case study design allows exploration of differences and similarities in descriptive and substantive representation across two different regime types.

Data collection took place in close collaboration with two African partners, the Center for Democratic Governance in 2013 in Ghana, and the Centre de Recherche et de Sondage d'Opinions in 2014–15 in Togo. The survey achieved comparatively high response rates: 92 percent in Ghana (253 of 275

MPs), and 79 percent in Togo (72 of 91 MPs). MPs were interviewed using a standardized questionnaire. The questionnaire comprised biographical questions, such as date of birth, ethnic group, and religion of the respondent. In addition, two open questions were asked: (a) In your opinion, what do the voters in your constituency expect from you? (b) In your opinion, what are the most important duties of an MP?

On the basis of these data, I address the two core questions that this chapter raises. The first one is, How *representative* are the two parliaments with regard to specific social groups? Descriptive representation is operationalized by using descriptive statistics on the share of MPs with certain personal characteristics. As the theoretical discussion has shown, a wide array of groups can be represented in a national assembly. Among the attributes that may distinguish these groups, gender will be included as one of the most widely discussed issues in the literature. Given the nexus between clientelism, representation, and ethnic groups discussed in the last section, ethnicity and religion are also incorporated in the analysis. Age is another relevant social category. For the sake of completeness, and to get a better understanding of MPs as a social group, some basic statistics on the level of their education will also be reported. Where possible, missing survey data on gender, education, or religion were completed by using other sources.[5] In order to compare these figures to national statistics, Afrobarometer Round 5 is used.[6] On the basis of these data, the Rose-Index of Proportionality is calculated (see also Ruedin 2013). The index ranges from 0 to 100 and is calculated in the following way: the differences between each group's share in the population and the national assembly are first summed up; the result is then divided by two and subtracted from 100 (Mackie and Rose 1991: 511). The closer the values are to 100, the more representative is the parliament.

The second question, that of substantive representation, is much harder to operationalize. As noted earlier, research on Western parliaments usually conceptualizes substantial representation as the congruence between voter preferences and party policy platforms or policy outcomes. Since ideological boundaries tend to be blurred in African party systems, this is not a viable strategy for this chapter. Another strategy would be to explore this question with regard to policy outcomes: for example, has the growing number of female parliamentarians contributed to more gender equality? There are, however, no readily available data to test this. Instead, following the example of Esaiasson's (2000) work on Nordic countries, the chapter uses task definition. The basic idea is that the tasks of an elected representative are flexible

(Esaiasson 2000: 52). Thus, "Depending on how MPs see their task . . . they will behave in parliament in a particular way" and "champion the interests they personally consider important to champion" (52). In this way, the self-definitions of MPs allow conclusions about their likely political behavior. To answer the question on substantive representation, therefore, data from the two open questions were inductively and manually coded into categories. In a first step, every new statement in the survey was coded as an original category. To reduce the number of categories and to ensure better cross-country comparability, categories with the same content were collapsed. In a third step, a research assistant independently recoded 10 percent of the questionnaires according to this coding scheme. To control for intercoder reliability, these codings were then compared to the original codings using Cohen's kappa. The average kappa value of 0.649 signifies a substantial agreement between the two independent coders.[7]

ANALYSIS

The Composition of the National Assemblies in Ghana and Togo

Ghana returned to multiparty democracy in 1992. The political landscape has since been dominated by two political parties, the NDC (National Democratic Congress) and the NPP (New Patriotic Party). The NDC won the 1992, 1996, 2008, and 2012 general elections, while the NPP won in 2000 and 2004. Voting in Ghana is determined by a complex mix of regional, ethnic, historical, and socioeconomic factors (Lindberg and Morrison 2005; Fridy 2007). While the salience of ethnic identities is debatable, the NPP clearly has its strongholds in the Akan-populated regions, especially in Ashanti and the Eastern Region. The NDC dominates in the non-Akan regions, most notably the Volta Region, but also the north of Ghana. It must nevertheless be added that all recent elections have been closely contested. Table 3.2 shows the composition of the Fifth Parliament of Ghana (see also Frempong and Siaw, this volume).

Togo, by contrast, has been ruled by the Gnassingbé dynasty for more than forty years. Under Gnassingbé Eyadema, who came to power in a military coup in 1967, the country was known as one of Africa's worst dictatorships. The regime relied on the military but also on the support from northern Togo, especially on the president's ethnic group, the Kabye. A limited opening in the 1990s reintroduced multiparty politics but left the structure of power largely unchanged. After Eyadema's death in 2005 the military installed his son Faure Gnassingbé as the president of the republic. Faure has since been able to win the 2005, 2010, and 2015 presidential elections. Today, the national assembly is composed of the ruling party, Union for the Republic (UNIR), which holds an absolute majority of sixty-two seats, and a number of smaller opposition parties (see table 3.3).

"Standing For": Descriptive Representation

This section will now use the MPs' biographies to evaluate how representative the national assemblies of the two countries are. If, as Pitkin (1967) holds, parliaments should mirror the social composition of the society, we would expect to this reflected in the MPs' biographical characteristics. As argued in the theoretical section, there is a supposed link between descriptive representation and accountability: if MPs do not share the social experiences of the groups they represent, they cannot act effectively in their interest. Low numbers of females in a parliament, for example, would mean that the experiences of women are not sufficiently present in the national assembly, and that the specific needs of these groups are not adequately addressed in policymaking. The same is true of other social groups: the needs of the young are sometimes poorly understood by the elderly, and the grievances of excluded ethnic or religious groups are not credibly addressed by dominant groups.

Table 3.2: Composition of the Parliament of Ghana

Party	National Democratic Congress (NDC)	New Patriotic Party (NPP)	People's National Convention (PNC)	Independent
Seats	148	123	1	3

Source: Electoral Commission of Ghana.

Table 3.3: Composition of the Parliament of Togo

Party	Union pour la République (UNIR)	Arc-en-ciel	Collectif Sauvons le Togo (CST)	Front des patriotes pour la Démocratie (FPD)	Sursaut National	Union des Forces de Changement (UFC)
Seats	62	6	19	1	1	2

Source: Data collected by the author in cooperation with CROP Togo, 2014.

AGE

The mean age of parliamentarians in both countries is surprisingly similar. On average, Ghana's MPs were born in 1963, and those of Togo in 1962. This compares well to other areas of the world. The members of the European Parliament, for example, are on average fifty-three years old (Sabbati 2014: 3).

GENDER

With regard to women's representation, Togo scores with 20.8 percent, much better than Ghana, with 11.3 percent (see table 3.4). The differences are statistically significant at the 5 percent level. Even more interesting is the breakdown into government and opposition. For Ghana the differences are rather small, with 10.1 percent females in the NDC and 13.1 percent in the NPP, but in Togo the ruling party has twice as many females (21 percent) as the opposition (10.3 percent).

EDUCATION

Unsurprisingly, MPs in both countries are better educated than the average population. While only 17.1 (Ghana) and 16.9 (Togo) percent have an education lower than the bachelor's level, the huge majority have at least a bachelor's degree (table 3.5). In the Afrobarometer survey, it is quite the opposite:

Table 3.4: Gender representation among MPs in Ghana and Togo (percent)

	Male	Female	N
Ghana	88.7	11.3	275
Togo	82.4	17.6	91

Source: Data collected by the author.
Note: $\chi^2 = 4.536; p = .033$.

Table 3.5: MPs' level of education in Ghana and Togo (percent)

	Ghana	Togo
1 Lower than BA	17.1	16.9
3 BA	48.0	32.4
4 MA	24.4	28.2
5 PhD	6.2	15.5
9 Other	4.4	7.0
N	275	72

Source: Data collected by the author.

only a minority of 12.3 percent of the respondents in Ghana and 12.0 percent in Togo have some sort of postsecondary qualifications.

ETHNICITY

One of the most interesting aspects is the representation of ethnic groups, which is detailed in table 3.6 and table 3.7. In each of the tables, the second column shows the distribution of ethnic groups among the Afrobarometer respondents, and the third column shows the ethnic composition of the respective national assembly. The last two columns give a breakdown into government and opposition.

Table 3.6: Ethnic representation in Ghana (percent)

Group	Afrobarometer	Parliament	NDC	NPP
Akan	50.0	57.6	38.5	81.0
Ga-Dangme	8.9	9.4	12.3	6.0
Ewe	15.4	10.7	17.2	3.0
Guan	1.7	4.0	6.6	1.0
Gurma	3.3	4.0	4.1	4.0
Mole-Dagbani	13.4	11.2	16.4	4.0
Grusi	1.6	2.2	3.3	0
other	5.7	0.9	1.6	0.9
N	2,400	224	122	100
Rose Index		90.70	76.97	72.95

Source: Data collected by the author.

Table 3.7: Ethnic representation in Togo (percent)

Ethnic group	Afrobarometer	Parliament	Ruling Party	Opposition
Ewe	36.33	28.57	21.28	47.83
Kabye	14.33	7.14	10.64	0
Ben (Moba)	8.42	8.57	4.26	17.39
Tem (Kotokoli)	7.33	5.71	4.26	8.7
Mina	4.17	4.29	2.13	8.7
Lamba	3.42	2.86	4.26	0
Ana	3.25	1.43	2.13	0
Adja	3.08	2.86	4.26	0
Akposso	1.83	5.71	8.51	0
N	1,200	70	47	23
Rose Index		80.83	81.10	71.20

Source: Data collected by the author.

Both national assemblies are, in their totality, fairly representative. If we look at the breakdown into parties, however, it becomes apparent that certain ethnic groups tend to be overrepresented. This is true for the Akan in the NPP and the Ewe and Mole-Dagbani group in the NDC in Ghana, but also for the Kabye in the Togolese ruling party, UNIR. Overall, the Togolese opposition is dominated by a few ethnic groups from the south of the country, namely Ewe and Moba, whereas certain groups, like the Kabye or Akposso, are completely absent. Interestingly, the ruling parties, UNIR and NDC, tend to be slightly more representative than the opposition.

RELIGION

When we turn to religion, the picture becomes a little different. For reasons of comparability, tables 3.8 and 3.9 give only the values for the three big religious categories, "Christian," "Muslim," and "other."[8] Overall, both national assemblies are fairly representative. Two patterns are, nevertheless, interesting. First, Muslims are slightly under- and Christians are slightly overrepresented in both countries. The deviations are rather small and therefore not alarming, especially since religion has never been a point of political cleavage in either Ghana or Togo. It is nonetheless remarkable that parliamentary elites are overrecruited from the Christian population.

Table 3.8: Representation of religious groups in Ghana (percent)

Group	Afrobarometer	Parliament
Christian	72.8	83.3
Muslim	15.4	12.7
Other	11.8	0.7
Rose Index		88.2
N	2,400	275

Source: Data collected by the author.

Table 3.9: Representation of religious groups in Togo (percent)

Group	Afrobarometer	Parliament
Christian	71.0	85.9
Muslim	12.4	7.0
Other	16.6	7.0
Rose Index		89.2
N	1,200	72

"Acting For": Substantive Representation

This section gives further insights into substantial representation. As described in the previous section, data from two open survey questions on voters' expectations and MPs' duties are used. Table 3.10 shows what MPs perceive as their constituents' expectations.

A large number of deputies in Ghana and Togo believe that their voters are first and foremost interested in public goods, development, and better living conditions. Typically, voters seek an improvement of the physical infrastructure in their communities, especially roads, hospitals, schools, water, or electricity. The answers given by the Ghanaian and Togolese MPs were surprisingly similar.[9] Two examples demonstrate this:

> I live in a constituency with a myriad of problems: electricity, provision of water, roads, health facilities as well as toilet facilities. Those are key expectations [of my constituency]. (MP from Ghana)

> They think that I can improve their socioeconomic situation (education of their children, health care, provision of infrastructure . . .), in short, they think that I can solve all the problems that they have. (MP from Togo)

While many MPs referred to particular public goods, such as roads and hospitals, others made more general statements:

Table 3.10: In your opinion, what do the voters in your constituency expect from you?

	Ghana	Togo
Provide public goods	55.5	45.7
Development/improve living conditions	42.0	51.4
Provide private goods	24.2	24.3
Be close to voters/listen to them	10.6	22.9
Represent the constituency	13.1	28.6
Make laws	0.4	7.1
Conflict mediation/Security and peace	1.1	7.1
Fight for political reforms	-	7.1
Being a role model	4.4	-
Build up party structures	1.1	4.3
Fight for social justice	-	4.3
Women's empowerment	-	1.4

They expect lots of development. (MP from Ghana)

They expect the development of their area. (MP from Togo)

A quarter of the voters in both countries are apparently also interested in private goods. Examples include paying school fees, giving traders capital to start businesses, giving scholarships to needy students, helping people to find a job, or paying their medical bills. Interestingly, a number of MPs commented critically on the demands of their populations:

> I think my constituency doesn't just see me as a lawmaker . . . it might not be their fault, because it is based on the way we campaign—we normally campaign as if we are capable of doing everything under the sun because we need political power. They expect all the basic things of life, water, sanitation facilities, good roads, solve everyday problems . . . . They see me as a development agent. (MP from Ghana)

> In theory, the people hope that the deputies advocate their interest vis-à-vis the government. In reality, they hope that the deputies help them to solve their personal everyday problems. (MP from Togo)

In addition, voters expect their MPs to be close to them, listen to their concerns, and represent their views in the national assembly:

> [They expect me to] articulate their concerns on the floor of parliament, to be on the forefront of their developmental agenda, to visit them on regular basis to explain government policies and programs to them, to help unite all people in the constituency from various political divides. (MP from Ghana)

> [They expect me to] listen to them, defend their interests, truly represent them, share their joy and pain, to be engaged in the developmental activities of the community. (MP from Togo)

Very few MPs refer to policies and programs. Only 7.1 percent in Togo and 0.04 percent in Ghana believe that their voters expect them to make good laws. In Togo, 7.1 percent think that their voters want better policies. Another 7.1 percent of the Togolese deputies—all of them belonging to opposition parties—refer to political reforms, and a single female deputy refers to the empowerment of women. In Ghana, these issues were completely absent in the interviews—while the large majority mentioned the need to develop the constituency in one or the other way, almost no one included any programmatic or concrete policy statement. Table 3.10 lists some additional answers that were given only by small minorities, such as being a role model, building up party structures, or mediating local conflicts.

With regard to the second question ("In your opinion, what are the most important duties of an MP?"), table 3.11 shows that a large majority of MPs regard lawmaking as one of their core tasks. In addition, a similar proportion in Ghana and Togo believes that an MP has the duty to represent and defend his or her constituents. The following examples demonstrate how the interviewed deputies see themselves:

> You are supposed to be the mouthpiece of your constituents. (MP from Ghana)

> For me the most important duty of an MP is to legislate and in the process liaise with the constituency to get their views on bills, so that you will be able to present their views so that it is reflected in the national laws. (MP from Ghana)

> [It is my duty to] be a good intermediary between the people and party authorities, [to be] their advocate and defender of their interests. (MP from Togo)

Table 3.11: In your opinion, what are the most important duties of an MP?

	Ghana	Togo
Make laws	85.8	75.7
Liaison between people and parliament	41.0	45.7
Provide the needs of the people, lobby for development new	56.9	11.4
Oversight over the executive	30.0	50.0
Political education	4.9	18.6
Help my party to hold on to power	0.8	5.7
Solve local conflicts	1.6	4.3
Be responsible to the nation as a whole	2.0	4.3
Fight for the empowerment of women	-	1.4
Cooperation with chiefs	-	1.4

[It is my duty to] inform the people about the laws that are made, [and] inform the government authorities about the local needs and problems. (MP from Togo)

In both countries, the task of an MP includes frequent visits to the constituency and participation in local events, such as funerals, festivals, sports events, and party meetings. Oversight over the executive—usually regarded as one of the core functions of parliaments—is mentioned by only half of the Togolese and only a third of the Ghanaians. In Ghana, more than half of the MPs are also convinced of the need to provide material benefits to their people:

In my opinion an MP is supposed to lobby for projects for his/her constituency and also to legislate in parliament. (MP from Ghana)

Only slightly over 10 percent of their counterparts in Togo think the same. Political education and parliamentary diplomacy are more highly regarded in Togo than in Ghana. Some Togolese MPs (4.3 percent) also mention the need to promote the party and help to secure another electoral victory. Other minor issues mentioned only by small minorities include women's empowerment and cooperating with local chiefs (see table 3.11).

CONCLUSION

As the theoretical section has laid out, representation is regarded as important for the functioning of modern democracies. Higher levels of democracy should theoretically be associated with higher levels of demographic representation and responsiveness. Empirical reality is more complex, however. In both Ghana and Togo, MPs share similarities regarding their demographic profile and perceptions of their duties and voters' expectations. Any analysis of representation must therefore not only take the social and historical background of a country into consideration, but also seek to understand what accountability in the local context actually means. Much more work is needed on parliaments in Africa, specifically on the relationship between voters and their representatives.

What can we learn from the analysis in this chapter? To begin with descriptive representation, it has become clear that women and youth are underrepresented in both countries. This finding is unsurprising and might not be confined to Africa. It is worth noting, however, that the electoral autocracy, Togo, has a higher share of females in the legislature than the democracy, Ghana. Even more interesting is the fact that Togo's ruling party, UNIR, has the highest share of females of all parties under investigation in this chapter. This shows that democracy is no guarantee of a greater participation of women in politics.

For ethnicity, the results are more in line with the theoretical expectations. Ghana's legislature is generally a good mirror of the ethnic composition of the country. There are, however, strong differences in the ethnic composition of the parties: the Akan are strongly overrepresented in the NPP and underrepresented in the NDC. The Rose Index score is lower for Togo, but the dynamics are quite similar: certain groups, like the Kabye, are underrepresented in the opposition but overrepresented in the ruling party—for the Ewe it is just the other way round. The data show impressively that national assemblies that are fairly representative can still be made up of rather unrepresentative individual parties. Furthermore, ruling parties in both countries reach a better Rose Index score than opposition parties. This corroborates the claim by Arriola (2012) and Wahman (2017) that ruling parties are usually more national in character than the opposition. Although religion is not a politicized cleavage in either Ghana or Togo, it is noteworthy that Muslims are slightly underrepresented in both countries.

The fact that parliamentarians in both countries are generally highly educated—much more highly than the rest of the population—might not be surprising. It is, however, an indication of a very important fact: MPs share, irrespective of gender, party affiliation, or ethnicity—a common social space. Their social similarity might also help to explain the very interesting parallels in their attitudes. Without any doubt, MPs in both countries see the development of their communities as the top priority. Just as Lindberg (2003, 2010) and van Vliet (2014) have observed, MPs are confronted with a myriad of demands from their voters. Contrary to what might be theoretically expected, the need to deliver material benefits to voters is even stronger in Ghana than in Togo. There is thus no support for the thesis that democracies are generally less clientelistic than autocracies. Quite contrary: policies, reforms, and programmatic appeals played almost no role in Ghana, whereas in Togo the need to reform the political system was articulated at least by some opposition MPs.

The findings on substantive representation in tables 3.10 and 3.11 highlight the generally low level of ideological competition in African party systems. Yet the results reflect only the views of the MPs themselves—they do therefore not mean that African voters are per se uninterested in different ideological platforms or policy proposals. On both sides of the relationship the priorities lie on the delivery of goods and services, not on ideas and programs. This can have both negative and positive consequences: on the one hand, MPs see the clear need to deliver development that can in fact lead to an improvement in service provision in a district. They do not seem to see themselves as representing particular interests—female MPs do not think that they explicitly stand for the empowerment of women, and opposition MPs do not feel that they are urged to oppose the government under all circumstances. This can also lead to an inclusive approach to the constituency as a group of people to whose welfare the representative is attending. On the other hand, it contributes to a low profile of political debate: in election campaigns, everyone promises to do "better" than the other. Given the very high turnover rates in the Parliament of Ghana, for example, voters do seem to punish politicians who do not deliver on their promises, but this opens a cycle of trial and error in which voters might think, "Well, this MP failed, let's try another one next time," which does not enhance the quality of policy formulation on the whole but encourages ever more promises for ever more goods delivery, and discourages innovative policy proposals. In political systems like Togo, where the punishment of failing MPs is difficult due to polarization along the ruling party / opposition cleavage, it effectively weakens the ability of the opposition to develop a visionary, united, and policy-driven approach to social and political problems. Seen in this way, democracies might seem to be more accountable by giving voters the opportunity to unseat unpopular politicians. Yet in both countries, the link between descriptive and substantive representation is important. MPs in Ghana and Togo share a number of descriptive similarities: they are predominantly male, very well educated, and relatively wealthy. They occupy a social space of their own that is distinct from the social space in which large sections of their constituents live. Elites are, by their social characteristics, a privileged group that is often disconnected from the daily struggles of their constituents. Only a low number of MPs highlight the importance of "being close to voters / listening to them" (table 3.10). This shows where the room for improvement is: exchange with voters is not just promising them a new road or a new hospital, but means being present in the community and providing an opportunity for citizens to talk about their needs. Unfortunately, we have little knowledge on whether effective voter-

Fig. 3.1. Interview of the author with the Honourable Ben Donkor, Accra 2012.

representative feedback mechanisms exist. Future studies should therefore investigate this topic and compare, for example, what different forms of relations between MPs and voters exist on the ground: How often do MPs travel home? Are there constituency offices with regular opening hours, or are there any other forms of consultation and feedback? This would further enhance our knowledge on political accountability in Africa.

Drawing general conclusions from only two cases is of course problematic. It is not possible to say whether the arguments made in this chapter are generalizable across other African cases. Another limitation consists of the fact that substantive representation is only measured by looking at MPs' perceptions. We still know little about the degree of congruence between the attitudes of representatives on the one hand and voters on the other hand. There is also still much work to be done on the relationship between descriptive and substantive representation—and the implications for elite accountability, both substantive and symbolic. What the chapter has achieved, however, is to give empirical insights into two cases. This can be a starting point for future research on the important topic of the political in Africa.

NOTES

1. The term "electoral authoritarianism" was coined by Schedler (2006). For an overview of the literature in this field, see Morse 2012.

2. Democracy is measured with the widely used Polity IV-Index (see www.systemicpeace.org/polityproject.html). The index uses a twenty-one-point scale to measure democracy/autocracy. The best value is 10 (consolidated democracy); the worst is −10 (hereditary monarchy). Ghana is ranked as a full democracy with a score of 8, while Togo receives a score of −2 and is ranked as a closed anocracy.

3. In their concept of "discursive representation," Dryzek and Niemeyer (2008) argue that not only people, but also discourses, can be represented. Mansbridge (2003: 515) distinguishes between "promissory representation," which is focused on the campaign promises made to constituents, "anticipatory representation," which anticipates the will of the people in the next election, "gyroscopic representation," in which the representative uses common sense and experiences from his or her personal background, and "surrogate representation," which occurs when legislators represent constituents outside their own district.

4. The Afrobarometer is a representative survey that measures the social, political, and economic atmosphere in Africa. Data can be accessed at www.afrobarometer.org. The question discussed here was included in Round 4 (2008–9) and reads as follows: "Representatives to the National Assembly have different responsibilities. Which of the following do you think is the most important responsibility of your representative to the National Assembly?"

5. For Ghana, some biographical information can be found on the parliament's website. For Togo, the website of the parliament contains only information on the MPs' gender, but not on other biographical characteristics.

6. For Ghana, official household survey data are available from the statistical service. For Togo, no such data are available. It was therefore decided to use the Afrobarometer for both countries.

7. Landis and Koch (1977: 165) characterize the strength of interrater agreement in the following way: kappa values from 0 to .2 as "slight," .21 to .4 as "fair," .41 to .6 as "moderate," .61 to .8 as "substantial," and over .8 as "almost perfect."

8. The "other" category includes animist religions but also a few cases where people adhere to religious groupings that are not widespread in Africa.

9. All statements by Togolese MPs were translated from French by the author.

REFERENCES

Achen, Christopher H. 1978. "Measuring Representation." *American Journal of Political Science* 22, no. 3: 475–510.

Ake, Claude. 2000. *The Feasibility of Democracy in Africa*. Dakar: Council for the Development of Social Science Research in Africa.

Arriola, Leonardo R. 2012. *Multi-ethnic Coalitions in Africa: Business Financing of Opposition Election Campaigns.* New York: Cambridge University Press.

Arriola, Leonardo R., and Martha C. Johnson. 2014. "Ethnic Politics and Women's Empowerment in Africa: Ministerial Appointments to Executive Cabinets." *American Journal of Political Science* 58, no. 2: 495–510.

Azevedo-Harman, Elisabete. 2012. "Parliaments and Citizens in Sub-Saharan Africa." *Journal of legislative Studies* 18, nos. 3–4: 419–40.

Barkan, Joel D. 2009. *Legislative Power in Emerging African Democracies.* Boulder, CO: Lynne Rienner.

Basedau, Matthias, Gero Erdmann, Jann Lay, and Alexander Stroh. 2011. "Ethnicity and Party Preference in Sub-Saharan Africa." *Democratization* 18, no. 2: 462–89.

Beck, Linda Jane. 2008. *Brokering Democracy in Africa: The Rise of Clientelist Democracy in Senegal.* New York: Palgrave Macmillan.

Beckwith, Karen. 2007. "Numbers and Newness: The Descriptive and Substantive Representation of Women." *Canadian Journal of Political Science / Revue canadienne de science politique* 40, no. 1: 27–49.

Beetham, David. 2006. *Parliament and Democracy in the Twenty-First Century: A Guide to Good Practice.* Geneva: Inter-Parliamentary Union.

Best, Heinrich, and Maurizio Cotta. 2000. *Parliamentary Representatives in Europe, 1848–2000: Legislative Recruitment and Careers in Eleven European Countries.* Oxford: Oxford University Press.

Bjarnegard, Elin. 2013. *Gender, Informal Institutions and Political Recruitment: Explaining Male Dominance in Parliamentary Representation.* New York: Palgrave Macmillan.

Bleck, Jaimie, and Nicolas van de Walle. 2011. "Parties and Issues in Francophone West Africa: Towards a Theory of Non-mobilization." *Democratization* 18, no. 5: 1125–45.

Carman, Christopher Jan. 2007. "Assessing Preferences for Political Representation in the US." *Journal of Elections, Public Opinion and Parties* 17, no. 1: 1–19.

Celis, Karen. 2009. "Substantive Representation of Women (and Improving It): What It Is and Should Be About?" *Comparative European Politics* 7, no. 1: 95–113.

Chabal, Patrick, and Jean-Pascal Daloz. 1999. *Africa Works: Disorder as Political Instrument.* Oxford: James Currey.

Dogan, Mattei, and Dominique Pélassy. 1990. *How to Compare Nations: Strategies in Comparative Politics.* London: Chatham House.

Dryzek, John S., and Simon Niemeyer. 2008. "Discursive Representation." *American Political Science Review* 102, no. 4: 481–93.

Erdmann, Gero, and Ulf Engel. 2007. "Neopatrimonialism Reconsidered: Critical Review and Elaboration of an Elusive Concept." *Commonwealth and Comparative Politics* 45, no. 1: 95–119.

Esaiasson, Peter. 2000. "How Members of Parliament Define Their Task." In Peter Esaiasson and Knut Heidar, eds., *Beyond Westminster and Congress: The Nordic Experience,* 51–82. Columbus: Ohio State University Press.

Fridy, Kevin S. 2007. "The Elephant, Umbrella, and Quarrelling Cocks: Disaggregating Partisanship in Ghana's Fourth Republic." *African Affairs* 106, no. 423: 281–305.

Gazibo, Mamoudou. 2012. "Can Neopatrimonialism Dissolve into Democracy?" In Daniel C. Bach, ed., *Neopatrimonialism in Africa and Beyond*, 79–89. London: Routledge.

George, Alexander L., and Andrew Bennett. 2005. *Case Studies and Theory Development in the Social Sciences*. Cambridge, MA: MIT Press.

Goetz, Anne Marie. 1998. "Women in Politics & Gender Equity in Policy: South Africa & Uganda." *Review of African Political Economy* 25, no. 76: 241–62.

Golosov, Grigorii V. 2014. "Is Electoral Authoritarianism Good for Women's Representation? Evidence from the 1999–2011 Regional Legislative Elections in Russia." *Post-Soviet Affairs* 30, no. 1: 51–66.

Hoffmann-Lange, Ursula. 1986. "Eliten und Demokratie in der Bundesrepublik." In Max Kaase, ed., *Politische Wissenschaft und politische Ordnung: Analysen zu Theorie und Empirie demokratischer Regierungsweise*, 318–38. Opladen: Westdeutscher Verlag.

Horowitz, Donald L. 1985. *Ethnic Groups in Conflict*. Berkeley: University of California Press.

Joshi, Devin K. 2013. "The Representation of Younger Age Cohorts in Asian Parliaments: Do Electoral Systems Make a Difference?" *Representation* 49, no. 1: 1–16.

Kitschelt, Herbert. 2000. "Linkages between Citizens and Politicians in Democratic Polities." *Comparative Political Studies* 33, nos. 6–7: 845–79.

Landis, J. Richard, and Gary G. Koch. 1977. "The Measurement of Observer Agreement for Categorical Data." *Biometrics* 33, no. 1: 159–74.

Landman, Todd. 2008. *Issues and Methods in Comparative Politics: An Introduction*. 3rd ed. New York: Routledge.

Levitsky, Steven, and Lucan A. Way. 2010. *Competitive Authoritarianism: Hybrid Regimes after the Cold War*. Cambridge: Cambridge University Press.

Lijphart, Arend. 1971. "Comparative Politics and the Comparative Method." *American Political Science Review* 65, no. 3: 682–93.

Lindberg, Staffan I. 2003. "'It's Our Time to "Chop"': Do Elections in Africa Feed Neopatrimonialism Rather Than Counter-act It?" *Democratization* 10, no. 2: 121–40.

Lindberg, Staffan I. 2010. "What Accountability Pressures Do MPs in Africa Face and How Do They Respond? Evidence from Ghana." *Journal of Modern African Studies* 48, no. 1: 117–42.

Lindberg, Staffan I., and Minion K. C. Morrison. 2005. "Exploring Voter Alignments in Africa: Core and Swing Voters in Ghana." *Journal of Modern African Studies* 43, no. 4: 565–86.

Lindberg, Staffan I., and Minion K. C. Morrison. 2008. "Are African Voters Really Ethnic or Clientelistic? Survey Evidence from Ghana." *Political Science Quarterly* 123, no. 1: 95–122.

Luna, Juan P., and Elizabeth J. Zechmeister. 2005. "Political Representation in Latin

America: A Study of Elite-Mass Congruence in Nine Countries." *Comparative Political Studies* 38, no. 4: 388–416.

Mackie, Thomas T., and Richard Rose. 1991. *The International Almanac of Electoral History*. London: Macmillan.

Mansbridge, Jane. 1999. "Should Blacks Represent Blacks and Women Represent Women? A Contingent 'Yes.'" *Journal of Politics* 61, no. 3: 628–57.

Mansbridge, Jane. 2003. "Rethinking Representation." *American Political Science Review* 97, no. 4: 515–28.

Miller, Wakken E., and Donald E. Stokes. 1963. "Constituency Influence in Congress." *American Political Science Review* 57, no. 1: 45–56.

Mkandawire, Thandika. 2015. "Neopatrimonialism and the Political Economy of Economic Performance in Africa: Critical Reflections." *World Politics* 67, no. 3: 563–612.

Morse, Yonatan L. 2012. "The Era of Electoral Authoritarianism." *World Politics* 64, no. 1: 161–98.

Mozaffar, Shaheen, and James R. Scarritt. 2005. "The Puzzle of African Party Systems." *Party Politics* 11, no. 4: 399–421.

Phillips, Anne. 1995. *The Politics of Presence*. Oxford: Oxford University Press.

Pitcher, Anne, Mary H. Moran, and Michael Johnston. 2009. "Rethinking Patrimonialism and Neopatrimonialism in Africa." *African Studies Review* 52, no. 1: 125–56.

Pitkin, Hanna Fenichel. 1967. *The Concept of Representation*. Berkeley: University of California Press.

Posner, Daniel N. 2005. *Institutions and Ethnic Politics in Africa*. New York: Cambridge University Press.

Putnam, Robert D. 1976. *The Comparative Study of Political Elites*. Englewood Cliffs, NJ: Prentice-Hall.

Randall, Vicky. 2007. "Political Parties in Africa and the Representation of Social Groups." In Matthias Basedau, Gero Erdmann, and Andreas Mehler, eds., *Votes, Money and Violence: Political Parties and Elections in Sub-Saharan Africa*, 82–104. Uppsala: Nordiska Afrikainstitutet.

Ruedin, Didier. 2009. "Ethnic Group Representation in a Cross-National Comparison." *Journal of Legislative Studies* 15, no. 4: 335–54.

Ruedin, Didier. 2013. *Why Aren't They There? The Political Representation of Women, Ethnic Groups and Issue Positions in Legislatures*. Colchester: ECPR Press.

Sabbati, Giulio. 2014. *Briefing. European Parliament: Fact and Figures*. Brussels: European Parliament Research Service.

Sartori, Giovanni. 1991. "Comparing and Miscomparing." *Journal of Theoretical Politics* 3, no. 3: 243–57.

Schedler, Andreas, ed. 2006. *Electoral Authoritarianism: The Dynamics of Unfree Competition*. Boulder, CO: Lynne Rienner.

Schwindt-Bayer, Leslie A., and William Mishler. 2005. "An Integrated Model of Women's Representation." *Journal of Politics* 67, no. 2: 407–28.

Stockemer, Daniel. 2011. "Women's Parliamentary Representation in Africa: The Impact

of Democracy and Corruption on the Number of Female Deputies in National Parliaments." *Political Studies* 59, no. 3: 693–712.
van de Walle, Nicolas. 2003. "Presidentialism and Clientelism in Africa's Emerging Party Systems." *Journal of Modern African Studies* 41, no. 2: 297–321.
van de Walle, Nicholas. 2012. "The Path from Neopatrimonialism: Democracy and Clientelism in Africa Today." In Daniel C. Bach, ed., *Neopatrimonialism in Africa and Beyond*, 111-123. London: Routledge.
van Vliet, Martin. 2014. "Weak Legislatures, Failing MPs, and the Collapse of Democracy in Mali." *African Affairs* 113, no. 450: 45–66.
Wahman, Michael. 2017. "Nationalized Incumbents and Regional Challengers Opposition- and Incumbent-Party Nationalization in Africa." *Party Politics* 23, no. 3: 309–22. https://doi.org/1354068815596515
Wängnerud, Lena. 2009. "Women in Parliaments: Descriptive and Substantive Representation." *Annual Review of Political Science* 12, no. 1: 51–69.
Yoon, Mi Yung. 2001. "Democratization and Women's Legislative Representation in Sub-Saharan Africa." *Democratization* 8, no. 2: 169–90.
Yoon, Mi Yung. 2004. "Explaining Women's Legislative Representation in Sub-Saharan Africa." *Legislative Studies Quarterly* 29, no. 3: 447–68.
Young, Daniel J. 2009. "Is Clientelism at Work in African Elections? Voting Behaviour in Kenya and Zambia." Afrobarometer Working Paper no. 106. Cape Town: Afrobarometer.

CHAPTER 4

Elite Conflict and Consensus in Ghana's Fourth Republic

ALEX K. D. FREMPONG AND EMMANUEL K. SIAW

INTRODUCTION

Elite conflict and consensus have been one of the overarching themes that run through diverse analyses of democratic stability, intra- or interstate conflicts, and development. Generally, it has been observed that elites are instrumental to democratic stability largely due to their enormous power and control over public opinion and citizenry behavior (Alder and Wang 2018; Diermeier and Li 2019; Wilson 2019). This influence over popular behavior and opinion can be deployed to either build and sustain democratic progress or for selfish objectives that can lead to democratic reversals. Thus, while elites in Africa often tend to perpetuate democratic reversals, there is also a strong inclination to ensure and safeguard democratic stability. Ghana's history is a mix of both. In the past twenty-six years, the Ghanaian political elites have shown greater commitment to ensuring and safeguarding the nation's democratic stability.

The struggle for independence in Ghana, the first country to gain independence in sub-Saharan Africa, was characterized by certain dynamics and complexities. The mode of this struggle began in mainstream politics with the formation of the United Gold Coast Convention (UGCC), a party touted as elite dominated. However, elite disagreements and misunderstandings led to the formation of the Convention People's Party (CPP), which later secured independence for Ghana. The CPP became the dominant party due to its unprecedented preindependence electoral successes in 1951, 1954, and 1956. Throughout these phases of elections, the general political milieu was characterized by a little cooperation between the elites and more conflict that led to the formation of various political groupings and splinter political parties (Frempong 2012). Therefore, it would be flawed thinking to assume that Ghana's independence struggle was achieved from a united front or was devoid of elite conflicts. These disagreements manifested in issues relating to national elections, constituency demarcation, constitution, and system of government, among others. However, upon attaining independence, Ghana became an example of African elite success for the elites of other colonies. The Ghanaian leader at the time, Kwame Nkrumah, expressed his bid to liberate African colonies through financial support and ideological mentoring of the African elites. His tenure was, however, short-lived due to crosscutting grievances among opposing elites (Thompson 1969).

Ghana is an example of democratic government in a continent noted for democratic reversals, upheavals, and authoritarian rule (Morrison 2004). Democratic government has been developing since its shaky beginning in 1992, the longest democratic regime since independence (Frempong 2007a). During the twenty-six years of democracy, Ghana has had three relatively peaceful power turnovers. Therefore, believers in Samuel Huntington's two-turnover test argue that Ghana's democracy is consolidated. However, other scholars and political actors have lamented the continuous existence of conflict drivers, stemming from interelite conflicts, that have the propensity to derail Ghana's democratic system (Tonah 2007).

Diverse studies on developed democracies and relatively underdeveloped ones have attempted to demonstrate these dynamics. These studies have established that elites are not only instrumental in securing democracy, but they also influence voter behavior and public opinion (Diermeier and Li 2019; Hoffmann-Lange 2012; Hoffmann-Lange, Neumann, and Steinkemper 1985; Sohlberg 2017; Suslov et al. 2015). A review of the literature reveals two main issues about elite behavior regardless of the context within which it was studied. First, the general patterns of state-society relations and the nature of international politics are mostly a product of the dynamics of elite politics (Lopez 2013). Second, globalization has increased the number of global elites, making accountability difficult to achieve (Hoffmann-Lange 2012). Intuitively, elites achieve their objectives through either direct engagement with the citizenry or the creation of viable institutions to facilitate engagement. In this chapter, we focus on exploring the latter in Ghana.

In this chapter, we approach elite accountability within liberal democracies as involving the institutionalization of the means and mechanisms that encourage and facilitate the masses' holding public officers answerable for their actions and inactions. Periodic and guaranteed elections, therefore, become an essential means of elite accountability, an avenue for the masses to either punish or reward behavior. Where these processes are compromised, there is a tendency to resort to coercive means of creating accountability (Körösényi 2009).

The debates in more recent studies such as Alder and Wang (2018: 1) have emphasized political elites as people who "strategically initiate conflicts to polarise society and sustain their power." Using Rwanda and Yugoslavia as case studies, they demonstrated this theory of civil conflict by arguing that both are examples of elite manipulations through divide-and-rule tactics that initiate conflicts and interethnic polarization that is consequently beneficial to elites in diverse ways. On elite accountability, Carvalho and Dippel (2020) theorize that elites' economic and social identities and configurations have a strong correlation with their support for extractive policies. Using ten British Caribbean sugar colonies as case studies, they demonstrated that elites of different social and economic identities tend to vote for or against extractive policies that benefit them at the expense of the general citizenry. It gets more complicated when the elite becomes too accountable as a whole. In this case, elites may have the propensity to "pursue extractive policies by altering the institutional framework" (Carvalho and Dippel 2016: 2). However, the cases examined by these authors are based on racially diverse elite stratifications whose history and immediate environment have an unparalleled influence on their behavior and configurations.

In this chapter, we focus on elites not as deliberate architects of conflict but as actors in the democratic process through conflict and cooperation. Since Ghana has never been in a civil war, the thesis of Alder and Wang (2018) will not suffice here. Instead, we argue that elite conflict and consensus are not mutually exclusive. Therefore, the elites that are capable of conflict are also capable of forging consensus for democratic consolidation. This assumption is well captured in the broader consociational theory by scholars who argue that the thriving of democracy rests on a consensually united elite who share general values and have been integrated into the governance system (Higley and Burton 2006; Lijphart 2018; Wilson 2019). Some have argued that due to limited elite consensus in different countries, the prospects for liberal democracy worldwide are limited. This has been the premise with which most works on elites in Ghana begin. Osei (2014), in a study of Ghanaian elites, revealed a structural weakness in this assumption. Her argument is that the dynamics of elite consensus differ, and that Ghana presents a rare case where elite settlements may not have been structurally integrated over time, yet democracy is being consolidated. One of the ways this is happening is through horizontal integrations across the social cleavages between members of parliament (MP) and vertical integrations of MPs and the wider population (see Osei in this volume). In this chapter, we go beyond the social compositions of the MPs and examine how elite conflict and consensus play out—inter- and intraparty—and how institutions such as the electoral commission set the rules of the game and function as a platform for value integration.

To understand these dynamics, two timelines can be distilled—1957–1992 and 1993–2017. While the former was characterized by military regimes with intermittent democracies, the latter has witnessed sustained democratic rule for over two decades. These different epochs were characterized by a unique constellation of elite conflict, cooperation, and accountability. These dynamics have had both adverse and positive effects on democratic stability. Therefore, it can be argued that democratic stability depends on the nature of elite consensus and accountability. Consequently, we delve into the nuances of elite conflict and cooperation that characterized the preindependence era; this account will serve as a foundation for understanding the postindependence era. This is based on the establishment of path dependence in elite conflict and cooperation from pre- to postindependence politics. We argue that the postindependence authoritarian interludes and democratic reversals are mainly due to elite conflict and lack of political accountability.

CONFLICT AND CONSENSUS IN GHANA: A HISTORICAL SKETCH

The Preindependence Era

In the politics of the 1920s–1940s, chiefs and Western-educated elites were opposed to each other in the struggle to determine the true representatives of Africans. In that struggle, the chiefs were the favorites of the colonial masters and were given greater representation on the legislative council (six to three in 1925 and thirteen to five in 1946). By the time the UGCC was formed in 1947 as the first political party, the rivalry between the two groups had somewhat subsided, not least because several of the leading members of the party had chiefly backgrounds (Boahen 1975; Austin 1964).

However, the road to independence was marked by more conflict than consensus, particularly with the emergence of the CPP in 1949. The CPP was a breakaway from the UGCC, led by its former general secretary, Kwame Nkrumah, and leading members of the UGCC's youth wing. This parting of the ways would remain a source of conflict. The CPP opposed the UGCC on several fronts. Whereas the UGCC wanted self-government within the shortest possible time and by constitutional means, the CPP preferred immediate self-government and the use of noncooperation with the colonial Governor and regulations (positive action). Shortest possible time does not mean the UGCC did not believe in immediate self-government. Rather unlike the CPP, it wanted to pursue independence through constitutional means regardless of how much that could elongate attainment of independence. While the UGCC preferred working with the chiefs, the CPP was opposed to them. This will explain why the Nkrumah constitution of 1954 abrogated statutory chiefs' representation in parliament (Frempong 2007a). The two groups were also somewhat divergent along ideological lines.

The demise of the UGCC after the 1951 election did not put an end to its rivalry with the CPP, for other parties would emerge from the ashes of the UGCC (the Ghana Congress Party, GCP, in 1952; and the National Liberation Movement, NLM, in 1954), whose subsequent demand for a federal government raised a constitutional question that needed to be resolved before independence could be granted. The NLM won an alliance with other regional/ethnic/religious-based opposition parties. It also opposed all attempts by the CPP to determine at a roundtable whether to adopt a federated structure. Indeed, the NLM and its allies boycotted the Frederick Bourne Commission, set up by the British government to probe the feasibility of a federal system for independent Ghana (Frempong 2007a).

It was against this background that the colonial government sought to break the impasse through the 1956 election. The CPP won 71 out of 104 seats (though with only 57 percent of the vote). The party expected the colonial authorities to accept its draft of a unitary constitution. But conscious of the fact that the NLM-led opposition alliance had won more than 40 percent of the vote, the colonial authorities in the independence constitution adopted a compromise formula of a unitary system with devolutionary powers that had been recommended by the Bourne Commission (Boahen 1975; Austin 1964; Frempong 2007b: 55). This crafted consensus satisfied neither the government nor the opposition. The ruling CPP reportedly accepted the constitution with grave misgivings but preferred to take what was offered rather than see independence delayed. For the NLM and its allies, anything short of a federal system was not desirable, and they continued to boycott the transition process, a strategy that the CPP cleverly exploited to its advantage (Austin 1964; Frempong 2007b: 56).

The Postindependence Era

After independence, the CPP resorted to an uncompromising attitude, using its majority in parliament to adopt measures aimed at weakening the opposition. Among them was the Avoidance of Discrimination Act, passed in December 1957, which sought to abolish all the opposition parties, forcing them to merge into the United Party (UP). There followed the Preventive Detention Act in 1958, which empowered the government to detain opponents without trial for five years and without right of appeal. Leading opposition members who were imprisoned on the orders of Nkrumah include Dr. J. B. Danquah, Joe Appiah, M. K. Apaloo, Baffuor Osei Akoto, R. R. Amponsah, and S. G. Antoh.[1] In 1960, the CPP, which had weakened the opposition, replaced the independence constitution with a republican constitution that gave broad powers to its leader. Later, the introduction of the one-party system left the CPP wholly in charge (Schwelb 1960; Dale 1993; Frempong 2007b: 56–57). These activities shredded the mechanisms for political accountability, as elections became ineffectual. This subsequently became a justification for the 1966 coup plotters.

Not only did the new military junta, the National Liberation Council of 1966, chaired by Lt. Gen. J. A. Ankrah, ban former CPP government and party functionaries from public office and detain others, it sought to keep the former CPP rulers permanently out of power.

The crisis that led to the collapse of the Second Republic and the January 1972 coup has already been explored in extant literature (see Frempong 2007b). The succeeding military regimes, the Acheampong regime (1972–78) and the Akufo regime (1978–79), experimented with the ideas of union and national governments but were eventually forced under pressure from civil society to allow a return to multiparty constitutional rule in 1979. The Rawlings-led Armed Forces Revolutionary Council allowed the 1979 elections to proceed on schedule but rescheduled the time of handover (Owusu 1979; Oquaye 1980). While justifications on grounds of corruption and nonaccountability have been the dominant excuses for democratic reversals, the same rationale was applied to the military-to-military overthrows.

Hilla Limann's People's National Party (PNP) government (1978–81) brought the Nkrumahists back to power but was forced to forge an ill-fated "coalition" with the United National Convention, led by a UP veteran, William Ofori Atta. The Limann government accepted the judicial verdict on the (re)appointment of Chief Justice Apaloo, but the ruling PNP had intense internal squabbles. The effort by the opposition parties in 1981 to merge as the All People's Party led to withdrawal of some parties over a leadership gridlock (Asamoah 2014; Addae-Mensah 2016). The fractionalization of the ruling elite, among other factors, resulted in the 1981 coup.

The Provisional National Defence Council (PNDC), under Rawlings's chairmanship, emerged following the December 31, 1981, coup. The PNDC would prove uncompromising in its more than one decade in power. It refused initially to tie itself to a timetable for a return to constitutional rule and was insistent on introducing a so-called people's democracy. When eventually, under domestic and external pressure, the PNDC agreed to a return to constitutional rule, it crafted a transition of self-succession in which it rejected all alternative proposals from opposition forces, keeping the transition timetable close to its vest. It then metamorphosed into a political party, the National Democratic Congress (NDC) with the sitting military head of state, Jerry Rawlings, as its presidential candidate (Gyimah-Boadi 1991; Frempong 2012).

Throughout this period of political development, the judiciary suffered from attempted political domination. Conflict occurred between the ruling political elite and the judiciary regardless of the political system. While the 1964 referendum sought to subjugate the judiciary, Busia's refusal to adhere to the Supreme Court ruling after "Apollo 568"—when more than five hundred civil servants (most of whom were Ewes) were sacked by the PP government—undermined the powers of the judiciary. The decision was challenged in court by M. K. Sallah, who, even though he won the case, was denied reinstatement because the Busia government ignored the court ruling. Prime Minister Busia stated that "no court" could compel him to work with anyone unprepared to help him pursue his policies. The height of these political manipulations and abuse of the judiciary was the killing of three judges under the PNDC.[2]

Up to the start of the Fourth Republic, in January 1993, politics in Ghana was marked more by conflict than by consensus. Elite accountability was weak owing to the weaknesses of the opposition throughout Ghana's political history. To what extent has this changed in the Fourth Republic?

CONFLICT AND CONSENSUS IN THE FOURTH REPUBLIC

The Contested Transitional Elections of 1992

As indicated earlier, the new ruling group, the PNDC under Rawlings's chairmanship, held power for eleven years, until January 7, 1993, when Ghana embarked on the current experiment under the 1992 constitution. The special interest the incumbent PNDC regime had, in the outcome of the transition, produced the heightened tensions and the unprecedented lack of compromise that became the hallmark of the process (Gyimah-Boadi 1991; Ninsin 1998; Frempong 2007a: 134). Nonetheless, the constitution became a framework for elite political participation. It also maintained a special place for traditional leadership through the National House of Chiefs, which was established under Article 154 of the 1969 constitution.

One major area of conflict in a transition process is agreeing on its modalities. In the Ghanaian context, this was characterized by biases and uncertainties. The PNDC refused to spell out a clear timetable for the transition. It packed the constitution-drafting Consultative Assembly with progovernment "identifiable bodies" to the virtual exclusion of those with antigovernment views. It also refused to grant a general political amnesty, release political detainees, or repeal repressive laws, and kept tight control of the whole process. For the first time in the country's history, the incumbent military head of state contested the presidency. This in effect turned the incumbent regime into a referee and a player at the same time (Gyimah-Boadi 1991; Frempong 2007b: 135).

Political and civil society groups protested these unilateral decisions, but without success. However, the protests brought consensus among groups of varying backgrounds, including political foes such as leaders from the Danquah-Busia-Dombo and Nkrumahist traditions. For instance, the Movement for Freedom and Justice (MFJ), a vocal critic of the transition process, had in its leadership elements of the Nkrumahist (CPP) and Danquah-Busia's (UP) traditions, as well as political groups ranging from moderate to extreme left-wing orientations (Ninsin 1998: 58).

The November 1992 presidential election resulted in a victory for Rawlings, who won 58.3 percent of the vote, and for the NDC's allies (the National Convention Party, the NCP, and Every Ghanaian Living Everywhere, the EGLE). The four defeated parties (the New Patriotic Party [NPP], People's

National Convention [PNC], National Independence Party, [NIP] and People's Heritage Party [PHP]) denounced the contest as fraudulent (Frempong 2007a: 136) and demanded a more even playing field as a condition for their participation in future elections and the then-pending parliamentary, which they subsequently boycotted amid failed attempts at consensus-building.[3]

The implications of this state of affairs were many for both the ruling alliance and the opposition. It was a clear manifestation of a flawed transition that risked disrupting the cherished democratic order. On the part of the government, the boycott produced a virtual one-party parliament since the three parties that contested were offshoots of the same family tree (Bluwey 1998: 114). On the surface, this looked good for the consolidation of power by the government, but the exceptionally low voter turnout of 29 percent in the parliamentary election reduced the legitimacy of the whole transition process. It became obvious that if the young political order was not secured on the basis of consensus among the political elites, the new government, like its predecessor, would suffer from a crisis of legitimacy. Above all, the vacuum arising from the lack of consensus could encourage another group of adventurers to seize power and reverse the democratic process (Ninsin 1998; Jonah 1998).

Their withdrawal from the parliamentary election put greater pressure on the opposition parties to achieve consensus with the NDC government and to propose alternative strategies to enhance their political effectiveness outside parliament. In this direction, early in 1993 the defeated parties came up with an Inter-Party Coordinating Committee and promised the nation a "shadow cabinet" outside parliament to monitor the activities of the government. The opposition appealed to the government to be consulted on major national issues and urged supporters to accept the NDC government for the sake of peace.[4] The boycott, thus, put pressure on the various stakeholders to secure some form of consensus. This, to some extent, explains why political conflict in the first term in the Fourth Republic did not become as acrimonious and destabilizing as the immediate postelection indicators suggested it might be (Bluwey 1998: 118; Frempong 2007b: 137).

CONTESTED ISSUES (1993–1996)

Against the background of the disputed 1992 election, the seven-member Electoral Commission (EC), which was inaugurated in August 1993, saw a clear need for electoral reforms with a view to greater transparency in all aspects of the election process and sought to create popular faith in the ballot and to build confidence in the EC itself. Thus, the EC, like the government and the opposition parties, as earlier indicated, was under some pressure to seek consensus. The most important mechanism the EC adopted was the innovative Inter-Party Advisory Committee (IPAC). The EC through the IPAC co-opted the parties into the process of election management beginning in March 1994. The IPAC brought together representatives of the political parties for regular monthly meetings with the EC to build consensus on contested electoral issues (Ayee 1997: 10).

The consensual state of affairs at the IPAC would have a moderate influence on the 1996 elections. Meanwhile, there were several other contested issues in the 1993–96 period that would impact on the 1996 polls. Two of them will suffice here to indicate the pressures for elite conflict and consensus.

First, in April 1995 the NDC government introduced the value-added tax (VAT) system, which imposed a 15 percent tax on selected goods and services. With little or no public education before implementation, even sellers exempted from the VAT increased their prices, bringing untold hardships on Ghanaians. In response, the Alliance for Change (AFC)—a coalition of opposition forces from the Nkrumahist and the Danquah-Busia camps, reminiscent of the PMFJ and MFJ—was formed to protest against the VAT through series of peaceful nationwide demonstrations (dubbed *Kume Preko*), which attracted what were alleged to be government-sponsored counterprotests, leading to four deaths in Accra on May 11, 1995. Prominent among its convenors was the current president of Ghana, Nana Akufo Addo.[5] The activities of the AFC upset the delicate balance between citizens' right to protest and the government's duty to maintain public order. However, the AFC was eventually successful, a feat that evolved into an alliance of all opposition forces to contest Rawlings and the NDC in the 1996 elections (Frempong 2007a: 142).

The second contested issue was the rivalry between President Rawlings and Vice President Arkaah and their respective parties, the NDC and the NCP.

The dominance of the three parties in the ruling alliance in parliament (the NDC, the NCP, and Every Ghanaian Living Everywhere) ensured cordial relations between the executive and the legislature. But the consensus was marred by interpersonal acrimony of unprecedented proportions within the presidency between the president and his vice president. The vice president found his party sidelined by the NDC, himself in a strained relationship with the president, and his position bereft of power. Not only was he denied his constitutional right of chairing the cabinet in the absence of the president, but he did not have an official residence. Arkaah survived a sexual scandal but was assaulted by Rawlings at a cabinet meeting. This last act was reportedly in reaction to a speech Arkaah had delivered critical of the government and intensified earlier calls for his resignation. But, in an uncompromising manner, Arkaah had argued against his resignation calling on the president to resign first. His party formally withdrew from the alliance, with a portion of it joining the newly formed People's Convention Party (PCP). But by sticking to his guns and staying in office, Arkaah in 1996 would make history as the sitting vice president who would also become the running mate of an opposition alliance.

The 1996 Elections

The success of the IPAC leaders in producing consensus on several areas of electoral politics in the two years preceding the 1996 elections enhanced the confidence of all the key actors and ensured that the conduct and outcome of the elections would be accepted by the contending parties as free and fair (Ninsin 1998: 190). This notwithstanding, the path leading to the elections was strewn with issues of conflict among political parties.

The NDC, which had lost its major partner in the 1992 alliance, the NCP, found a replacement in the Democratic People's Party. Two other issues confronted the ruling NDC: the choice of a new running mate and the need to strengthen the quality of its parliamentary candidates, with the embittered Arkaah out of the way. While the selection of John Atta Mills did not raise any public protest at this time, he would, in 2000, become a source of the conflict in the race to succeed Rawlings. In addition, the ruling NDC, with the advantage of incumbency, managed the delicate matter of replacing its stopgap candidates by placating about eighty incumbents with cash and other inducements. The NDC's problems, however, paled compared to what transpired on the other side of the political divide: the Great Alliance (Aubynn 1997: 21, 34; Frempong 2007a: 145).

The Great Alliance, an alliance of traditional political adversaries—the Danquah/Busiaist NPP and the Nkrumahist PCP—represented an elite consensus of sorts, but lack of consensus on the modalities including who becomes the flagbearer created friction among the opposition parties (Frempong 2007a: 145). In the NPP there were opposing views on the alliance. While some members had publicly decried it, others were prepared to leave the party if it was not pursued.[6] When eventually the NPP joined the alliance, the limelight had shifted from the party's 1992 "radical" flagbearer Adu Boahen to the "moderate" John Kufuor as a "compromise" candidate who presumably would be more acceptable to the two traditions.

The PCP also had its internal squabbles. The PCP was only a fraction of the Nkrumahist family, with the PNC on its own and a chunk of the former NCP in the NDC fold. It also lacked consensus on the alliance; some argued it was a defeatist strategy since it implied that neither the PCP nor NPP by itself could defeat the NDC. But the worst baggage that the PCP brought into the alliance was the election of Arkaah as its presidential candidate. Clearly, he had ridden on the crest of his assault by Rawlings (Aubynn 1997: 22; Frempong 2007a: 146). The struggle between Arkaah and Kufuor for the top slot delayed consummation of the alliance until September, barely three months before the election.

Far worse was the struggle over parliamentary seats. The PCP, in spite of its weaknesses, made an initial demand for fifty-fifty share of the seats. When the 112–86 formula (with 2 seats reserved for incumbent independents) was agreed on, the two parties had in many places registered separate candidates, and it was difficult getting some to step down; the battle, therefore, raged till election day (Aubynn 1997: 22). A tragic aspect of this "comedy of alliance" was bickering over ministerial posts before the elections were held. The net effect of all this was disastrous for the opposition. The NDC capitalized on the wrangling and drummed up possibilities of instability and chaos should the government lose to the bickering opposition alliance (Ayee 1997: 15).

These intra- and interparty squabbles gave the NDC considerable advantage at both the parliamentary and presidential levels. The voter turnout was an impressive 73.5 percent, and in the three-way presidential contest, Jerry Rawlings (NDC / Progressive Alliance) obtained 57.4 percent; John Kufuor (NPP / Great Alliance) 39.6 percent; and Edward Mahama (PNC) 3.0 percent. For parliament, the NDC won 133 seats (one short of the two-thirds majority), the NPP 61, the PCP 5, and the PNC 1 (Ayee 1997: 17; Ninsin 1998: 185).

The general mood following the election confirmed that the contending political leaders had agreed, to an appreciable extent, upon the basic rules of electoral politics (Ninsin 1998: 194). Unlike 1992, the losing candidates, Kufuor and Mahama, conceded defeat and congratulated the winner; Rawlings, in turn, congratulated the losers for their competitive spirit (Ayee 1997: 12–13). Parliamentary candidates, across all parties, who had complaints expressed their intention to seek redress through the EC and the courts rather than resorting to dubious tactics (Gyimah-Boadi 1999: 412). The defeated political parties and their supporters seemed geared up for the election of 2000, a further indication of a broad consensus that the ballot box was the sole legitimate instrument for seeking power (Gyimah-Boadi 1999: 412). Thus, on the whole, the 1996 elections produced a far more favorable outcome than those of 1992, suggesting that even a flawed transition could set the stage for democratic progress if the political elite could build some consensus.

Election 2000 and the First Power Alternation

One issue that cast long shadows on the Ghanaian political scene from the early part of Rawlings's second term was whether he would abide by the constitutional term limit and relinquish power at the end of election 2000. In fact, Rawlings's effort to demonstrate his intention to depart in 2000 created problems for his party and contributed in no small measure to its defeat (Agyeman-Duah 2000: 23).

At an NDC rally at Agona Swedru in the Central Region in June 1998, two and half years ahead of the elections, Rawlings publicly expressed his preference for Vice President John Atta Mills as the party's flagbearer for the next elections. This declaration had serious implications for the NDC (Agyeman-Duah 2000: 23). First, it effectively foreclosed competition from within the party and dashed the presidential ambitions of other stalwarts in the government. The support of these veteran politicians, who saw themselves outwitted and outpaced by the new entrant, Mills, waned considerably. But far worse was the split that the declaration created in the NDC. One faction, the Reform Movement, demanding democracy within with the NDC, formed the splinter National Reform Party. Its emergence encouraged the opposition to attack the democratic credentials and policies of the NDC, and it also acted as a spoiler. It caused the NDC's defeat (and the NPP's victory) in a number of constituencies, without winning any seats by itself. The NDC could have maintained its parliamentary majority had it effectively managed its internal differences (Frempong 2007a: 152–53).

On the other hand, the opposition NPP, reeling under the disastrous effects of the Great Alliance and seeking to avoid a third consecutive defeat, took some positive steps: it decided it would contest the next election without an alliance and conducted its presidential primary two years ahead of the election. The August 1998 primary contest retained Kufuor, the candidate defeated in 1996. The early primary had the therapeutic effect of healing internal divisions in the party (Gyimah-Boadi 2001: 108). At the parliamentary level, the party, generally impressed by the performance of its MPs, retained 90 percent of them. Only in six of the sixty-one constituencies were the incumbents replaced. This consensus formula worked relatively well for the NPP. And with the one exception, the NPP retained all its 1996 seats in 2000 (Frempong 2007a: 153).

The 2000 presidential contest was undecided in the first round. Kufuor (NPP) led by 48.2 percent, with Mills (NDC) trailing with 44.5 percent and the remaining 7 percent spread across five other contestants. In the parliamentary poll, NPP had one hundred seats, the NDC ninety-two, the PNC three, the CPP one, and independents (all NDC protesters) four. Most significantly, in the runoff, Kufuor (NPP) with the publicly declared support of the third parties, defeated Mills by 56.9 percent to 43.1 percent, leading to the first civilian-to-civilian transfer of power in Ghana's electoral history (Ayee 2001; Gyimah-Boadi 2001). It worth noting that Ghanaian voters exacted accountability from an incumbent party that had become unresponsive, complacent, and arrogant and flaunted its apparent "invincibility."

Election 2000 offered some useful lessons in consensus-building. First, the opposition's show of resilience and fortitude in the face of extreme provocation, involving accusation of attacks during the campaign and election processes, and the incumbent's gracious concession and peaceful handing over of power were a manifestation of growing elite consensus on the rules of the democratic game. Second, the coalition of opposition forces, particularly for the second ballot, was not only invigorating but also a step toward political inclusiveness. Third, the pivotal role that civil society (including traditional and religious leaders) can play in moderating political tensions was demonstrated. Lastly, the fact that the government and opposition had virtually the same number of parliamentarians required consensus-building, unlike the impunity of the majority that characterized the previous parliaments (Gyimah-Boadi 2001: 114; Frempong 2007a: 155–15).

One postelection issue that created controversy in the early days of the new administration was the retirement settlement of Rawlings and his entourage. The Kufuor administration was plunged into the unfamiliar terrain of an appropriate settlement, an issue that was made thornier because the outgoing government officials had been in power for almost two decades but failed to provide appropriate retirement settlement for previous leaders. But the somewhat unexpected alternation of power and the very limited transition period turned the whole process into a messy affair.[7] The Joint Transition Team to sort out some of those issues had less than two weeks between the presidential runoff and the inauguration (Agyeman-Duah 2000: 56).

The situation in parliament was even more intriguing. The first few months were marked by disagreements over many issues, with the singular exception of a $20,000 car loan for each MP. For example, Speaker Justice Annan was replaced by a former NPP national chairman, Peter Ala Adjetey; but the NPP in 1997 had preferred somebody less partisan. Other points of disagreement included the assumption of responsibilities by ministerial nominees before their approval by parliament; the use of a new but controversially bought presidential jet; vehicle and oil agreements with Nigeria without parliament's prior approval; and the rumored renovation of the president's private residence with state funds.[8] In all these matters, the once-vociferous opposition now on the majority bench (an alliance of the NPP, PNC, and CPP) supported the government, while the formerly subservient NDC group vehemently opposed. Because the NPP seats were exactly half the membership of the House, it won the support of most of the non-NDC members, some of whom were rewarded with ministerial and other positions. These included Freddie Blay (PCP, Ellembelle constituency), Moses Dani Baah (PNC, Sissala constituency), Rashid Bawa (IND, Akan constituency), Joseph Akudibillah (Garu-Tempane constituency), and Boniface Saddique (Salaga constituency).

In a rare exception to the rule, the NDC MP for Bimbilla, Mohammed Ibn Chambas, praised the president's State of the Nation address as having a "heavy dose of realism."[9] Either by design or fate, Chambas was later supported by the NPP government to become the executive secretary of the Economic Community of West African States. While the NPP trumpeted this as a manifestation of its all-inclusive governance, the NDC saw it as a calculated ploy to weaken the opposition. In the resultant by-election in Bimbilla, the NPP wrestled the seat from the NDC (Frempong 2007a: 160).

After the initial furor, parliament settled down and worked through consensus on several issues. But it must be emphasized that in 2002 and 2003, respectively, the minority boycotted the debate and voting on the National Reconciliation and the National Health Insurance bills. The former sought to deal with unresolved issues of truth, justice, and reconciliation, while the latter replaced the existing "cash and carry" health care system with an insurance system. The boycott of the bill on national reconciliation was considered most unfortunate for the country. While both sides agreed on the need for some form of reconciliation, they could not agree either on the mode of appointment of the commissioners or the period their work was to cover. The majority wanted commissioners to be appointed by the president with parliamentary approval and investigations restricted to Ghana's unconstitutional governments, but the minority preferred a less partisan mode of appointment and to cover all regimes before the Fourth Republic. The perception that parliament could not set the pace by reconciling itself remained and haunted the work of the National Reconciliation Commission (Frempong 2007a; Boafo-Arthur 2006).

Another issue that demonstrated the dangers of nonconsensus and exploitation of the parliamentary majority was the US$1 billion loan agreement with a private consortium brought to parliament in mid-June 2002. The opposition and the media raised concerns about the loan, but the Finance Committee, by a majority vote, all members of the minority dissenting, recommended the proposed loan agreement for approval by the House. Parliament in turn, amid intense controversy, "fast-tracked" the approval process in partisan acquiescence to the wishes of the executive, which would not tolerate too many probing questions. The loan turned out to be a scam.[10]

Election 2004

The NDC was compelled by its defeat in 2000 to form a Revamp Team, headed by Obed Asamoah, in March 2001, to come up with ideas for the reorganization of the party.[11] But its work stalled over a role in the party for ex-president Rawlings, a bone of contention that haunted the NDC during the 2004 elections and beyond. By the time the NDC held its first postdefeat national congress in April 2002, the party had divided into pro-Rawlings and anti-Rawlings camps. The former were the defenders of the status quo for whom the party was inseparable from Rawlings and any attempt to diminish his grip on the party would make the NDC something other than the NDC. The latter were the champions of a new and depersonalized NDC that looked beyond Rawlings.[12] Unfortunately for the NDC, in the run-up to the election in 2004, the anti-Rawlings camp controlled the national executive and the pro-Rawlings group the presidential ticket. This internal divide, in part, caused the NDC a second defeat in 2004. The situation within the ruling NPP was different. Ahead of the election, incumbent party succession did not become an issue because President Kufuor was unanimously endorsed to seek reelection.

With the NPP winning 128 seats, compared to 94 by the NDC, in the enlarged 230-member House, an intriguing conflict emerged from an unexpected quarter: the election of the Speaker. Incumbent Speaker (and former NPP chairman) Ala Adjetey lost the support of the majority caucus, which nominated a former member of the Council of State, Begyina Hughes. In an unprecedented manner, the minority caucus, instead of endorsing the majority nominee, renominated Ala Adjetey and forced the vote onto a secret ballot, which ended in the defeat of the incumbent Speaker. This had repercussions down the line when the NPP, in turn, used its majority to defeat the NDC nominee for Second Deputy Speaker, which hitherto had been a normative preserve for the minority.

Election 2008

The second term of Kufuor was overtaken by issues of who to succeed him as the NPP's presidential candidate. While Kufuor could not singlehandedly "anoint" his successor, as Rawlings did, he remained at the center of the storm that blew over his succession. His somewhat muted preference for Trade Minister Alan Kyerementen over his two-term vice president, Aliu Mahama, and the party's "heir-apparent," Akufo-Addo, led to a divisive primary that featured seventeen aspirants. The primary left the eventual winner, Akufo-Addo, bruised for the presidential contest. Senior Minister J. H. Mensah and NDC general secretary, Asiedu Nketia, referred to the presidential race as a "beauty contest" due to the number of aspirants.[13] On the other hand, the opposition NDC, after some initial hiccups, united behind John Mills, who was making his third bid for the presidency (Frempong 2017).

The 2008 elections produced an intriguing outcome. Akufo-Addo (NPP) led Mills (NDC) by 49.1 percent to 47.9 percent in the inconclusive first-round poll. But the NDC had a parliamentary majority of 116–107, with seven seats spread across third parties and independents. In the runoff, Mills turned the tables with a stunning 50.2 percent to 49.8 percent victory, and with that Ghana experienced a second civilian-to-civilian transfer of power, but this time with no broad consensus among the third parties in terms of which party to support in the runoff.

As in the first such transfer in 2000, the incumbent NPP lost because of mismanaged party succession and the attendant intraparty disunity. But it was also punished because it had grown complacent after two consecutive victories and had lost touch with the electorate.

Election 2012

After assuming office, Mills was consistently criticized by his mentor, ex-president Rawlings, for sidelining him and Mills' perceived lack of leadership. As it turned out, Mills became the first sitting president to be challenged within the incumbent party, albeit unsuccessfully, in his second-term bid, and by no less a person than the wife of Rawlings, Nana Konadu Agyeman Rawlings (flagbearer of the National Democratic Party, NDP). With Mills's demise six months ahead of the 2012 elections, his vice president, John Mahama, assumed the presidency for the unexpired term and also became the NDC's presidential candidate through a broad intraparty consensus. On the part of the NPP, Akufo-Addo had been renominated, without public rancor, by an enlarged electoral college.

John Mahama was declared the winner of the 2012 presidential election by 50.7 percent to 47.7 percent, and at the parliamentary level the NDC secured 148 of the enlarged 275-member House against the NPP's 123 seats. The NPP disputed the presidential outcome, leading to a nine-month petition trial at the Supreme Court, which confirmed Mahama's victory. Akufo-Addo, while indicating his disagreement, accepted the verdict. The petition no doubt tested Ghana's electoral system to its limit but ended up strengthening it. Not only did the petition symbolize elite trust and confidence in democratic institutions, it also facilitated the adoption of new reforms for Ghana's electoral system. Over twenty of these reforms were implemented before the 2016 elections (ERMAG 2017).

Election 2016 and the Third Alternation

In a rematch between John Mahama (NDC) and Akufo-Addo (NPP) in 2016, the latter emerged victorious in a single round by 53.9 percent to 44.4 percent, and in parliament the NPP won 169 seats against NDC's 106. Once again, it was a punishment for a government that had lost touch with the electorate. Before the election, the internal rivalries in the NPP had led to the suspension of its party chairman and secretary. While this open disunity was evident, the papered-over unity of the NDC proved more detrimental.

Significantly, this election secured for Ghana its third transfer of power in the Fourth Republic. Mahama conceded defeat and peacefully handed over power. However, a number of issues of conflict have sprung up since the inception of the third alternation. Postelection politics have been characterized by unresolved conflict over "pro-NPP" vigilantism or hooliganism—a phenomenon characterized by dissident groups that, in some instances, engage in violent acts to, presumably, serve the interest on their affiliated political parties. In other circles, they are unregistered private security groups for political parties who hope to enter mainstream security services or secure jobs once their party wins power. On the part of the NPP, activities of vigilante groups like Invisible Forces, Delta Force, Bamba Boys, and Bolga Bulldogs have been inimical to the government's first tenure in office, with incidents such as Kumasi court raid by Delta Force.[14] Although the national security minister, Albert Kan Dapaah, asserted in parliament that "there are no legally registered political vigilante groups in the country, and for that matter, there are no such groups to be disbanded,"[15] their violence has been a major feature of the new NPP government.

In addition, until November 2017 both majority and minority in parliament were caught up in a legal-political banter over the much-awaited Office of the Special Prosecutor bill. However, a consensus was achieved and the bill's passage, as broad consultations were done across the political divide (Gadugah 2017).

EMERGING ISSUES

The significant differences between the 1957–1992 and the 1993–2017 periods have been the extent to which broad consensus across the elite divide has been achieved amid conflict. Again, democratic institutions such as the Electoral Management Body and the judiciary, which hitherto were an extension of the ruling elites or under pressure to do the bidding of the government, have been instrumental. Their unique independence is vital for democratic stability. This section addresses what these issues mean for Ghana's democracy, positively and negatively.

On the positive side, consensus-building on the rules of the electoral game through the IPAC mechanism has proved useful in Ghana's electoral and political progress. As indicated earlier, it continues to provide an avenue for interparty discussions on sensitive political and electoral issues. Second, the Electoral Commission and the courts have generally played their roles effectively in election management and dispute resolution. This has been evident in their settling of election disputes in the Fourth Republic. On the system of governance, the two-party system has ensured that the losing major party can restrategize and recapture power. Even the third parties have not been completely left out. On some occasions, they have become kingmakers in presidential runoffs. In addition, several times opposing groups, even traditional political foes, have forged alliances to contest against a stronger force. Ghana has also enjoyed what we term "ethnic fortune." Ghana's largest ethnic group, the Akans, has not always voted in unison. If they did, the NPP would always win power, which would lead to marginalization of the other political parties.

Lastly, civil societies have been important. Various civil society groups (think tanks, domestic observers, traditional authorities, religious bodies, and the media) have played growing roles in voter education, presidential and parliamentary debates, election observation and monitoring, and "peacemongering," among other functions, and in the process become a moderating influence in the country's electoral politics.

On the negative side, however, the dominance of the ruling party in each of the seven parliaments of the Fourth Republic has not helped consensus-building in the House. Instead, at each turn, the majority caucus has acquiesced to the wishes of the executive and ignored questions from the minority. Indeed, MPs who are vociferous in opposition have often turned subservient to the majority, and even when the minority has its say, the majority has its way. Indeed, this legislative rubber-stamping of government policies does not serve any useful public interest. Moreover, the frequency of parliamentary boycotts casts doubts on how deeply the political elite have imbibed the ethos of consensus-building. The two dominant parties are equally guilty. The NPP in opposition in the second parliament boycotted the vetting of ministerial nominees and the budget, and for nine months in the Sixth Parliament boycotted all major issues while the presidential election petition was ongoing. The NDC also has to its "credit" boycotts over national reconciliation, national health insurance, extension of the franchise to Ghanaians abroad, and, in one instance, the imprisonment of one of its members by a court of competent jurisdiction.

CONCLUSION

This chapter has illustrated both intra- and interparty elite conflict and consensus in Ghana while tying them to political accountability and assessing the extent to which it influences democratic stability in Ghana. We argue that the deliberate creation of institutions of elite consensus, establishing both formal and informal elite links, has been instrumental in addressing elite conflict and safeguarding Ghana's democracy. However, the institutions of elite accountability have yet to function as expected. We also established a dichotomy between the 1957–1992 and 1993–2017 epochs as vital in explaining how the dynamic mix of elite conflict and consensus has streamlined Ghana's democratic stability. Yet every phase of elections and leadership succession has been marked by acrimony and, in some cases, the formation of splinter parties. This has not been unique to the two main parties (NPP and NDC) but has also been a feature of smaller parties, such as the Nkrumahist parties. It is one of the main reasons why Ghana does not have a formidable third party, and why the current parliament is made up of only the NPP and NDC.

On the whole, Ghana has made considerable progress in terms of elite consensus, elite accountability, and democratic stability. The democratic experiment that begun in 1993 has continued for more than a quarter century, the longest stretch in the country's electoral history. Over the period, consensus on the electoral system has been built through the IPAC, and with three peaceful alternations in power, Ghana has passed Huntington's (1991) two-turnover test of democratic consolidation. Still, a lot of progress remains to be accomplished if democracy is to become "the only game in town" (to borrow from Linz and Stepan 1996: 15), behaviorally, attitudinally, and constitutionally. There is, therefore, the urgent need to engage in progressive electoral reforms while discouraging violent factional politics. In addition, elite consensual platforms should be created to address policy issues to avert elite marginalization and extreme antagonism.

The de facto two-party system has limited the choice of Ghanaian voters to either the NPP or the NDC. This brings it closer to the idea of a choiceless democracy (Mkandawire 2010; Ninsin 2006; Obi 2008). The results of the 2017 Afrobarometer survey, for instance, demonstrate that calls to make the municipal metropolitan district chief executive positions elective are driven by citizens' concern for accountability (Armah-Attoh and Norviewu 2018). There is, therefore, a need for a concrete shift to policies that represent the interests of the people, to whom elected representatives are held accountable. In addition, institutions of democratic accountability should be strengthened and made impartial, so citizens can hold their leaders accountable without having to wait for elections every four years.

NOTES

1. Human Rights, Individual Freedoms and Democracy in Ghana- The Preventive Detention Act and After By Prof Justice A. K. P. Kludze Retrieved from http://www.justiceghana.com/index.php/en/law-a-justice/7443-human-rights-individual-freedoms-and-democracy-in-ghana-the-preventive-detention-act-and-after?showall=1&limitstart=. Accessed April 29, 2018.

2. K A. Busia: His Politics of Demagoguery By Kwame Botwe-Asamoah Retrieved from https://www.ghanaweb.com/GhanaHomePage/NewsArchive/K-A-Busia-His-Politics-of-Demagoguery-120360. Accessed May 20, 2018.

3. *Pioneer* (Accra), November 26, 1992.

4. *Uhuru* 5, no. 7, 1993.

5. Postdemonstration press conference by the AFC, "Alliance for Change Speaks Out," GhanaWeb, May 23, 1995, https://www.ghanaweb.com/GhanaHomePage/NewsArchive/Alliance-for-Change-Speaks-Out-174

6. *Daily Graphic*, July 15, 1996.

7. *Evening News*, January 20, 2001.

8. "Millions Spent on Kufuor's Private House," GhanaWeb, March 10, 2001,

https://www.ghanaweb.com/GhanaHomePage/NewsArchive/Millions-Spent-on-Kufuor-s-Private-House-13997

9. "Dr Chambas Applauded for Objective Analysis of Sessional Address," GhanaWeb, February 24, 2001, https://www.ghanaweb.com/GhanaHomePage/NewsArchive/Dr-Chambas-applauded-for-objective-analysis-of-sessional-address-13749

10. *Democratic Watch*, September 2002, 1–5.

11. Obed heads NDC revamping team https://www.modernghana.com/news/12758/obed-heads-ndc-revamping-team.html, March 5, 2001.

12. *Democratic Watch*, September 2002, 9–10.

13. "Presidential Race Is No Beauty Contest—J.H. Mensah," *Radio Recogin*, January 8, 2007, http://www.recogin.com/newsdetails.asp?id=2262&cat_id=1; and http://theheraldghana.com/nkrabeah-effah-dartey-misses/, accessed May 20, 2018.

14. Sammy Darko, "Vigilante Groups in Ghana; a Necessary Evil," CitiTV, April 19, 2017, http://citifmonline.com/2017/04/19/vigilante-groups-in-ghana-a-necessary-evil-article/; and https://www.myjoyonline.com/news/2017/April-10th/un-condemns-kumasi-circuit-court-raid-by-delta-force.php Accessed May 20, 2018.

15. Arrest political militants – Kan Dapaah tells Police Retrieved from https://www.ghanaweb.com/GhanaHomePage/NewsArchive/Arrest-political-militants-Kan-Dapaah-tells-Police-526873 Accessed May 20, 2018.

REFERENCES

Addae-Mensah, Ivan. 2016. *A Biography of Hilla Limann: Scholar, Diplomat & Statesman*. Accra: Africa Biographies Consult.

Agyeman-Duah, Baffour. 2000. *Elections in Emerging Democracies: Ghana, Liberia and Nigeria*. Accra: Ghana Center for Democratic Development.

Alder, Simeon, and Yikai Wang. 2018. "Divide and Rule: An Origin of Polarization and Ethnic Conflict." Working paper, Center for Institutions, Policy and Culture in the Development Process.

Armah-Attoh, Daniel, and Newton Norviewu. 2018. "Demand for Transparency, Accountability Drives Call for Electing Local Leaders in Ghana." *Afrobarometer Policy Paper* No. 48. http://afrobarometer.org/sites/default/files/publications/Policy papers/ab_r7_policypaperno48_should_ghana_elect_its_mmdces_2.pdf

Asamoah, Obed Yao. 2014. *The Political History of Ghana (1950–2013)*. Bloomington, IN: AuthorHouse.

Aubynn, Anthony Kwesi. 1997. "Beyond the Transparent Box: The Significance of the 1996 Elections in Ghana." *Working Paper* No. 5/7. Helsinki: Institute of Development Studies.

Austin, Dennis. 1964. *Politics in Ghana, 1946–1960*. London: Oxford University Press.

Ayee, Joseph R. A. 1997. "Ghana's 1996 General Elections: A Post-mortem." *Occasional Paper Series*, vol. 1, no. 1. Harare: AAPS.

Ayee, Joseph R. A., ed. 2001. *Deepening Democracy in Ghana: Politics of the 2000 Elections.* Vol. 1. Accra: Freedom Publications.

Badu, Kwasi Afriyie, and John Larvie. 1996. *Elections 96 in Ghana.* Part 1. Accra: Gold Type.

Bluwey, G. K. 1998. "State Organizations in Transition to Constitutional Democracy." In Kwame Akon Ninsin, ed., *Ghana: Transition to Democracy.* 167–85. Accra: Freedom Publications.

Boafo-Arthur, Kwame. 1995. "Managing Inter-party Conflict in Ghanaian Politics: Lessons from the NDC and NPP Dialogue." In Mike Oquaye, ed., *Democracy and Conflict Resolution in Ghana.* 212–30 Accra: Gold Type.

Boafo-Arthur, Kwame. 2006. "The Quest for National Reconciliation in Ghana: Challenges and Prospects." In Kwame Boafo-Arthur, ed. *Voting for Democracy in Ghana: The 2004 Elections in Perspective, Thematic Studies,* Vol. 1. 127-55. Accra: Freedom Publications.

Boahen, A. Adu. 1975. *Ghana: Evolution and Change in the Nineteenth and Twentieth Centuries.* London: Longman.

Bratton, Michael, and Nicholas van de Walle. 1997. *Democratic Experiments in Africa.* Cambridge: Cambridge University Press.

Transitions and Breakdowns." *American Sociological Review* (February).

Carvalho, Jean-Paul, and Christian Dippel. 2020. "Elite Identity and Political Accountability: A Tale of Ten Islands." *Economic Journal.*

Dale, William. 1993. "The Making and Remaking of Commonwealth Constitutions." *International and Comparative Law Quarterly* 42, no. 1 (January).

Diamond, Larry J. 1994. "Toward Democratic Consolidation." *Journal of Democracy* 5, no. 3: 4–17.

Electoral Reform Monitoring and Advocacy Group (ERMAG). 2017. *Final Report on the Implementation of ECs Electoral Reforms.* CDD-Ghana.

Diermeier, Daniel, and Christopher Li. 2019. "Partisan Affect and Elite Polarization." *American Political Science Review* 113, no. 1: 277–81. https://doi.org/10.1017/S0003055418000655

Frempong, Alex K. D. 2007a. "Constitution-Making and Constitutional Rule in Ghana." In J. R. A., ed., *Ghana at 50: Government, Politics and Development.*, 51–76. Accra: Department of Political Science, UG/Friedrich Ebert Stiftung-Ghana.

Frempong, Alex K. D. 2007b. "Political Conflict and Elite Consensus in a Liberal State." In K. Boafo-Arthur, ed., *Ghana: One Decade of the Liberal State.*, 128-164. Dakar: CODESRIA; London: Zed Books.

Frempong, Alex K. D. 2012. *Electoral Politics in Ghana's Fourth Republic in the Context of Post–Cold War Africa.* Accra: Yamens Press.

Frempong, Alex K. D. 2017. "Trajectories of Intra-party Succession: The New Patriotic Party and Ghana's Election 2008." In Bossman. E. Asare and Alex K. D. Frempong, eds., *Aspects of Democracy in Ghana,* vol. 1: 19-49. Tema: Digibooks.

Gadugah, N. 2017. *Special Prosecutor's Bill Finally Passed.* November 14. https://www.myjoyonline.com/news/special-prosecutors-bill-finally-passed/

Gebrewold, Belachew. 2003. *Passion, Politics and State-Building: The African Case.* https://www.uibk.ac.at/theol/cover/archives/innsbruck2003/abstracts/innsbruck2003_gebrewold_paper.doc. Accessed May 25, 2018.

Gould, J., and S. Szomolanyi. 1997. "Elite Fragmentation in Industry and the Prospect for Democracy." *Intermarium* 1, no. 2: 1–23.

Gyimah-Boadi, Emmanuel. 1991. "Tensions in Ghana's Transition to Constitutional Rule." In Kwame Akon Ninsin and Francis K. Drah, eds., *Ghana's Transition to Constitutional Rule.* 35–40. Accra: Ghana Universities Press.

Gyimah-Boadi, Emmanuel. 1999. "Ghana: The Challenges of Consolidating Democracy." In Richard A. Joseph, ed., *State Conflict and Democracy in Africa.* 409–29. Boulder, CO: Lynne Rienner.

Gyimah-Boadi, Emmanuel. 2001. "A Peaceful Turnover in Ghana." *Journal of Democracy* 12, no. 2 (April): 103-17.

Higley, John. and Michael Burton. 2006. *Elite foundations of liberal democracy.* Lanham: Rowman & Littlefield Publishers.

Hoffmann-Lange, Ursula. 2012. "Vertical and Horizontal Accountability of Global Elites: Some Theoretical Reflections and a Preliminary Research Agenda." *Historical Social Research* 37, no. 1: 193–208.

Hoffmann-Lange, Ursula, Helga Neumann, and Bärbel Steinkemper. 1985. "Conflict and Consensus among Elites in the Federal Republic of Germany." *Research in Politics and Society: A Research Annual.* Vol. 1: 243–83. Stamford: JAI Press Inc.

Huntington, Samuel., 1991. Democracy's Third Wave. *Journal of democracy* 2, no. 2: 2-34.

Jeffries, Richard. 1998. "The Ghanaian Elections of 1996: Towards the Consolidation of Democracy?" *African Affairs* 97, no. 387(April): 189–208.

Jonah, Kwesi. 1998. "Political Parties and the Transition to Multi-party Politics in Ghana." In Kwame Akon Ninsin, ed., *Ghana: Transition to Democracy.* 72–94. Accra: Freedom Publications.

Körösényi, András. 2009. "Beyond the Happy Consensus about Democratic Elitism." *Comparative Sociology* 8, no. 3: 364–82.

Kotey, E. N. A. 1995. "The Supreme Court and Conflict Resolution in Ghana's Fourth Republic." In Mike Oquaye, ed., *Democracy and Conflict Resolution in Ghana.* 276–309. Accra: Gold Type.

Le Vine, Victor T. 1968. "Political Elite Recruitment and Political Structure in French-Speaking Africa." *Cahiers d'études africaines* 8, no. 31: 369–89. https://doi.org/10.3406/cea.1968.3133

Lijphart, Arend. 2018. "Consociationalism After Half a Century." In Michaelina Jakala, Durukan Kuzu, and Matt Qvortrup., eds. *Consociationalism and Power-Sharing in Europe. International Political Theory.* 1-9. Cham: Palgrave Macmillan.

Linz, Juan J. (Juan José), and Alfred C Stepan., 1996. "Toward Consolidated Democracies." *Journal of Democracy* 7, no. 2: 14-33.

Lopez, Matias. 2013. "Elite Theory." *Sociopedia.Isa*, 1–12. https://doi.org/10.1007/978-3-658-02935-7_7

Miller, Robert A. 1974. "Elite Formation in Africa: Class, Culture, and Coherence." *Journal of Modern African Studies* 12, no. 4 (December): 521–42.

Mkandawire, Thandika. 2010. "Aid, Accountability, and Democracy in Africa." *Social Research* 77, no. 4: 1149–82.

Morrison, Minion K. 2004. "Political Parties in Ghana through Four Republics: A Path to Democratic Consolidation." *Comparative Politics* 36 no. 4: 421–42.

Ninsin, Kwame Akon, ed. 1998. *Ghana: Transition to Democracy*. Accra: Freedom Publications.

Ninsin, Kwame Akon 2006. "Introduction: The Contradictions and Ironies of Elections in Africa." *Africa Development* 31, no. 3: 1–10.

Obi, Cyril I. 2008. "No Choice, but Democracy: Prising the People out of Politics in Africa?" *Claude Ake Memorial Paper Series* no. 2. Uppsala.

Oquaye, Mike. 1980. *Politics in Ghana, 1972–1979*, Accra: Tornado Publications.

Osei, Anja. 2015. "Elites and Democracy in Ghana: A Social Network Approach." *African Affairs* 114, no. 457: 529–54.

Owusu, Maxwell. 1979. "Politics without Parties: Reflections on the Union Government Proposal in Ghana." *African Studies Review* 22, no. 1 (April): 89–108.

Schedler, Andreas. 1998. "What Is Democratic Consolidation?" *Journal of Democracy* 9, no. 2: 91–107.

Schwelb, Egon. 1960. "The Republican Constitution of Ghana." *American Journal of Comparative Law* 9, no. 4 (Autumn): 634–56.

Sohlberg, Jacob. 2017. "The Effect of Elite Polarization: A Comparative Perspective on How Party Elites Influence Attitudes and Behavior on Climate Change in the European Union." *Sustainability* (Switzerland) 9, no. 1: 1–13. https://doi.org/10.3390/su9010039

Suslov, Evegeniy V., Valeriy B. Golubev, Sergei A. Zhyravlev, and Vitaliy T. Mihailov. 2015. "Formation of Elite [*sic*] in Russia: Conflict and Consensus." *Mediterranean Journal of Social Sciences* 6, no. 3: 71–78. https://doi.org/10.5901/mjss.2015.v6n3s7p71

Tonah, Steve. 2007. *Ethnicity, Conflicts and Consensus in Ghana*. Accra: Woeli Publishing Services.

Thompson, W. Scott. 1969. *Ghana's Foreign Policy, 1957–1966: Diplomacy Ideology, and the New State*. Princeton, NJ: Princeton University Press.

Wilson, Matthew C. 2019. "A Closer Look at the Limits of Consociationalism." *Comparative Political Studies* 53, no. 5: 700–23. https://doi.org/10.1177/0010414019858956

CHAPTER 5

Is the African University a Site of Elite Reproduction or Disruption?

What the Senegalese Experience Tells Us

MICHAEL C. LAMBERT

Africa is home to some of the world's oldest continuously operating institutions of higher education. Morocco's University of Al-Karouine was established in AD 859 and Egypt's Al-Azhar University in AD 972. However, almost a millennium would pass before institutions of higher education similar to those that had developed north of the Mediterranean would find their way from Europe to sub-Saharan Africa. In 1827 Sierra Leone's Fourah Bay College became the first African institution of higher education designed in the image of the European university. This was followed in 1829 by the University of Cape Town, established to serve white South Africans. Other early African institutions of higher education include Cairo University, founded in 1908, the University of Algiers, founded in 1909, and Makerere University, founded in 1922.[1] Most African institutions of higher education would be developed later, many coming in the years following World War II. During this period, the Universities of Ghana and Ibadan in 1948, Zimbabwe in 1952, and Dakar in 1957 were established. During the 1960s, a host of other African universities would be founded, including two in the Portuguese colonies of Angola and Mozambique. And during this same period a large number of institutions of higher education opened their doors in newly independent nations of Africa. Among them were the Universities of Malawi in 1964, Benin in 1970, Nairobi in 1970, and Congo-Brazzaville in 1971.

Many of these institutions of higher education were established either shortly before or after independence. With the colonial era either winding down or having ended, the newly independent African nations faced a pressing manpower gap, and it was seen as imperative in African nations that their own nationals have the formal education and background deemed necessary to assume the administrative and technical positions that had been filled by Europeans during the colonial era. African universities were in part conceived to educate this class of African administrators and technicians. It was also foreseen that hand in hand with this educational mission would be the expansion of an elite class of Africans comprising individuals who would move from their respective educational institutions into comparatively high-salary occupations that would allow them to maintain a standard of living that was higher than that of their compatriots.

The political leadership in Africa sought to create an elite African administrative class that would advance their political projects and agendas without challenging their leadership. Universities, however, have a long history of incubating movements that question and hold accountable elites who hold political power. In Africa, this tendency dates back to the colonial era, when higher education was not widely available on the African continent and when only a select few students received the opportunity to pursue higher education outside of the continent. Some of these students would eventually become political leaders who would confront colonialism and lead their nations into independence. Ghanaian nationalist Kwame Nkrumah sharpened his political acumen and critique of British colonialism as a student at Lincoln University, the University of Pennsylvania, and the London School of Economics. Kenya's first president, Jomo Kenyatta, honed his critique of colonialism at a number of European institutions of higher education, including the London School of Economics, where he earned a master's degree in anthropology. Senegalese intellectual, trenchant critic of colonialism, and leader of the Rassemblement démocratique africain (African Democratic Assembly) Cheikh Anta Diop developed his political positions as a student pursing an education in France in no less than seven distinct fields of study (see Bassey 2009). And, of course, without his opportunity to pursue higher education in France, Frantz Fanon, theorist of the anticolonial revolution and adopted son of Algeria, would likely have never penned his acerbic texts on colonialism, *Black Skin, White Masks* and *The Wretched of the Earth*.[2]

The list of revolutionary political leaders whose sense of engagement was in some way shaped by the experience of higher education does not, of course, end there. There is no question that the need for Africans with formal education during the colonial era presented a contradiction to the colonial powers. On the one hand they needed to foster an educated class of indigenous Africans to whom they could pass some responsibilities of colonial administration. On the other hand, this education furthered in this nascent elite class a disquiet with the political situation. This should not have been a surprise to anyone, as during this era, largely unfolding after World War II in the wake of the rise and fall of European fascism, European institutions of higher education developed their own intellectual critiques of imperialism, capitalism, and racism. Many of these African intellectuals would find allies in Caribbean and African American intellectuals such as George Padmore and W. E. B. Dubois, who saw the struggle against the European colonial project in Africa as integral to a global struggle of all peoples of African descent.

At independence, it might not have occurred to the African leadership that their universities would spawn opposition to their power in the same way that many of these leaders honed their critiques of colonialism through their university experiences. It is possible that both the political leadership and the populace were too swept up by the euphoria of independence to see how challenges to the political leadership would take root in these locations. It is more likely, however, that this leadership was aware of these risks, but also knew that they needed a workforce with formal education to fill administrative positions and to realize their ambitious development plans. In the 1960s, demand for African administrators was high and the supply was low. There were not many Africans who had the formal education to occupy the growing positions in the African administrative apparatuses, and it appeared that the ability of these nations to absorb their university graduates into the elite class of these nations was endless. Writing in *The New Elites of Tropical Africa* in the mid-1960s, P. C. Lloyd pointed out that in no African state did more than 2 percent of the population reach secondary school (1966: 22) which speaks to the dearth of Africans with the requisite formal education to move into privileged elite positions.

In the 1960s through to the mid-1970s, as Leo Zeilig (2007: 21) describes it, "University students were part of a privileged transitory group waiting to be allotted graduate employment in an expanding civil service and across the state sector." For many if not most of these students, education was the revolution. Coming out from under the yoke of colonialism and emerging, in many cases, from impoverished rural communities, they saw education as a vehicle for both political and economic empowerment. The new political leadership likely understood the political and economic positionality of these new elites in the making. They might have assumed that these students knew that they had much to lose by using the university as a platform to attack and dismantle the structures of leadership in their respective nations.

Even in that time, when the ability of African nations to absorb the energy of the educated elite seemed limitless, some could see that the direction of political engagement of those on the university campuses in Africa was not stable. P. C. Lloyd pointed out that, while at that time there was a dearth of African university graduates, there remained political hazards to rapidly expanding the education system (1966: 26). He foretold that as the number of Africans with credentials increased, employers would increase the qualifications candidates would need in order to be hired into positions. He predicted that eventually school graduates, too educated to remain in their rural homes, would "drift to towns" where many would not be able to find employment. Those who did find jobs would find themselves, by virtue of their education, hired to work for individuals with much less formal education—the latter were hired earlier, when you would not have needed the same credentials in order to be hired. Lloyd (1966: 26) mentioned that he had already seen evidence of this happening. He foretold that rather than being a tool for political stability, African systems of education, and universities in particular, might eventually become loci of political opposition and dissent.

It is this thread, how African universities have become locations of political dissent, that I will explore in this chapter. I will use a case study of the University of Dakar[3] in Senegal to explore universities as a semi-autonomous force in Senegalese politics.[4] In particular, I am interested in the way that this institution of higher education, on the one hand, is designed to prepare its students to occupy positions in Senegal's elite class, and, on the other, has served as a site for engagement and activism through which student leaders have been able to disrupt elite politics in Senegal. The core question is whether students, as potential elites, see themselves as accountable to the current political leadership, which is in a position to pave their path to elite status and economic security, or as accountable to other political ideals, institutions, and socioeconomic classes.

In Senegal, as will be described, for many students the latter appears to have been the case. Students, through their protests in 1968, laid the groundwork for political reforms in the 1970s. In the wake of the fiscally austere structural adjustment programs introduced in the 1980s they would prove to be important actors in 2000, when they were part of a movement to end the control that the Socialist Party had over the Senegalese government. And again in 2012 they showed their political muscle when they were critical actors in ending the presidency of Abdoulaye Wade.

HIGHER EDUCATION AND STUDENT ACTIVISM IN SENEGAL

The University of Dakar was founded by the French in 1957 on the eve of Senegalese independence as a constituent part of the French university system. It continued to be part of that system until 1971. This relationship was more than symbolic, and during the 1960s a substantial minority of the student body and many of its faculty members were French citizens. Similar to its antecedents in Dakar, such as the École normale William Ponty and the Institute des hautes études, in the 1960s the university attracted students not just from Senegal but also from other African nations, rendering Senegalese students a minority on their own campus (Zeilig 2007: 178–79). This, combined with the small size of the student body at the time (1,081 in 1960), would have likely muted the ability of these students to influence Senegalese politics, even if they had wished to do so.

By 1967, while still multinational, the size of the university's student body had almost tripled to 3,047 (Zeilig 2007: 179). By then students at the university had become politically organized, and in 1966 the Union démocratique des etudiants sénégalaise (Democratic Union of Senegalese Students), in reaction to the coup d'état in Ghana against Kwame Nkrumah, organized anti-imperialism protests against the American and British embassies. This, for the first time, placed Senegalese students in direct confrontation with Senegalese police, and in the ensuing days the student protests refocused from the issue of imperialism to the issue of the repression of student political expression on the part of the Senegalese state (Diop 1992: 442–43).

The closing years of the 1960s saw economic decline in Senegal that by 1968 had begun to impact the daily living conditions of students at the University of Dakar. In May of that year, in part inspired by student activism in the United States and in France, students staged a protest over a seemingly pedestrian campus concern: the decision of the Senegalese government to reduce student stipends. The frustration of the students resonated with the general sense of frustration in the city, and the protest quickly spilled out of the university campus and into the streets of Dakar. The Union nationale des travailleurs du Sénégal (National Union of Senegalese Workers) and others took to the streets in support of the students, presenting one of the greatest political challenges to Leopold Senghor during his two decades as Senegal's president. From then on what was happening on Dakar's campus had to be understood as a refraction of concerns more broadly held by those throughout the city and nation. The 1968 student protests are widely seen to have been the starting point for the political reforms adopted in the mid-1970s that moved the country from one-party rule to what scholars have described as a restricted democracy.[5]

The structural question for students was whether or not their interests clearly aligned with those of the state. This point was driven home in the aftermath of the 1968 student protests in Senegal when those associated with the protests were expelled from the university, effectively blocking their path to elite status.[6] As long as the understanding was that a university degree guaranteed salaried employment in the formal sector, the potential of the university to become a site for challenges to the Senegalese political leadership would be held in check. The protests of 1968 exposed fissures in this arrangement.

The 1970s would see much of the African continent besieged by debt, drought, soaring fuel prices, and a challenging global economy. Many African nations, as a way to deal with crippling debt-servicing obligations and in the hopes that they could jump-start sluggish economies, would, at the urging of the World Bank and other lenders, adopt structural adjustment programs. Austerity was at the core of these programs, and they meant substantial cuts to the government's educational programs at all levels. The cuts were also extended to the administrative structure of the national governments, which effectively meant that there would be fewer formal sector jobs available to university graduates. Coming at a time when African universities were serving increasing numbers of students (UCAD had ten thousand students in 1978), the social contract that guaranteed university graduates formal sector jobs was placed under stress, leaving university graduates insecure about their postgraduation professional future (Zeilig 2007: 181).

Students at the Cheikh Anta Diop University were not the only students to be placed in this precarious position. During this era, as the promise of the African university as an avenue to elite status began to fade, campuses throughout the African continent experienced shrinking government financial support, ballooning student body numbers, and contracting formal sector employment opportunities. By the 1990s, this institution had betrayed its roots as one that would give form to and populate Africa's privileged elite class. In this atmosphere of declining professional expectations for university students it was no longer possible to assume that they (and African students at all educational levels) would be politically "captured" by the political objectives of the state. As Leo Zeilig (2007) documents, the implementation of structural adjustment policies would lay the groundwork for student involvement in politically engaged protests in a number of African countries. In 1989, in the context of vast political change, students in Benin protested against the states' abandonment of assured formal sector jobs for university graduates. Students in Zaire (now the Democratic Republic of Congo) were among the first to take to the streets in the uprising that led to the eventual fall of Mobuto Sese Seko. In Zimbabwe in 1989 students protested against IMF- and World Bank–imposed economic policies. In 1990 in Mali the protest that led to the fall of Moussa Traore's regime was initiated by a small group of unemployed graduates whose ambitions for elite status had been frustrated. And similar student unrest and protests were witnessed during in the early 1990s in Cameroon, Ethiopia, Kenya, and Nigeria, among other countries (see Zeilig 2007: 81–93).

Senegal would prove to be no exception. By the end of the 1980s the structural adjustment programs had had their impact on the living conditions and career expectations of students at Cheikh Anta Diop University. One of the more meaningful changes for the students in Dakar was the end of the policy of guaranteeing coveted public service employment to students who managed to complete their university studies in Senegal's highly competitive education system. To soften the blow of not ensuring salaried employment to university graduates, programs were designed to provide students with training and financing so that they could establish themselves as self-employed entrepreneurs. During this time, it was not uncommon to come across university graduates behind the counters of neighborhood retail stores or working in bakeries. These were graduates who had been encouraged to become entrepreneurs rather than salaried public officials. In some cases, this placed freshly minted university graduates in direct competition with other retail stores owned and staffed by individuals who had little if any formal education. This was a far cry from the lifestyles they had imagined they would have after their years at UCAD. The failure of these entrepreneurship programs can in part be explained by the fact that the Senegalese government and the donors who financed them underestimated the extent to which they dashed the hopes that Senegalese youth had harbored to use their university education to achieve elite status.

When Africa's universities were established with the expectation that they would create an elite class, that class was not large enough to reproduce itself. There were not enough elite children to fill the growing number of places in the universities. This meant that many of these universities had to recruit students from the ranks of the urban and rural poor. As the size of the elite class grew, it was never able to shift this pattern and monopolize university positions for its children to the exclusion of the poor. Indeed, African universities have been marked by a comparatively high percentage of students who are from rural or working-class urban backgrounds (Zeilig 2007: 36, 179). At the same time, Africa's elite began sending their children more often to American and European universities, both raising the bar for credentials in their own countries and allowing African elites to set new expectation for prestige and secure new ways to ensure the reproduction of their class status for their children.

In Senegal the end of the expectation for public sector jobs for university graduates, a long-standing social contract between the state and students, severed the direct connection between attending university and elite status. However, these same students maintained social connections to their birth communities. In terms of their long-term economic prospects, many of these students found they had more in common with their kin who did not have the same opportunity to pursue formal education, a fact underlined by the entrepreneurship programs that placed graduates in competition with those who did not have formal education.

Yet the students still embodied experiences that marked them as distinct from their kin who did not have the opportunity to attend university: they formed expectations of formal sector employment that for many were not realistic; they were concentrated in one location, the university campus, where they could organize and share their grievances; they were housed in a state-run and state-owned institution; and their grievances against the government would be made concrete as they saw the budget cuts have direct, material impacts on their living conditions.

What becomes apparent in Senegal is that under the policies of structural adjustment many students and graduates of Cheikh Anta Diop University were put in a position where they identified less with the privileged Senegalese elites than with the urban underemployed and unemployed, with whom they shared more economic structural similarities. Under these conditions, many of these students pursued a form of political engagement that was accountable to non-elite interests. These students increasingly directed their energies toward holding the political elite accountable for their decisions.

Thus by the end of the 1980s the campus of the university tilted away from being a site for the reproduction of state power, to becoming a site for the questioning of state power and for the organization of protests. During this period, while still to an extent distinct from Dakar's broader political landscape, political activism on the university campus became embroiled in politicized Senegalese youth movements that were not restricted to university students and their concerns. This broad activism was abetted by a well-organized student union whose scope extended beyond the university campus, reaching out to remote rural public schools (Diop 1992). The protests following the 1988 presidential election would raise the tenor of the students' grievances and would move the protests from more parochial student concerns to issues that challenged national politics.

THE FALL OF THE PRESIDENT DIOUF AND THE SOCIALIST PARTY

The stage for what unfolded in Senegal in 1988 was set during the two decades following independence in 1963. Similar to the experience of many African nations, in Senegal in the years following independence, President Leopold Senegal and his political party, the Union progressiste sénégalaise,[7] dismantled democratic institutions and consolidated political power. From 1966 until 1976 neither legal opposition nor contested presidential elections were allowed by the Senegalese constitution. In 1974, under pressure to reopen the political system, and in part in response to the student-initiated protests of 1968, President Senghor introduced a restricted multiparty system, allowing Abdoulaye Wade to form the Parti démocratique sénégalais (Senegalese Democratic Party). In 1976, the restricted multiparty democracy was given form when the constitution was revised to allow for three parties that would represent three distinct political ideologies: liberal democratic, socialist, and Marxist-Leninist (Gellar 2005: 47).

By the late 1970s, Senegal was confronting a host of problems, including drought, economic decline, political discontent, and seemingly unsurmountable debt (Diop and Diouf 1990). In face of these challenges, in early 1981 President Senghor ceded the presidency to his handpicked successor, Abdou Diouf, who Senghor believed was better suited to negotiate the economic and budgetary challenges faced by Senegal, such as the implementation of structural adjustment programs (Diop and Diouf 1999: 145–46). Senghor's resignation allowed Diouf two years to consolidate power and run as an incumbent in the 1983 presidential election, which he handily won with almost 80 percent of the votes (Gellar 2005: 81).

By the 1988 presidential elections, Diouf and his party had begun to feel the political impact of the austerity measures of the structural adjustment programs. Senegalese Islamic leaders' support for Diouf, which Senghor had skillfully managed, had eroded. Students, facing limited postgraduation employment opportunities and experiencing the effects of eroding financial support for the schools, had become disenchanted with him as well. These students were joined in their opposition to Diouf by many urban youth who were disenchanted with their economic prospects after forty years of Socialist Party rule. Many of these students and urban youth cast their support for Abdoulaye Wade, the leading opposition figure and the most visible and viable candidate to challenge Diouf in the presidential election.

The results of the 1988 election, which Abdou Diouf officially won with 73 percent of the votes, were immediately challenged by Abdoulaye Wade and the economically disenfranchised youth of Dakar. During the months following the election Dakar's youth staged protests during which symbols of the state were attacked. Mobs of youths set upon buses, forcing the government to suspend Dakar's public transportation service. Government vehicles were overturned and burned. The government responded by declaring a state of emergency and imposing a dusk-to-dawn curfew (see Cruise O'Brien 1996; Diouf 1996).

By 1988 the government already had experience with student protests and had developed strategies for dealing with them. The scope of the 1988 protests, however, was different from those that had occurred in earlier eras, such as the protests of 1968. The government apparently did not appreciate the extent to which structural adjustment had shifted the social landscape of youth politics. The Socialist Party had always assumed that it could depend on the loyalty of the students, or school-leavers, a category the party distinguished from the urban unemployed, the *encombrement humains*, or social marginals (Diouf 1996: 230–31). What this distinction between "school-leavers" and "social marginals" missed, however, is that by 1988 the difference between these two groups had become increasingly blurred. The contraction in state employment opportunities meant that university students often did not perceive themselves as having economic prospects that were significantly different from those who did not have the same education. This blurring was compounded by the degree to which student activists in Senegal's high schools had become more centralized, organized, and politicized (Diop 1992:

466). This blurred the organizational distinction between students at all levels, from elementary school through to the university.

During the early morning of the day of the first round of voting in the 1988 presidential election, the government preemptively raided the campus of Cheikh Anta Diop University and emptied it of all students so as to prevent the campus from becoming the focus of protests. But this strategy to control the campus did nothing to quell the youth protests against the election result. This strategy was undermined by the extent to which the concerns of university students had a national scope that was shared by youth regardless of whether or not they were students (see Cruise O'Brien 1996).

The protests surrounding the 1988 elections failed to change the official results, and Abdou Diouf and the ruling Socialist Party retained power. But for the second time in Senegal's history protests led by students would in part push the government to adopt political reforms it likely would not have otherwise considered. In 1991 President Diouf assembled a multiparty electoral reform commission. Among the significant reforms it proposed were that all political parties would receive certified results directly from precincts, a secret ballot would be guaranteed to all voters, the voting age would be lowered from twenty-one to eighteen (increasing the size of the youth electorate), coalitions would be allowed, and an independent electoral commission would monitor the electoral process. In 1993, the ability of the political opposition to communicate directly with the public was enhanced when the government ended its monopoly on broadcast media. This change opened the door to the establishment of independent radio stations (Geller 2005: 81–83).

Despite these reforms, Diouf, the incumbent Socialist Party candidate, was able to handily win the 1993 presidential election in what was widely considered to have been the fairest election Senegal had organized since independence. The 2000 election, however, would be a different story, and students, allied with other youth, would figure as major players in unraveling the Socialist Party's grip on power. The position of the youth in this election can be seen as an expression of their rejection of the Socialist Party's control over access to elite status. In the second round of the 2000 election, longtime opposition leader Abdoulaye Wade defeated Diouf in a landslide.

It was widely recognized in Senegal that Wade had ridden a wave of youth support to victory. Much of this support came from the hard work of students at Cheikh Anta Diop University, many of whom retained strong social ties to their rural roots. They spent much of the campaign season back in their home villages mobilizing the rural vote for Abdoulaye Wade. Many of these students persuaded their parents to vote against the ruling party by describing how living conditions on the university campus had deteriorated under the leadership of the Socialist Party (Zeilig 2007: 200, 206). The day following the election, a large mob of youth had gathered at Wade's residence to celebrate what they felt was their victory. The irony was not lost on anyone that the candidate who was seen to represent the hopes and aspirations of the youth was, by conservative estimates, at least seventy-three years old.

The question that remained, however, is whether or not he would be able to depend on the continued support of the youth and other students. If anything, with the end of the informal policy of automatically advancing university graduates into the ranks of the salaried elite, students were freed to challenge the political status quo. They could no longer be depended on to legitimize the power of those who controlled access to elite privilege. They were now in a position to question political power no matter who might be at the helm.

THE FALL OF PRESIDENT WADE AND THE SENEGALESE DEMOCRATIC PARTY

The goodwill and support that the youth had provided to Wade during the election would not last long, and many questioned whether the new president and his party were truly committed to either defending democracy or improving government support for institutions of higher education. Students had supported Wade largely on the promise that he would improve conditions on the university campus. By then, however, international lenders had shifted their funding priorities from tertiary to primary education in Africa (Brannelly, Lewis, and Ndaruhutse 2011: 7).[8] A year into his presidency, as the government was considering a World Bank loan whose conditions would have meant additional cuts to the university budget, students staged a protest against the loan. During the protest a student was shot and killed by a gendarme. In the ensuing public outrage over the incident the government agreed to meet some of the students' demands and rejected some of the financial constraints on the funding of higher education that had been imposed by the World Bank. Significant among the changes was that the university dropped its entrance exam and returned to the practice of granting admission to all students who successfully completed the baccalaureate. The result was an ever-expanding student body, which by 2007 had ballooned to sixty thousand students, rendering university students an ever more potent political force (Zeilig 2007: 208–18).

It was not long into his presidency before opposition to Wade extended well beyond students at the university. Journalists, political activists, and filmmakers began to share with students, and more broadly the youth, doubts about the political intentions of the new regime. Wade came to be known for initiating high-profile construction projects that were seen primarily to benefit wealthy elites, while many in Senegal were unemployed, faced daily power outages, and encountered crumbling public facilities, among other problems.

Many Senegalese speculated on and were disconcerted by the support that President Wade had shown for his son Karim's political ambitions. In 2002, Wade appointed Karim to be one of his personal advisers and, in 2004, to be head of the mission to organize the Eleventh Islamic Summit. It appeared that the elder Wade was trying the pave the way for his son's entry into Senegalese politics. In 2009, Karim Wade ran in Dakar's mayoral race and suffered a humiliating defeat. Undeterred, President Wade appointed him to the position of minister of state for international cooperation, regional development, air transport, and infrastructure. Karim held the largest portfolio ever by a minister in Senegal, estimated at 46 percent of the national budget (Aljazeera 2015). It seemed apparent that Wade was laying the groundwork for a lineal transfer of power in which Karim would assume the presidency. If anything, Wade's effort to promote his son was a public relations disaster, as it indicated a return to the patterns of elite patronage that many had been pushing so hard against. In the 2012 presidential elections, these issues inspired many Senegalese youths again to engage politically. This time they took aim at the presidency of Abdoulaye Wade, who had presented himself just twelve years earlier as the candidate who represented their interests.[9]

While disquiet had been building in Senegal over Wade's high-profile projects that seemed to bring benefits only to elites, what sparked widespread protests were proposals to change the constitution that would have entrenched Wade's iteration of the elite Senegalese politics. In 2011, he proposed lowering the percentage of votes a candidate needed to win in the first round of voting from 50 percent to 25 percent. This would have assured him a first-round victory. He also proposed creating the office of vice president, the occupant of which would ascend to the presidency if the current president resigned. Many speculated that Wade intended to appoint Karim vice president and then resign.

The youth protests leading up the 2012 elections contrasted with those following the 1988 elections. In 1988 student organizers tended to work behind the scenes, leaving the impression that the political activities of the youth were orchestrated by Abdoulaye Wade and his opposition party. This indeed was the basis for charges that were brought against Wade by the Senegalese government in the aftermath of the protests following the 1988 presidential election. By contrast, in 2011, youth movements with named leadership emerged to contest the political moves of President Wade. Nouveau type de Sénégalais (New Type of Senegalese), Y'en a marre (I'm Fed Up, or Enough Is Enough), and, later, the broad Mouvement du 23 juin (Movement June 23) would galvanize opposition against the president. These youth movements were led by a coalition of hip-hop musicians and journalists who, despite differences in their background and professional identities, shared a sense of frustration and alienation under the leadership of Abdoulaye Wade.

The anti-Wade youth protests exhibited striking parallels to the Arab Spring protests and uprisings that were then sweeping through North Africa and the Middle East. Y'en a marre leader Fadel Barro acknowledged this connection but at the same time underlined that what was unfolding in Senegal was more closely connected to student protests throughout the world (Haeringer 2012: 158; Nelson 2014: 26). In his opinion, challenging structures that entrenched elite privilege was the signature political position of youth globally.

Hip-hop groups and artists such as Keur Gui Crew and Fou Malade figured prominently in the effort to unseat Wade, and their musical sensibility was seen to have had deep roots in the urban alienation and political disillusionment that marked Senegal's "lost generation," which came of age during the austere years of structural adjustment. This generation included students who had seen their path to elite status blocked by diminishing access to public sector jobs. Many in Senegal see this generation of hip-hop activists as having had their political consciousness formed on the campus of Cheikh Anta Diop University during the *année blanche* of 1987–88, the academic year in Senegal that was canceled during the youth protests following the 1988 presidential election. Many attribute the emergence of hip-hop in Senegal, marked by the arrival of Positive Black Soul and the release of their hit song "Boul Falé," to the political turbulence of this period and the economic and political alienation of Senegal's urban youth in the late 1980s and early 1990s. Given the deep connection between the protests of 2012 and the events that unfolded on the university campus in 1988, it is little surprise that the latter movement had deep intellectual roots. The leaders of this movement had immersed themselves in social theory and drew inspiration from the writings of Frantz Fanon and other critical social theorists (Touré and Seck 2014).

Faux! Pas forcé[10] became a major slogan of the 2012 presidential election, galvanizing the Senegalese public against the attempt by Abdoulaye Wade to remain in power for a third term. This was not a slogan for any particular candidate; in fact the Y'en a marre leadership did not endorse anyone. As Thiat, a member of Keur Gui Crew, described it, they instead campaigned *against* what they considered the sitting president's illegitimate attempt to remain in office and pass the mantle to his son (Touré and Seck 2014). In 2000, Thiat was among the youth who campaigned against Abdou Diouf to bring Wade to power. Over the course of Wade's presidency, Thiat became disillusioned with political parties and explicitly maintained distance from them. At the outset, in 2011, Y'en a marre toyed with the idea of forming a political party but ultimately decided against it and even declined to endorse Macky Sall, the president's opponent in the second round. Instead they focused their energy on citizenship and galvanizing the Senegalese public to assume responsibility for politics in their country. They spearheaded a voter registration campaign that added an estimated three hundred thousand new voters to the rolls. In the second round of the election, Macky Sall defeated Abdoulaye Wade in a landslide.

For the leadership of the movement, Y'en a marre was about much more than just removing Abdoulaye Wade and his party from power. As Aliou Sane, journalist and cofounder of the movement, described it, the movement was about creating a new political consciousness in Senegal, to create what they called a "new type of Senegalese" (Nelson 2014: 14). They wanted to inspire the Senegalese to adopt a heightened sense of citizenship, to question power, and to take responsibility (UNRIC 2012). A major focus of Y'en a marre after the election of Macky Sall was neighborhood organizing through workshops focused on citizenship, democracy, environment, health, culture, leadership, and peace.

As for members' attitude toward the current government: while they were instrumental in bringing Macky Sall and his Alliance pour la république to power, they have remained true to their decision not to endorse any political candidate and did not fall into line behind him. If anything they remained highly critical of the current ruling party. In 2014, Keur Gui Crew released the controversial song "Diogoufi" (2014). The English translation of the title is "Nothing Has Changed."

AFRICAN UNIVERSITIES AND ELITE ACCOUNTABILITY

When it was founded in 1957, the University of Dakar, like other universities in Africa, was seen by many to be an institution that would reinforce the political status quo. It was designed to meet what at the time was a shortage of educated nationals to fill positions in the increasingly Africanized postcolonial administrative structure. The African university was intended to play the role of legitimizing the African state by creating the manpower and expertise necessary for Africa's ruling class to bring to fruition their economic development projects. For university students, it represented the promise of elite status and economic security.

By the end of the 1960s, students at Senegal's University of Dakar had already become embroiled in political protests, and they would serve as a bellwether for what would happen on campuses throughout the continent in the coming decades. This position of universities, as a sites of discontent, would be exacerbated with the implementation of the fiscally austere structural adjustment program. Higher education throughout the continent was hit hard by these policies, which were part of a broader shift in international funding from tertiary to primary education (Brannelly, Lewis, and Ndaruhutse 2011). This rendered every campus protest over tuition, stipends, food, or housing facilities inherently political. It is little surprise that in Senegal student activism played an important role in ending the rule of both the Socialist Party in 2000 and the Democratic Socialist Party in 2012. And it not surprising that similar scenarios have played out in other African countries.

If anything, African university campuses now have an ambivalent position with respect to the political elite. This is in part conditioned by the fact that the institution is not fully controlled by the state; much of the student body remains rooted in and accountable to non-elite social and economic formations, such as those of the students' families or of Dakar's broad urban youth culture. While access to elite status might remain the principal lure that draws students onto the university campuses, the case of Senegal illustrates that one cannot assume that these students will raise their voices to legitimize the political status quo. Unlike the early days of African independence, these students are entering these campuses well aware that a university degree is no longer a sure path to elite status. In fact, they are aware that the material condition of the university campuses, and their material well-being as students, speaks directly to their relationship to the political elite.

Stated otherwise, the social and political significance of institutions of higher education in Africa cannot be reduced to an assessment of how successfully they reproduce elite social classes on the continent. Such an approach fails to fully consider the political agency of students during the time that they occupy the particular and bounded social status of university student. As described earlier, students in a number of African nations have exercised their power to disrupt the political status quo. This has occurred too frequently for student political activism not to be taken seriously as a semi-autonomous political force that is an expression of the unique social position that students occupy. At times, as has occurred in Senegal and in other African nations, these students have exercised their political agency to hold political elites accountable.

The question is when, and under which circumstances, students will focus their actions on defending elite politics, and when they will focus their energy on dismantling the status quo of elite politics in their respective countries. Will students perceive themselves as accountable to the political elite, or will they see it as their responsibility to hold the political elite accountable? In recent years, in light of the pressure of fiscal austerity that has dimmed the economic prospects for graduates and resources for higher education in Africa, in a number of instances, and certainly in Senegal, many of these students have chosen the latter course.

NOTES

1. Makerere was established as a technical school in 1922. In 1963, it became the University of East Africa and offered degrees from the University of London. In 1970, the University of East Africa was divided into Makerere University; University of Nairobi, Kenya; and Dar-es-Salaam University, Tanzania. See Wale Adebanwi, "Africa as a 'Dissimilar' System? Africa and Knowledge Production in the UK," talk presented at the Centre for African Studies Weekly Seminar, University of Cambridge, October 16, 2017.

2. In *Revolt and Protest*, Leo Zeilig correctly points out the anticolonial position of African intellectuals prior to independence was informed by much more than just their opportunity to study in Western institutions of higher education. See Zeilig 2007, 25–35, for an excellent discussion of the various factors that influenced the thought of this generation of African leaders.

3. In 1987 the Université de Dakar (University of Dakar) was renamed Université Cheikh Anta Diop (Cheikh Anta Diop University). In this chapter I use the name that corresponds to the date being discussed or, alternatively, the acronym UCAD.

4. By examining the university as a semi-autonomous political force, this chapter does not provide an analysis of the functional position of institutions of higher education in reproducing (or failing to reproduce) elite classes in Africa. This has been the subject of much research on tertiary and secondary education in Europe and the United States (see, for example, Howard and Gaztambide-Fernández 2010; Rubinstein

1986; Meyer 1977; Van Zanteen 2010; and Harrigan 1980). An examination of how African institutions of higher education function in this respect, while not addressed in this chapter, would be a fruitful topic of future research.

5. See the opening part of this chapter for an outline of these reforms, and Bathily 1992 for a discussion of the 1968 protest.

6. Martial Diémé, interview by the author, 1989, Dakar, Senegal.

7. By 1976 the Union progressiste sénégalaise (Senegalese Progressive Union) had been renamed the Parti socialiste (Socialist Party).

8. It was significant that in 2000 the Dakar Framework for Action was adopted by the World Education Forum. This framework endorsed the Millennium Development Goals, which placed a specific focus on primary rather than tertiary education (Brannelly, Lewis, and Ndaruhutse 2011: 7).

9. See Lambert 2016 for a discussion of these events from the perspective of youth politics in Senegal.

10. This polysemic slogan, when read as text, translates as "False! Not forced," yet when heard it translates as "Must not force" or, alternatively, as "False step forced." It is both an accusation against and a command to Abdoulaye Wade and his party.

REFERENCES

Adebanwi, Wale. 2017. "Africa as a 'Dissimilar" System? Africa and Knowledge Production in the UK." Talk presented at the Centre for African Studies Weekly Seminar, University of Cambridge, October 16.

Aljazeera. 2015. "Senegal Jails Former President's Son for Corruption." March 23. http://www.aljazeera.com/news/2015/03/Senegal-jails-president-son-corruption-150323143956239.html

Bassey, Magnus O. 2009. "Higher Education and the Rise of Early Political Elites in Africa." *Review of Higher Education in Africa* 1, no. 1: 30–38.

Bathily, Abdoulaye. 1992. *Mai 1968 à Dakar: Ou, la révolte universitaire et la démocratie.* Paris: L'Harmattan.

BBC. 2011. "Senegal Soldier Dies after Setting Himself on Fire." February 19. http://www.bbc.com/news/world-africa-12516438

Brannelly, Laura, Laura Lewis, and Susy Ndaruhutse. 2011. "Higher Education and the Formation of Developmental Elites: A Literature Review and Preliminary Analysis." Development Leadership Program Research Paper no. 10.

Cruise O'Brien, Donald. 1996. "A Lost Generation? Youth Identity and State Decay in West Africa." In Richard Werbner and Terence Ranger, eds., *Postcolonial Identities in Africa*, 55–74. London: Zed Books.

Diop, Momar Coumba. 1992. "Le syndicalisme étudiant: Pluralisme et revendications." In Momar-Coumba Diop, ed., *Sénégal: Trajectoires d'un état*, 441–77. Dakar: CODESRIA.

Diop, Momar Coumba, and Mamadou Diouf. 1990. *Le Sénégal sous Abdou Diouf: Etat et societé.* Paris: Karthala.

Diop, Momar Coumba, and Mamadou Diouf. 1999. "Sénégal: Par-delà de la sucession Senghor-Diouf." In Momar Coumba Diop and Mamdou Diouf, eds., *Les figures du politique en Afrique: Des pouvoirs hérités aux pouvoirs élus*, 139-188. Paris: Karthala.

Diouf, Mamadou. 1996. "Urban Youth and Senegalese Politics: Dakar 1988–1994." *Public Culture* 8: 225-49.

Fanon, Frantz. 2004. *The Wretched of the Earth*. Translated by Richard Philcox. New York: Grove Press.

Fanon, Frantz. 2008. *Black Skin, White Masks*. Translated by Richard Philcox. New York: Grove Press.

Gellar, Sheldon. 2005. *Democracy in Senegal: Tocquevillian Analytics in Africa*. New York: Palgrave Macmillan.

Haeringer, Nicolas. 2012. "Y'en a marre, une lente sédimentation des frustrations: Entretien avec Fadel Barro." *Mouvements* 1, no. 69: 151-58.

Harrigan, Patrick J. 1980. *Mobility, Elites, and Education in French Society of the Second Empire*. Waterloo, ON: Wilfrid Laurier University Press.

Howard, Adam, and Rubén A. Gaztambide-Fernández, eds. 2010. *Educating Elites: Class Privilege and Educational Advantage*. Lanham, MD: Rowman & Littlefield.

KeurGuiCrew. 2011. *Faux!Pasforcé*. https://www.youtube.com/watch?v=cHM7db193Mw

Keur Gui Crew. 2014. *Diogoufi*. https://www.youtube.com/watch?v=2Ky8hnq2F-Y. Accessed June 15, 2016.

Lambert, Michael C. 2016. "Changes: Reflections on Senegalese Youth Political Engagement, 1988–2012. *Africa Today* 63, no. 2: 32–51.

Lloyd, P. C. 1966. *The New Elites of Tropical Africa*. London: Oxford University Press.

Meyer, John. 1977. "The Effects of Education as an Institution." *American Journal of Sociology* 83, no. 1: 55–77.

Nelson, Sarah. 2014. "The New Type of Senegalese under Construction: Fadel Barro and Aliou Sané on Yenamarrisme after Wade." *African Studies Quarterly* 14, no. 3: 13–32.

Rubinstein, W. D. 1986. "Education and the Social Origins of British Elites 1880–1970." *Past & Present* 112: 163–207.

Touré, Cheikh Cyrille (Thiat), and Mbessane (Kilifeu) Seck. 2014. "Y'en a marre: Activists for Democracy in Senegal." Lecture, Carolina Seminar in African Ecology and Social Processes, University of North Carolina at Chapel Hill, February 19.

United Nations Regional Information Centre (UNRIC). 2012. "The Movement Y'en a marre—'we've had enough.'" December. http://www.unric.org/en/right-to-participation/28099-the-movement-yen-a-marre-weve-had-enough

van Zanteen, Agnès. 2010. "The Sociology of Elite Education." In Michael W. Apple et al., eds., *The Routledge International Handbook of the Sociology of Education*, 329–39. New York: Routledge.

Zeilig, Leo. 2007. *Revolt and Protest: Student Politics and Activism in Sub-Saharan Africa*. London: Tauris Academic Studies.

PART 2

Elites, Race, and Class

CHAPTER 6

Who Holds the Power?

Elites and Accountability in Democratic South Africa

ROGER SOUTHALL

South Africa is notorious for being the most unequal country in the world.[1] Credit Suisse (Kersley and Koutsoukis 2016) reported that in 2015 forty-five thousand South Africans were dollar millionaires, and that sixty-six thousand South Africans were members of the top 1 percent of global wealth holders. In 2017, Oxfam (2017) asserted that just 1 percent of the population owned 42 percent of the country's total wealth, and three dollar billionaires owned assets equivalent to those held by the bottom half of the population. The three billionaires were all white, emphasizing that, over two decades after the end of apartheid, the distribution of wealth remains heavily racialized. According to the annual *Sunday Times* Rich List for 2016, 174 of the top 200 corporate wealth holders in South Africa were white, while 146 out of the top 200 most highly remunerated executives of the state-owned enterprises (SOEs, or parastatals) were black (*Times Live* 2016).[2]

That the ownership of wealth is imbalanced in South Africa and that it remains highly racialized should come as no surprise. At one level, it reflects global trends, with Oxfam reporting that in 2015 just 62 individuals possessed the same amount of wealth as 3.6 billion people, the bottom half of humanity. Oxfam and numerous authorities, most famously Thomas Piketty (2014), ascribe the galloping trend toward extreme global inequality as the result of unrestrained capitalist market economics (neoliberalism). At the domestic level, the imbalance of wealth in South Africa is the product of history—the total dominance of a white oligarchy prior to 1994, with its partial dilution by the rise of a small group of black oligarchs following the onset of democracy.

There are divergent interpretations of these trends. The first examines the convergence of established white with liberation movement elites through a process of *elite transition*. A second approach argues for merging of black political and white economic elites into an identifiable *South African power elite*. In contrast, a third asserts that little has changed since 1994, and that *white monopoly capital* continues to ensure the dominance of a white capitalist elite. Each of these will be briefly elaborated to assess the changing character of South Africa's elites and the extent of their accountability.

ELITE CONVERGENCE THROUGH AN "ELITE TRANSITION"

Elite rule in South Africa has moved through four stages. A first identifiable era was that of the "Randlords" who amassed huge fortunes by gaining control over the diamond- and gold-mining industries in the late nineteenth century and whose political influence was buttressed by British imperialism. A second period, after Union in 1910, saw Afrikaner political power driving *volkskapitalisme* (people's capitalism) to challenge domination by foreign (predominantly British) capital within a broader process of capitalist consolidation. This reached its apogee during the 1960s, with the rise of an Afrikaner bourgeoisie and its merger with "English-speaking" capital. This was then followed by a third period when, with white minority rule forced into crisis by popular and international challenges to apartheid, there was a growing disjuncture between the ruling National Party (NP) political elite and corporate elites. The fourth era, with which this chapter is concerned, was initiated by the white elites' conceding white minority rule in exchange for the incoming African National Congress (ANC) elite's accepting the tenets of neoliberal economics, although both public and private power was now made subject to South Africa's becoming a constitutional state—that is, one that provided authority to the courts to demand that citizens adhere to the constitution.[3]

The "elite transition" was implemented through a process of "elite pacting." By 1989, the apartheid regime had concluded that it was unable to quell popular power. For its part, the ANC came to the recognition that it was unable to overthrow white minority rule through armed struggle. Both sides to the conflict acknowledged the high risk of the country's descent into total civil war, with consequent destruction of the economy. Accordingly, the NP and ANC, along with other political actors, entered a negotiation phase that was to extend over four years. Although the focus of global attention was upon the political negotiations and the transition to democracy, equally important discussions concerned the future of the economy. Patrick Bond (2000) discusses how from the early 1970s, South African capital was facing a crisis. On the one hand, the poverty of the black majority population severely limited the scope of the internal market; on the other, global pressures against apartheid were leading to disinvestment by international corporations, purchase of their assets by domestic conglomerates, resulting monopolization of the economy, international sanctions, and domestic capital being locked up within the country. A transition to democracy therefore offered the prospect of resolution of what Sampie Terreblanche (2002) depicted as South Africa's twin crisis of accumulation and legitimation, although for this to happen, the ANC needed to drop its socialist ambitions in favor of an accommodation with capital.

Concerted pressures were exerted by global elites who argued that the collapse of the Soviet Union heralded the triumph of capitalism. In response, the ANC dropped plans for nationalization of key sectors of the economy to assure international investors that a democratic South Africa would be open for business. In turn, the International Monetary Fund and World Bank worked hand in hand with business-oriented think tanks to argue the potential for a socially redistributive capitalism. This culminated in the adoption by the ANC of the Redistribution and Development Programme (RDP), drawn up in collaboration with its trade unions allies, as its April 1994 election manifesto. However, within two years (June 1996), the RDP was to be abruptly replaced by the Growth, Employment and Redistribution (GEAR) program. Whereas the RDP pointed in the direction of a social-democratic-style social contract, GEAR espoused fiscal austerity and market-friendly policies, the ANC leadership and the Treasury stressing the urgency of reducing South Africa's international indebtedness and citing the dangers of losing control of the economy to foreign creditors. Strongly backed by large-scale capital, GEAR pursued a neoliberal menu. This featured reduction of the deficit, countering inflation, cutting public expenditure, adopting a strict monetary policy, committing to a competitive exchange rate, liberalizing the trade regime, promoting exports, privatizing "nonessential" state enterprises, and seeking wage restraint.

In practice, the ANC government's shift to neoliberalism was ameliorated by its introduction of pro-labor legislation, affirmative action ("equity employment"), and the substantial expansion of social grants and other aspects of a welfare state. Nonetheless, its commitment to GEAR widened already existent fault lines within the party and its "tripartite alliance" with the Congress of South African Trade Unions (COSATU) and the South African Communist Party (SACP). Ultimately, this was to lead to the defeat of Thabo Mbeki when he stood for a third term as party president at the ANC's National Congress in 2007 and his subsequent early removal from the state presidency in September 2008. However, prior to those dramatic events, the ANC had elaborated a policy of black economic empowerment (BEE) that constituted a key plank of the elite transition.

The goal of BEE was to promote a class of black capitalists and to facilitate black entry into the white-dominated corporate sector. However, although promoted as ANC policy, BEE had been originated by "white capital." Large firms had sought to reposition themselves by co-opting leading figures from the ANC through the transfer to them of assets (shareholdings) (largely debt-funded) and/or by appointing them to positions on corporate boards. In so doing, argues Moeletsi Mbeki (the former president's brother), the white elite was intent on weaning the ANC away from socialism while ensuring that they retained policy influence. The corporates wanted to ensure access to government contracts and protection from foreign competition even as neoliberalism dictated that the economy be opened to the global market. Some also sought (and gained) permission to transfer their primary listings to London. In response, the ANC was enabled to "deploy" party loyalists to the corporate sector, claiming this as indicative of "transformation" (Mbeki 2009). Subsequently, in response to complaints from black business strata that this first phase of BEE did not go far enough, legislation formalizing BEE (via demands that corporates employ more black managers and outsource contracts to black businesses) was enacted in 2003 (and was to undergo successive revisions).

Critics were to argue that BEE propelled the ANC leadership into an alliance with corporate capital, enriched a small coterie of black oligarchs, promoted "crony capitalism," stiffened its commitment to neoliberalism, and did nothing to address fundamental issues of inequality (Southall 2006). For its part, large-scale capital has increasingly criticized the demands made in the name of BEE for discouraging further investment (Institute of Race Relations 2012). The debate goes on—although what is widely agreed is that BEE was central to the elite transition: if capitalism in South Africa was to survive, it needed to change its racial complexion.

SOUTH AFRICA'S POWER ELITE: DISJUNCTURE BUT COEXISTENCE

Building upon the "elite transition," a further approach proposed that despite significant disjuncture between South Africa's political and corporate elites after 1994, they nonetheless constituted a relatively coherent "power elite" (Southall 2013a). Its starting point was provided by the work of C. W. Mills (1956), who, in seeking to divine the distribution of power in 1950s America, argued that analyzing *who holds power* requires a close look at who holds the capacity to make the *decisions* that structure the patterns of inequality.

Mills argued that the development of capitalism had seen a progressive enlargement and centralization of the means of oppression and exploitation as well as of production. This had led to the rise in power in the United States of the 1950s not only of corporate elites, presiding over historically unrivaled productive power, but also of military elites who wielded destructive power greater than at any time previous in history. The "corporate chieftains," "warlords," and a "political directorate" formed a power elite whose occupation of the "command posts" of society enabled them to make decisions that affected the lives of ordinary men or women. While the military and political power holders possessed considerable autonomy from the economic domain, the domination of the US power elite of the day involved "the uneasy coincidence of economic, military and political power" (Mills 1956: 276).

Below this topmost level of power, US society featured "middle levels of power" (featuring congressional and state politics, as well as their relationships with small businesses and unions) that constituted the stuff of much "politics" reported upon in the media. At the bottom of the heap there was a "mass society" that was on the receiving end of decisions and information from above.

While contemporary South Africa is far removed from 1950s America, the value of Mills lies in the directness of the questions he posed about the United States of the time. In what institutions was power located? Who occupied their "command posts" and made their decisions? To what extent were they accountable to those below them in institutional hierarchies and wider society? Did they constitute a coherent "power elite"? After all, underlying the notion of South Africa's "elite transition" was the idea that, notwithstanding democratic forms, an elite or elites continued to govern at the expense of the majority: rather than a genuine shift to democracy, South Africa had merely undergone what classic elite theorists would have described as a "circulation of elites."

The Political Elite

When applied to post-1994 South Africa, this approach discounted the utility of Mills's notion of the "warlords" as a separate silo of power. Certainly, the military had risen to greater prominence during the 1980s, when the apartheid regime had deployed it into the townships to combat popular uprising, yet it had always remained under ultimate civilian political control. Similarly, the ANC's own armed wing, Umkhonto we Sizwe (MK), had remained politically subordinated to the liberation movement. Consequently, although the democratic government inherited a substantial war machine, its concern was to contain the influence and size of the apartheid-era forces, while reconfiguring them under civilian control and merging them with MK. This left South Africa's "political directorate" and "the corporate chieftains" as the two pillars of the country's power elite.

The starting point for analysis of the former was the recognition that the elite transition had brought a predominantly ANC and black elite into office to replace the outgoing NP. At the highest level, this new political elite was distinguished by the nature of its decisions, which both were *formative* (concerning high policy) and had *national* implications. Yet even within this elite, power was differentially distributed among inner and outer circles of power holders. The inner circle was composed of the president, senior cabinet ministers (always Finance, along with holders of other major portfolios, notably defense, intelligence, and security), and the most influential members of the ANC and tripartite alliance; the outer circle was made up of ministers outside the inner circle, other influential members of the ruling party, and chairs of boards and chief executive officers (CEOs) of the most important parastatals. Both levels were sustained by the top ranks of the civil service. This was a recognition that although the ANC insisted that the president and the cabinet were its "deployees" and were governed by its policy directives, it was its control over the state machinery, and the resources it disposed, that ultimately provided the political elite with its power. Even so, it was argued that the relationship between the two components of the ANC's "party state" was continuously fluctuating, especially under the Zuma presidency, as party factionalism has increasingly penetrated the state.

Premiers of South Africa's nine provinces, their executives, as well as those presiding over local government, exercised their authority over nonnational spheres. Although this could be extensive, it was nonetheless subject to state and party control from above. Furthermore, such officeholders had far less scope to shape policies and were largely restricted to the sphere of implementation—although their control over significant resources enabled them to construct significant networks of patronage. Together with the broad body of the Tripartite Alliance (notably COSATU and its individual union affiliates), they operated at the equivalent of Mills's middle level of power, where their influence over the elite was largely one of *constraint*.

The implication of this approach was that, although supposedly empowered by the vote and the regularity of elections, the broad mass of society in post-1994 South Africa was overwhelmingly subject to the will of political elites and had little or no influence over them, although they might well be mobilized by politicians as a resource.

The Corporate Elite

Not holding public office, the corporate elite was less easy to identify. As in other capitalist societies, there was the difficulty that control of corporations had to a considerable extent moved away from the owners of capital to managers, the most senior of whom were generally the ones to most actively exercise corporate power. Furthermore, private ownership of corporations had largely given away to institutional ownership, with bodies like banks, unit trusts, and pension funds holding the major portion of investments in the actual companies that made things or dug minerals out of the ground. This in turn suggested a shift of power to asset managers and those who made investment decisions.[4]

The democratic era had seen significant changes in a corporate structure that had historically revolved around a minerals-energy complex (Fine and Rustomjee 1996) that by the end of apartheid had become dominated by a small group of major conglomerates. The opening of the economy postapartheid led to major processes of "unbundling," as conglomerates shed their "noncore" assets in search of "shareholder value," while many of them went "global" (some by moving their headquarters overseas). Meanwhile, as foreign money poured in (some to purchase unbundled assets, some to invest in an expanding financial sector, some to make short-term returns from high interest rates), the role of the banks and private investment institutions steadily increased. Indeed, by 2010, financial institutions (14.4 percent)—along with mining houses (37.9 percent)—accounted for over half of the market capitalization of the Johannesburg Securities Exchange (calculated from *Who Owns Whom* 2011: 45–51).

The *investment and pricing decisions* made by those who owned and ran the corporations had major implications for not only the political elite but ordinary citizens as employees, workers, and consumers. Yet identifying those who made such decisions was complicated by distinctions between wealth and control. Some could be identified by the massive extent of their shareholding in giant corporations (which in some cases they had founded) and over which they exercised control by serving as CEOs, chairman of boards, or directors. Others could be identified by the extent and the forms of their remuneration. As neoliberalism took hold, South African corporates proved adept at claiming the need to retain the scarce skills of their highest-flying executives by providing them with globally competitive financial packages, often topping these up with huge "termination benefits" (golden handshakes) when they left (Crotty and Bonorchis 2006).

These were practices that were seamlessly borrowed by the parastatals. Although generally remunerating their highest earners less than their private sector counterparts, they justified their actions by the need to retain talent that was not only scarce, but black—for the reality was that, overall, the corporate sector remained overwhelmingly dominated by whites. All but a tiny handful of top earners in the private sector were white, while direct ownership of share capital by blacks remained, by one calculation, as just 7 percent of the total in 2010. This reflected the brutal reality that, twenty years into democracy, whites continued to own the overwhelming proportion of South Africa's private wealth. However, the major portion of that wealth was owned by just a small proportion of those whites.[5]

The Coexistence of Elites

While elaborating the racialized composition of the political and economic elites and acknowledging that this resulted in significant tensions between them, this approach nonetheless concluded that South Africa's elites enjoyed an uneasy coexistence. Although differing on many issues, they had come to an accord around the market economy, with the large corporations using "disciplinary" power through their capacity to choose whether to invest or to withhold investment, and even to export capital in response to government policies. To be sure, the massive disjuncture between political and corporate power made for lots of "noise," notably at the middle levels of society, where significant elements of the ANC, COSATU, and civil society remained deeply suspicious of, if not actively hostile to, the large corporations. This meant that the ANC leadership was constantly required to resort to radical (and often racialized) rhetoric to assuage the demands of its mass (black) constituency.

Inevitably, whatever the agreement between the political and corporate elites, the massive gulf between rich and poor and the deep divisions between white and black continued to make for awkward relationships. It was a context ripe for exploitation by those within the ANC who, in their own class and material interests, took up the cry that black South Africans remained at the mercy of "white monopoly capital."

WHITE MONOPOLY CAPITAL

The notion of "white monopoly capital" was to be most elaborately articulated by Chris Malikane, a University of the Witwatersrand economist in early 2017. He had just been appointed adviser to Malusi Gigaba, who had himself just been appointed finance minister by President Zuma to replace Pravin Gordhan in highly controversial circumstances (see below). His argument was that the first phase of the democratic transition, which was characterized by "the unfettered dominance of white monopoly capital over all levers of power in all spheres of society," was approaching its end (Malikane 2017a).

White monopoly capital owned and controlled all South Africa's resources and had the strong backing of international capital. This in turn ensured its hold over the state. The wages earned by all employees, whether public and private, along with the taxes they paid and the money the state borrowed, all derived from the resources owned and controlled by the monopolies. No credence should be extended to claims that there had been a deracialization of the white monopolies through such devices as the growth in black pension funds, for the latter were themselves under the control of white asset managers. Likewise, although blacks had been enabled to acquire private sector funding to purchase shares, this scheme had been used to capture the top leadership of the ANC and other political parties. Meanwhile, although affirmative action, BEE and the tender system had leveraged opportunities for a growing black middle class, the independence of this stratum had been undermined by white capital's assault on black businesses. These were enabled neither to compete with the monopolies nor to escape massive indebtedness brought about by monopoly pricing of goods and services and the high interest rates charged by monopoly capitalist banks. Not only the state but the entirety of society was under white control.

Malikane conceded that a small black capitalist class had been enabled to grow through the tender system of the state. However, this scheme of accumulation had been constrained by the Treasury's conservative fiscal policy. Hence the dismissal of Gordhan had been interpreted by white monopoly capital as designed to unlock the Treasury and to promote reckless spending to enrich this tender-based capitalist class. This constituted a massive threat to white monopoly capital, which was thus fighting back to prevent the "capture" of its state by the black capitalist class and its potential allies.

Prime among the allies of the black capitalist class was the black working class. This remained trapped in squalid conditions: by low wages, low skills, insecure employment, and massive unemployment. Objectively, therefore, it was necessary, if the national democratic revolution was to be completed, for the formation of an antimonopoly capitalist front, led by the working class but supported by the black middle class, black professionals, black business, and other progressive elements of society. The way forward was to mobilize popular support (inclusive of progressive anti-imperialist sentiment) for the expropriation of the white monopolies (the Reserve Bank, commercial banks, insurance companies, mines, and farms without compensation) and their replacement by state-owned banks and industries, along with the redistribution of land and the provision of free quality social services (Malikane 2017a, 2017b).

Malikane's analysis harkened back to ANC theorizing during the liberation struggle, notably the argument that South Africa was an "internal colony" where race and class oppression coincided, with the resultant legitimation of alliance of the small black capitalist class with the much larger black working class. Consequently, it attracted similar criticisms, notably for its Soviet-style class analysis and its de facto subordination of class to race (with the result that it was more Africanist than Marxist). Even so, it stood in sharp contrast to the earlier approaches arguing elite transition and the merging of black political and white economic elites by an insistence that democratic South Africa remains firmly under the domination of a small white elite. Correspondingly, it sat in close alignment with a simultaneous campaign that had been launched by President Jacob Zuma demanding that the ANC pursue a program of "radical economic empowerment."

THE ZUMA PRESIDENCY AND THE "CAPTURE" OF THE STATE BY PRIVATE INTERESTS

The initial years of democracy had seen South Africa enjoy steady, albeit unspectacular, economic growth (an average of 3 percent between 1995 and

2003). Although this was just half the rate of growth promised by GEAR, it stood in major contrast to the negative growth of the later years of apartheid and provided for significant levels of black upward mobility as well as a reduction in the number of people living in poverty. However, after twenty years of democracy, there was growing popular dissatisfaction with what the economy was delivering, especially among the generation of "born frees," those born after 1994. The mantra took hold in political discourse that freedom had done nothing to tackle "inequality, poverty and unemployment."

Critics complained that while the ANC had continued to "talk left" to appease its mass constituency, it had chosen to "walk right" in policy terms (Bond 2000: 15–52). In short, ANC-style neoliberalism had worked to reinforce rather than transform the fundamentals of apartheid political economy. The indiscriminate opening of a previously isolated and protected economy to global competition had led to a flight of investment capital and associated deindustrialization of key sectors of manufacturing (notably textiles); although the service sector had expanded considerably, many of the new jobs it created were precarious and poorly paid; public finance had become increasingly dependent upon inflows of short-term investment funds; and an appallingly high level of unemployment had remained entrenched (at anything between 25 and 40 percent, dependent on the definitions adopted) with the inevitable accompaniments of widespread poverty and food insecurity. Meanwhile, despite black upward mobility and black entry into the top elite, racial inequalities remained stark. Private wealth was still very largely white owned and still heavily concentrated in the hands of a relative handful of enormously wealthy white oligarchs (Southall 2013b).

It was in this context that Jacob Zuma had risen to the ANC and state presidencies on the back of an ideological rejection of neoliberalism by COSATU and the SACP that piggybacked on to a wider mix of Africanism and populism to secure the defeat of Mbeki (Southall 2009). However, COSATU and the SACP were to become steadily disillusioned by the Zuma presidency. Rather than tackling capitalism, Zuma entrenched a far-reaching network of patronage and corruption whereby he and his cronies plundered the state, draining resources via massive abuse of procurement procedures in parastatals and at all three levels of government (national, provincial, and local). Although this was to involve numerous actions of the state being referred to independent authorities such as the Public Protector (or Ombudsperson) and the courts, Zuma and his government were to prove highly adept at limiting their reach by using official resources to fend off legal restraint (by taking appeals from one court to another) or simply by failing to implement, or subverting, the requirements of adverse judgments.

A major scandal erupted around massive official expenditure upon Zuma's own rural homestead in KwaZulu-Natal and the ANC's ultimately futile attempts, inside and outside parliament, to keep it covered up. Yet the feature of Zuma's rule that attracted most adverse attention was the association he, his close family, and key members of his faction within the ANC developed with the three Gupta brothers. Arriving in South Africa in 1993, they had rapidly built a major empire, based around computers, IT, and mining. These prospered on the back of political connections and dubiously won procurement contracts from major parastatals, notably Transnet and Eskom. Indeed, so great did their influence become that they secured influence in the appointment of ministers to Zuma's cabinet (notably to head the Department of Minerals and Energy). When this was referred by opposition parties and civil society to the Public Protector, it resulted in a major report upon "state capture" that broadly endorsed the view that Zuma was doing their bidding and had conceded the independence of the state to them (Public Protector 2017). Eventually, this was to lead on to a major clash over control of the Treasury (Myburgh 2017).

Even under Zuma, the Treasury, under successive finance ministers, had sought to contain the tide of kleptocracy sweeping the different tiers of government. This inevitably led to growing tension with the presidency. Most notably, the Treasury stood in the path of Zuma and Eskom concluding the deal whereby the Rosatom, the Russian nuclear agency, would build South Africa a fleet of nuclear power stations, insisting that it could only go ahead if it was affordable. Coming with an enormous price tag of over $50 billion (Yelland 2017), which many argued would haunt the economy for decades to come, this constituted a major problem for the Guptas (Ajay, Atul, and Rajesh) and their associated network. Planning that a nuclear deal would provide extensive opportunities for procurement and corruption, they wanted a deal sealed and signed before the end of the Zuma presidency. This led on to a major trial of strength between Zuma and the Treasury.

In December 2013, Zuma shocked the country with the dismissal of Nhanhla Nene, his highly respected minister of finance, replacing him with Desmond van Rooyen, an obscure ANC backbencher. The immediate reaction from many, even from within the ANC, was that Zuma and the Guptas had overreached themselves by attempting to "capture" the Treasury. Accordingly, certain senior members of the ANC aligned themselves with CEOs of

Fig. 6.1. "State capture": From left, the Guptas, Ajay and Atul, Jagdish Parekh, and President Zuma's son, Duduzane. Photo by Martin Rhodes, used with permission from *Business Day*, Tiso Blackstar Group.

some of the country's largest corporations who pressured Zuma to reverse the decision, which he was now compelled to do. Much against his will, he was required to recall Pravin Gordhan, who had preceded Nene at the Treasury, with van Rooyen being shuffled aside to replace him as minister of local government and traditional authorities. Resolutely determined to impose fiscal discipline, Gordhan sought to fight corruption vigorously and maintained the Treasury's opposition to an unaffordable nuclear deal. In turn, once they had recouped their strength, Zuma and the Guptas fought back, with Gordhan now being subjected to a campaign to undermine him. This included trumped-up charges of corruption relating to his time at the head of the South African Revenue Service, charges that, lacking substance, eventually had to be dropped. Furthermore, his deputy minister, Mcebisi Jonas, alleged publicly that he had been offered R600 million were he to agree to replace Gordhan, the condition presumably being that he would approve the nuclear deal. In this context of skullduggery and rumor, Gordhan now earned the status of a national hero, receiving extensive plaudits from opposition parties, the independent media, and civil society, who saw him as the final defense against "state capture."[6]

The tense relations between Zuma and Gordhan reached a climax after the country's four largest banks gave notice to the Guptas that they were going to close their accounts, thereby hugely limiting the ability of their companies to do business. The banks justified this by reference to suspect transactions (code for the Guptas money-laundering huge sums out of the country). In turn, the Guptas alleged a conspiracy against them. Gordhan replied by turning to the North Gauteng High Court, seeking a declaratory order to show that he was not legally allowed to interfere with a decision by the banks. Increasingly desperate, the Guptas sought to buy their own bank, one of their associates seeking permission from the Reserve Bank and Registrar of Banks to purchase the Habib Overseas Bank, only to be rebuffed by an insistence that there could be no expedition of complex legal and financial requirements. It was in this context that Zuma launched an effective coup in April 2017. Without consulting with the ANC's National Executive Committee (which it was party policy for him to do), he recalled Gordhan and Jonas from an overseas investment trip and sacked them before they reached home. He appointed Malusi Gigaba, hitherto the home affairs minister and known as one of Zuma's allies, in Gordhan's place.[7]

By this time, the ANC had become massively factionalized between those backing Zuma and those opposed to him. Limited to two terms as state president, Zuma had by now embarked upon a concerted campaign to secure the election of his former wife, Nkosazana Dlamini-Zuma, as ANC president at the party's national congress in December 2017. Having previously used South Africa's continental influence to secure her election as chairperson of the African Union, Zuma's motivation seemed to be that, notwithstanding their past differences, Dlamini-Zuma would subsequently succeed to the state presidency, from which vantage point (as mother of some of Zuma's numerous children) she would protect and further the interests of the Zuma clique and block attempts to prosecute Zuma himself for corruption.

Zuma's campaign to promote Dlamini-Zuma was justified by the narrative that the ANC needed to demonstrate that it was now ready to be led by a woman, a refrain that was taken up enthusiastically by the party's women's league (whose commitment to feminism was historically highly dubious). Notwithstanding the supposed ANC practice that pretenders to the presidency do not declare their ambition openly (for the party liked to insist that they merely responded to pleas by members that they be prepared to serve), Dlamini-Zuma's campaign (although formally undeclared) had moved into full swing had moved into full swing by as early as early 2017, as she addressed party gatherings all around the country.

Her proposed elevation to the party leadership was strongly opposed by the anti-Zuma faction, many of whom argued that it was established party practice for the deputy president to succeed to the presidency. Consequently, although there were other aspirants to the post, it was to Deputy President Cyril Ramaphosa that the main body of the anti-Zuma lobby looked to counter the Dlamini-Zuma bandwagon. Initially, he had proved reluctant to show his hand. However, within weeks of Gordhan's dismissal, he was on the road, addressing mass meetings, garnering support within the party, and issuing strong warnings about the dangers and dire consequences of the capture of the state by private interests (although without explicitly mentioning the Guptas' name).[8]

The moment for Ramaphosa to launch his own campaign was ripe, for Gordhan's dismissal had lit the fuse of mounting public frustration with the Zuma presidency, ANC-condoned corruption, and the Guptas. This had been foreshadowed by the ANC's poor performance in local government elections in 2014, when its overall vote had dropped sharply, and it had lost control over thirty local councils, including three metropolitan governments (in Durban, Port Elizabeth, and Johannesburg). This concentrated ANC minds. As ANC MPs were forced to contemplate the possibility of a sharp reduction in support in the forthcoming 2019 general election, a raft of party elders gave voice to concerns that the party had lost its way and risked the loss of power. Major figures within the party therefore gave public backing to Gordhan when he spoke forthrightly against corruption at memorial gatherings for Ahmed Kathrada (a revered associate of Nelson Mandela) whose death had fortuitously coincided with Zuma's "capture" of the Treasury. Meanwhile, as Gordhan rode a wave of sympathy and support, mass rallies were organized by civil society organizations and opposition parties across the country, taking place in all the country's major cities and numerous smaller towns. Worryingly, for the president, they mobilized support that was both cross class and cross race, and took on a revivalist atmosphere, reminiscent of the heady days of the United Democratic Front, which had spearheaded the internal struggle against apartheid during the 1980s. They were backed by opposition parties calling for a vote of no confidence in Zuma in parliament.

It was to counter the mounting public opposition to him, as well as to give momentum to Dlamini-Zuma's bid for the ANC leadership, that Jacob Zuma had launched an aggressive campaign in favor of "radical economic transformation." His immediate motivation was to outflank the Economic Freedom Fighters (EFF), a breakaway from the ANC headed by Julius Malema.

As head of the ANC Youth League, Malema had initially been one of Zuma's most fervent backers in his own campaign to replace Mbeki. Seem-

Fig. 6.2. Past tense: Zuma (*left*) in the early 1990s as deputy secretary-general of the ANC, with President Mandela and Tambo Mbeki. Photo by Jon Hrusa, used with permission from *Business Day*, Tiso Blackstar Group.

ingly, Zuma and Malema, fitted well together, Malema himself having to counter claims that he was deeply tainted by procurement scandals in his home province of Limpopo. However, under his leadership, the Youth League had adopted increasingly radical positions; these including the seizure of white-owned land without compensation and the nationalization of the banks, mines, and other major sectors of industry. Initially, the ANC was broadly tolerant of these calls. Yet as they became more strident during Zuma's first term, relations deteriorated (notably after Malema embarrassed the president within the region by calling for the overthrow of the government of Ian Khama in Botswana, which he claimed was collaborating with US imperialism). Ultimately, this resulted in Zuma throwing Malema to the wolves by initiating disciplinary proceedings that, after extensive process, led to his expulsion from the ANC (Southall 2013b: 306–11).

Malema thereafter spearheaded the formation of the EFF in October 2013. Bringing together a diversity of disgruntled elements (inclusive of platinum-belt mineworkers following the tragedy of Marikana),[9] the EFF presented the ANC as mired in corruption, espoused a radical-cum-populist-cum-Africanist economic program, made grandiose promises to the poor, and sought to appeal to the youth. Although, ultimately, the 6.4 percent vote it obtained in the 2014 election fell far short of its ambitions, these were largely claimed from the ANC (Robinson 2014).

The EFF was to prove a formidable opponent in parliament. It adopted a flamboyant style and disruptive tactics that on more than one occasion led to its MPs' expulsion from the national assembly. Zuma was the constant butt of its attacks, its most famous jibe being that he must "pay back the money" to compensate for the illegal expenditure upon Nkandla. Furthermore, as the ANC became increasingly compromised by its defense of a president who appeared to many as irredeemably corrupt, the EFF denounced his legitimacy. In this the EFF was backed by mounting public criticism about Zuma's resort to dubiously constitutional means to fend off numerous court-based challenges to various of his appointments, actions, and decisions. Meanwhile, the EFF joined with other opposition parties and the media in focusing their highly critical attentions upon Zuma's close connections with the three Gupta brothers.

Yet Zuma's abrupt conversion to "radical economic transformation" was meant to do more than dish the EFF. In addition, it was to provide a cause that would give impetus to the Dlamini-Zuma campaign. Zuma provided no content to match the slogan, yet it was clear that in appealing particularly to black Africans (the overwhelming proportion of the population),[10] he was seeking to mobilize the sort of cross-class coalition from within the ANC that had backed his rise to power. Most particularly, by attacking continued white domination of the economy, he was seeking to mobilize the backing of the increasingly vocal black business lobby whose well-being was dependent upon state procurement. Attacks upon the Guptas were therefore, by implication, attacks upon black business. Simultaneously, "radical economic transformation" also implied that Ramaphosa, who had accumulated a massive fortune through BEE and had held multiple directorships prior to becoming deputy president, was a friend and representative of "white monopoly capital."

The problem for Ramaphosa was that, despite his by now having received endorsements from both COSATU and the SACP, this was almost certainly true.

THE ANC AND BUSINESS: WHO HOLDS THE POWER?

The rise of the Gupta empire and its acquisition of far-reaching political influence provides important clues as to "who holds the power" in contemporary South Africa.

The extent to which procurement contracts came to be directed to Gupta-owned or associated companies by parastatals indicated that the ANC under Jacob Zuma exercised a significant degree of state power independently of, and indeed contrary to the interests of, large-scale capital (which had hogged such deals under apartheid). This provides a strong challenge to any suggestion that "white monopoly capital" is wholly dominant. While it may be credibly argued that any attempt by black business to challenge the dominance of the large corporates will need concerted state backing, this does not negate the fact that the democratic transition handed control over South Africa's powerful state-owned companies (responsible for around 15 percent of GDP) to the ANC government, and that this has been utilized to very considerable effect. Just as the ratcheting up of BEE has required private capital (albeit with limited success) to direct procurement to black businesses, the leverage provided by parastatal spending has been used systematically to boost black enterprise (Southall 2007).

The legitimacy of this is not in question. However, what is questionable is how the allocation of contracts—by government departments as well as SOEs—has become central to the patronage networks and the political factionalism that have increasingly come to characterize the ANC after two decades in power. Against this, the way in which parastatal procurement was manipulated, usually by dubiously constitutional means, to favor the Guptas (foreign nationals who had conveniently been granted citizenship), only for them to ship the profits out of the country, could scarcely qualify as BEE. Furthermore, the direct influence the Guptas managed to acquire, notably in steering Eskom (the electricity-generating and transmission parastatal) in the direction of the Russian-backed "nuclear" option, the massive gains their companies (and numerous ANC acolytes) would have made if it was to be implemented, and the say they acquired in the appointment of ministers and their attempted subversion of the independence of the Treasury bore heavy responsibility in the downgrading of South Africa's investment rating to "junk" by two major rating agencies during 2017. This in turn implied a major knock-on in terms of the rising cost of government borrowing and a dangerously rising extent of government debt. Nor, indeed, was the risk to the economy that this represents in the interests of large-scale capital.

It was for these reasons that CEOs of major banks and corporates joined in demanding that Zuma retract the appointment of Van Rooyen as finance minister and his immediate replacement by Gordhan. Yet even this fails to illustrate the supposed unbridled power of "white monopoly capital," for to succeed in this bid, they were required to act jointly with ANC heavyweights, inclusive of Deputy President Ramaphosa, when their objections, if lodged on their own, would probably have received an outright rebuff. Again, that Zuma ultimately staged his own coup a year later, by replacing Gordhan with Gigaba, demonstrates that the presidency cannot be usefully portrayed as a tool of the corporates, or as immediately subject to their will.

This is far from illustrating that the corporate sector is politically powerless. The mining industry is particularly powerful, an emergent literature demonstrating how it works hand in hand with the Department of Mineral Resources, often with traditional leaders in tow, at the expense of the rights of rural communities (e.g., Manson 2013; Capps and Mnwana 2015). Similarly, it has secured the transfer of the responsibility for environmental oversight of mines from the Department of the Environment to the Department of Mineral Resources. Justified by the need to cut red tape and to speed up investment, the inevitable outcome has been that environmental protection has been greatly reduced, to the massive detriment of local communities (Kings 2017). More generally, although usually avoiding critical comment on political affairs, corporates engage with government over numerous issues through such bodies as Business Unity South Africa. Overall, they enjoy a very real capacity to influence policy through their ability to invest or disinvest. Even so, this capacity to induce or constrain government actions depends significantly upon the political calculus of power holders. What was to prove so alarming to many was that, as Zuma approached the end of his presidency, he had manifestly abandoned the national interest and even the electoral interest of the ANC in favor of his personal interests, those of Guptas, and those of his faction.

Zuma's espousal of "radical economic transformation" in early 2017 provided the ideological justification for his backing Dlamini-Zuma to succeed him as president (with the unstated assumption that she would keep him out of jail by blocking any attempts to prosecute him for corruption while protecting if not furthering the interests of the Zuma family and its immediate acolytes). Given the concurrent stagnation of the economy, with the attendant ills of "poverty, unemployment and inequality," the call for radical economic transformation was not one that any major figure within the ANC would be prepared to disavow. Furthermore, although Zuma gave no explicit backing to Malikane's manifesto, its ideological assault upon "white" capital suited his purposes admirably (Mutize and Gossel 2017). The danger, it was suggested, was not so much that Zuma and his faction actively subscribed to

Fig. 6.3. Dlamini-Zuma sought unsuccessfully to replace her ex-husband as ANC leader and then president of South Africa. Photo by Simphiwe Nkwali, used with permission from *Business Day*, Tiso Blackstar Group.

Malikane's analysis (Gigaba explicitly kept his distance), but that it signaled a potential shift of state policy. If this were to feature an attack upon established capital, with a resultant bid to empower the state-dependent black capitalist class, it would lead to a massive flight of capital, fiscal crisis, and the impoverishment of all except those tied into the system of state patronage (Bernstein 2017). South Africa, argued one particularly cogent critic, would stand on the edge of its "Zimbabwe moment" (Satgar 2017).

The reality was not that the government was under the unmitigated sway of "white monopoly capital," but rather that the deal between the incoming ANC elite and the major corporates had been significantly eroded. The crony capitalism to which it had given rise had garnered limited legitimacy and ushered in no fundamental change to apartheid economy. While the acquisition of state power by the ANC had enabled it engage on stronger (if still unequal) terms with established capital, and during the Mbeki years to forge a broad consensus between government and large-scale business, the Zuma presidency and its favoring of narrowly private interests in the form of the Gupta empire indicated a widening disjuncture.

It was against this background that the ANC arrived at its national congress in December 2017. Although the congress proceeded to adopt various key resolutions designed to flesh out its commitment to "radical economic transformation," its real business was the election of the party's new president. In the event, Ramaphosa squeaked home ahead of Dlamini-Zuma. However, his triumph came only at the expense of his having to make a backroom deal with David Mabuza, the premier of the province of Mpumalanga. Mabuza's reputation was distinctly shady, tainted by allegations not only of corruption but even of involvement in the assassination of political rivals. Nonetheless, he had his province's delegate votes in his pocket, and was to throw these behind Ramaphosa at the last moment (Southall 2018).

Ramaphosa's victory was widely welcomed outside the ANC. Nonetheless, it was recognized that the narrowness of his victory meant that he had to move extremely cautiously if he was to reunite the party in the wake of Dlamini-Zuma's defeat. Initially, this required him to undertake cautious maneuvering within the party as he worked toward his objective of removing Zuma as state president before the expiry of his term in 2019. In the event, he succeeded in doing this by early January 2018, by which time Zuma faced such irresistible power to leave office that he was unable to secure from Ramaphosa the guarantees that he would not be prosecuted for past misdemeanors that he had hoped for. In essence, once Dlamini-Zuma had lost the race for the party leadership, Zuma's support had begun to drain away and gravitate toward Ramaphosa as the new fulcrum of party power.

Ramaphosa's challenge was to do much more than just unite the party if the ANC was to secure another majority at the forthcoming general election in 2019. His first task was to repair the party's relations with large-scale capital and to restore South Africa's reputation as an attractive location for investment. Central to this was his pursuit of moves designed to roll back "state capture" and to demonstrate commitment to tackling the corruption and patronage patterns that had become the ANC's hallmark. Initially he earned wide acclamation for his reappointment of Nene to the Treasury, Gordhan to the Ministry of Public Enterprise (where he was charged with refurbishing the credibility and efficiency of the parastatals), and his dismissal or marginalizing Zuma allies when he announced his first cabinet. At the same time, his appointment of Mabuza as deputy president signaled the potential capacity of compromised party bosses to stall much-needed reforms. Consolidating his support within the ANC while simultaneously battling corruption within its ranks was to constitute one of Ramaphosa's most difficult challenges.

Key to this exercise was his need to counter any suggestion that he was simply the "white man's black man" by engaging with corporate capital to usher in "radical economic transformation." This was going to demand more than just the attainment of more constructive relations with capital than obtained under Zuma and achievement of significantly improved rates of economic growth. It would also rest upon his ability to render corporate capital accountable to the diverse constituencies of South Africa's unruly democracy.

ELITES AND ACCOUNTABILITY IN SOUTH AFRICA

In modern democracies, governments are supposedly accountable to "the people," while public companies are similarly accountable to their shareholders. In reality, the former have become elective oligarchies in which popular power is largely restricted to the occasional replacement of one set of political elites by another, while the latter are rarely constrained by "shareholder democracy," for corporate decision-making has usually become concentrated in the hands of a tiny minority of shareholders who dominate boards and/or the topmost layers of senior management. Furthermore, given that the well-being of modern capitalist economies is massively dependent upon the investment decisions made by huge financial institutions or major corporations (with these often being intimately interlinked), the survival of governments becomes dependent upon not only securing the goodwill of large-scale capital, but competing with other countries for their investments. This in turn demands that governments render their countries suitable sites for investment, this very often involving systematic reductions of the costs and benefits of labor. It is in this context, of global competition for scarce finance and investment, that corporate elites proclaim the acute scarcity of their talent and skills and demand (and receive) historically unequalled levels of remuneration. In this way, wealth is funneled upward, and levels of inequality increase to obscene proportions. Meanwhile, given that public office is generally rewarded well, yet at far less generous levels, politicians are regularly drawn into making covert deals that favor corporate interests if they wish to access financial largesse.

It is no accident, therefore, that the distribution of wealth and incomes in South Africa is so remarkably extreme. The elite transition ensured that the ownership and control of a highly monopolized economy remained in the hands of a tiny white elite whose wealth was to be increased as their conglomerates joined in the fray of global competition. Correspondingly, the globalization of South Africa's corporations has had two major outcomes. First, its topmost corporate elites have demanded, and obtained, remuneration at levels commensurate with those that obtain in New York or London. Second, while a tiny handful of individuals retain ultimate control of certain important companies, South Africa's corporate elites have become increasingly accountable to foreign investors and finance capital (in the form of pension funds and asset managers) rather than to individual domestic shareholders (who in any case, constitute only a tiny fraction of the entire population) (Massie, Collier, and Crotty 2014).

Yet corporations are also subject to national laws and governance. These require that they engage in relations with governments that can range from the highly collaborative to the highly contested. In South Africa, since 1994, the conditions for continued corporate profitability were laid down by the elite transition and a constructive accommodation with the incoming ANC elite. Despite much political rhetoric by ANC politicians about the need for "transformation," the new political elite was primarily bent on rapid accumulation, either through incorporation into the ranks of "white capital" or by accessing the booty of the state. Meanwhile, the large corporations wielded sufficient power to ensure that their interests continued to be well served. Concessions were made to the ANC in terms of equity employment and BEE "charters" and so on, whether negotiated in backroom deals or formal structures, but broadly their influence was such that a favorable investment climate was retained. However, this largely comfortable and collaborative coexistence of corporate with political elites was to be undermined by the Zuma presidency.

Zuma succeeded to the presidency by manipulation of the narrowly constrained workings of ANC internal democracy. Formally, the ANC's five-yearly National Congress is the party's sovereign body, with 90 percent of its delegates elected by party branches, with balance elected by aligned organizations such as the ANC Women's and Youth Leagues. In turn, the Congress elects a one-hundred-strong National Executive Committee (NEC) to ensure implementation of party policy. The NEC then elects a smaller National Working Committee to oversee the party from day to day. In practice, this means that the ANC is dominated by a tiny elite. Branch elections have become hugely corrupted, with elections to party positions hugely dependent upon money, patronage and the power of factions. It was by generation of sufficient support within branches by mobilization of anti-Mbeki sentiment, backed by COSATU and the SACP reaction to Mbeki's endorsement of neoliberalism, that Zuma was enabled to secure the party presidency in 2007. Subsequently, because South Africa's proportional representation electoral system effectively dictates that the leader of the largest party in parliament becomes state president, Zuma ascended to the country's highest office (Booysen 2015).

Zuma was to personalize the power of the presidency largely unconstrained by the ANC. Through the shrewd deployment of patronage and individuals to positions in state and party, he was enabled to extend the reach of his faction. With ANC MPs dependent upon the retention of the goodwill of party bosses, the ANC caucus in parliament became reduced to a cypher, defending Zuma and ministers (however incompetent or corrupt) through one scandal after another. It was because precisely because of the subversion of both party and state that Zuma was enabled to further the interests of the Guptas, whose remarkable rise to fortune was crucially dependent upon the access to parastatal contracts that was provided by their political connections and the protection granted to them.[11]

That the Zuma and Gupta network is now unraveling is a result of a combination of circumstances. The foremost of these, obviously, is Ramaphosa's succession to the party and state presidencies, this consolidated by his leading the ANC to a further victory in the April 2019 election (albeit with a reduced majority) (Schulz-Herzenberg and Southall 2019). This enabled him to increase the freedom of state agencies and prosecutorial services to pursue corruption, the extent and nature of which have begun to be exposed by revelations to major commissions of inquiry established by Ramaphosa, and which formed a backdrop to the election.[12] They are having to do so without the assistance of the Guptas, who at time of writing, have fled to Dubai, seemingly having exported the bulk of their loot with them, although the assets they have left behind in South Africa have been largely frozen or reclaimed by the state. Zuma himself has had charges of corruption relating to an arms deal concluded by the Mbeki government in 2008, dropped during his presidency, reinstated against him and, if found guilty, may eventually face jail time. Simultaneously, the corporate sector has been caught up in a myriad of corporate scandals, central to which is the apparent connivance of major international as well as local auditing companies in state capture and the looting of the parastatals and other public entities.

Ramaphosa's early efforts to combat corruption were to earn him much domestic and international acclaim, although by mid-2019 (when this chapter was being completed), concern was mounting that he was failing to counter a vigorous "fight back" campaign launched by his opponents within the party. Although defeated at the 2017 party congress, they remained powerful and now threatened to derail the Ramaphosa presidency, and even to unseat him. Were they to succeed, they would rupture the contested yet broadly collaborative relationship that underpinned the power elite of the Mbeki years, and thrust the state and the economy into a downwardly spiraling crisis, perhaps collapsing South Africa into the arms of the International Monetary Fund.

It is clear that the immediate fate of South Africa depends heavily upon the capacity of Ramaphosa to assert his authority, rehabilitate and reform state corporations, empower independent state institutions to prosecute corruption, and hence regain the trust of large-scale capital. A restoration of the contested yet broadly collaborative relationship that obtained between the ANC's state and corporate capital during the Mbeki years could provide for a return to much-needed increased economic growth (global conditions allowing). Ultimately, the ANC remains heavily dependent upon the investment flows that only large-scale capital can generate. Yet, while welcome, higher rates of growth would not in themselves change the highly concentrated, highly monopolized, highly centralized structure of South Africa's political economy.

Greater accountability to the mass of ordinary South Africans is required if the brutal extent of inequality and mass poverty are to be seriously addressed. However, the restructuring of the political economy that this would require—inclusive of far-reaching land reform, rapid transition away from coal to green energy, pushback against the domination of one economic sector after another by large companies, and the loosening of the grip of predatory ANC politicians over allocation of state contracts—will meet with the major resistance of vested interests. Yet without such far-reaching change in the patterns of the political economy, massive inequality and the limited accountability of both political and corporate elites seem destined to continue.

NOTES

1. The oft-made assertion rests upon South Africa having the highest Gini coefficient (.56), which measures income inequality in the world (United Nations Development Programme 2015).

2. The "Rich List" lists the capital value of directors of companies listed on the Johannesburg Securities Exchange, as well as the remuneration paid to executives of the SOEs.

3. Useful sources for tracking this progression of South African elites include Adam and Giliomee 1979; O'Meara 1983; and Terreblanche 2002.

4. Compared with most other African countries South Africa offers a considerable richness of data concerning ownership of corporate assets and the rewards offered to corporate assets. These include annual volumes of *Who Owns Whom*, whose data allow the drawing up of annual Rich Lists for the *Sunday Times*.

5. Van Heerden (1996), using estate data, found that whites owned 90 percent of South Africa's private wealth, but just 20 percent of whites owned 70 percent of that wealth. Although there has been a substantial narrowing of racial disparities since 1994 (Mike Schussler cited in Institute of Race Relations 2011: 288), the data provided by Credit Suisse and Oxfam suggest that a relatively small proportion of whites continues to own the major proportion of private wealth.

6. Gordhan's removal was not the first instance of the Guptas' influence over cabinet appointments. The most blatant previous example was the appointment of Mosebensi Zwane, an obscure provincial minister from the Free State, as minister of mineral resources, a position that he used to assist the Guptas to acquire Glencore's Optimum mine (and lucrative coal supply contracts to Eskom to go with it) in late 2016. "New Minister of Mines Tainted by Gupta Family," *Mail & Guardian*, September 24, 2015, https://mg.co.za/ . . . /2015-09-23-new-minister-of-mines-tainted-by-gupta-family-link

7. This summary of events is composed from extensive reading of the South African media, notably *Business Day*, *Mail & Guardian*, and the (online) *Daily Maverick*.

8. Ramaphosa's cause was assisted by a judgment of the Western Cape High Court (responding to a case brought by an environmental group) that the agreement reached between Presidents Zuma and Putin to build the power stations was unlawful because the government had failed to consult parliament and public opinion. Although the government subsequently indicated its intention to proceed with the nuclear option, this constituted such a major setback that it seemed probable that the nuclear deal would never happen. *Financial Times* (London), April 26, 2017.

9. When police killed forty-three striking workers on a Lonmin platinum mine (Alexander 2013).

10. According to the 2016 census, black Africans accounted for 80 percent of the population, compared with nearly 9 percent Coloureds, 2.5 percent Indians, and 8 percent whites. The apartheid-era racial categories continue to form a basis for much government policy.

11. The intimate details of the state capture exercise were to be dramatically revealed during the last days of the Zuma presidency in an explosive book by the courageous investigative journalist Jacques Pauw (2017) and soon elaborated by Ivor Chipkin and Mark Swilling (2018).

12. The major probes were conducted by the Commission of Inquiry into Allegations of State Capture, headed by Deputy Chief Justice Raymond Zondo, and the Commission of Inquiry into Allegations of Impropriety Regarding the Public Investment Corporation, headed by Justice Lex Mpati, former president of the Supreme Court of Appeal.

REFERENCES

Adam, Heribert, and Hermann Giliomee. 1979. *The Rise and Crisis of Afrikaner Power*. Cape Town: David Philip.

Alexander, Peter. 2013. "Marikana, Turning Point in South African History." *Review of African Political Economy* 40, no. 138: 605–19.
Bernstein, Ann. 2017. "Gigaba's Adviser Entirely at Odds with Economic Policy since 1994." *Business Day*, April 26.
Bond, Patrick. 2000. *Elite Transition: From Apartheid to Neoliberalism in South Africa*. Sterling, VA: Pluto Press; Pietermaritzburg: University of Natal Press.
Booysen, Susan. 2015. *Dominance and Decline: The ANC in the Time of Zuma*. Johannesburg: University of Witwatersrand Press.
Capps, Gavin, and Sonwabile Mnwana. 2015. "Claims from Below: Platinum and the Politics of Land in the Bakgatla-la-Kgafela Traditional Authority." *Review of African Political Economy* 42, no. 146: 606–24.
Chipkin, Ivor and M. Swilling, eds. 2018. *Shadow State: The Politics of State Capture*. Johannesburg, Wits University Press.
Crotty, Ann, and Renée Bonorchis. 2006. *Executive Pay in South Africa*. Cape Town: Double Storey.
Fine, Ben, and Zavareh Rustomjee. 1996. *The Political Economy of South Africa: From Minerals-Energy Complex to Industrialisation*. London: Hurst.
Institute of Race Relations. 2011. *South Africa Survey 2011*. Johannesburg. Institute of Race Relations.
Institute of Race Relations. 2012. "Submission on Broad Based Black Economic Empowerment Act: BEE Should Be Scrapped, Not Reformed." December 4. irr.org.za/ . . . /policy-submission-bee-should-be-scrapped-not-reformed-4th-december . . .
Kersley, Richard, and Antonios Koutsoukis. 2016. *Global Wealth Report 2016*. November 22. Credit Suisse Research Institute. https://www.credit-suisse.com/articles/news-and . . . /the-global-wealth-report-2016.html
Kings, Sipho. 2017. "The Day That Mining Won." *Mail & Guardian*, May 19–25.
Malikane, Chris. 2017a. "The Unfettered Power of White Monopoly Capital." *Sunday Independent*, April 3.
Malikane, Chris. 2017b. "Call for Anti-imperialist Workers to Unite." *Sunday Independent*, April 23.
Manson, Andrew. 2013. "Mining and Traditional Communities in South Africa's 'Platinum Belt': Contestations over Land, Leadership and Assets in North-West Province, c1996–2012." *Journal of Southern African Studies* 39, no. 2: 409–23.
Massie, Kaylan, Debbie Collier, and Ann Crotty. 2014. *Executive Salaries in South Africa: Who Should Have a Say on Pay?* Auckland Park: Jacana.
Mbeki, Moeletsi. 2009. *Architects of Poverty: Why African Capitalism Needs Changing*. Johannesburg: Picador.
Mills, C. Wright. 1956. *The Power Elite*. New York: Oxford University Press.
Myburgh, Pieter-Louis. 2017. *The Republic of Gupta: A Story of State Capture*. Johannesburg: Penguin Random House.
Mutize, Misheck, and Sean Gossel. 2017. "'White Monopoly Capital': An Excuse to Avoid South Africa's Real Problems." *Daily Maverick*, March 24.

O'Meara, Dan. 1983. *Volkskapitalisme: Class, Capital and Ideology in the Development of Afrikaner Nationalism 1934–1946*. Cambridge: Cambridge University Press; Braamfontein: Ravan Press.

Oxfam. 2017. "An Economy for the 99%: It's Time to Build a Human Economy." Oxfam Briefing Paper, January. https://www.oxfam.org/sites/ . . . oxfam . . . /bp-economy-for-99-percent-160117-en.pdf

Pauw, Jacques. 2017. *The President's Keepers: Those Keeping Zuma in Power and out of Prison*. Cape Town: Tafelberg.

Piketty, Thomas. 2014. *Capital in the Twenty-First Century*. Translated by Arthur Goldhammer. Cambridge, MA: Belknap Press of Harvard University Press.

Public Protector. 2017. "State of Capture." Report No. 6 of 2017/17. Public Protector State Capture Report-Saflii. saflii.org/images/329756472-State-of-Capture.pdf

Robinson, Jason. 2014. "The Economic Freedom Fighters: Birth of a Giant?" In Collette Schulz-Herzenberg and Roger Southall, eds., *Election 2014, South Africa: The Campaigns, Results and Future Prospects*, 72–88. Auckland Park: Jacana.

Satgar, Vishwas. 2017. "Zuma's Cabinet Reshuffle Inaugurates South Africa's Zimbabwe Moment." *Mail & Guardian*, April 21–27.

Schulz-Herzenberg, Collette, and Roger Southall, eds. 2019. *Election 2019: Change and Stability in South Africa's Democracy*. Auckland Park: Jacana.

Southall, Roger. 2006. "Ten Propositions about Black Economic Empowerment in South Africa." *Review of African Political Economy* 33, no. 111: 67–84.

Southall, Roger. 2007. "The ANC, Black Economic Empowerment and State-Owned Enterprises: A Recycling of History?" In Sakhela Buhlungu, John Daniel, Roger Southall, and Jessica Lutchman, eds., *State of the Nation: South Africa 2007*, 201–25. Cape Town: HSRC Press.

Southall, Roger. 2009. "Understanding the 'Zuma Tsunami.'" *Review of African Political Economy* 121: 317–33.

Southall, Roger. 2013a. "The Power Elite in Democratic South Africa: Race and Class in a Fractured Society." In John Daniel, Prishani Naidoo, Devan Pillay, and Roger Southall, eds., *The New South African Review 3: The Second Phase—Tragedy or Farce?*, 17–38. Johannesburg: Wits University Press.

Southall, Roger. 2013b. *Liberation Movements in Power: Party and State in Southern Africa*. Woodbridge, Surrey: James Currey; Auckland Park, Jacana.

Southall, Roger. 2018. "Why Ramaphosa's Moment of Hope Is Built on a Fragile Foundation." *The Conversation*, February 19. theconversation.com/why-ramaphosas-moment-of-hope-is-built-on-a-fragile-foundati . . .

Terreblanche, Sampie. 2002. *A History of Inequality in South Africa, 1652–2002*. Pietermaritzburg: University of Natal Press; Johannesburg: KMM Review Publishing.

Times Live. 2016. "Money, Shares and Fame: Here's the Full Business Times Rich List." December 11. www.timeslive.co.za/sundaytimes/businesstimes/2016/ . . . / Money-shares-and-fame-Her

United Nations Development Programme. 2015. *Human Development Report*.
van Heerden, J. 1996. "The Distribution of Personal Wealth in South Africa." *South African Journal of Economics* 64, no. 4: 278–91.
Who Owns Whom in South Africa. 2011. 31st ed. Johannesburg: Who Owns Whom.
Yelland, Chris. 2017. "Analysis: How Much Will New Nuclear Electricity Cost South Africa." *Daily Maverick*, May 25.

CHAPTER 7

Land, Freedom, and Legal Elites

Rights Debates in South Africa

TIMOTHY GIBBS

INTRODUCTION: LAND AND FREEDOM—AND LAWYERS

This chapter concerns the public interest and "struggle lawyers" who took up land rights and chieftaincy cases and defended dissidents in rural South Africa, the Native Reserves, and the Bantustans during the apartheid era. My particular interest is to outline the distinct elite trajectories and the wide-ranging ideas of human rights and freedoms that were espoused by these diverse, disputatious, legal elites.

The role played by land and legal rights activists of the 1980s has been discussed extensively (Abel 1995: 385–494)—not least because many of the scholars writing on land rights today were young activists then! My ambition in this chapter is to provide a longer history of legal activism that (1) emphasizes multiple threads of argument and action, and (2) stresses the complex relationships between elite lawyers and other land activists and the rural communities they sought to represent.[1] The first section discusses the politicized struggle lawyers of the mid-twentieth century—particularly lawyers linked to the non-European Unity Movement in the Eastern Cape, and the Liberal Party in Natal—who pioneered distinctive forms of land rights activism in rural South Africa. The second section considers the diverse new ideas of dissent that were shaped inside the Bantustans during the 1970s. Here I focus not only on the well-known liberal land rights activists in Natal, but also important groupings of Black lawyers and activists working inside the Bantustans who were often associated with the Black Consciousness Movement. In the third section I suggest that these diverse strands of legal dissidence were folded into the well-known human rights organizations that emerged in the final decade of apartheid. This was a moment when organizations such as the Legal Resources Centre and Lawyers for Human Rights moved beyond their narrow base in the cities and embraced a wider set of professionals based in rural South Africa and the Bantustans.[2] In the final section, I conclude with a brief discussion of how these Bantustan legacies have shaped rights debates in postapartheid South Africa.

In making these arguments I engage with three broader debates about questions of elite agency and accountability in tight corners (Lonsdale 2000)—the central themes of this edited collection. First: historians have often described how colonialism constructed repressive codes of Native and customary law (Chanock 1985; Benton 1999; Mann and Roberts 1991), and "invented" patriarchal systems of traditional authority (Ranger 1983). Apartheid was an archetypal example: its policies of separate development turned Native Reserves—in which around half the Black African population had homes—into self-governing, "tribal" Bantustans. Thus Lungisile Ntsebeza (1999), a noted land rights activist and academic, has described apartheid's chieftaincies as "decentralised despotisms"—a term that has been applied more broadly by Mamood Mamdani (1996). This critique of the chieftaincy runs like a red thread through many of the land rights debates and controversies in South Africa today (Claassens and Cousins 2008; Minisi Weeks 2011; Ntsebeza 2006; Pityana 2015).

Yet, while colonial and apartheid authorities drafted patriarchal and repressive laws, these codes were not hegemonic. Subalterns, peasant intellectuals, and dissenting traditional leaders imagined alternative visions of justice and community—and sometimes faced jail for their pains. A second important strand of scholarship has thus, to paraphrase John Lonsdale's resonant expression, studied these subaltern ideas of land and freedom (Ekeh 1990; Feierman 1990; Lonsdale 1992; Ranger 1993). Such ideas have been important in South Africa, where the writings of many land rights scholars, activists, and lawyers were shaped by their own engagements: initially with the widespread rural resistance inside the Bantustans; and today in the complex, contested processes of land restitution (e.g., James 2007; Walker 2005). Thus South African land rights activism and scholarship have fed into broader debates about "legal pluralism" in the postcolony: the relationship between rural communities, traditional/indigenous authorities, and land rights (Comaroff and Comaroff 2009; Oomen 2005).

This chapter, however, takes its impulse from a third strand of research that has rather focused on the professional trajectories, political engagements, and ideas articulated by lawyers and legal elites themselves (cf. Dezalay 2015, 2017). While codes of apartheid and Native law were extremely repressive, courtrooms were also places in which dissidents "spoke back . . . [in] the language of the law" (Karekwaivanane 2011: 333; see also Abel 1995; Broun 2000; Comaroff 2001; Ibhawoh 2013). Thus it is important to trace the genealogies of various ideas of rights and freedoms that were formulated on the peripheries (Dubow 2012). For land activism has been an important stream of legal dissidence across twentieth-century South Africa and has shaped South Africa's powerful human rights movement (Abel 1995).

This argument comes with caveats. As Dubow (2012) and Moyn (2010) have noted, it is facile to make the teleological argument that equates all struggles for political emancipation and freedoms as ultimately a quest for human rights. Indeed, one central concern running through this chapter is the vexed question of how lawyers and land activists variously conceived or defined the rights and freedoms they were fighting for (James 2007: 9–12, 34–50). An interwoven thread concerns the ambivalent relationship between elite lawyers and the chiefs, landowners, and rural communities that they sought to represent in court. Sometimes struggle lawyers claimed they were defending the true traditional leaders and tribal dissidents from chiefs imposed by the apartheid authorities. In other instances, (white) liberal legal activists used the language of Christian brotherhood when they defended *kholwa* (Christian) communities, led by Black Christian landowners, against apartheid's forced removals. It was only in the 1970s and 1980s that elite lawyers and land activists organized themselves around the concepts of defending human rights; identifying themselves with the "poorest of the poor." The postapartheid era has seen the rise of the influential Congress of Traditional Leaders (CONTRALESA)—crucially, an organization led by cosmopolitan *lawyers*—making the case for communal rights in which traditional leaders are the true representatives of their peoples.

The dissonance between these different ideas of freedoms and rights is crucial. For I conclude with the suggestion that one of the reasons that postapartheid rural reform programs have stalled is because policy elites, lawyers, and judges have disagreed on how to conceive of the rural communities that are due to benefit from land rights restitution.

DEFENDING PEASANTS, CHRISTIANS, AND THE "TRUE" CHIEFS

In the first part of the twentieth century, recourse to law had largely been the privilege of a small group of chiefs and African landowners who could afford representation. But from the 1940s, a succession of laws associated with the coming of apartheid and the Bantustans bit deep into rural society, drawing a wider set of peasant communities into South African courtrooms (Basner 1993: 100–104). First, in the name of improving peasant productivity, "Rural Betterment" directives granted magistrates authoritarian powers to cull cattle, demand corvee labor, and relocate villagers. A least three million rural people were subject to Rural Betterment across the apartheid era (de Wet 1995: 28 n. 24; Westaway 2010: 138). Second, programs of forced removals evicted rural communities from land that apartheid policies had designated for white South Africa. These forced removals would eventually displace 1.1 million labor tenants over the course of the apartheid era (Platzky and Walker 1985). Third, apartheid policies concentrated power in the hands of the chieftaincy (Evans 1997; Ntsebeza 2006). In particular, the 1952 Bantu Authorities Act instituted tribal authorities as a new layer of local government. Traditional leaders were granted sweeping powers to squeeze taxes and labor from their subjects and fine recalcitrant villagers in their newly recognized tribal courts. (Indeed, the newly instituted taxes and fines were often used to build tribal courtrooms.) Additionally, the 1959 Bantu Self-Government Act transformed the Native Reserves into ten self-governing homelands—derisively known as Bantustans—which were typically ruled by men who hailed from chiefly lineages. Under the prime ministership of Chief Kaiser Matanzima, the Transkei Territories became the first apartheid Bantustan in 1963.

In response, there were a series of rural revolts: at Zoutpansberg (1941–44), Witzieshoek (1950), Zeerust (1957–58), Sehukhuneland (1958), southern Natal (1959), Ciskei (1950s), and the Mpondo (1960) and Thembu (1962–63) regions of Transkei. Typically, dissident communities clubbed together and hired lawyers to defend rebels in court and to challenge apartheid directives. One policeman's report written at this time described a rebellious village holding meetings that were addressed by a city lawyer who had been solicited by a herbalist. Another government loyalist asked the local magistrate for armed protection from rebels opposed to rural betterment, who were burning out the householders who refused to pay lawyer's fees (Redding 2006: 193).

Often labor migrants from rural communities sought out struggle lawyers (i.e., politically active lawyers) based in the big cities (Bizos 2007: 102–18, 145–48; Mandela 1994: 173).[3] Johannesburg was the largest hub of this important grouping of South African struggle lawyers—most famously (Nelson) Mandela & (Oliver) Tambo, attorneys-at-law (est. 1952). Importantly, this group of lawyer-politicians included growing numbers of Black attorneys, whose entry in the legal profession occurred in the context of the rapid urbanization of South Africa. The number of Black lawyers increased from eighteen in 1946 to fifty by 1960 (Gibbs 2014: 36). Johannesburg's communist and nationalist lawyers primarily fielded clients from across Transvaal and the Free State. Nelson Mandela, for instance, built his professional reputation and political base as a struggle lawyer in Johannesburg; but he also handled rural cases from Carolina in the Eastern Transvaal to Engcobo in the Eastern Cape (Mandela 1994: 172–73, 176; Mda 2012: 16–19). In some notable instances—notably at Sekhukhuneland and Zeerust—local activists and struggle lawyers acted as political brokers, deeply entrenching the ANC's influence in particular chieftaincies and districts (Lodge 1983: 261–94).

While mid-century Johannesburg's ANC-aligned struggle lawyers have commanded most attention, there were also a couple of important cases in which lawyers rooted in South Africa's regions took up rural cases in the 1950s and 1960s. Most notable was the legal activism associated with the Non-European Unity Movement (a political grouping) in the Eastern Cape, and the Liberal Party in Natal. These three political groupings—the ANC, the NEUM, and the Liberals—were largely rivals on the national stage. Yet while the ANC was largely based in the burgeoning cities, the Unity Movement and Liberal Party took up land cases and concentrated much of their political efforts on rural South Africa. The Unity Movement's and Liberal Party's separate efforts to make apartheid's courtrooms a focus of political mobilization deserves scrutiny because it provides a striking insight into how elite lawyers sought to represent rural South Africans.

Intriguingly, the professional foundations of the Unity Movement lawyers were in the Native Reserves of the rural Eastern Cape. Many had started-off as high school teachers in the rural missionary schools that had produced South Africa's Black elites since the late nineteenth century. They had then turned to law in the mid-1950s when forced out of the teaching profession by the apartheid authorities. Thus by 1960 around one-third of African lawyers were based in Transkei Territories, where African lawyers—elsewhere confined by the strictures of segregation—could build a decent commercial practice in the small, bustling, trading towns. This set the stage for an important grouping of around a dozen struggle lawyers from the Unity Movement to take up land cases across the rural Eastern Cape. In particular, Wycliffe Tsotsi, Richard Canca, and Mda Mda became deeply involved in the politics of the Transkei Territories, which became apartheid South Africa's first tribal Bantustan in 1963 under the leadership of Chief Kaiser Matanzima.[4]

The Unity Movement has often been seen as a debating society for middle-class Black professionals, long on left-wing rhetoric, short on practical action (Lodge 1983: 87; Simons and Simons 1983: 546), so their attempt to use the courtrooms as a focus of popular political mobilization is intriguing. Intellectually, they had been formed by the radical currents of the 1930s and 1940s (Gevisser 2007: 31–45). Mda Mda, for instance, remembered that his interest in politics stemmed from learning the history of the French Revolution when at mission boarding school.[5] While at the University of Cape Town, Richard Canca (1948) had written an MA thesis on the Transkei *Bunga*: the segregated district councils in the Transkei Territories that were dismantled in the 1950s to make way for the even less democratic tribal authorities and Bantustans. (He was one of only half-a-dozen Black students in that university.) Similarly, another prominent Unity Movement lawyer, Livingstone Mqotsi, later wrote *House of Bondage* (1990), a loosely fictionalized account that told the story of a group of peasants driven into poverty by traditional leaders co-opted by the apartheid government. These Unity Movement critiques of the tribal authorities in many ways anticipate the famous polemic written by Govan Mbeki, *The Peasants Revolt* (1964), against the Bantustan project and the chieftaincy, which would be smuggled into exile and published by Penguin. For while Mbeki was a leader in the rival ANC, he had worked closely with Transkei's Unity Movement leaders in the 1940s and certainly shared their radical critique of the chieftaincy (Bundy 1998; Mbeki 1992).

Canca, Mda, and Tsotsi saw themselves as protagonists in "the progressive wing of the Unity Movement"—part of "the new generation of African intelligentsia that [saw] their own disabilities as being inextricably bound up with the disabilities of their own people."[6] Such rural lawyers commonly "dispensed free advice to needy people . . . and often made their car—[typically] the only one in the area—available for the use of others" (du Preez 2003: 49). Yet this professional elite was well aware of the tenuous threads that connected them to the poor communities that they sought to represent in court. Black professionals were a tiny minority: African lawyers numbered no more than a few dozen in a society where the vast majority had received only a few bare years of education. Lawyers were marked as distinctive elite by their professional status, their extensive education, their comparative wealth, and their homes and motor cars. Mda Mda later remembered how Black lawyers driving across the Transkei on political cases would be welcomed by illiterate villagers with a double-edged compliment: "These educated people are not lost; they are truly on our side."[7] Indeed popular sayings mocked "'the show-off, educated': For too much learning could purged one of humanity" (Gibbs 2014: 36).

A couple of documents provide evocative suggestions as to how the rural Eastern Cape's radical Unity Movement lawyers understood the complex relationship between elite legal activism and the rural communities that they served. Richard Canca, for instance, wrote a legal deposition in support of Sabata Dalindyebo, a dissident Thembu paramount chief, which included the striking comment: "Chiefs have been reconciled to their position of equality with educated commoners in the leadership of their people."[8] Other attorneys boasted: "Lawyers have very high prestige and you will find at weddings people are anxious to please them. . . . They invite me into their homes for advice. . . . People take it for granted that I am a leader" (Kuper 1964: 79).

There was a final irony. Because the Bantustan project imposed an authoritarian vision of indirect rule onto the Native Reserves, the course of rural struggles sometimes pitted dissenting traditional leaders and rural communities against "sellout" chiefs who enjoyed the backing of the apartheid state. We see this in the western districts of Transkei, where lawyers such as Richard Canca and Mda Mda played a significant role in the attempts of the Thembu king, Sabata Dalindyebo, to defend his authority from Chief Kaiser Matanzima—a jumped-up chief, lacking royal legitimacy. Throughout the 1950s and early 1960s, Chief Kaiser Matanzima aggressively expanded his chieftaincy, using it as a springboard to the prime ministership of the Transkei Bantustan. Thus radical Unity Movement lawyers—described by rivals as Trotskyites—found themselves defending "the true traditional leaders" and owners of the land.[9]

The Liberal Party (est. 1953), largely based in Natal, provided another focus of land rights activism in the first decades of apartheid. Unlike the "Trotskyite" and Africanist ideologies of the assertively *Non-European* Unity Movement lawyers, it was a self-consciously multiracial organization. Some of its leaders—for example, Alan Paton and Peter Brown—had formed the party, disillusioned about the United Party's inability to mount a meaningful opposition to the National Party, which came into power in 1948. Other important leaders, such as Selby Msimang and Archie Gumede, had drifted away from the ANC as the predominant Johannesburg faction, under Nelson Mandela, had drawn closer to the Communist Party in the 1950s (Lodge 1983: 87; Vigne 1997).

The Liberals concentrated particularly on protecting the land rights of so-called "Black Spot" communities: land owned or held by Africans that was threatened by apartheid's forced removals. Natal's checkerboard geography was an important factor (Hart 2004: 73; Walker 1981): for it included nineteen mission reserves (totaling 147,000 acres) and forty-eight locations (totaling 2.2 million acres) Accordingly, the Liberals formed associations with Black landowners threatened by eviction—with men such as Eliot Mngadi. Mngadi's father had been part of a syndicate that bought a farm at Roosboom in the early years of the twentieth century; and in 1958 he became secretary of the Northern Natal Landowners Association, an organization sponsored by the Liberals (Brown 1989). Strikingly, Mngadi had once worked as a messenger in the magistrates' courts; he now left this job—rather than implicate himself in the "machinery of oppressive laws"—explaining in a letter (Sato 2002: 4):

> I would, therefore, be too pleased to resign in favour of becoming an organiser of African Landowners. I feel Africans desperately need an organiser, before they are removed to the [Native] reserves, where they will fall under the Bantu Authorities Act, and that will be the end of their freehold title deeds.[10]

The Liberal Party's vision of land rights activism also drew on the deep traditions of Christian humanitarianism in Natal. Many African landowners lived on land established by Christian (*kholwa*) communities in the late nineteenth and early twentieth century. Thus the series of court cases defending the threatened rural communities were accompanied by mass prayer meetings and petitions. The most famous was at Roosboom in September 1963. "We make this appeal to our White fellow Christians and fellow citizens" (Sato 2002 11):

> *Pray for us that we may be given courage and be left in peace on our lands.*
> *Speak for us who have no voice to speak for ourselves.*
> *Intercede for us with the Government and the authorities.*
> *Work for us so that this terrible plan of removal may be abandoned.*
> *In the name of God, and of our Lord Jesus Christ. Amen.*

In the 1960s these struggle lawyer networks were unraveled by apartheid oppression. Across South Africa the apartheid government's political crackdown—most famously the 1963 Rivonia trial that jailed Nelson Mandela—forced many into prison, exile, or quiescence. Working in the Native Reserves carried additional dangers. Armed with repressive Native legal codes, even more despotic than the emergency regulations of "White South Africa," the chief magistrates of the Native Reserves (and later the chief ministers of the Bantustans) crushed dissidence. This was epitomized by "banishment": an extrajudicial process, instituted in the 1927 Native Authorities Act, which exiled dissidents to remote districts (Badat 2013: 33). Thus the Unity Movement was crushed in the Eastern Cape as many leaders, including Mqotsi and Tsotsi, fled into exile (Tsotsi n.d.).[11] Similarly, many Liberal leaders were also detained and banned during this period, and the party eventually disbanded in 1968 after apartheid legislation forbade multiracial political parties.

Nonetheless, the genealogies of legal activism were not entirely unstitched. Most broadly, memories of these mid-century legal struggles suffuse the accounts of many contemporary Black lawyers and judges born in the Bantustans. The memoirs of Dumisa Ntsebeza—the human rights lawyer and Truth and Reconciliation Commission commissioner—are saturated with the stories of how his home in Cala district held out against the chieftaincy claims of Kaiser Matanzima (Bell and Ntsebeza 2003: 129–41).[12] We can also trace individual professional genealogies. The experience of Richard Canca is emblematic. After his health was broken by repeated arrest and detention in the early 1960s, he retreated from political activism and built a thriving commercial practice in the Transkei Bantustan. Yet he continued to take the occasional political case—for instance, bailing student activists of the 1970s. He also extended articles of clerkship (i.e., legal apprenticeships) to a younger generation of political dissidents whom most other lawyers were too scared to train (Pikoli and Weiner 2013: 33–34).[13] Thus important strands of legal activism would continue deep into the Bantustan era and beyond—as we shall see below.

RADICAL DOCTRINES OF DISSENT

If white magistrates in the Native Reserves had operated in a patriarchal, sometimes brutal, manner in the middle years of the twentieth century, then the exercise of state authority in the legal sphere became even more clannish in the Bantustan era (1963–94). The ten "self-governing" Bantustan territories agglomerated from the old Native Reserves took over the legal machinery of the magistrates' courts and administration. The four that opted for "full independence"—Transkei (1976), Bophuthatswana (1977), Venda (1979), and Ciskei (1981)—carved out their own judicial divisions. These were the decades when homeland prime ministers used the courtrooms and legal processes for patrimonial aggrandizement, sometimes brutally.

The courtroom struggles within chieftaincies and rural communities, which had been characteristic of the mid-twentieth century, intensified in the Bantustan decades. Because the homeland project was based on notionally tribal lines, Bantustan prime ministers, whose authority partially derived from their positions in the chieftaincy, were obsessed by the possibility of rival claimants and dissenting chieftaincies. Andrew Manson and Bernard Mbenga's (2011) studies of Bophuthatswana emphasize Prime Minister Lucas Mangope's paranoia. He used apartheid codes of customary law to push rivals out of chieftaincies. His loyalist traditional leaders had dissidents arraigned before the newly instituted chief's courts where defense lawyers were forbidden. Rural Betterment directives—cattle culling measures, forced removals, and so on—were punitively used against rebellious districts. Today, the Bophuthatswana / North West archives are stuffed full of documents detailing these measures—all signed by Chief Lucas Mangope.[14]

A capricious, patriarchal vision of legal process lay at the heart of the Bantustan project. "All is not well . . . [and] we call upon the ancestors to come and arbitrate," lamented the praise singer during the trial of one dissenting paramount chief, King Sabata Dalindyebo (Streek and Wickstead 1981: 314). It was to no avail. In 1980 King Sabata was humiliated in court—accused of treason against the Transkei Bantustan—and then forced into exile with the African National Congress in Lusaka.

At the same time, the Bantustan project offered new opportunities for Black lawyers to rise within professional and government hierarchies: as magistrates, government prosecutors, and state law advisers. Indeed, the majority of Black law students in the 1970s and 1980s went to university on Bantustan bursaries. There was also plenty of commercial legal activity for homeland lawyers (Gibbs 2017). Within the confines of segregated South Africa, law remained the profession for a narrow elite: as late as 1993 there were seven thousand lawyers in the country, of which only seven hundred were Black. Law (along with medicine) was the acme of professions open to Black Africans in the Bantustans and, more widely, apartheid South Africa (Agbakoba and Carver n.d.; Moseneke 2016; Ndima 2004).

In the mid-1970s there was an intriguing revival of struggle lawyer networks inside and connected to the Bantustans. Matthews Phosa (today an ANC heavyweight) set up his law firm in Eastern Transvaal. An important knot of KwaZulu magistrates—including Pius Langa and Sandile Ngcobo—left government service and joined the Durban bar, from which they would oppose the KwaZulu Bantustan government that had once employed them.[15] (Langa and Ngcobo would become the second and third chief justices of the postapartheid constitutional court.) The rural Eastern Cape remained the main hub of the Black legal profession. Thus the largest African law firm of the 1970s and early 1980s, Sangoni Partners, was based in Transkei. Sangoni's firm used the profits they made from Transkeian independence to cross-subsidize the many political cases they defended in the courts.[16] The firm's founding partner, Themba Sangoni, would later become judge president of the Eastern Cape court.

More broadly, the 1970s was a time when land rights activism was being broadly redefined in rural South Africa. With the collapse of peasant productivity during the Bantustan era, educated activists became increasingly interested in the new doctrines of community development—for example, Paulo Freire's *Pedagogy of the Oppressed*—that confronted deepening levels of rural poverty. Most notably, Steve Biko's Black Community Programmes built health clinics, schoolrooms, and cooperatives across Transkei and the rural Eastern Cape (Hadfield 2016). His partner, Mamphela Ramphele, continued this work when she was banished to the rural Transvaal. She later wrote striking project reports critiquing the deeply unequal patterns of patriarchy and customary law that, in her opinion, stymied meaningful community development and left the weakest members of society most vulnerable (Ramphele and Ramalepe 1984; Ramphele 1991).

We find these strands of rural activism in the biographies of many prominent Black lawyers—particularly if we look at their activities beyond the courtroom. Dumisa Ntsebeza, for instance, had started his legal studies while jailed in Transkei for treason in the 1970s. (The charges against him included claims that he had run a subversive poultry program in his home of Cala—a plausible allegation given that the district remained a hotbed of rural dissidence.) While Dumisa concentrated on political cases when working at Sangoni Partners—for instance, he helped found the Prisoner Welfare Education Programmes that supported political detainees—rural activism remained important for the Ntsebeza family. His cousin, Bathandwa Ndondo, was working as a fieldworker for the Health Care Trust in Cala district when

Fig. 7.1. Mamphela Ramphele. She was banished to the rural Transvaal. Photo courtesy Nelson Mandela Foundation and NMF/Eccentrics.

he was assassinated by apartheid police in 1985. Dumisa's younger brother, Lungisile, worked in land rights NGOs and later wrote a searing history of the chieftaincy in Cala district (Bell and Ntsebeza 2003: 141–78; Ntsebeza 2006).[17]

The biography of yet another Unity Movement lawyer, Fikile Bam, who had been jailed on Robben Island from 1964 to 1975, provides one more example of how the Bantustans shaped the political trajectories of the small coterie of struggle lawyers. In the mid-1970s Fikile Bam served his articles as an attorney with Richard Canca, retrained as an advocate at the Johannesburg bar, and then returned to the Eastern Cape, where he made a prosperous living, becoming chair of the Transkei Bar Association. During the course of his successful legal career, he had many run-ins with authority. Bam became one of the prominent leaders within the Black Community Programmes, setting up an agricultural cooperative in his home village. When Matanzima's government cracked down on the Black Consciousness Movement in 1977,

Fig. 7.2. Fikile Bam, Unity Movement lawyer. Photo by Brett Eloff, used with permission from Tiso Blackstar Group.

Bam was briefly swept into Transkei's jails. Yet Bam's rural activism continued throughout the 1980s, and in 1995 he was made the first judge president of South Africa's Land Claims Court, serving until his death in 2011.[18]

Perhaps the most important institutional development in land rights activism of the 1970s was the formation of the Association for Rural Advancement (AFRA) by stalwarts associated with the (disbanded) Liberal Party in Natal. In one sense, AFRA drew deeply on long-standing traditions of liberal land rights activism in Natal. Importantly, Peter Brown, AFRA's founding chairman, had been deeply involved in the Liberal Party's attempts to prevent forced removals at Roosboom in the 1960s. At the same time, many of the people connected to AFRA broadly drew from the same radical intellectual currents that had galvanized Black Consciousness and Unity Movement activists in the Eastern Cape in the 1970s. In particular, the younger generation of fieldworkers employed by AFRA were shaped by the radical student movements. Cherryl Walker, for instance, had started as a student volunteer with the Church Agricultural Project, tasked with challenging forced removals in the Weenen district of Natal. Her memoirs include a photograph of a lanky, young student activist and trainee lawyer, Geoff Budlender, sitting in the thornveld, collecting depositions from evicted farmworkers (Walker 2008).[19] At the time, Budlender was a prominent leader in the radical National Union of South African Students (NUSAS). He would later become a founding member of the human rights NGO the Legal Resources Centre; in the 1990s he would lead the Department of Land Affairs, before returning to human rights law (Budlender 2007). Walker too would have a prominent postapartheid career as KwaZulu Natal's first land (restitution) claims commissioner.

The well-documented tensions within AFRA also provide an insight into how the radical doctrines of the 1970s sometimes jarred the older liberal traditions of land activism. Peter Brown's vision of land rights had been shaped by his lifelong friendship with the chair of the Northern Natal Landowners Association, Elliot Mngadi. Thus Brown persistently argued that AFRA's limited resources were best directed toward court cases they were likely to win. He thought legal fees were best spent defending rural communities that lived on land owned by African landowners or church authorities (Cardo 2010: 279–81). By contrast, younger radicals saw Black landowners as rentier elites and paid far more attention to the deep inequalities within these rural communities (Alcock 2014: 2449–509).[20] They argued that AFRA's mission lay more broadly in conscientizing and politicizing the rural poor. We see these concerns in the trajectory of Sizani Jean Ngubane, AFRA's second fieldworker. She would go on to run a legal rights advice office in rural Natal (Cardo 2010: 286), convene the Women's National Coalition, found the Rural Women's Movement, and, later, win numerous international human rights awards, including the Ruth Selwyn Award for Achievement in Empowering Women and Girls.[21]

A second line of tension concerned the strategic purpose of land rights court cases. Human rights lawyers self-consciously took court cases that would carve out legal precedents thus enlarge the spaces of human freedoms. Yet some proponents of this strategic, legalistic approach tended to stay away from "sticky" land rights disputes that involved multiple, antagonistic claimants.[22] This was one reason why the Church Agricultural Project (CAP), which had been a prime mover in bringing land and eviction cases to court in the 1970s, later found itself marginalized by some of Natal's human rights lawyers. In the mid-1980s, CAP was embroiled in internecine disputes and faction fighting, sparked by rivalries over land and resources, after twenty thousand black labor tenants were evicted from Weenen's white farms into the neighboring Msinga district of the KwaZulu Homeland. One notorious dispute involved the Zwane and Sithole clans. The latter was backed by an influential minister in the KwaZulu government, Chief Owen Sithole, who used the authoritarian powers of Native legal codes to banish his Zwane rivals. However, the CAP's appeal for legal aid in support of the Zwanes—"a small tribe . . . bullied by a big neighbour"—largely fell on deaf ears.[23] Apparently the object of land rights activism was to expose white oppression, not interfere in internecine faction fighting.[24]

Thus the questions about the purpose and scope of legal activism—which elite Unity Movement lawyers had wrestled with in the 1950s and 1960s when they worked with illiterate rural communities—also confronted the land rights activists of the 1970s and early 1980s.

LAWYERS FOR HUMAN RIGHTS

In the final decade of apartheid, human rights organizations, particularly Lawyers for Human Rights (est. 1979) and the Legal Resources Centre (est. 1980), emerged as a significant force in South Africa. At first critics of this human rights activism argued that it was the vehicle of a coterie of prosperous, liberal, white lawyers largely based in South Africa's main cities. Initially, the Black Lawyers Association (est. 1977) distanced itself from Lawyers for Human Rights. There were also complex racial tensions among the lawyers working for the LRC—symbolically played out in hard-fought table tennis matches between Geoff Budlender and Mohammed Navsa—not least because the Johannesburg office was dominated by "the NUSAS boys": young white lawyers who had grown up together inside the small, clubby world of radical NUSAS politics.[25]

However, the South African legal field was rapidly expanding on many fronts in the 1980s, not least in the Bantustans. Symptomatically, in these years the LRC established three new offices that took on rural casework and hired heavyweight Black lawyers.[26] Its Grahamstown office, for instance, employed Adv. Lex Mpati (now judge president of the Supreme Court of Appeals) as its in-house counsel. The Durban office's lawyers included Sandile Ngcobo, who would go on to become the third chief justice of the postapartheid constitutional court. Most significantly, Fikile Bam became the founding director of the LRC's Port Elizabeth office in 1986—the first Black principal of any South African human rights organization. By the end of the 1980s—after a passionate, sometimes sharp, series of debates (Bizos 2007: 429–32)—a much broader group of lawyers and activists were affiliated to what might be broadly described as human rights organizations and legal initiatives.[27] The National Association of Democratic Lawyers (est. 1987) provided a home for many of these lawyers. Its founding president was Dumisa Ntsebeza.[28]

Importantly, legal rights activists reached into the Bantustans, confronting the patriarchal legal codes that underpinned homeland authorities on three broad fronts. First, the well-resourced LRC offices—which received much of their funding from the Ford Foundation, the doyen of international human rights activism—took up land and chieftaincy cases across rural South Africa.[29] The Johannesburg offices took cases across the Transvaal; Durban reached into rural Natal and the KwaZulu Homeland; Port Elizabeth and Grahamstown offices were active in the rural Eastern Cape. These legal cases were also buttressed by a slew of land rights NGOs, established in the 1980s, such as the Transvaal Rural Action Committee, the Grahamstown/Border Rural Committee, and the Surplus People Project. By the late 1980s these NGOs had formed campaigning coalitions, such as the National Committee Against Removals. Perhaps their most notable victory occurred in the rural Eastern Cape, where a campaign led by the Border Rural Committee prevented the forced removal in the Peelton district (Cardo 2010: 271–300; James 2007: 36–40; Wotshela 2001).

Second, the LRC led "social rights" court cases concerning the payment of government pensions, a vital mainstay for most poor rural households. This started with a commission of inquiry and a series of reports into the KwaZulu Homeland—some written by AFRA fieldworkers (Ngubane 1984)—that uncovered entrenched patterns of corruption. Chiefs and headmen demanded bribes to sign vital identity documents; local officials stole monies; senior officials balanced the books by removing pensioners from the payroll. Following this issue across South Africa's Bantustans, the LRC uncovered more politicized patterns of abuse. In the Ciskei Bantustan, for instance, loyalist chiefs and headmen refused to provide identity documents to pension claimants who were suspected ANC supporters. In Bophuthatswana, dissident villages opposed to the rule of Chief Lucas Mangope were boycotting their state pensions. Eventually, a series of high-court judgments ruled that all pensioners had a right to receive pensions from the Bantustan authorities, and a wave of cases brought to local advice centers checked many of the most egregious forms of patriarchal abuse.[30]

Third, in the final years of apartheid, civic activists challenged chiefly power in many districts of South Africa: they led squatter movements onto unused commonage; they chased away (and sometimes killed) unpopular chiefs (Bank and Southall 1996). In the wake of the wave of counter-repression that followed—organized by Bantustan chiefs, vigilantes, and security forces—a slew of human rights organizations, such as Lawyers for Human Rights, sprang up in the Bantustans (Manson 2011).[31] Cumulatively, these allegations of human rights violations, relayed through powerful international NGOs such as Human Rights Watch, played an important role in checking chiefly power and defenestrating the Bantustan supporters of the apartheid government.

These legal challenges to the Bantustans also initiated a new generation of lawyers into legal activism. The local branch of Lawyers for Human Rights in Bophuthatswana, for instance, was founded by Pansy Tlakula and Mogoeng Mogoeng.[32] The former went on to take a high-profile series of human rights posts in postapartheid South Africa; the latter became South Africa's fourth chief justice of the constitutional court.

THE TRIUMPH OF COMMUNAL RIGHTS

In one sense, the resurgence of human rights activism in the 1980s played an important role in shaping the constitutional order of postapartheid South Africa. The expertise that legal and land rights activists had amassed in the 1980s gave them entrée into the technical committees that drafted key parts of the constitution, as South Africa moved toward its first democratic elections in 1994. Many also served spells in various parts of postapartheid government, working on issues such as land rights, social rights, and human rights legislation. Minister Derek Hanekom's leadership of the Department of Land Affairs from 1994 to 1999 marked the apogee of the land rights movement. Hanekom's director general was Geoff Budlender, the former director of the Legal Resources Centre. Many more activists from the land rights movement also took senior posts in the department.

The officials working for Hanekom and Budlender, shaped by their experience of land activism in the 1980s, took a distinctive view of the land question (James 2000, 2007). Questions of land rights and citizenship (and not productive relations) were given central prominence.[33] "The resolution of the land question ... lies at the heart of our quest for liberation from political oppression [and] rural poverty," Hanekom told parliament (Walker 2005: 820). In their first years in office, they focused on protecting the rights of labor tenants and farmworkers. Thereafter, the department drove forward an ambitious series of land restitution cases (Cousins and Claassens 2005). Indeed, one of the first large land restitution cases restored farmlands in Weenen district to evicted farmworkers and was managed by the Church Agricultural Project.

The centerpiece of Hanekom's and Budlender's legislative efforts was a new Land Rights Bill, which sought to democratize the system of tenure in the Native Reserves by shifting power from chiefs to communities. The legislation—which was predominantly written by white, middle-class activists—did not replace the patriarchal chiefs with individualized notions of land rights. Rather, it attempted to codify an idealized version of African land rights: one in which property would not be exclusive and proprietary, but shared within overlapping social networks. James (2007: 9) wryly suggests that this complex vision of land reform inevitably led to "the restocking of the South African countryside with legal experts and judicious mediators." The legislation—which sought to balance the executive power invested in communal property associations against the human rights of individuals—was extremely lengthy and convoluted (Cousins and Claassens 2005). Additionally, individual restitution cases often required endless arbitration. This "nested" vision of African land rights, in which property was held by many claimants, inevitably led to multiple, conflicting land claims that were sometimes dragged into the courts.[34]

Cherryl Walker's memoir (2008: 107–42) of her time as KwaZulu Natal's land commissioner carries a beautifully told case study of one intricate land claim on the shores of Lake St Lucia, which was resolved after last-minute negotiations involving different branches of the Mbuyazi clans. Yet elsewhere she detailed how other land claims spontaneously combusted, having "enflame[d] destructive local conflicts about the process of community definition, boundary demarcation and land allocation" (Walker 2005: 820; also Delius 1996: 224). Indeed, a series of land claims just below the St Lucia nature reserve, at Reserve Four, stalled for over a decade as rival clans and claimants fought over the lucrative revenues from mining and forestry that were due to be paid into tribal authority coffers. Commercial lawyers, scenting lucrative legal fees, aligned themselves with rival factions.[35]

In 1999, Hanekom and Budlender were ousted, and their centerpiece Land Reform Bill scrapped. The new team at land affairs under Thoko Didiza—who hailed from a landowning *kholwa* family—were far more sympathetic to the arguments made by the Congress of Traditional Leaders of South Africa (CONTRALESA): that chiefs were guardians of the land. In the following decade, land reform debates were dominated by Didiza's Traditional Courts Bill (2003) and accompanying Communal Land Rights Act (2004). Controversially, this legislation sought to place land in the old Native Reserves / Bantustans in the hands of traditional leaders and their newly instituted traditional councils. It was contested in the courts for the best part of a decade in a legal challenge led by the Legal Resources Centre.

Perhaps one aspect of this much-discussed controversy deserving more attention is that the leading protagonists on both sides of these land rights debates were drawn from the legal profession.[36] Land activists associated with the Legal Resources Centre—such as Geoff Budlender—were veterans of the 1970s and 1980s land and legal activism. The same was true of their adversaries. While not a lawyer by training, Thoko Didiza had worked at the Diakonia Ecumenical Church Agency when it shared offices with the Legal Resources Centre in the 1980s, and hired a number of old land rights lawyers to help prepare the government case.[37] Moreover, the two best advocates for CONTRALESA were Chiefs Pathekile Holomisa and Mwelo Nonkonyana, both lawyers practicing at the Transkei Bar, who owed their prominence to their legal knowledge (Gibbs 2014: 161–62, 164–65).

Lawyers such as Holomisa and Nonkonyana explained themselves, not as defenders of patriarchal traditions, but as promoters of African/indigenous rights (Holomisa 2007, 2009).[38] Pathekile Holomisa, in particular, was deeply rooted within struggle lawyer circles and well versed in the lexicon of rights. In the early 1980s he had trained with Hintsa Siwisa (a notable ANC-linked lawyer in the Eastern Cape), taking cases against the apartheid authorities and the Ciskei Bantustan. Only when the Bantustan project was collapsing inside Transkei did Holomisa take up his chieftaincy and the leadership of CONTRALESA. Initially, Holomisa was involved in ANC-led attempts to extricate the chieftaincy from the Bantustan project. In the Transkei, for instance, CONTRALESA activists and lawyers undermined Matanzima's authority by promoting the rival Dalindyebo chieftaincy. This was a continuation of the legal struggles that went back to the 1950s (Holomisa 2009: 159–62).[39]

This so-called Africanist group drew their own conclusions from South Africa's long history of land struggles. They made the argument that the chiefs, no longer encumbered by apartheid laws, should govern the postcolony according to their own customary ways (Holomisa 2007, 2009). Sonwabile Mancotywa—a trained lawyer and close ally of Pathekile Holomisa—epitomizes the subtleties of their positioning. In the closing years of apartheid, Mancotywa had made his name in ANC circles by speaking out against "tribalism" and "secessionism" at a moment when many chiefs were calling for the Bantustans to enjoy devolved, federal powers in the postapartheid dispensation.[40] But as head of the National Heritage Council in the 2000s, he turned to the chieftaincy as a symbol African nationalism. In 2008 his "Ubuntu for Nation-Building" campaign came to the Thembuland districts of Transkei to hold a celebration of King Sabata Dalindyebo's life and legacy. Pathekile Holomisa and Mwelo Nonkonyana flew into Mthatha to sit on the main stage next to Mancotywa. Their speeches described King Sabata Dalindyebo as a "humble leader, who . . . sacrificed his life . . . for the emancipation and the freedom of his people," and who epitomized the values of ubuntu, "the most precious heritage of African culture that can contribute to nation-building."[41]

Such was the philosophy underpinning the Traditional Courts Bill (2003) and Communal Land Rights Act (2004), which sought to make chiefs, as representatives of their people, the guardians of the land. These neotraditionalist lobbyists were cosmopolitan, articulate lawyers—able to cite examples of indigenous rights legislation from around the world when making their case (especially Holomisa 2009: 41–44, 108–11). For, as Barbara Oomen (2005: 2) has noted, Pathekile Holomisa's neotraditional attempt to revive the chieftaincy was congruent with global developments: "the fragmentation of the nation state, the embracing of culture, the applauding of group rights."

However, the "Africanists" would not have their way. The land rights activists who had been forced from government in 1999 regrouped in the institutions of academia and NGO activism. "Old hands" from the 1980s land rights and civic movements, such as Annika Claassens, Nomboniso Gasa, and Mazibuko Jara, for instance, played prominent roles in the University of Cape Town's Centre for Law and Society, which cranked out scores of reports on the threats to democracy posed by the Communal Land Rights Act. Umbrella groups, such as Custom Contested and the Association for Rural Democracy, provided a platform for activists such as Sizani Jean Ngubane, by now the chair of the Rural Women's Movement, to denounce the Traditional Courts Bill as abusive of the rights of women.[42] Geoff Budlender, working once again at the Legal Resources Centre, led a legal challenge that would ultimately block the government's legislative efforts.

Strikingly, two different notions of rights were argued through the courts: the government's Communal Land Rights Act was challenged by land activists in the name of women's rights. In 2010 the constitutional court ruled against the government legislation. Four years later the bill was decisively struck down by the National Council of Provinces after the parliamentary legal adviser found many passages of the bill unconstitutional. One ANC legislator vividly explained his reasons for voting against his own government: "This bill can't even be panel-beaten. We must go back and start again with a new bill and consult people who will live under this bill, [and] not just traditional leaders."[43] The question of how to define—indeed, who would define—concepts of community, land, and freedom in South Africa's chieftaincy areas remained as contested as it ever had been.

CONCLUSIONS: A EULOGY FOR JUDGE PRESIDENT FIKILE BAM

Land rights debates and legal struggles have played an important part in South Africa's history since the 1940s and 1950s, when the first generations of struggle lawyers defended rural communities from new laws and decrees of the apartheid state. Questions of land and freedom continue to resonate in contemporary South Africa too. Even if peasant production plays a relatively marginal economic role in South Africa compared to other African societies, "the land question" remains a potent symbol of dispossession and oppression in current political discourse. Moreover, many of the legal activists who started their careers working on land rights have played an important role in shaping South African constitutional thinking. The struggle lawyer in the courtroom, speaking on behalf of the poor and the marginalized, is a classic trope of the antiapartheid literature, justly celebrated by legal historians such as Richard Abel (1995).

At the same time, uncomfortable questions remain on how lawyers—an elite, clubby profession—can claim to represent the poorest, most marginal communities in South Africa. The central strand threading through this chapter has been the vexed subject of how legal elites—from the Unity Movement and the Liberal Party, to Black Consciousness activists, the land rights movement, and CONTRALESA—variously conceived or defined the rights and freedoms they were fighting for. Strikingly, all of these activists across the apartheid era articulated various ideas of communal land rights. The Unity Movement lawyers of the 1950s sometimes, despite their distaste for the chieftaincy, found themselves defending "the true chiefs" from government-backed imposters. During the same decades, Liberal Party activists made alliance with *kholwa* landowners who were leaders of tenant communities. In the 1970s and 1980s, a new generation of Black Consciousness and land rights activists promoted a more grassroots vision of community mobilization and land rights. From the late 1980s, CONTRALESA argued that chiefs were the guardians of their peoples' land rights. In consequence, perhaps it is not surprising that different ideas of communal and indigenous conceptions of rights—rather than the classic, liberal vision of individual land rights—dominated South Africa's postapartheid land reform debates after 1994 (cf. Beinart, Delius, and Hay 2018: 100–102; James 2000).

Accordingly, this chapter offers a counterpoint to the observations that are often made about "the *surprising* resurgence of traditional authority and customary law in South Africa" (Oomen 2005: 2, my emphasis). Lungisile Ntsebeza (2006) powerfully writes in *Democracy Compromised* of the antidemocratic revival of the chieftaincy (see also Claassens and Cousins 2008). From a slightly different theoretical perspective, Barbara Oomen (2005) argues that the revival of traditional leadership in South Africa follows broader global trends that have seen the resurgence of identity politics and communitarian philosophies of rights in the postcolony (also Comaroff and Comaroff 2009). By contrast, my suggestion is that if we bring a longer historical perspective to these issues, it is striking to note that land rights activists and legal elites have been grappling with these questions of how to define concepts of community, land, and freedom since the middle of the twentieth century. Continuity has been as important as change.

Therefore, one place to finish is with the eulogies delivered at the funeral service of Judge Fikile Bam. His professional vocation encapsulated the full spectrum of rural activism in all its vigor and complexity. He was first a Unity Movement stalwart in the 1950s, then a Black Community Programmes leader in the 1970s, a director of the Legal Resources Centre in the 1980s, and a founding member of a local chapter of Lawyers for Human Rights in the 1990s. He ended his career as judge president of the Land Claims Court. When Bam died of cancer in Johannesburg in 2011, the flags over the Union Buildings in Pretoria flew at half-mast. The funeral party—including some of South Africa's leading lawyers, politicians, traditional leaders, and churchmen—journeyed back to his ancestral home, Lower Goqwana, in the rural Transkei, where his body was interred. Villagers told journalists of his involvement with Black Community Programmes that had led to the building of the only primary school in the Goqwana area; of how he visited poor families and gave food parcels to the sick.[44] The archbishop of Cape Town, Thabo Makgoba, preached the sermon (Makgoba 2011):

God in Christ, the second person of the Trinity, was not afraid to leave the power and the glory of heaven, to be born amongst sheep and cattle. . . . [Fikile Bam was] a parishioner, a friend of the family . . . and a wise advisor to us, the Makgoba [clan], in our ongoing land claim. . . . Closest to his heart was how this land could be used to help the rural people of the Eastern Cape. He gave all of himself and the family should have comfort in that.

NOTES

1. Deborah James (2000) and Cherryl Walker (2008) have examined these themes, looking at the ideas of land rights espoused by the land NGOs that emerged in the 1980s.

2. I primarily draw on interviews with lawyers and land activists, both my own and those conducted by the Legal Resources Centre Oral History Project (LRCOHP) and the Constitutional Court Oral History Project (CCOHP) and found at the Historical Papers at the University of Witwatersrand. Published memoirs and the biographical files of the Gerhart-Karis Collection were my other main sources. Additionally, the Liberal Party and the Association for Rural Advancement (AFRA) deposited substantial archives at the University of KwaZulu Natal's Alan Paton Centre (APC).

3. The limited resources of litigant communities meant that commercial lawyers rarely handled these cases.

4. Author interviews: Richard Canca, Dutywa, November 7, 2008; Mda Mda, Viedgesville, November 3, 2008, September 3, 2011; Livingstone Mqotsi, East London, November 13, 2008; Carter-Karis Collection, Reel 18, Canca, R.S. (1958), "Memorandum on the difficulties and tensions arising from the implementation of the BAA in Thembuland."

5. Author interview, Mda, Viedgesville, November 3, 2008.

6. University of Fort Hare, National Heritage and Cultural Studies Centre, Livingstone Mqotsi Collection: L. Mqotsi (n.d.), "Dr W.M. Tsotsi."

7. Author interview, Mda, 2008.

8. Canca, "Memorandum."

9. Canca "Memorandum." Govan Mbeki (1964: 47)—instinctively an opponent of the chieftaincy—also reflects on this irony in some of his writings. Kaiser (2002) and Ntsebeza (2011: 35–42) provide a broad account of the Unity Movement's approach to the land question, including districts in which activists supported peasant revolts against incumbent chiefs.

10. APC, Liberal Party Collection, PC 2/9/14, Elliot Mngadi to Peter Brown, November 5, 1956.

11. Author interview, Mqotsi.

12. Likewise, Nathi Mxenjane, who later worked for the liberal Legal Resources Centre, had been given the name Mthethozima (Heavy Laws / Lawyer for Hard Times) by

his grandfather, a counselor to a traditional leader who was persecuted by the Transkei Bantustan government. Cf. LRCOHP interview, Nathi Mjenxane, September 5, 2008.

13. Author interview, Canca.

14. Indeed, Justice Bess Nkabinde hails from a chiefly family that faced such harassment—cf. CCOHP interview, Bess Nkabinde, December 14, 2011.

15. CCOHP interview, Pius Langa, December 1, 2011.

16. Author interview, Dumisa Ntsebeza, Sandton, August 26, 2009. Of course, the opportunities for commercial law in the Bantustans were nothing compared to the fees earned in legal centers such as Johannesburg. Intriguingly, human rights lawyers who practiced at the Johannesburg bar, such as George Bizos and Sydney Kentridge, received lucrative briefs from the captains on mining and industry even when they were persona non grata with the apartheid government. Ismail Mahomad, who also practiced at the Johannesburg bar, was probably the only Black lawyer in all of South Africa who tapped into these lucrative networks (Bizos 2007: 143, 307, 403, 428).

17. Karis-Gerhart Collection, reel 94, biographical files (Dumisa Ntsebeza): "The Chicken Coop Trial."

18. LRCOHP interview, Fikile Bam, November 29, 2007, Karis-Gerhart Collection, reel 98, biographical files (Fikile Bam); Bam F (n.d.). "Legal problems of the rural poor in South Africa," unpublished manuscript.

19. Author interview, Creina Alcock, Mdukatshani, January 3, 2012.

20. AFRA's files of this period are also stuffed full with farm eviction cases—e.g., APC, AFRA Collection, file PC29/10/55/2 (Impendle); file PC29/10/55/3 (Compensation). Also APC, John Aitcheson Collection: PC14/5/7/29+32 (Weenen); PC14/5/5/1 (Impendle).

21. S. J. Ngubane LinkedIn profile: https://www.linkedin.com/in/sizani-ngubane-a1b67b10/?ppe=1, accessed June 15, 2017.

22. LRCOHP interviews: Chris Nicholson, December 24, 2007; Peter Rautsch, September 10, 2008.

23. University of Witwatersrand, Historical Papers, Legal Resources Centre, file 1.14.4.2, "Church Agricultural Project"; APC, Peter Brown Collection, PC16/12: Church Agricultural Project newsletter, December 1980; "Report on proposed removal of Zwane tribe, Msinga," March 1984; Creina Alcock to Chris Nicholson, LRC, March 2, 1984; Richard Lyster, LRC, to Creina Alcock March 2, 1984; Creina Alcock to Peter Brown, n.d. (1983). Cardo (2010: 290) provides another viewpoint.

24. Author interview, Alcock.

25. These complex issues were discussed in LRCOHP interviews: Bam; Geoff Budlender, December 14, 2007; Mohammed Navsa, December 4, 2007; Sydney Kentridge, February 15, 2006; Jeremy Pickering, December 18, 2007. Abel (1995) and Moseneke (2016: 3261–5740) also touch on these issues.

26. CCOHP interview, Lex Mapti, December 8, 2011; LRCOHP interview, Bam.

27. CCOHP interview, Langa.

28. Ntsebeza resigned in 1988 when the National Association of Democratic Lawyers

(NADEL) adopted the ANC's freedom charter. In the early 1990s he was a spokesman for Azanian Peoples' Organisation, a Black Consciousness Movement offshoot.

29. LRCOHP interviews: Budlender; Kentridge.

30. LRCOHP interviews: Nicholson; Clive Plaskett, September 2, 2008; Brian Sephton, December 6, 2008; Sarah Sephton, December 18, 2007.

31. CCOHP interviews: Langa; Yvonne Mokgoro, November 24, 2011.

32. CCOHP interview, Mogoeng Mogoeng, February 2, 2012; LRCOHP interview, Pansy Tlakula, July 22, 2008.

33. An early initiative, supported by the World Bank, which would have made productive family farms the center of the restitution program, was scrapped—cf. Williams 1996.

34. James (2007: 12) suggests that this program reflected land activists' "utopian" vision of land rights. Walker (2003: 820), by contrast, argues land activists were knowingly attempting the delicate task of "advancing the rights of women within customary tenure systems that are strongly patriarchal, without undermining the social networks on which these systems rely."

35. The land removals from Reserve Four in the 1980s were covered by AFRA: File PC29/10/78/1 (Reserve Four). The contentious process of postapartheid land restitution made more recent headlines: "Richards Bay Investment Millions at Risk," *Daily Maverick*, May 12, 2016; "Rich Land, Poor Man," *Mail and Guardian*, April 4, 2013. Also author interviews, Mavusa Majola, Richards Bay, August 24, 2012; Peter Rautsch, Salt Rock, August 3, 2012; Thami Shange, Durban, August 6, 2012.

36. James (2007: 22, 34–50, 156–57) addresses this issue directly. It is mentioned in passing in a number of other accounts, e.g., Southall and Kropiwnicki 2003: 79.

37. LRCOHP interview, Rautsch.

38. Also: Mark Gevisser, "That Other Holomisa," *Mail & Guardian*, September 13, 1999; Pathekile Holomisa, "Resolving Communal Land Rights a Vital Link in the Reform Process," *Business Day*, May 21, 2003.

39. Author interview, Pathekile Holomisa, Cape Town, September 18, 2009.

40. Author interview, Jeff Peires, October 22, 2008; "Mindful of Our History," *Mail and Guardian*, December 7, 2012.

41. National Heritage Council, "Fourth Annual Ubuntu Campaign" (2009), 3–4. Also Gibbs 2014: 176.

42. For instance: "Traditional Courts Bill Is Dead!," February 21, 2014, http://www.customcontested.co.za/traditional-courts-bill-dead/

43. "Traditional Courts Bill Is Dead!"

44. "Judge Fikile Bam Buried," *City Press*, December 27, 2012.

REFERENCES

Abel, Richard L. 1995. *Politics by Other Means: Law in the Struggle against Apartheid, 1980–1994*. Oxford: Taylor & Francis.

Agbakoba, Olisa, and Richard Carver. n.d. "The Status of Human Rights Organisations in Sub-Saharan South Africa." http://www1.umn.edu/humanrts/africa/safrica.htm. Accessed October 10, 2017.

Ainslie, Andrew, and Thembela Kepe. 2016. "Understanding the Resurgence of Traditional Authorities in Post-apartheid South Africa." *Journal of Southern African Studies* 42, no. 1: 19–33.

Alcock, G. G. 2014. *Third World Child: Born White, Zulu Bred*. Kindle ed. Jonathan Ball.

Badat, Saleem. 2013. *The Forgotten People: Political Banishment under Apartheid*. Leiden: Brill.

Bank, Leslie, and Roger Southall. 1996. "Traditional Leaders in South Africa." *Journal of Legal Pluralism* 28, nos. 37–38: 407–30.

Basner, Miriam. 1993. *Am I an African? The Political Memoirs of H.M. Basner*. Johannesburg: Witwatersrand University Press.

Bell, Terry, and Dumisa Ntsebeza. 2003. *Unfinished Business: South Africa, Apartheid and Truth*. London: Verso.

Beinart, William, Peter Delius, and Michelle Hay. 2018. *Rights to Land: A Guide to Tenure Upgrading and Restitution in South Africa*. Johannesburg: Jacana.

Benton, Lauren. 1999. "Colonial Law and Cultural Difference: Jurisdictional Politics and the Formation of the Colonial State." *Comparative Studies in Society and History* 41, no. 3: 563–88.

Bizos, George. 2007. *Odyssey to Freedom: A Memoir by the World-Renowned Human Rights Advocate, Friend and Lawyer to Nelson Mandela*. New York: Random House.

Broun, Kenneth S. 2000. *Black Lawyers, White Courts: The Soul of South African Law*. Athens: Ohio University Press.

Brown, Peter. 1989. "Elliot Mngadi: A Tribute." *Reality* 21, no. 1: 10–11.

Bundy, C. 1998. "Breaking the Midnight Slumber: Govan Mbeki in the Transkei, 1940–48." Seminar paper, Institute for Historical Research.

Canca, R. S. 1948. "A History of the Origin, Growth and Structure of the Transkeian Council System." MA thesis, University of Cape Town.

Cardo, Michael. 2010. *Opening men's eyes: Peter Brown and the liberal struggle for South Africa*. Jonathan Ball: Johannesburg.

Chanock, Martin. 1985. *Law, Custom and Social Order: The Colonial Experience in Malawi and Zambia*. Cambridge: Cambridge University Press.

Claassens, Aninka, and Ben Cousins. 2008. *Land, Power and Custom: Controversies Generated by South Africa's Communal Land Rights Act*. Cape Town: University of Cape Town Press.

Comaroff, John L. 2001. "Colonialism, Culture and the Law: A Foreword." *Law and Social Enquiry* 26, no. 2: 305–14.

Comaroff, John L., and Jean Comaroff. 2009. *Ethnicity, Inc*. Chicago: University of Chicago Press.

Cousins, Ben, and Aninka Claassens. 2005. "Communal Land Rights and Democracy in Post-apartheid South Africa." In Peris Jones and Kristian Stokke, eds., *Democ-*

ratising Development: The Politics of Socio-economic Rights in South Africa, 245–70. Leiden: Martinus Nijhof.

Delius, Peter. 1996. *A Lion amongst the Cattle: Reconstruction and Resistance in the Northern Transvaal*. Oxford: James Currey.

De Wet, C. 1995. *Moving Together, Drifting Apart: Betterment Planning and Villagisation in a South African Homeland*. Johannesburg: Witwatersrand University Press.

Dezalay, Sara. 2015. "Les juristes en Afrique: Entre trajectoires d'etat, sillons d'empire et mondialisation." *Politique Africaine* 138, no. 2: 5–23.

Dezalay, Sara. 2017. "Lawyers' Empire on the (African) Colonial Margins." *International Journal of the Legal Profession* 24, no. 1: 25–32.

Dubow, Saul. 2012. *South Africa's Struggle for Human Rights*. Athens: Ohio University Press.

du Preez Bezdrob, Anné Mariè. 2003. *Winnie Mandela: A Life*. Cape Town: Zebra.

Ekeh, Peter. 1990. "Social Anthropology and Two Contrasting Uses of Tribalism in Africa." *Comparative Studies in Society and History* 32, no. 4: 660–700.

Evans, Ivan. 1997. *Bureaucracy and Race: Native Administration in South Africa*. Berkeley: University of California Press.

Feierman, Steven M. 1990. *Peasant Intellectuals: Anthropology and History in Tanzania*. Madison: University of Wisconsin Press.

Gevisser, Mark. 2007. *Thabo Mbeki: The Dream Deferred*. Johannesburg: Jonathan Ball.

Gibbs, Timothy. 2017. "Mandela and Matanzima, Attorneys-at-Law." University of London, Southern Africa Seminar Series, April 24.

Gibbs, Timothy. 2014. *Mandela's Kinsmen: Nationalist Elites and Apartheid's First Bantustan*. Oxford: James Currey.

Hadfield, Leslie Anne. 2016. *Liberation and Development: Black Consciousness Community Programs in South Africa*. East Lansing: Michigan State University Press.

Hart, Gillian. 2004. *Disabling Globalisation: Places of Power in Post-apartheid South Africa*. Berkeley: University of California Press.

Hendricks, Fred T. 1990. *The Pillars of Apartheid: Land Tenure, Rural Planning and the Chieftaincy*. Stockholm: Almqvist and Wiksell International.

Holomisa, S. Pathekile. 2007. *A Double Edged Sword: A Quest for a Place in the African Sun: Records of the Congress of Traditional Leaders of South Africa, 1989–1998*. Cape Town: Lotsha Publications.

Holomisa, S. Pathekile. 2009. *According to Tradition*. Essential Books: Somerset West.

Ibhawoh, Bonny. 2013. *Imperial Justice: Africans in Empire's Court*. Oxford: Oxford University Press.

James, Deborah. 2000. "'After Years in the Wilderness': The Discourse of Land Claims in the New South Africa." *Journal of Peasant Studies* 27, no. 3: 142–61.

James, Deborah. 2007. *Gaining Ground: "Rights" and "Property" in South African Land Reform*. Abingdon: Routledge-Cavendish.

Kaiser, Robin. 2002. "Land and Liberty! The Non-European Unity Movement and the Land Question, 1933–1976." MA thesis, University of Cape Town.

Karekwaivanane, George H. 2011. "'It Shall Be the Duty of Every African to Obey and Comply Promptly': Negotiating State Authority in the Legal Arena, Rhodesia 1965–1980." *Journal of Southern African Studies* 37, no. 2: 333–49.

Kuper, Leo. 1964. *An African Bourgeoisie: Race, Class and Politics in South Africa.* New Haven: Yale University Press.

Lodge, Tom. 1983. *Black Politics in South Africa since 1945.* London: Longman.

Lonsdale, John. 1992. "The Moral Economy of Mau Mau: Wealth, Poverty and Civic Virtue in Kikuyu Political Thought." In John Lonsdale and Bruce Berman, eds., *Unhappy Valley: Conflict in Kenya and Africa,* 265–468. London: James Currey.

Lonsdale, John. 2000. "Agency in Tight Corners: Narrative and Initiative in African History." *Journal of African Cultural History* 13, no. 1: 5–16.

Makgoba, Thabo. 2011. "Funeral Sermon for Judge Fikile Bam." December 28. http://archbishop.anglicanchurchsa.org/2011/12/funeral-sermon-for-judge-fikile-bam.html

Mamdani, Mahmood. 1996. *Citizen and Subject: Contemporary Africa and the Legacy of Late Colonialism.* Princeton, NJ: Princeton University Press.

Mandela, Nelson. 1994. *Long Walk to Freedom.* London: Abacus.

Mann, Kristin, and Richard Roberts, eds. 1991. *Law in Colonial Africa.* Portsmouth, NH: Heinemann.

Manson, Andrew H. 2011. "'Punching above Its Weight': The Mafikeng Anti-Repression Forum (Maref) and the Fall of Bophuthatswana." *African Historical Review* 43, no. 2: 55–83.

Manson, Andrew & Bernard Mbenga. 2011. "'An albatross about the new government?' Bophuthatswana and the North-West Province". Paper to "Let's talk about Bantustans" Conference, Wits University.

Mbeki, Govan. 1964. *South Africa: The Peasants Revolt.* Harmondsworth: Penguin.

Mbeki, Govan. 1992. *The Struggle for Liberation in South Africa.* Cape Town: David Philip.

Mda, Zakes. 2012. *Sometimes There Is a Void: Memoirs of an Outsider.* New York: Farrar, Straus and Giroux.

Minisi Weeks, Sindiso. 2011. "The Traditional Courts Bill: controversy around process, substance and implications," *South African Crime Quarterly,* no 35: 3–10.

Moseneke, Dikgang. 2016. *My Own Liberator: A Memoir.* Kindle ed. Pan Macmillan South Africa.

Moyn, Samuel. 2010. *The Last Utopia: Human Rights in History.* London: Belknap.

Mqotsi, Livingstone. 1990. *House of Bondage.* London: Karnak.

Ndima, Dial Dayana. 2004. *Law of Commoners and Kings: Narratives of a Rural Transkei Magistrate.* Pretoria: HSRC Press.

Ngubane, S. Jean. 1984. "Pensions: The Case of Natal." Carnegie Conference Paper no. 142. Cape Town.

Ntsebeza, Lungisile. 1999. "Land Tenure Reform, Traditional Authorities and Rural Local Government in Post-apartheid South Africa." Research Report no. 3, University of the Western Cape.

Ntsebeza, Lungisile. 2006. *Democracy Compromised: Chiefs and the Politics of Land in South Africa*. Cape Town: HSRC Press.

Ntsebeza, Lungisile. 2011. "Resistance in the Countryside: The Mphondoland Revolts Contextualised." In Thembela Kepe and Lungisile Ntsebeza, eds., *Rural Resistance in South Africa: The Mpondo Revolts after Fifty Years*, 21–42. Leiden: Brill.

Oomen, Barbara. 2005. *Chiefs in South Africa: Law, Power and Culture in the Post-apartheid Era*. Oxford: Currey.

Pikoli, Vusi, and Mandy Weiner. 2013. *My Second Initiation: The Memoir of Vusi Pikoli*. Johannesburg: Picador.

Pityana, Sipho M. 2015. "The Land Question: The South African Constitution and the Emergence of a Conservative Agenda." In Ben Cousins and Cherryl Walker, eds., *Land Divided, Land Restored: Land Reform in SA for the 21st Century*, 161–74. Johannesburg: Jacana.

Platzky, Laurine, and Cherryl Walker. 1985. *The Surplus People: Forced Removals in South Africa*. Johannesburg: Ravan Press.

Ramphele, Mamphela. 1991. "Empowerment and Symbols of Hope: Black Consciousness and Community Development." In N. Barney Pityana, Mamphela Ramphele, and Lindy Wilson, eds., *Bounds of Possibility: The Legacy of Steve Biko and Black Consciousness*, 154–87. Cape Town: David Philip.

Ramphele, Mamphela, and R. Ramalepe. 1984. "Rural Healthcare: The Tears and Joy." Carnegie Conference Paper no. 204. Cape Town.

Ranger, Terence. 1983. "The Invention of Tradition in Colonial Africa." In Eric Hobsbawm and Terence Ranger, eds., *The Invention of Tradition*, 211–59. Cambridge: Cambridge University Press.

Ranger, Terence. 1993. "The Invention of Tribalism Revisited: The Case of Colonial Africa." In Terence Ranger and Olufemi Vaughan, eds., *Legitimacy and the State in Twentieth Century Africa: Essays in Honour of A.H.M. Kirk-Greene*, 62–111. London: Macmillan.

Redding, Sean. 2006. *Sorcery and Sovereignty: Taxation, Power and Rebellion in South Africa, 1880–1963*. Athens: Ohio University Press.

Sato, Chizuko. 2002. "'Pray for Us and Speak for Us': Liberals and African Landowners in Northern Natal, 1953–1965." History seminar paper, University of Durban, Natal.

Southall, Roger, and Zosa Kropiwnicki. 2003. "Containing the Chiefs: The ANC and Traditional Leaders in the Eastern Cape, South Africa." *Canadian Journal of African Studies* 37, no. 1: 48–82.

Simons, Harold Jack, and Ray Esther Simons. 1983. *Class and Colour in South Africa: 1850–1950*. London: International Defence and Aid Fund.

Streek, Barry, and Richard Wicksteed. 1981. *Render unto Kaiser: A Transkei Dossier*. Johannesburg: Ravan Press.

Tsotsi, W. M. n.d. "I Was a Refugee or Was I?" repository.forcedmigration.org/pdf/?pid=fmo:2136. Accessed June 15, 2017.

Vigne, Randolph. 1997. *Liberals against Apartheid: A History of the Liberal Party in South Africa, 1953–68*. Basingstoke: Macmillan.

Walker, Cherryl. 1981. "Mass Removals in Natal: Consolidation and Farm Evictions." AFRA Special Report no. 1, Pietermaritzburg.

Walker, Cherryl. 2003. "Piety in the Sky? Gender Policy and Land Reform in South Africa." *Journal of Agrarian Change* 3, nos. 1–2: 113–48.

Walker, Cherryl. 2005. "The Limits to Land Reform: Rethinking 'the Land Question.'" *Journal of Southern African Studies* 31, no. 4: 805–24.

Walker, Cherryl. 2008. *Landmarked: Land Claims and Restitution in South Africa*. Athens: Ohio University Press.

Westaway, Ashley. 2010. "Bare Life in the Bantustans: Remembering the Centennial South African Nation-State." PhD thesis, University of Fort Hare.

Williams, Gavin. 1996. "Setting the Agenda: A Critique of the World Bank's Rural Restructuring Programme for South Africa." *Journal of Southern African Studies* 22, no. 1: 139–66.

Wotshela, Luvuyo. 2001. "Homeland Consolidation, Resettlement and Local Politics in the Border and the Ciskei Region of the Eastern Cape, South Africa, 1960-1996." PhD thesis, University of Oxford. Unpublished.

CHAPTER 8

Elites and the Practice of (Non) accountability in Mauritius

RAMOLA RAMTOHUL AND ROUKAYA KASENALLY

INTRODUCTION

A major critique of the Mauritian democracy is the frequent incidence of corruption and nonaccountability among the elites—in both the public and private sectors. In this chapter, we approach accountability as a "liability to reveal, to explain, and to justify what one does; how one discharges responsibilities, financial or otherwise, whose several origins may be political, constitutional, hierarchical, or contractual" (Normanton 1971: 311). In recent times, accountability is often associated with the concept of good governance—a term that has been popularized in the corporate, political, and social worlds (Bovens 2007). In a democratic system, public accountability serves four key functions or purposes, namely, democratic control, enhancing the integrity of public governance, improving performance, and enhancing legitimacy (Bovens 2007). Accountability constitutes a primary restraining force on power, both political and economic or business. It also determines the quality of governance and democracy. It can be a process and an outcome where process ensures procedure, rules, and transparency in decision-making, whereas outcome concerns performance results that accrue from that process (Burnell 2008: 11). Goetz and Jenkins (2005: 45) argue that accountability failures that particularly affect the poor arise from elite "biases" as well as from elite "capture."

Mauritius, a 720-square-mile island, located in the southwestern Indian Ocean with a population of approximately 1.3 million inhabitants, is strategically positioned on the route of seafarers and merchants and has experienced successive waves of colonizers from the Dutch to the French and finally the British.[1] Mauritius did not have a native population when it was first "discovered," and its current population is principally constituted of European settlers as well as African, Indian, and Chinese immigrants. The French were the first permanent settlers on the island following French colonization in 1715. The independence of Mauritius was the result of a long series of political negotiations between local elites and British colonial authorities. At the time of independence in 1968, Mauritius was known for its heterogeneous population with a Hindu Indian majority. Moreover, until recently, the small but powerful Franco-Mauritian community controlled political and economic power in the island followed by the light-skinned Creole or colored professional and middle class. At the bottom of the hierarchy were the dark-skinned Creoles and Indo-Mauritian laborers. Class and ethnic (or ethnoracial) divisions in the population of Mauritius remain pertinent in contemporary times. The Mauritian population is composed of four ethnic groups and four major religious groups.[2]

Over the last two centuries, Mauritius has been able to use its size, geographical location, and people, among other factors, to emerge as one of the most celebrated democracies and economically sound countries in Africa. The island has been consistently ranked as one of Africa's top performers in human development, democracy, and economic freedom (Bertelsmann Foundation 2014). In fact, the Mauritian exceptionalism (Brautigam with Diolle 2009) or enigma (Miles 1999) is rather surprising, as the only real resource that the island has possessed is its people. Under postcolonial rule, Mauritius made a determined effort to ensure equal rights for all ethnic groups on the island. Equality is enshrined in the laws of the country, and the constitution explicitly outlaws all forms of discrimination based on race, sex, or religion and has provisos to guarantee parliamentary representation to minority groups through the best-loser system (UNDP 1994: 45).[3] Moreover, the state has invested heavily in the social sector, with a comprehensive welfare state that offers free health services, universal pensions, and free education to its citizens. The Mauritian economy underwent major structural adjustments after independence, moving from a monocrop sugar economy to a more diversified base of economic activities and sources of revenue that included manufacturing, tourism, and, more recently, information technology and offshore financial services (Eriksen and Ramtohul 2018: 5). Visionary political and economic leadership together with the support of the local elite have led to the successful transformation of the economy (Bunwaree 2014: 579). Despite the remarkable progress made by the country, Mauritius still has wide economic disparities. More than 50 percent of harvested land in the sugar estates, for instance, is still controlled by a few powerful Franco-Mauritian families (UNDP 1994: 45). A recent publication from the World Bank points to the fact that inequality is on the rise: "The gap between the incomes of the poorest and the richest 10 percent of households has increased by 37 percent from 2001 to 2015" (World Bank 2018: 1).

This chapter examines the interplay of ethnicity and class in the composition, development, and advancement of elites in Mauritius, analyzing how these identities extend into the operations of economic and political elites of the country. We argue that the different elites collude to protect their interests (class and ethnic) and thereby encourage and endorse nonaccountability. We examine the workings of three facets of accountability—vertical, horizontal, and social accountabilities—in illuminating the dynamics of elite corruption and anticorruption efforts in Mauritius. The chapter also situates anticorruption efforts in Mauritius as a key site in the political production of social accountability by the local media and civil society. Primary data were sourced from semistructured interviews of politicians, investigative journalists, and civil society and NGO representatives, as well as leaders of leftist groups, legal professionals, with relevant experience on this issue, and consultants working in this field both locally and internationally. Given the high level of sensitivity associated with the topic, all names have been withheld in order to protect respondents.

THE MAKING OF MODERN MAURITIUS: THE EMBEDMENT OF ELITES

Elites are generally small groups within the upper strata of society and are often related to positions of power and prestige and also to social mobility and complex procedures of inclusion and exclusion. They tend to use a variety of resources to exert and maintain their positions (Schijf 2013: 29). Elites often hold key decision-making positions in both the public and private sectors, including parliament, cabinet, political parties, economic institutions, large corporations, and cultural organizations, among others. Elites can also refer to a wider range of people such as sports champions, intellectuals, and powerful families. There is a diversity among elites, but one key aspect of commonality among them is their resistance to change (Salverda and Abbink 2013: 10). Many members of elites follow a lifelong career, moving from one sector to another (Schijf 2013: 32).

In many former colonies, elites played a vital role in mediating and driving the complex processes that ultimately led to decolonization and independence. At the same time, after independence some elite groups lost influence and power under the new regimes, while others had to reinvent themselves in new surroundings (Dülffer and Frey 2011: 2). Local or indigenous elites emerged with decolonization and independence, often led by nationalist leaders—and their groups or parties—who later became the new political and economic elites in the former colonies. However, accountability of the new ruling and economic elites in much of postcolonial Africa has been problematic. In the case of Mauritius, given its colonial history, which includes the absence of an indigenous population and the reality of settler or migrant population, the island had distinct phases in the establishment of elites, characterized by clear divisions along ethnic (ethnoracial) and class lines.

Franco-Mauritians: The Historical Elites

The very first elite on the island were the white settlers who became the *plantocrats* under the expansionist approach of the French governor, Mahe de La Bourdonnais, known for establishing a culture of rigor and discipline in making the colony a prosperous sugar colony. This elite ultimately became classified as the Franco-Mauritians and are often referred to as the "historical elites." According to the 1972 census,[4] Franco-Mauritians constitute about 1 percent of the population. Their position as elites was consolidated during the French period and further legitimized under British rule (Salverda 2015). In addition to owning large swaths of agricultural land, the white plantocrats exercised major influence in the professions, such as banking, commercial sectors, and the political and administrative arms of the government. In fact, their hold on power was absolute, but this slowly started to lessen with new clauses that were introduced to the 1885 and 1948 constitutions—which widened the franchise. With decolonization, the Franco-Mauritian elite lost its political position and status, but remained powerful in the private and business sector in the postindependence period. In the contemporary era, despite their small numbers, the Franco-Mauritians hold sway and influence. More specifically, the five families that constitute the landowning elite in the country and run a portfolio of companies in the hospitality, sugar, energy, and real estate sectors are Franco-Mauritian.

Indo-Mauritians: New Elites or Counterelites?

Slavery and coolitude[5]—two very harsh moments in human history, particularly in Mauritius—were key to the development of Mauritius as a sugar colony. Following the abolition of slavery in 1835, the huge void in labor prompted the "Great Experiment" on the part of the British to replace slaves with free workers from Asia, specifically India. At the beginning, there was a slow flow of laborers (known as indentured laborers), but by 1912 some 453,063 had been brought to Mauritius (Allen 1999; Mishra 2009). Both the free and indentured laborers were exploited by the plantocrats. But it is interesting to note that the indentured laborers were able to better organize themselves essentially through education and property acquisition. In fact, the constitutional reform of 1885 and more specifically that of 1948 introduced electoral franchise based on property that favored a progressive political inclusion of elites of all groups except the most deprived ones—the Afro-Creoles (Boudet 2016: 191). This points to the ethnoracial context of the emergence elites in Mauritius. Anthropologist Thomas Hylland Eriksen, who has written on postindependence Mauritius, argues that

> ethnic groups in Mauritian society vary in terms of degrees of group organization. This has an impact on social mobility and access to state resources. The Hindus and Sino Mauritians being the most organized communities, they can rely on group networking for access to employment resources and on their associations for lobbying on state offices. The Afro-Creoles being the least organized group, they cannot efficiently rely on association and membership for political lobbying. (1994: 14)

The social mobility and consequently the political emancipation of Indo-Mauritians were aided by two important moments. The first one was the "Grand Morcellement" process that happened between 1880 and 1920. This, to a large extent, enabled many Indo-Mauritians to change their status from wage-earning laborers living in estate camps to independent smallholders (Carter 2002: 93). As time unfolded, a small group of influential Indo-Mauritian families made their mark by purchasing land and property. Some even ventured into the sugarcane plantations and factories, but this was with limited success due to the quasi-monopolistic power of the Franco-Mauritians. The second key marker was the visit of Gandhi in 1901 followed by that of Manilal Doctor, who stayed on the island between 1907 and 1910.

These visits were instrumental as they helped the Indo-Mauritians to politically mobilize themselves.

Social mobility and political emancipation were also closely linked to the fact that many of the Indo-Mauritians invested in the education of their children, allowing a relatively quick shift from parents as laborers to sons and daughters as professionals. The embourgeoisement of this group was the very foundation of what would ultimately constitute the new political elites. When discussing the rise of the Indo-Mauritian political elite, we cannot discount the fact that it was to a certain extent supported by a small section of the colored elite. The creation of Mauritius Labor Party (MLP) is an attestation to that. Created in 1936 by Maurice Curé, a colored medical doctor, as a political party to represent the rights of workers, the MLP quickly became an antiestablishment symbol and a platform for the struggle for independence. However, as the colony slowly moved toward its independence in 1968, the MLP under the stewardship of yet another young medical doctor, Seewoosagur Ramgoolam, was seen as a Hindu-dominated party.

The Politics of Consociationalism: The Accommodation of the Elites

As the colony of Mauritius moved toward independence, there was a clear split between the pro- and anti-independence activists. This split was ethnic or ethnoracial, with the Franco-Mauritians, colored elites,[6] and Afro-Creoles resisting independence, whilst the Hindus and a large section of the Muslim community voting in favor. The general election of 1967, which mirrored a referendum on independence, saw the MLP win 54 percent of the popular votes.

The fear of what became termed as the "Hindu hegemony" was both vocal and tangible and most visible among the Franco-Mauritians and colored elites. However, Mauritius is a case study of the ballot and not the bullet (Bunwaree and Kasenally 2005), and this, to a large extent, was made possible by consociationalism that was gradually set up between 1945 and 1968. This was to ensure a smooth political transition to independence. Boudet (2016) argues that consociationalism hinges on the idea of power-sharing, a sense of autonomy, and ultimately a sense a national unity. This was evidenced by the grand alliance that constituted the first government of independent Mauritius, where all past adversaries were brought together. This speaks to the fact that the Mauritian elites are ready to make concessions and compromises across ethnic lines to safeguard their interests—a point also highlighted by Salverda (2015) when discussing the economic survival of Franco-Mauritians. The process of national unity through power-sharing among the different elites and ethnic groups was central to the immediate postindependence years. The first postindependence prime minister, Sir Seewoosagur Ramgoolam, extended a hand to include Franco-Mauritians and Sino-Mauritians in developing the hospitality and sugarcane industries as well as an export processing zone (EPZ) (Bunwaree 2005; Brautigam with Diolle 2009). This was key to ensuring a balance between the political elite (Hindus or Indo-Mauritians) and the economic elites (Franco-Mauritians).

In the decade following independence, the control of the economy by the plantocrats and the white elites showed no real sign of abatement. Government resorted to the establishment of a swath of parastatal bodies, state-owned companies and other governmental institutions that would compete in activities normally ascribed to the private sector. These included telecommunications, air transport, banking, and import of strategic goods such as rice, flour, and petroleum products, among others. These would, over time, gradually act as parallel state activities challenging the monopoly of the white elites over the economy. One of the respondents who has had a long political career mentioned that a senior minister within the first government of postindependence Mauritius confided in him that the purpose of these bodies and public companies was to allow the Indo-Mauritian elite of the country to compete in activities denied to them by the colonial authorities. A laudable initiative, it transformed with time into a parallel economy that was not always accountable to public scrutiny. In fact, such organizations are headed by political appointees who alternate within the two political parties forming government. Their governance is often shrouded by a veil of secrecy and (non)accountability on the pretext that the deals are of government to government in nature. It should be noted that since the 1990s, an increasing level of (non)accountability has been felt in the management of a number of parastatal bodies, especially when it comes to the procurement of contracts and this despite the presence of accountability legislation, such as the Public Procurement Act (2006).

New Blood in Politics: The Advent of Mouvement Militant Mauricien

Elite accommodation had strengthened itself considerably during the first postindependence government (1967–76) which witnessed a number of worrying features, namely: an economy highly fragilized by external shocks, the postponement of the general elections due in 1972, political repression and a growing intolerance against the media. From the general state of protest

Fig. 8.1. Paul Bérenger, the Franco-Mauritian current leader of the MMM. Photo courtesy La Sentinelle Ltd.

emerged a young party that espoused Marxist ideology, the Mouvement Militant Mauricien (MMM). Its founders were also inspired by the May 1968 protest march of students in Paris. Founding members of the party who were interviewed stated that what demarcated the MMM from the political parties of the time was that it was people-driven and had at heart the problems, concerns, and issues of the common person—be it the cane laborer, the port worker, or the EPZ factory worker. Another influential member of the party mentioned the capacity of the MMM to rally the voices of the common person with the intellect and capacity of young professionals ready to serve their country. In fact, when the MMM contested its first general elections in 1976, the majority of its candidates were first-timers, and a fair number hailed from the professional class.[7]

The case of the MMM is interesting for multiple reasons. Its birth and ascendency were part of an anti-establishment/anti-elite movement—similar to that of the MLP in 1936—essentially as a class-based party. However, it slowly (just like the other mainstream political parties) lost its commitment to being the soundboard of the common people to being essentially a parliamentary party. The other element is linked to the issue of the "agreed" balance between the elites when it comes to political and economic matters. The leader of the MMM since 1983, Paul Bérenger, is a Franco-Mauritian (although he does not hail from the plantocrats families). Thus, his "whiteness" (Salverda 2015) has been a systematic hindrance in claiming the post of prime minister. In the recent past, he has been subject to vitriolic hate speech, given the fact that the top job has come to be regarded as the preserve of Hindus. Therefore, it seems that elite accommodation at the level of ethnicity is limited where politics is concerned, and the crossing of elite boundaries is discouraged or rejected.

The Neoliberalism of the 1990s and 2000s

Elite power in both the political and economic spheres were to a large extent legitimized and further entrenched with the advent of the boom years of the 1990s and early 2000s, which saw a stable growth rate, practically full employment, and the setting of new sectors, namely in the offshore financial services and ICT. The business world witnessed a real expansion and the opening of new opportunities for what one of the key informants called the creation of new elites working primarily in the booming offshore sector. In fact, hundreds of management companies were created and serviced by Hindu and Muslim professionals, employing thousands of graduates. In general, the private sector maintains a good working relationship with the different governments of the day (Zafar 2011). This was confirmed by two private sector executives who were interviewed.

What is clear is that the political elites (mainly Hindu) need the economic elites (largely Franco-Mauritians) and vice versa, although the latter are at times used as the punching bag of some of the political leaders. In fact, in the recent past, their whiteness, their link to colonial powers, and their massive wealth have been exploited as part of political slogans to transfer more wealth and land to Hindu elites. In 2005, under the Navin Ramgoolam (Seewoosagur's son)[8] government, a new program was introduced called "Democratization of the Economy." The aim was to widen the circle of opportunities to Hindu and Muslim entrepreneurs. Unfortunately, the program did not achieve much except encourage a culture of patronage, and those close to the power brokers reaped favors, contracts, and other privileges. In fact, neoliberalism has to a great extent tainted the political parties and, by extension, political elites. A number of observers link the advent of clientelism, patronage, and big money in politics to the early 1990s. This will be further discussed in a later section and linked to the symbiotic relation between elites and the game of capture.

Therefore, in chronicling the trajectory of elites in Mauritius, it is evident that at the level of business and economic dealings, the relationship between the different elites transcends ethnicity and is fostered, strengthened, and ultimately maintained in the spirit of mutuality and survival. However, this is not the case in politics. A number of attempts have been made at enlarging the circle of opportunity to allow new entrants, but this has not always been done for the best of intentions. One noticeable absence has been the Afro-Creoles. This "crowding out" has its roots in colonial Mauritius and has persisted in postindependence Mauritius. A detailed assessment of Afro-Creoles is beyond the scope of this chapter, but it is perhaps relevant to mention what is described as the "Malaise Creole," a termed coined in 1993 by the Creole priest Roger Cerveaux to refer to the persistence of poverty, social problems, and political marginalization among Creoles of mixed, African, or Malagasy descent (Boswell 2006).

ELITE ACCOUNTABILITY

Accountability involves two main dimensions—answerability and enforcement (Schedler 1999). Answerability entails mechanisms of monitoring and oversight of political institutions, and includes the right to demand information as well as explanation of and argumentation for them, whereas enforcement involves rewarding good behavior and punishing unfitting behavior through sanctions. In most systems of government, the task of holding accountable those to whom power has been delegated is again delegated to a relatively small number of individuals such as senior judges, auditors general, and members of legislative public accounts committees (Goetz and Jenkins 2010: 1). Accountability is further operationalized through horizontal, vertical, and social accountability.

Horizontal accountability refers to the capacity of state institutions to check abuses by other public agencies and branches of government, primarily through the interbranch relations among the judiciary, legislature, and executive (Diamond, Plattner, and Schedler 1999: 3). These are supposed to be separate and function as institutions of checks and balances toward each other, although the reality is often different. The list of institutions or agencies of accountability in democracies has expanded to include electoral commissions, electoral tribunals, anticorruption bodies, auditing agencies, ombudsman offices, human rights commissions, and constitutional courts, among others (Diamond, Plattner, and Schedler 1999). These institutions of horizontal accountability aim to give voice and power to the people by promoting citizens' participation, but institutions such as the human rights commission and anticorruption commission are often either corrupted or deliberately weakened by the executive. The result is often democratic decline or dysfunction.

Horizontal accountability complements vertical accountability. In fact, it operates according to a bottom-up approach where citizens, the media, and civil society seek to enforce standards of good and ethical conduct for public officials. Vertical accountability is the ability of the population to hold the state accountable through elections and political parties. Vertical accountability thus focuses on the relationship between citizens and their elected representatives (Schedler 1999). The effectiveness of institutions of vertical and horizontal accountability can nonetheless be limited, as they lack the capacity to continuously oversee the day-to-day functioning of the wider state apparatus (Goetz and Jenkins 2010: 234). In such situations, civil society, often through independent media and investigative journalism, whistleblowers, and NGOs, plays a crucial role in trying to ensure that some form of accountability happens in a country. Malena et al. (2004: 3) refer to this practice as "social accountability," which is characterized by the direct involvement, beyond formal political participation, of civil society organizations and the media in the realization of accountability for politicians and state institutions. While social accountability does not directly involve sanctions on culprits, it exposes the deeds or corrupt acts committed and creates pressure on decision-makers to institute sanctions.

Accountability necessitates active agency from citizens in the democratic and civil processes of governance as well as strong institutions that deliver effectively. Political accountability often receives key focus from the media, civil society, and the international community. It is the means of control through which elected officials, parliamentarians, and public officials, including civil servants, are brought to account for their actions or inactions in the public spaces they operate in (Adejumobi 2018a: 1) and also acts as a constraint on the use of power (Lindberg 2013). Strong democratic institutions provide an incentive and environmental and political context facilitating political participation and accountability, but they may not necessarily guarantee the desired results (Adejumobi 2018a: 1). In much of Africa, weaknesses of institutions, participation, and accountability have led to a fragile liberal democracy. So far, institutions are weak and accountability limited, and weak electoral and political institutions compromise effective political and civil participation, distorting people's choices, subverting their wishes, and silencing their voices (Adejumobi 2018a: 1). In fact, weak institutions and the often unresponsive bureaucratic administrative systems are the sources of many of Africa's developmental woes, including poor enforcement of the rule of law, corruption, and mismanagement, the absence of a strong civil society, lack of competitive pressure in the delivery of public goods and services, and the inefficiency of the public sector (Kumssa and Mbeche 2004: 852).

Accountable governance is central for democratic stability and consolidation (Adejumobi 2018b: 115). A deficit in accountability at the level of governance erodes public trust and confidence, which may adversely affect the performance of governments and public institutions. Promoting credible accountability in governance will necessitate genuine efforts to strengthen state institutions, including the parliament, judiciary, public bureaucracy, and electoral body. Furthermore, nonstate actors such as the media, trade unions, professional groups, and NGOs need to be able to enjoy freedom in their activities and to challenge government actions as well. These groups also need to internalize the virtues of accountability, transparency, and internal democracy within their organizations.

As mentioned earlier, Mauritius is one of the most performant democracies in Africa (EIU Report 2018; IIAG 2017). However, democracies are far from perfect, and there has been a sustained crisis in the state of democracy across the world. One of the key features of a functioning democracy is the presence of elections—how regularly they are held, whether they are free, competitive, and fair. While Mauritius does not have rigged elections or election-related violence, as is the case in a number of African countries, its democracy is showing worrisome trends: the emergence of big-money politics, growing lack of accountability from those elected, the subjugation of the legislature by an arrogant executive operating through the tyranny of numbers, a highly ethnicized polity, and the advent of dynastic leadership within political parties (Kasenally 2017).

Mauritius scored 50 out of 100 on the 2017 Corruption Perceptions Index report by Transparency International, where 0 represents a highly corrupt state of affairs and 100 indicates negligible corruption.[9] Cables that have leaked from the US embassy refer to corruption as "pervasive and ingrained" (US Embassy in Port Louis 2008). Accordingly, a lack of accountability, including increasing corruption, is becoming a problematic feature of postcolonial Mauritius. The main drivers of corruption include the complicated connection between business interests and politics, an opaque party-financing system, as well as lack of citizen oversight and, at times, the partisan nature of investigative bodies (Jenkins 2004: 3). At the legislative level, the integrity framework of the country has long-standing weaknesses, especially the absence of an act on the right to information or regulations dealing with private sector corruption and the funding of political parties (Jenkins 2014: 1). These issues are discussed in greater detail in the next sections.

ELITES AND MAURITIAN ACCOUNTABILITY FRAMES: IMPACT AND EFFICIENCY?

So far this chapter has provided an assessment of the functioning of elites as well as an overview of accountability mechanisms in Mauritius. These two cannot and should not exist as stand-alone features in societies that aspire to be progressive, inclusive, and just. In an earlier section, allusion was made to the collusion that exists among elites across racial and economic classes to retain the status quo and thus ensure that their "rights" are unchallenged. In fact, one can observe a continuum that has evolved from the preindependence to postindependence era where the historical elites (Franco-Mauritians), the political elites (Hindus), and the new economic elites (Hindus, Muslims, and Sino-Mauritians) collude. Another worrisome trend that further legitimizes the "right to collusion" is the role that sociocultural religious bodies play in Mauritius. The latter are essentially religious bodies that champion the idea of ethnic rights and recognition. Political elites have, however, turned to these organizations to ensure that their vote banks are not jeopardized. The question that therefore begs attention is whether this collusion can be exposed and challenged and, if so, with what impact.

Stakeholders interviewed tended to link elites in contemporary Mauritius to power (institutional, economic, and political), authority, policymaking, and, most pertinently, "the power to influence policies, perceptions and decisions." Elites were seen to be represented by government—politicians and high-level civil servants—the private sector, NGOs, and academics. One respondent from the NGO sector stated that "most of the time elites have the tendency to unify their force due to their vested interests and common background in order to have control and enable them [to] further their interests in society." Membership in elites is determined by different criteria. For trade unions and similar organizations, membership tends to be open, whereas in the private and business sector, it is largely based on interests, and admission is often by selection. Some respondents stated that membership in other elite groups is determined by religion, ethnicity, and even caste in the case of the Hindu community. There was also mention of elite membership being based on the degree of closeness to politicians and political parties. In fact, one respondent from the NGO sector said that it was not easy for elites to have their ideas accepted unless they were in the good books of the government of the day.

Most of the stakeholders interviewed felt that accountability is not really

Fig. 8.2. Dr. Ameenah Gurib-Fakim, former president of Mauritius. Photo courtesy La Sentinelle Ltd.

exercised in a rigorous and sustained manner in Mauritius. One informant who has had a long political career spoke about "pseudoaccountability." It seems that the most problematic area of accountability is political accountability. Executive and legislative officeholders, once elected, tend to forget the electorate. This view, to a large extent, corroborated the recent findings of Afrobarometer Round 7, where nearly four out of five respondents felt that members of parliament (MPs) never or rarely "did their best to listen to what people have to say." Another informant from the NGO sector stated that "there is no accountability in Mauritius." In response to a question asking for an example of a successful case of accountability in Mauritius, most respondents said that they were not aware of any. One respondent from the media sector mentioned the stepping down of the former president, Dr. Ameenah Gurib-Fakim, who was compelled to resign in March 2018 following pressure from government and civil society—after the exposure in the press of her involvement in a scandal linked to her close connection with the controversial Angolan investor and businessman Alvaro Sobrinho, and the misuse of a credit card of an educational trust set up by Sobrinho for personal expenses.[10] The case is still under investigation.

DELIVERING VERTICAL ACCOUNTABILITY

As one of the levers of vertical accountability, elections have been regularly held on the island—eleven since independence—and they have all been deemed free and fair,[11] allowing for regular changes in government. Elections have been both important and popular in Mauritius, with voter turnout of 80 percent and above for most of them. However, in more recent times, voter turnout has dropped, to 77 percent for the 2019 general election and under 50 percent for a by-election in late 2017. This is, however, far from alarming, especially when compared to voter turnout in established Western democracies. This brings us to the quantity-versus-quality argument, which is increasingly being made. What is needed is to be able to assess the quality of democracy (Diamond and Morlino 2005) and that of elections (Bratton and Logan 2014).

In the case of Mauritius, the findings from Afrobarometer Round 7 provide interesting insights. Although there is an overall endorsement of the importance of democracy, just about 50 percent of the respondents expressed satisfaction with the quality of the Mauritian democracy. Significant was the growing demand for accountability, with about seven in ten respondents mentioning that accountability is more important than efficiency in government. What seems clear is that there is a notable gap between the demand for and supply of accountability, especially among political elites who do not always bother with the electorate between elections.

While Mauritius has regular changes in government through elections, a closer look indicates that there is alternation without change. In fact, over the last five decades, the same mainstream political parties have dominated the electoral scene, often through forming pre-electoral coalitions[12] (Kadima and Kasenally 2006). Political leaders face little or no contestation within their parties, a culture of dynastic politics and an electoral system (first past the post) that favors mainstream parties, as opposed to smaller ones. Reforms to the current electoral system were initiated early in this century, but the process has been stalled by some of the key political elites who fear change. This has created a stalemate, with dwindling trust in key positions within the executive and legislature.

In fact, even the legislature, which follows the Westminsterian model where parliamentary questions (PQs) give the opportunity to MPs to demand accountability from the executive, has been weakened over the different legislative assemblies. Often PQs filed for responses are left unanswered due to inadequate time and precedence given to other parliamentary matters. According to Darga (1998: 7), the capacity of parliament to ensure accountability and transparency on the part of the executive by way of PQs remains limited by the willingness of the government to provide information. He states that "nothing and no one can force a minister to give a reply to a question, except however by the pressure of civil society opinion which in Mauritius is of critical consideration" (Darga 1998: 7). This is an example of nonaccountability to an institution that is supposed to perform oversight of the executive. The weakening of these bodies of accountability has translated into dwindling trust among Mauritian citizens: where seven in ten respondents to the Afrobarometer questions said that they had "no/little trust" in the prime minister, president, MPs, ruling party, or opposition parties (Afrobarometer Round 7).

Therefore, vertical accountability in the form of elections does not seem to be very effective in Mauritius. There seems to be a lot of posturing and rhetoric from the political elites to the effect that they believe in accountability, fairness, and equality but they are far from walking the talk. The bottom line is that they have too much to lose and therefore prefer to continue the status quo. This leads to the question of whether horizontal accountability performs better as a system of checks and balances.

HORIZONTAL ACCOUNTABILITY: A MYTH?

Mauritius was one of the first states to sign the United Nations Convention Against Corruption in 2003. The current government, as well as previous ones, have listed the fight against corruption as a priority, and initiatives have been taken to tackle this challenge, although progress remains to be observed (Bertelsmann Stiftung 2018: 37). Apart from regulatory legislation, Mauritius possesses a panoply of institutions of horizontal accountability: a National Audit Office (NAO), a Public Accounts Committee (PAC), an Independent Commission Against Corruption (ICAC), a host of regulatory agencies, ombudsman offices, a National Human Rights Commission, and an Equal Opportunities Commission. Other measures include adaptation of the National Code of Corporate Governance for Mauritius (2016), endorsed by the National Committee on Corporate Governance, which is expected to contribute to transparency and the fight against corruption.[13] No doubt the list is impressive and has allowed Mauritius to receive kudos from international monitoring agencies. However, a closer look at the workings of these institutions reveals a different story, of ineffectiveness, inefficiency, absence of operational autonomy, lack of willpower to act, and a general inability to call the powerful to task. A respondent from a leftist political party and pressure group highlighted the fact that although Mauritius has legal checks and balances that should produce accountability, in practice "the elite gets away with crime." What is disquieting is the inability of one of the arms of legislature to rein in the culture of waste, which often proceeds with impunity. In fact, this has been going on for years under successive governments. The weaknesses of some of the main institutions with a mandate to ensure horizontal accountability are discussed in greater detail in what follows.

The NAO is outlined in section 110 of the Constitution of Mauritius, which also guarantees its existence as an independent public organization tasked with promoting good governance in the public sector and reporting to the national assembly on the management of public funds in all public institutions. This office was established at the time of independence and audits government expenditure on a yearly basis. Every year, the report of the NAO on public spending reveals the catalog of waste and mismanagement of public funds. Upon its publication, public opprobrium is heightened for a couple of days and then matters go back to business as usual.[14] The NAO is, unfortunately, not empowered to investigate cases of corruption, although these can be reported to the Financial Intelligence Unit, which can investigate and refer the case to ICAC. The PAC, to which the NAO report is sent, in principle should act as an oversight body when it comes to government expenditures. Unfortunately, the PAC is often a site for party faction and bickering and only rarely is able to function effectively. For many observers, the PAC is a joke. Interviewees highlighted the absence of "ownership of problems" and of "consequences for people who mismanage," citing lack of vision, incompetence, recklessness, irresponsibility, and improper planning as causes of the wastage by public institutions. Some respondents also mentioned political interference as a key factor that leads to inaction and nonaccountability. A respondent with a legal background stated that "a sense of personal responsibility in relation to the use or misuse of public funds is not part of the culture" and "to address these problems, there should be greater empowerment and personal accountability of civil servants and other public officials."

The ICAC was established in 2002 under the aegis of the Prevention of Corruption Act, as one of the anticorruption measures adopted by the government. Previous institutions with a similar mandate included the Anti-Corruption Tribunal (1984–98) and the Economic Crimes Office (ECO) (dismantled in 2001). None of these institutions has really delivered or secured any serious convictions, and they are perceived to be subject to political manipulation (Darga 2008: 93). In fact, the ECO was dismantled abruptly just as it closed in on powerful political and business leaders (Darga 2008: 93). Officially, the ICAC is accountable only to a parliamentary committee that monitors administrative aspects of its work, in view of protecting the institution from partisan political interference (Jenkins 2014). However, in reality, the lack of operational oversight implies that there is no easy way to ensure that investigations are neither buried nor used to target political opponents of the government (Transparency International 2007: 49). Furthermore, there have been a number of allegations of political bias directed at the ICAC, especially from members of the opposition, who claim that it serves as a political tool for the ruling party in government (Bertelsmann Foundation 2014). A leaked diplomatic cable from the US embassy from 2008 also reported that the ICAC was highly partisan, as "ICAC officers are all appointed by and owe their career and loyalty to the Prime Minister's Office" (US Embassy in Port Louis 2008). Interviewees confirmed the negative consequences of political nominations for accountability. One respondent from the NGO sector stated that "if institutions do have political nominations, it has been found that there are gateways for the elite and politically connected people to get through the system even after committing damages."

At the level of business elites, the private sector has been an important engine of growth in key sectors and a provider of jobs. They are required to abide by the law (which they do) and have over time created structures that allow them to coalesce to ensure that their interests are preserved. As mentioned earlier in the chapter, the most dominant players hail from the Franco-Mauritian community. In terms of accountability, their first port of call remains their shareholders. Fairness and competition are key features to ensure a level playing field. However, this has not always been the case, especially with the big players. One of the informants mentioned the absence of antitrust laws and alluded to a recent case where three listed companies (with significant common ownership and cross-board directorships) colluded to crowd out a potential foreign takeover. This did not prompt the regulators to intervene, and an inquiry was only initiated following a public outcry. It is equally interesting to note that a Competition Commission was created in 2008 with the mandate to promote competition by enforcing the Competition Act, in the interest of consumers, businesses, and the Mauritian economy. Unfortunately, the commission has been lukewarm in its intervention and has been mired in controversy concerning the nomination process of its top management. Although section 16 of the Prevention of Corruption Act deals with the private sector and can be used to prosecute corruption committed entirely within this sector, in reality the number of criminal acts in the private sector is far more limited than in the public sector, as only acts carried out without the consent of one's hierarchical superior are illegal in the private sector (Jenkins 2014: 9).

Yet no doubt the biggest bone of contention with regard to business elites is the financing of political parties. Influential businesses have perpetuated a "tradition" of giving money (most of the time undisclosed and unofficially) to the mainstream political parties and specifically their leaders. This is a means to ensure that elite interests are safeguarded irrespective of those who get into power. This practice goes against the norms of good governance, as it encourages corruption, influence peddling, and nepotism. As face-saving devices, the business world has created a "Code of Corporate Governance" and an "Integrity Pledge Project,"[15] which are essentially voluntary mechanisms that most companies have signed up to. In recent years, in the spirit of espousing a culture of transparency, many of the top one hundred Mauritian companies have started recording in their annual reports the amount they give to political parties. However, the question that must be asked is how genuine is this commitment to transparency and accountability. Judging by certain of the comments of those interviewed, there are mixed feelings:

> In many instances the private sector has been leading in terms of good governance principles, but at the same time, it can be argued that some of the prominent private sector organizations have two faces. One of them has a very ethical discourse and the other continues the culture of glass ceiling for anyone not belonging to their circle/community/caste and continues with cash donations to political parties and politicians. (Interview conducted by email on June 22, 2018)

Respondents also linked (non)accountability to the activities of sociocultural organizations where certain sociocultural religious bodies wield influential power within the Mauritian polity. One respondent with a legal background stated that "some sociocultural lobbies use political pressure as they claim to have the numbers to influence electoral outcomes." Indeed, one of the contradictions of the Mauritian setup is its duality as a secular country in which the government provides subsidies to religious bodies to promote religion and culture (APRM 2010). The government's decision to subsidize sociocultural and religious organizations may be one of the factors that deepened the involvement of these socioreligious groups in political affairs (Chan

Low 2012).¹⁶ This has created a controversial connection between the leaders of sociocultural religious bodies and mainstream political leaders, who in return for support have bestowed favors and patronage. Leaders of these religious organizations are often nominated as board members of parastatal bodies and state companies, leading to frustration among the population about a lack of meritocracy (Hilbert 2012). The link between politicians and sociocultural organizations assumes greater intensity at the approach of general elections, when some of these organizations endorse a given political party or lobby for or sponsor candidates from their linguistic or ethnic group so that the latter obtain electoral tickets from the main political parties (Ramtohul 2015: 32). Despite reassurances by political leaders that they will stop courting these groups, the relationship is still strong.

SOCIAL ACCOUNTABILITY:
THE MEDIA, CIVIL SOCIETY, AND ALTERNATIVE PLATFORMS

Social accountability can be defined as an approach toward building accountability that relies on civic engagement, in which it is ordinary citizens and civil society organizations that exact accountability (Malena et al. 2004). The media are an important feature within the social accountability matrix, especially the right to information. Often referred to as the fourth estate or the watchdog of society, independent and balanced media are considered an essential feature of any functional democracy.

Mauritius has some of the oldest written media in the southern hemisphere. The media played an important role during the preindependence phase. Media in contemporary Mauritius have evolved significantly, offering a diversity of titles and different ownership patterns. Commercial and public media are distinctive in terms of their ideological stand. Written media and radio are commercial entities run by private groups,¹⁷ while television runs as a public monopoly. The Mauritian media generally operate in a free and open environment. However, in recent times Mauritius has lost its good rating, as government has over the years tried to rein in the media (especially the written press). The most recent report from the Reporters Without Borders speaks about growing tensions and a decline in the freedom to inform. It also highlights the fact that "investigative coverage of certain subjects can be risky for Mauritian journalists" (RWB 2018). In fact, it should be noted that under previous governments and indeed the current government, journalists have experienced intimidation (arrests, imprisonment, searches of premises, government advertising boycotts). Legislation is heavy-handed: an Official Secrets Act (1972), as well as libel, defamation, and sedition legislation, part of the Criminal Code Act (1838). These laws can act as deterrents in the pursuit of truthful and incisive journalism, creating a culture of self-censorship.

Showing the impact of investigative journalism, one of the leading newspapers on the island broke a story that led to the resignation of three government ministers as well as the president. All the cases were linked to the abuse of power (Sivaramen 2016). One of the interviewees, who occupies a senior editorial position, expressed dismay that despite all the evidence, the police have yet to investigate the matter. Therefore, there is no doubt that a section of the media has exposed certain political wrongdoings within the public sphere. However, can the same be said of the private sector? Do the privately owned media provide the same level of scrutiny when it comes to the dealings of the private sector? An analysis of the shareholding structure of some of the privately owned media indicates a significant presence of the private sector, and some of the big scandals that have hit the private sector are not always given fair and balanced coverage where at times stories are either minimized or blatantly ignored. This brings us to the issue of the media's ownership pattern, making it an inherent part of the elite structure. The main aim of accountability is to ensure that all parties are scrutinized equally without any fear or favor. Unfortunately, it seems this is not always the case in Mauritius as elite interest often undermines public interest.

What about civil society? Can it exercise enough social pressure to generate elite accountability? The concept of civil society is itself problematic, as it is at times difficult to define who forms part of civil society. In Mauritius it is fragmented, often interest driven, and unorganized. This sentiment was expressed by one respondent who has held a key leadership position within civil society. However, what is interesting is the presence of a number of postmaterialist movements driven by a philosophy of social justice, equity, and inclusive rights, among others. They operate across all the different spheres—political, social, and economic. When asked about the impact of such movements and platforms, most of the respondents responded that these were laudable incentives. However, they expressed skepticism as to their capacity to influence the government, as they have not reached a point "where governments would be inclined to really listen and agree to all of their demands."

A point of concern highlighted by respondents was that these groups do not always get their facts right, as they are too driven by "the need to expose and make a big PR announcement out of it." One of the respondents, who holds a leadership position in the media, said that it was important for these movements to reflect on the fact that "their confrontational attitudes toward certain economic interests are probably useful to actual or potential competitors of those companies."

CONCLUSION

With its outstanding record of sustained democracy, growth, and development in the African region, Mauritius is a case study where elite accountability remains elusive and (non)accountability pervasive at all levels, despite the establishment of structures and mechanisms to safeguard accountability. Elites tend to collude across ethnic barriers in order to protect their vested interests and thereby foster (non)accountability. In fact, the two dimensions of accountability—answerability and enforcement—appear to be relatively nonexistent. One of the key causes of such a situation is the weak voice and passivity of civil society. For instance, as rightly pointed out by an informant from a leftist party, despite all the evidence of wastage and mismanagement at the highest level in government and the public sector, Mauritians still vote for the same political parties and political leaders. Nonetheless, the stance and voice of civil society have recently assumed greater visibility on social media, which is closely monitored by politicians and political parties. Although social media activism tends to be limited to the internet, it has added some pressure and created a demand for accountability. With the internet and social media, news travels very fast, and the reactions and feedback from society are also rapid, thereby putting pressure on elites to react. In fact, the missing link in this form of activism is translating intention, protest, and dissent into action. Civil servants also have a role to play in ensuring accountability in the public sector. Yet one of the key institutions in the public service, the Mauritius Police Force, is consistently reported to be one of the most corrupt institutions in the country (Transparency International 2007: 13). There is also the fear of sanctions, such as punitive transfers among civil servants, that silences dissident voices. Conversations with respondents pointed to the need to train and equip the civil servants to be accountable to the system and not to the masters of the day.

The nomination of political appointees at the head of public institutions, especially parastatal bodies, is a further obstacle blocking accountability of the political elites, as it leads to clientelism and political patronage. This trend has accentuated over the years, and the motto "the right person in the right job" is rarely considered. To make matters worse, a senior minister of the previous government often affronted the population with the saying: "Government is Government and Government decides" (Prayag 2015). Even in the business sector, which finances political parties, there is no accountability in the use of funds, nor is there a demand for it. According to an informant from the media sector, business elites prefer to toe the line so as not to be in the bad books of government, highlighting the collusion between the different elites. The one sector where accountability has been apparent is in the judiciary. The number of high-profile cases that the director of public prosecutions has filed gives hope that accountability can rein in the impunity of the powerful.

In both empirical and theoretical terms, the politics of elite accountability in Mauritius highlights the fraught character of contemporary thinking on democracy. Scholars and policy actors tend to assume that there are straightforward paths by which democracy delivers greater elite accountability and good governance. As Thomas Carothers and Saskia Brechenmacher (2014: 3) of the Carnegie Endowment for International Peace recently remarked, in the work of international institutions to promote democracy and development, "accountability, transparency, participation, and inclusion" have emerged as "four key principles," representing the emphasis on democracy and democratization since the 1990s. Specifically, there is a central assumption that "greater governmental transparency will allow citizens to determine where their political leaders are going astray and exert well-targeted pressure to put them back on track" (Carothers and Brechenmacher 2014: 5).

In this chapter, we have emphasized that Mauritius is almost universally recognized as a shiny example of democracy and sustained democratization in Africa. This greater democratization undoubtedly generates heightened expectations of accountability for both citizens and donors alike. However, contrary to popular understanding, Mauritian elites have remained largely unaccountable. As Carothers and Brechenmacher (2014: 6) recognize, commitment to the actual implementation of any of their key principles in everyday political processes remains "superficial." In the specific case of Mauritius, the elites appear to be uninterested in, and resistant to, change. There is also collusion across ethnic lines in maintaining the status quo. To a large extent, the long-standing (non)accountability appears to be the result of "elite capture," as highlighted by Goetz and Jenkins (2005: 45). The analysis in this chapter thus sheds light on a country that, over the decades, has projected a highly romanticized version of democratic and economic progress. However, beneath the image lies the inconvenient truth of (non)accountability.

NOTES

1. Although the British colonized Mauritius, they did not settle on the island. Each of these colonizing phases was important, as each shaped the direction and character of the small island—the Dutch (logging of vast ebony plantations, the extinction of the dodo, and the introduction of sugarcane), the French (the development of a plantocracy economy), and the British (a culture of administration and governance).

2. These include the Franco-Mauritians and Creoles, who are Catholic; the Indian community, Muslim and Hindu; and the small Chinese or Sino-Mauritian community, either Buddhist or Catholic. The Franco-Mauritians, Hindus, Muslims, and Sino-Mauritians have retained cultural ties to their original homelands, whereas the Creoles, who are descendants from the slaves brought to Mauritius from East Africa, have no such ties (Simmons 1982).

3. The best-loser system allows up to eight additional members of parliament from candidates belonging to minority groups who narrowly lost in the election. The best-loser system has, however, been critiqued for promoting divisions in the population and institutionalizing communalism (Mathur 1991; Nave 1998).

4. This was the last time that Mauritians were asked to classify themselves along the four main ethnic groups—Hindus, Muslims, Sino-Mauritians, and General Population (to which Franco-Mauritians belong).

5. This is a term coined by Khal Torabully, a Mauritian poet. It became a shorthand for describing the cultural integration or interaction of the Indian or Chinese "coolie" (laborer) diaspora. The word "coolie" is now regarded as not just pejorative, but a racial slur.

6. The "Coloreds," also known as the free people of color, or gens de couleur, are an ethnic category that emerged during French colonial rule. The Colored population was largely a mixed-race group, often the children of Franco-Mauritian plantation owners and slave women (Eriksen 1998: 9).

7. We thank Nad Sivaramen, the director of Publications of *L'Express*, for permission to use both Berenger's and Gurib-Fakim's photographs.

8. Navin Ramgoolam came to power in 1995. He was prime minister from 1995 to 2000 and 2005 to 2014. He lost the general election in December 2014 but still leads the Mauritius Labor Party.

9. Source: Transparency International, https://tradingeconomics.com/mauritius/corruption-index (accessed October 6, 2018).

10. "Sobrinho—Gurib-Fakim: Tout sur l'affaire Platinum Card, " *L'Express* (2018) (various articles)—https://www.lexpress.mu/node/327306/sobrinho-gurib-fakim-tout-sur-laffaire-platinum-card (accessed December 7, 2018).

11. Elections have been held on a regular basis—every five years as prescribed in the Representation of People's Act (1958). The only time when an election was postponed was in 1972.

12. Ten out of the eleven postindependence elections have featured pre-election coalitions.

13. The main objectives of the code are to encourage organizations to comply with good governance practices and empower participation of stakeholders in ensuring that these practices are effectively implemented (Bertelsmann Stiftung 2018).

14. In the 2018–19 budget speech, the prime minister mentioned the government plan to amend the Finance and Audit Act to ensure greater accountability and transparency by making it mandatory for ministries and departments to report on corrective measures taken to address the weaknesses identified by the director of audit and prevent wastage of public funds (Jugnauth 2018).

15. The Integrity Pledge Project (IPP) is led by the Mauritius Institute of Directors and its partners, the Independent Commission against Corruption, Business Mauritius, Transparency Mauritius, and other private sector stakeholders. The aim is to assist Mauritian companies in assessing their anticorruption measures and reducing areas of risk, in compliance with international best practices. http://www.miod.mu/services/integrity-pledge-project

16. Interview with Jocelyn Chan Low in "Sociétés socioculturelles: Lobbyistes à l'oeuvre," *Le Défi Quotidien*, May 3, 2012.

17. In 2001 licenses were allocated to three private commercial radios. Private television does not exist, although web television is gaining in popularity.

REFERENCES

Adejumobi, Said. 2018a. "Unbundling Liberal Democracy: Institutions, Participation and Accountability." In Said Adejumobi, ed., *Voice and Power in Africa's Democracy: Institutions, Participation and Accountability*, 1–14. New York: Routledge.

Adejumobi, Said. 2018b. "Promoting Accountable Governance in Africa: Issues, Challenges and Policy Reforms." In Said Adejumobi, ed., *Voice and Power in Africa's Democracy: Institutions, Participation and Accountability*. New York: Routledge. pp. 115–34.

Allen, Richard B. 1999. *Slaves, Freedom and Indentured Labourers in Colonial Mauritius*. Cambridge: Cambridge University Press.

African Peer Review Mechanism. 2010. *Country Review Report Number 13: Republic of Mauritius*. Addis Ababa: African Union

Afrobarometer. 2017. *Mauritius Country Report*. Ghana: CCID.

Bertelsmann Foundation. 2014. *Bertelsmann Transformation Index: Mauritius Country*

Report 2014. http://bti-project.de/uploads/tx_itao_download/BTI_2014_Mauritius.pdf. Accessed March 2, 2015.

Bertelsmann Stiftung. 2018. *BTI 2018 Country Report: Mauritius*. Gütersloh: Bertelsmann Stiftung. http://www.bti-project.org/fileadmin/files/BTI/Downloads/Reports/2018/pdf/BTI_2018_Mauritius.pdf. Accessed June 30, 2018.

Boswell, Rosabelle. 2006. *Le Malaise Creole: Ethnic Identity in Mauritius*. New York: Berghahn Books.

Boudet, Catherine. 2016. "Case Study: Mauritius." In Fabio Bargiacchi and Victoria Florinder, eds., *Preventing and Mitigating Electoral Conflict and Violence: Lessons from Southern Africa*, 180–204. European Union. URL: http://democracysupport.eu/southafrica/template/Preventing_and_Mitigating_Electoral_Conflict_and_Violence.pdf. Accessed July 10, 2018.

Bovens, Mark. 2007. "Analyzing and Assessing Accountability: A Conceptual Framework." *European Law Journal* 13, no. 4: 447–68.

Bratton, Michael, and Carolyn Logan. 2014. "From Elections to Accountability in Africa." *Governance in Africa* 1, no. 1: 1–12.

Brautigam, Deborah, with Tania Diolle. 2009. "Coalitions, Capitalists and Credibility: Overcoming the Crisis of Confidence at Independence in Mauritius." Development Leadership Programme Research Paper no. 4, April.

Bunwaree, Sheila. 2005. "State-Society Relations: Re-engineering the Mauritian Social Contract." Paper presented at the 2005 CODESRIA General Assembly, December 6–10, 2005, Maputo, Mozambique. www.codesria.org/IMG/pdf/bunwaree.pdf

Bunwaree, Sheila. 2014. "The Fading Developmental State: Growing Inequality in Mauritius." *Development* 57, nos. 3–4: 578–90.

Bunwaree, Sheila, and Roukaya Kasenally. 2005. *Political Parties in Mauritius*. Johannesburg: EISA.

Burnell, Peter J. 2008. "The Relationship of Accountable Governance and Constitutional Implementation, with Reference to Africa." *Journal of Politics and Law* 1, no. 3: 10–24.

Carter, Marina. 2002. "Subaltern Success Stories: Socio-economic Mobility in the Indian Labour Diaspora—Some Mauritian Case Studies." *Internationales Asienforum* 33: 91–100.

Carothers, Thomas, and Saskia Brechenmacher. 2014. "Accountability, Transparency, Participation, and Inclusion: A New Development Consensus?" October. Washington, DC: Carnegie Endowment for International Peace. https://carnegieendowment.org/files/new_development_consensus.pdf

Darga, L. Amadee. 1998. "Mauritius: Governance Challenges in Sustained Democracy in a Plural Society." http://unpan1.un.org/intradoc/groups/public/documents/cafrad/-unpan00859.pdf. Accessed August 28, 2020.

Darga, L. Amadee. 2008. *Consolidating Democratic Governance in the SADC Region*. Johannesburg: EISA. https://www.eisa.org.za/pdf/RR37.pdf

Diamond, Larry, Marc F. Plattner, and Andreas Schedler. 1999. "Introduction." In Andreas

Schedler, Larry Diamond, and Marc F. Plattner, eds., *The Self-Restraining State: Power and Accountability in New Democracies*. Boulder, CO: Lynne Rienner. pp. 1–10.

Diamond, Larry, and Leonardo Morlino. 2005. *Assessing the Quality of Democracy*. Baltimore, MD: John Hopkins University Press.

Dülffer, Jost, and Marc Frey. 2011. "Introduction." In Jost Dülffer and Marc Frey, eds., *Elites and Decolonization in the Twentieth Century*. New York: Palgrave Macmillan. pp. 1–10.

Economist Intelligence Unit (EIU). 2018. *Democracy Index 2017: Free Speech under Attack*. EIU Publications. http://pages.eiu.com/rs/753-RIQ-438/images/Democracy_Index_2017.pdf. Accessed July 15, 2018.

Eriksen, Thomas Hylland. 1994. "Nationalism, Mauritian Style: Cultural Unity and Ethnic Diversity." *Comparative Studies in Society and History* 36, no. 3: 549–74.

Eriksen, Thomas Hylland. 1998. *Common Denominators: Ethnicity, Nation-Building and Compromise in Mauritius*. New York: Berg.

Eriksen, Thomas Hylland, and Ramola Ramtohul. 2018. "Introduction." In Ramola Ramtohul and Thomas Hylland Eriksen, eds., *The Mauritian Paradox: Fifty Years of Development, Diversity and Democracy*, 1–13. Réduit: University of Mauritius Press.

Goetz, Anne Marie, and Rob Jenkins. 2005. *Reinventing Accountability: Making Democracy Work for Human Development*. Basingstoke: Palgrave Macmillan.

Goetz, Anne Marie, and Rob Jenkins. 2010. "Hybrid Forms Of Accountability: Citizen engagement in institutions of public-sector oversight in India." *Public Management Review* 3, no. 3: 363–83.

Hilbert, Patrick. 2012. "Suite à la declaration du père Véder—l'état et la religion, deux entités indissociables?" *Le Défi Quotidien*, August 29.

Ibrahim Index of African Government (IIAG). 2017. *Index Report: Mauritius*. IIAG Publication.

Jenkins, Matthew. 2014. *Overview on Corruption in Mauritius*. October 20. Anti-Corruption Helpdesk, Transparency International. https://knowledgehub.transparency.org/assets/uploads/helpdesk/Country_Profile_Mauritius_2014.pdf

Jugnauth, Pravind Kumar. 2018. "Budget Speech 2018–2019: Pursuing Our Transformative Journey." Port Louis, Mauritius: Ministry of Finance and Economic Development. http://mof.govmu.org/English/Documents/Budget%202018-2019/2018_19budgetspeech.pdf. Accessed June 16, 2018.

Kadima, Denis, and Roukaya Kasenally. 2006. "The Formation, Collapse and Revival of Political Party Coalitions in Mauritius." In Denis Kadima, ed., *The Politics of Party Coalitions in Africa*, 73–109. Johannesburg: EISA & KAS Publication.

Kasenally, Roukaya. 2017. "Democratic Shortfalls in Mauritius." In Khabele Matlosa et al., *Democratic Development in Africa*, 37–51. EISA 20th Anniversary Occasional Paper Series no. SYMP16_3. Johannesburg: EISA.

Kumssa, Asfaw, and Isaac M. Mbeche. 2004. "The Role of Institutions in the Development Process of African Countries." *International Journal of Social Economics* 31, nos. 9–10: 840–55.

Lindberg, Staffan I. 2013. "Mapping Accountability: Core Concept and Subtypes." *International Review of Administrative Sciences* 79, no. 2: 202–26.

Malena, Carmen, Reiner Forster and Janmejay Singh. 2004. *Social Accountability: An Introduction to the Concept and Emerging Practice*. Participation and Civic Engagement Paper No. 76. Washington DC: The World Bank.

Mathur, Hansraj. 1991. *Parliament in Mauritius*. Rose Hill, Mauritius: Éditions de L'Océan Indien.

Miles, William F. S. 1999. "The Mauritius Enigma." *Journal of Democracy* 10, no. 2: 91–104.

Mishra, Amit Kumar. 2009. "Indian Indentured Labourers in Mauritius: Reassessing the New System of Slavery vs Free Labour Debate." *Studies in History* 25, no. 2: 229–51.

Nave, Ari. 1998. "The Institutionalisation of Communalism: The Best Loser System in Mauritius." In Marina Carter, ed., *Consolidating the Rainbow: Independent Mauritius, 1968–1998*, 19–22. Mauritius: Centre for Research on Indian Ocean Societies.

Normanton, E. L. 1971. "Public Accountability and Audit: A Reconnaissance." In Bruce Smith and Douglas C. Hague, eds., *The Dilemma of Accountability in Modern Government: Independence versus Control*, 311–45. London: Macmillan.

Prayag, Touria. 2015. "Strange Case of Dr. Anil and Mr. Gayan." *Weekly*, April 1, 2015. https://www.lexpress.mu/idee/260619/strange-case-dr-anil-and-mr-gayan

Ramtohul, Ramola. 2015. "Intersectionality and Women's Political Citizenship: The Case of Mauritius." *Journal of Contemporary African Studies* 33, no. 1: 27–47.

Reporters without Borders. 2018. *RWB News: Mauritius*. https://rsf.org/en/news/rsf-condemns-harsh-penalties-online-content-mauritius. Accessed on November 17, 2018.

Salverda, Tijo. 2015. *The Franco-Mauritian Elite: Power and Anxiety in the Face of Change*. New York: Berghahn Books.

Salverda, Tijo, and Jon Abbink. 2013. "Introduction: An Anthropological Perspective on Elite Power and the Cultural Politics of Elites." In Jon Abbink and Tijo Salverda, eds., *The Anthropology of Elites: Power, Culture and the Complexities of Distinction*, 1–28. New York: Palgrave Macmillan.

Schedler, Andreas. 1999. "Conceptualizing Accountability." In Andreas Schedler, Larry Diamond, and Marc J. Plattner, eds., *The Self-Restraining State: Power and Accountability in New Democracies*, 13–28. Boulder, CO: Lynne Rienner.

Schijf, Huibert. 2013. "Researching Elites: Old and New Perspectives." In Jon Abbink and Tijo Salverda, eds., *The Anthropology of Elites: Power, Culture and the Complexities of Distinction*, 29–44. New York: Palgrave Macmillan.

Simmons, Adele S. 1982. *Modern Mauritius: The Politics of Decolonization*. Bloomington: Indiana University Press.

Sivaramen, Nad. 2016. "It Is Their Time to Eat." *L'Express*, April 30, 2016. https://www.lexpress.mu/idee/280733/it-their-time-eat

Transparency International. 2007. "National Integrity System, Transparency International Country Study Report: Mauritius." Transparency International.

United Nations Development Programme (UNDP). 1994. *Human Development Report 1994*. New York: Oxford University Press.

US Embassy in Port Louis. 2008. *Not So Subtle Corruption in Mauritius*. Wikileaks Cable 08PORTLOUIS205. http://www.wikileaks.org/plusd/cables/08PORTLOUIS205_a.html. Accessed July 5, 2018.

World Bank. 2018. *Mauritius Addressing Inequality through More Equitable Labor Markets*. Washington, DC: World Bank Group Publications.

Zafar, Ali. 2011. *Mauritius: An Economic Success Story*. Washington, DC: World Bank Group Publications.

PART 3

Elites, Ethnoregional Competition, and (Counter)hegemonic Politics

CHAPTER 9

Elite Associations in Cameroon

SWELA, Development, and the Cultural Politics of Redistribution

ROGERS OROCK

INTRODUCTION

How do elite groups work to produce accountability in contemporary Africa, especially after the transitions from one-party states to multiparty autocracies? "Elite" and "accountability" are notions associated with the exercise of public power. "Elite" generally refers to a leading group of actors in any field of power (social, cultural, economic, or political). Accountability underlines an aspirational quality in regards to how any elite exercises its power: do the group's actions meet the expectations of those that the elite claim to represent? That is, common to both elites and accountability is a moral or ethical expectation. Contemporary descriptions of state-society relations in Africa generally suggest the acute absence of accountability on the part of the elite. The result is what Richard Werbner (2004) has described as a "Machiavellian suspicion of elites." This is largely because scholars overemphasize the action of elites within state bureaucracies, and these are especially defined by corruption and critical deficiencies in the delivery of public services (Blundo and Olivier de Sardan 2006).

In this chapter I propose that the arenas and fields of elite accountability in sub-Sahara Africa largely lie outside the state. Elites perform their actions of accountability in the wider society, through and within social arenas and fields of collective action. I analyze the role of elite associations in Cameroon in the politics of ethnic and regional claim-making over expectations for collective social improvement. Whereas these elite associations attend primarily to the narrow interests of their elite membership, they also make considerable demands for the social and material improvement of their ethnic/regional communities vis-à-vis the state. In turn, elites within these elite organizations tend to be under pressure from their local communities (villages and towns) within their ethnic communities to provide material and other kinds of resources that will enhance social welfare in these constituencies.

Both the local communities' expectations and the demands made by the elites against the state in Cameroon are framed through the discourse of development. I argue that in both its ideological orientation and its practical expressions as a relational form, development talk and claims for development made upon and by elites against the state express a politics of redistribution that emanates from social forces as they affect the state. These redistributive claims (pressures) are nevertheless made within a culturally specific ethos of political accountability, one that is consistent with the workings of a state that depends on complicity with society (cf. Bayart 1993; Mbembe 1992).

As Tim Kelsall has suggested, we need to be looking critically at societal forms of indigenous and indexical mechanisms and practices of accountability. Kelsall argues that these necessarily enrich conventional stories about accountability, which tend to rely on universal templates associated with state bureaucracies and democratic institutions. However, doing so requires our attunement to the different forms of everyday social institutions and practices that constitute what Kelsall called "rituals of verification" (2003; cf. Power 1994). This approach is especially pertinent for interrogating the modalities of political verification that may occur and are fostered alongside or even outside (even though not entirely beyond) the normal workings of state bureaucratic institutions and processes. I follow this approach to examine how Cameroonian elites account for themselves or seek to hold the state accountable through the idea of development. This Cameroonian story of development and accountability is particularly important in regards to the role of elites in Africa, where struggles in the domain of politics, economy, and culture are matters of "do or die" for those at the apex of societies.

Following Mbembe, for example, Charles Gore and David Pratten remark that political struggles in Africa indeed interrogate the state as a "public good" as well as the meanings of political rights and citizenship. These struggles, almost invariably localized around different identity-based claims on the state, question the logics and practices of the state in the politics of redistribution (cf. Parkin 1978). Essentially, these political struggles interrogate the state based on some nebulous notions of a "national economy" and national citizenship. Such struggles are inscribed within a politics of accountability whose logics must therefore be contextualized in relation to every claim. Gore and Pratten suggest that in order to fruitfully "locate these contests in the cultural politics of accountability," we should look to the collective activities undertaken "outside the regulatory frameworks maintained by the state." Rightly, they suggest that such collective activities "take place within associational forms and their interactions with the state" as well as within "histories of localized idioms of power, knowledge and accountability" (Gore and Pratten 2003: 213–14).

The material in this chapter is based on my field observations on one such elite association, the South West Elite Association (SWELA). I have conducted fieldwork on elites and development in Cameroon intermittently between 2007 and 2015, for a total of fifteen months. Much of this field research has been devoted to understanding issues, questions, and political struggles associated with elite practices of power in Cameroon. This ethnographic research has typically relied on different methods of data collection, including participant observations of political meetings, open-ended ethnographic interviews with key informants, and documentary (particularly textual) material such as speeches, memorandums, and newspaper articles. I combine these sources to examine the dynamics of SWELA's politics of accountability in relation to the question of redistribution in the Cameroonian state. SWELA's politics of accountability as examined here is only one example of the role that elite organizations have had on political mobilizations, since the formal return to democratization in Cameroon in 1990.

ELITES, DEVELOPMENT, AND POLITICAL ACCOUNTABILITY IN AFRICA

SWELA is an elite association created by urban-based educated men in the professions and business, with the main criteria of membership being common origins from the South-West Region of Cameroon. Since its creation in 1991, the organization has remained largely open to southwesterners, though its membership has been dominated by mostly powerful men in the legal, medical, and educational professions as well as business, although some urban-based educated women have also joined. These are described as "sons" and "daughters" of one or the other of the various ethnic groups within the South-West Region. In the Cameroonian context, SWELA's members are undoubtedly viewed as "elites." They have relatively high levels of formal education and hold secure jobs in the professions and business. In addition, they command influence by virtue of holding or having held some political office or being connected to those that do. This elitist outlook can be hobbling to the organization's formally declared intention to attract a wider membership. In 2006, its secretary-general at the time, Dr. Enow-Orock George Enonchong (a specialist medical doctor and professor of surgery and oncology), complained that "the appellation 'elite' has been misconstrued to mean white collar executives" (SWELA 2006a).

The idea for creating SWELA is credited to a lawyer, barrister A. T. Enaw (Nyamnjoh and Rowlands 1998: 227; Nkwi 2006). Enaw's ideas are said to have inspired a meeting of five political figures from the South-West. These include David Iyok (businessman), Chief Emmanuel Tabi Egbe (a former lawyer, a former minister, and roving ambassador at the time), Chief Ephraim Inoni (a public accountant who was serving as a minister at the time), Chief Fomenky (businessman), and Enaw himself, who was the least known of these five figures. SWELA emerged in the early 1990s, right from the onset of the political struggles for democratization in Cameroon. As an association of powerful men and women from the South-West Region, the organization undertakes different kinds of collective activities, including lobbying the government on behalf of regional interests, convening public meetings for its members, or even attracting the "general public."

In January 2011, I witnessed a remarkable example of such pursuit of regional interests. It was a political meeting of elites in the South-West, an anglophone region. More than a thousand or so elites gathered for a "Mega Forum" in the large Pavilion Hall of the National Social Insurance Fund in Mile 17, Molyko, Buea. The event was organized by the two regional organizations, SWELA and the South West Chiefs Conference. The Pavilion Hall was completely filled with some of the most prominent members of these South-West elite, including ministers, former ministers, mayors, former provincial governors, village chiefs, executives of public and private corporations, and so on. Canopies were set out in the yard to accommodate less powerful members of the elite, such as university professors and administrators, bank managers, deputies to the mayors of the various towns in the region, as well as curious ordinary people who thought they should come and see what this highly advertised event was all about.

Elsewhere, I have shown that at least some of the leading figures who staged this event sought to draw the attention of the country's president, Paul Biya, to their cause. They wished that Biya would declare their region as the site for the commemorations, scheduled for later in 2011, of the fiftieth anniversary of the reunification of former British Southern and French Cameroons. Major political figures in the region, such as Mbella Moki (then mayor of Buea), hoped that hosting national celebrations in the region would be an economic boon to the regional economy (see Orock 2014). For South-West elites, then, a main concern of their Mega Forum was to reflect on the development problems facing the South-West Region and potential political solutions they could design.

Why do elite groups such as SWELA make rather parochial and socially exclusive and exclusionary ethnic and regional claims through an appeal to a discourse of development, a concept that has typically been identified with inclusion and universalist aspirations for wellness, welfare, and social empowerment (cf. Sen 1988; 1999)? After all, isn't a predominant public, scholarly, and even international development discourse about African elites anchored on a master narrative that these elites are unconcerned with the development and the welfare of their people and society (see, e.g., Mbeki 2009; Deutsche Welle 2009; cf. Mkandawire 2015)? Moreover, how do these elites work to attain this public pursuit of development? In addition, how do such claims by elite groups express their understanding of the sociocultural fabric of the state and the modalities of political accountability in Cameroon? Lastly and even more broadly, in the context of sub-Saharan Africa, why do subnational claims on ethnic or regional bases appear to have intensified after the economic and political liberalizations of the 1990s?

Anthropologist Arjun Appadurai (2007) provides an interesting claim as to why development might become entangled in the dynamics of politics and culture. He remarks that development expresses "the idea of aspiration as a cultural capacity" (Appadurai 2007: 32). Accordingly, development must be studied in relation to the multiple registers of cultural politics enacted to give material expressions to the aspirations that animate it. According to Appadurai, then, development provides a useful language for enacting what Charles Taylor has called the "politics of recognition." SWELA's interactions with the government of Cameroon express such a politics of recognition, couched as it is in a discourse of belonging and rights (cf. Englund and Nyamnjoh 2004).

Following Appadurai, I examine the questions above by appraising SWELA's interactions with the government of Cameroon in relation to both its particular elite interests and the broad social concerns of the regional community it purports to represent. While addressing these questions, however, I am also interested in this volume's focus on economic and political liberalizations of the post–Cold War moment (Piot 2010) and their relationship to processes of political deliberation and rule in Africa. Precisely, challenging the previous ideological emphasis on national unity by state authorities and in response to the new conditions of crisis, the political and economic changes brought with them or reinvigorated a plethora of actors that continue to affect and, in turn, are affected by an elite politics defined by fragmentation and strife.

In understanding the significance of these changes, we must remember that such "liberalizations" might not necessarily result in greater democratization (cf. Huntington 1991). For example, popular electoral processes are not necessarily freer or fairer just because these are held more regularly— although Steffan Lindberg (2004, 2006) has suggested that there has been an improvement to the democratic quality of elections in many African contexts over the years. The assumption, however, is that contrary to the situation under long-standing one-party rule, political liberalizations have either ushered in new, or empowered older, actors and institutions in the processes of political participation.

A key question to be determined in this regard is the relationship between the broader political culture, the role of elites, and the kinds of *accountabilities* that might be fostered within or through the new political spaces and institutions enabled by democratization. Hence, I seek to address some of these questions raised in the introduction to this volume. Specifically, I ask two questions related to elite politics in African settings since the return to multiparty politics in the 1990s. First, how do elite groups re/present themselves as "responsible" and therefore accountable and socially relevant to their local, constituent communities? Second, how might such elite groups make and legitimize themselves as political representatives?

After all, political accountability must be determined by how much a government can be said to be "responsible" (Lonsdale 1986: 127) for the welfare of people under its authority. This "measure of responsibility," John Lonsdale reminds us, is determined in material terms because the politics of accountability is essentially about "the relationship between politics and production." That is, the politics of accountability is at the heart of debates and struggles over redistribution in any given political setting. In contemporary West Africa, the capacity for ethnic or regional communities to engage in the contentious politics of accountability—scrutinizing and even challenging governmental decisions and actions over resource allocations—depends on their capacity for political representation of their interests. This, in turn, is contingent on their capacity to mobilize through different kinds of organizations. John Dunn underlines the crucial role that political mobilization plays for political representation and accountability. As he remarks, "Because the capacity to secure political representation depends upon the capacity for self-organisation and upon the coherent and accurate understanding of interests (individual, group, class, national), it can be assessed only by a highly specific and ethnographically delicate investigation of particular examples" (Dunn 1986: 163). Examining this vexed question in relation to the postcolonial state in Africa demands that we advance "the anthropology that underlies both issues of representation and issues of unequal allocation of utilities, the negotiation of heterogeneity, and the refinement of passions" (Mbembe (2001: 39).

Tracking and understanding elite political claims through their modes of organization and in relation to discourses of development, I suggest, opens up the multiple registers of specific struggles for political accountability and inclusion in states like Cameroon that have systematically routinized patrimonial, corrupt, and unaccountable forms of redistribution of national wealth. To examine how SWELA (as a concrete ethnographic example for other elite associations) articulates accountability within the idiom of development, I discuss the expressive modalities of SWELA's politics of claim-making on the state. Specifically, I discuss how SWELA and its members question the state or give their support for the state's decisions that affect them through their written statements and public declarations by SWELA in the various ways that the organization . I begin by situating the origins of SWELA and its groundbreaking Mundemba Declaration. This is an important marker in the landscape of ethnoregional claim-making during the country's early moments of democratization. I then contrast this politics of development through ethnoregional claim-making in the era of democratization to the different meanings of development during an earlier phase of Cameroon's postcolonial state and its visions of nation-building under the one-party state.

SWELA'S MUNDEMBA DECLARATION

On March 28, 1992, SWELA issued the Mundemba Declaration to both the government of Cameroon and the public. This declaration, issued from the small and isolated town of Mundemba in Ndian Division, was the culminating point of SWELA's Fifth General Assembly, meeting less than a year after its official establishment as an "elite association." During research at the

National Archives in Buea in November 2007, I found this twenty-five-year-old declaration, published in the May–June 1992 issue of an obscure regional newsmagazine called *The Oracle*. Only in its second issue then, the magazine was undoubtedly a mouthpiece of the "gods" of political life in the South-West Region. Although as an "oracle" it could not prophesy the political future of the South-West Region, its editorial line and opinion pieces were supportive of the political interests and causes of the South-West vis-à-vis the rest of the country.

Phrased in an accusatory language, the declaration shifts between protest and performance. It represents to a great extent the aspects of political discourse and practice typical of elite political culture in Cameroon following the early years of political liberalization in the 1990s. For example, as far as political performance is concerned, the elites underlined that the choice of Mundemba as the town in the South-West Region to host the Fifth SWELA General Assembly was not by accident. Rather, they argued, they made this choice "under very peculiar circumstances dictated by the peculiar nature of the place," given that Ndian Division, of which Mundemba is the chief town, is "the most marginalized division in the most marginalized province—the South West Province" (the "provinces" of Cameroon became "regions" in 2008).

Having spelled this out, SWELA's communiqué underscored the multifaceted character of this "general neglect" of the region. To express their "dissatisfaction," SWELA questioned the morality and fairness of the government's politics of redistribution. The declaration invoked an overriding principle of "*derivation*" to argue that while the South-West contributed "almost 70 % to the Gross National Product (GNP)" of the country, it was the object of "general neglect" by the national government. This was especially so in regards to "roads, telecommunications and socio-human development" (SWELA 1992: 30). Thus, in light of the principle of derivation, SWELA claimed that government actions or inactions spelled a "drain of revenue for the South West Province."

To buttress this, point, SWELA declared,

> Conscious that the Government Treasury is considered one and in view of the fact that revenue collected by government should be distributed according to need and capacity of the various Treasuries, SWELA frowns at the recent action of the Ministry of Finance where the entire revenue accruing

from taxes from SONARA (Sociètè Nationale de Rafinerie) are air-lifted to Yaoundé Treasury General, without regard to the needs of the Treasuries of the South West Province. (SWELA 1992: 33)

Besides immediate fiduciary concerns, in this declaration SWELA also questioned government action or inaction on other regional concerns in the politics of state redistribution regarding infrastructural development. A notable example concerns plans for the establishment of a second, "deep" seaport for the country, to decenter the congestion in the lone seaport in the Wouri River at Douala. SWELA remarked that "reports of expert studies from International Marine Engineers recommended Limbe"—the fledgling coastal city of the South-West Province and the location of the country's lone state oil refinery corporation, SONARA—as the most suitable site for the proposed port. Disappointed by the government's choice, the South-West elites decried the government's decision to overlook this expert recommendation when it chose to direct its public investment to the South Province town of Kribi. The chosen city is located in the Ocean Division, an area that is part of President Paul Biya's ethnic Beti-Bulu communities. Accordingly, SWELA viewed "this act as a stab in the back." The South-West elite "accuses government of favouritism, deceitfulness, and tribalism" (SWELA 1992: 33).

Essentially, the Mundemba Declaration enumerated "grievances" by South-West elites over what they felt was a conscious politics of injustice in relation to material or infrastructural development by the central government vis-à-vis their region. As such, it is a powerful example of elite scrutiny and critique of the Cameroonian government in the early 1990s. But it is by no means unique. Instead, it must be recognized as the product of a particular moment, a painful transition in Cameroon from the one-party state toward multiparty politics in 1990. As SWELA explained in the declaration, these ethnic or regional grievances contributed to a palpable sense of marginalization among southwesterners that, in turn, explained their political behavior during the first multiparty elections. According to SWELA, embittered voters in the region used this first-ever multiparty parliamentary election in March 1992, after the democratic reforms of May 1990, to signal their frustrations. At this election, in the South-West the ruling party of President Paul Biya, the Cameroon People's Democratic Movement (CPDM), lost to the National Union for Democracy and Progress, an opposition party led by Bello Bouba Maigari.

As SWELA explained it, over the years "different socio-political and cultural groups have addressed, in different ways, to the government, the grievances of the people as concerns the evolution of development in this province. More recently, SWELA joined this struggle." However, because "government gave a deaf ear" to these "requests," it is no surprise that "during the last parliamentary elections the South West people had a chance to demonstrate their unity of thought, word and deed . . . according to their conscience." In light of this reality, SWELA warned: "Any government, present or future, must consider the development of the South West Province to be their pre-occupation, as a condition for our continual loyalty" (SWELA 1992: 33).

In all, elites in the SWELA let it known in no uncertain terms that they were "most disappointed" by this state of affairs in the political life of the region because they had previously tried to draw the attention of the prime minister, Sadou Hayatou, and President Paul Biya to the region's plight when they discussed two memorandums with them. Firstly, in June 1991 they had discussed a memorandum with Sadou Hayatou in Yaoundé. And in September 1991 they discussed a second memorandum with Biya when the president visited Buea during his tour of the South-West Province in the buildup to the first multiparty elections in 1992. But as the South-West elites remark bitterly in the Mundemba declaration, "Neither the Prime Minister nor the President of the Republic has shown any sign of what action is being contemplated on the problems raised in the two memoranda, despite their oral promises during audiences" (SWELA 1992: 30–31).

These were strong words in a context such as Cameroon, long defined by the authoritarianism of one-party rule and brutal crackdowns on dissidents. Yet, as I demonstrate below, SWELA's bold Mundemba Declaration must be situated within the broader atmosphere of crisis and the push for liberalizations that defined the early moments of democratization in the early 1990s. Crucially, these began with civil unrest and boycotts but culminated in constitutional reforms that protected the freedoms of speech and association (see Geschiere 2009; Nyamnjoh 2005; Mbembe and Roitman 1995). Crucially, also, this freedom of association facilitated the outgrowth of nongovernmental organizations and especially saw the rise of ethnoregional elite associations in Cameroon, in complete reversal of the situation under the old order of the one-party state.

DEMOCRATIZATION AND ELITE ASSOCIATIONS: SWELA'S FORM AND MISSION

> We, the indigenes of the South West Province of the Republic of Cameroon,
>
> Having firmly and solemnly resolved: To live in unity and harmony, conscious of the need for self-development, conscious of our talent, skill, specialized training and our material resources, dedicated to the improvement of the lot of our people as well as to the well-being of our nation Cameroon.
>
> DO hereby make, enact, and give to ourselves the following constitution. (SWELA 1991: 1)

The above is the preamble of SWELA's constitution, adopted by the General Assembly on August 7, 1991. Two weeks later, on August 21, SWELA was officially registered as a civil society organization (CSO), with its headquarters in the South-West town of Kumba. This official registration of an ethnoregional association as a CSO was only possible following the democratic reforms of December 1990, notably those provisions on freedoms of speech and association. With these familiar words of constitution-making, SWELA endowed itself with a ten-page constitutional document. Among the different provisions of this elite organization, two are important to my purpose in this chapter. The first, Article 3, outlines the objective of the elite organization. This is stated to be, among other concerns, primarily about advocating for "*unity and development* amongst its members, the South West Province and the nation at large" and particularly so by advocating for "the *balanced socioeconomic and cultural development of the South West Province* in line with Government policy" (SWELA 1991: 1).

George Marcus (1983: 11) suggests that exclusivity and agency are two central attributes associated with both scholarly and popular conceptions of elites and their actions. Marcus's view is a helpful way to understand SWELA in both its form and mission. As the excerpts above show, SWELA is a patent example of how contemporary African elites may draw from exclusionary ideologies of bounded community to organize institutions for political action in a context of political liberalization (cf. Orock 2015). Both its vision of interests and modalities of membership recruitment are structured to enact a politics of belonging on assumptions that shared South-West regional identity and interests exist (cf. Geschiere 2009; Nkwi 2006; Nyamnjoh and Rowlands 1998).

Crucial to this politics of belonging is the production of a powerful "we" discourse associated with faith not only in "the magic of performative" constitution-making (Urban 2001: 20), but also in various public political discourses. SWELA's constitution defines both its mission and membership in exclusive and exclusionary terms. SWELA is strictly concerned with promoting the "unity and development" interests of the South-West, and primarily it seeks southwesterners with parents whose origins can be traced to the region. Membership for those without such direct parental ties is subject to an adjudicatory process.

Almost everywhere and particularly so in the West, elite exclusivity is elaborated through associations, clubs, and secret societies established with specific goals, missions, and purposes (Mills 1956). These are generally predicated on an elite's sense of a shared subculture based on common registers of social distinction from which they attain economic, cultural, or social capital (Bourdieu 1984; cf. Daloz 2009). Generally, however, these elite associations tend to carry with them a different sense of civic openness that transcends ideologies of kinship, whether familial, tribal, or ethnic-based structures of affiliation. Such transfamilial or transethnic elite associations have historically also been part of African social landscapes. Some have evolved from old trading networks into secret societies such as the Ekpe (also known as Ekpo) societies in West African societies of the Cross-River Basin (Röschenthaler 2011; Ruel 1969). Even in more contemporary times, elite culture in Cameroon has also been defined by different kinds of exclusive elite associations that transcend ideologies of kinship. A notable form of these has been the alumni associations of some of the most exclusive private (especially mission) schools for men and women, such as Sasse, Bali, Saker, and Okoyong, which have produced some of the country's elite from anglophone Cameroon (see Nyamnjoh and Rowlands 1998).

However, as Peter Ekeh (1975) argued long ago, associations founded on the basis of shared educational or professional interests exclusive to its members only foster one dimension of the idea of the "public" in Africa, that of the civic public. Recognized as a highly "amoral" public realm, this domain of publicness is more commonly associated with the structures of the (post)colonial state. Social actors feel no moral obligation to this public and are therefore not invested in the expectations attendant to it. That is, in the civic public in Africa, social actors are not anxious to give accounts of themselves even though they expect the state and other actors working as public authorities to account for their decisions and actions. In contrast, elite associations such as SWELA are defined by a kind of "primary patriotism" (Geschiere and Gugler 1998; Evans 2010).

Here, exclusivity of membership is primarily anchored in a kin-based ideology of belonging to a village, ethnic, or regional identity and belonging considered as the part of the community of interests for which the association is established. For Ekeh, such primarily kin-based associations define a rather "primordial" and much more "moral" public in Africa. According to Ekeh, social actors (and especially elites) in these settings find this dimension of publicness to be much more socially and politically meaningful. In these associations elites seek social recognition. They expend great energies and material resources to "perform" functions of leadership in the social improvement of their narrowly defined (village, town, regional) communities of interest. In this realm of primordial public interests, elites feel bound to social and political obligations to enhance the collective good. Here, too, these elites give accounts of, as well as hold each other and the state accountable for, their actions.

Within this primordialist orientation, SWELA positioned itself as a representative of a bounded community of interests along the lines of an administratively defined territorial boundary, called at that time the South-West Province. One of the two English-speaking regions of Cameroon (the other is the North-West Region), it is situated on the Gulf Coast of Cameroon but extends inward far enough to share boundaries with Nigeria. Both regions were part of the British colonial administration between the end of World War I and 1961, as part of the postwar settlement that saw the entire German colony of Kamerun partitioned between Britain and France.[1] Beyond the fact of bureaucratic territorialization, SWELA's claims of representation over this area also assumed some kind of sociocultural contiguity for people of this entire province that SWELA attributed to a shared geography. Explaining the symbolism of the organization's logo, SWELA remarked that this shared cultural and geographic expression of the area represented peoples commonly inhabiting "forested mountain ranges with rivers emptying into the ocean" (SWELA 1991: 1). In reality, instead of an ethnically homogenous area, the region is constituted by various ethnic communities that include the Orocko, Bayang, Ejagham, Bakweri, Bangwa, Bassosi, Bakossi, Bafawa, Balong, Mbo, and others (Nkwi 2006: 135; cf. Yenshu-Vubo 2006).

Despite this apparent cohesiveness in self-presentation, in its formative phase SWELA was especially defined by internal strife and factionalism (Orock 2015; Nkwi 2006). These struggles revolved around the appropriate political distance that should be established between this elite organization and the central government in Yaoundé. Those who sought to endow it with some measure of autonomy tried to limit the influence of leading members who were highly placed in government as ministers, and the latter thought the organization would be better served by a closer alignment with the government (see Onuoha in this volume for interesting parallels among the Igbo in Nigeria). Notwithstanding these different positions on how to undertake its political action publicly, there appears to be consensus among SWELA leadership on how to present itself. A notable aspect of this public self-representation has been to avoid the perception that it is simply a lobbying organization or "pressure group" for the interests of the South West-Region.[2] Although in a public statement SWELA (2006a: 1) recognized that it "acts as a lobby/pressure group through advocacy," it has consistently issued memorandums, communiqués, and speeches that articulate an eclectic tool kit in its pursuit of accountability in the government.

SWELA'S MEMORANDUMS AS POLITICS OF VERIFICATION

One of SWELA's specifically identified missions lies in promoting the interests of South-West elites, especially its politically influential members. Essentially, this concerns political appointments made by the central government in Yaoundé. SWELA often scrutinizes governmental decisions on political appointments to ministerial and other highly elevated positions within the state bureaucracy or directorships of public corporate entities and others of the sort. The moments of democratization in Cameroon were defined by political turmoil, civil unrest, and outright violence. These were particularly evident in the North-West Region, leading up to the "unlawful" launch of the Social Democratic Front in Bamenda in May 1990 under the leadership of John Fru Ndi. In contrast, South-West elites—many of whom were members of the ruling CPDM party, led by Paul Biya—organized "anti-democratic" protest marches in some towns and cities of the South-West Region. These marches were directed against political actors calling for the reintroduction of multiparty democracy and Biya's resignation. During those marches they famously chanted their support for Biya in pidgin: "Dimabola! Paul Biya na we president!" ("Dimabola, Paul Biya is our president"). These South-West elites were therefore quite surprised that Biya appointed Simon Achidi Achu, a man from the North-West Region, as prime minister on April 9, 1992. This was part of Biya's efforts to appease the radical political posture of the North-West Region.

SWELA's defiant posture in the Mundemba Declaration against Biya and his government (of which some among the SWELA elite were a part) must therefore be partly understood as a reaction to Biya's display of political "ingratitude" by appointing Achu as "head of government." Particularly, the "warning" issued to the government in this declaration regarding the CPDM's loss in the 1992 parliamentary elections in the South-West Region was intended to draw the regime's attention to a "protest vote" by southwesterners over this "neglect" in favor of their historic rivals. As already indicated, SWELA stated in the Mundemba Declaration that during Biya's provincial tour to Buea on September 27, 1991, he had been presented with a memorandum to which the president had remained unresponsive. On this particular occasion, too, the municipal administrator of the Buea Rural Council—a prominent member of SWELA—told "His Excellency" about "a few of our grievances," including "dismay that our province has never had a fair consideration in top administrative and political appointments" (SWELA 1992: 18).

In reality, anglophone elites in both the South-West and North-West Regions have historically defined themselves in terms of political rivalry within the national political arena (see Orock 2009, 2015; cf. Nyamnjoh and Rowlands 1998; Nkwi 2006). Hence, when SWELA articulates its politics of verification of government on appointments, it tends to do so mainly by evaluating the situation of southwesterners in relation to positions held by elites from the neighboring English-speaking region of the North-West (cf. Nyamnjoh 1999). For example, during the early years of democratization (1992–96) Cameroon's prime minister was a man from the North-West Region, Simon Achidi Achu. SWELA largely perceived this appointment as a humiliating political outcome because Achidi was thought to privilege his native North-West Region.

Accordingly, when Paul Biya fired Achidi Achu in August 1996 and appointed Peter Mafany Musonge, a man from the South-West, to replace him as prime minister, the change was greeted with great joy by the South-West elite. The latter perceived this as a long-sought victory over political rivals, the elite of the North-West Region. This feeling of victory was strengthened when, on December 7, 1997, Biya reappointed Musonge. One of the pro-SWELA periodicals, *The Pilot*, conveyed the boastful political tone of the South-West elite. An editorial was titled "After Biya's New Gov't, Who Holds Power?" The editorial answered the question in a satisfied tone. "The son" of the South-West Region,

> Peter Mafany, did not only survive the storm to get re-appointed as Prime Minister but went further to put his imprint as the Grand master of the political game in his South West constituency.... The North-West came out completely marginalized this time around. (*The Pilot* 1997: 7)

This feeling of satisfaction with governmental action in relation to political appointments of ministers remained strong between 2004 and 2009. During these years Biya replaced Musonge as prime minister with Chief Ephraim Inoni. Chief Inoni was not only another "indigene" of the South-West Region but, like Musonge, of the same Bakweri ethnic group in the same administrative unit of Fako Division. Consequently, such changes in government composition would attract positive statements of "evaluation" or "reviews" from SWELA. For instance, following the announcement of Paul Biya's cabinet change in September 2006, SWELA (2006b) issued a statement that strikes a tone remarkably different from the Mundemba Declaration of 1992:

COMMUNIQUE ON THE RECENT GOVERNMENT RESHUFFLE

> *Considering the renewal of confidence by the Head of State His Excellency President Paul Biya on Chief Ephraim Inoni, by reconfirming him as Prime Minister Head of Government;*
> *In view of the reappointment of H.E. Prof. Ngolle Ngolle Elvis as Minister of Forestry and Wildlife; and H.E. Chief Dr.Dion Ngute as Minister delegate to the Ministry of Foreign Affairs in charge of the Commonwealth;*
> *Mindful of the appointment of H.E. Mengot Victor Arrey Nkongho as Minister in charge of Missions at the presidency of the Republic;*
> *The General Secretariat of the South-West Elite Association (SWELA) deliberated on the government reshuffle of September 22 2006, and resolved as follows:*
> —*Remark that the South-West province came out unscathed after the exercise,*
> —*Heartily thank the Head of State for this honor and renewal of confidence to the people of the South-West Province,*

> —Reconfirm their total and unconditional support to the policies and institutions of the state,
> —Vehemently condemn any detractors and intoxication within the province,
> —Pray that in future appointments, South-Westerners be assigned to more strategic positions.
>
> Secretary General
Dr. Enow-Orock George.

Although SWELA's politics of scrutiny in the area of political appointments is evidently self-interested and self-promotional, it is only one facet of SWELA's overall politics of claim-making. Since its creation SWELA has made several claims (and in various forms) on the government for collective regional interests of the South-West. The Mundemba Declaration is only one among many others. Another prominent example is SWELA's "Memorandum on the Issues in the University of Buea," then the lone English-speaking university in the country. It was written in early 2006. For a long time, Cameroon's only medical school was lodged within the Faculty of Biomedical Sciences at the University of Yaoundé I, in the capital city. Graduates from this medical school are automatically employed as medical doctors with the coveted status of civil servants. Particularly since the economic crisis of the 1990s has limited the ability of Cameroonians to seek medical training abroad, admission into this lone state-sponsored medical school had become increasingly mediated by bribery, corruption, and influence peddling by the mighty in Cameroonian society. Many poor and middle-class Cameroonian families, especially in anglophone Cameroon, aware of the relatively dominant position of the francophone elite, have historically lamented their exclusion from such prestigious "grandes écoles," including the National School for Administration and Magistracy, popularly known by its French acronym, ENAM.[3]

In late 2005 the government announced its plans to decenter medical school training in the country by establishing new medical schools in some of the other state-sponsored universities in the country. The Ministry of Higher Education signed orders establishing these new medical schools at the Universities of Buea, Douala, Ngaoundèrè, and Dschang. It also stipulated that the mode of recruitment would be by competitive entrance examinations, as it is in the case with the medical school in Yaoundé. For many Cameroonians, their dreams of having medical doctors in their families seemed to have greater chances at becoming real. But typical to its mode of operation, the government delayed implementation of these plans and went mute. The proposed entrance examinations, set to be organized by the authorities of the universities under the approval of the Ministry of Higher Education, were stalled. This created an atmosphere of uncertainty regarding these plans. In response, SWELA addressed a memorandum to the newly appointed vice-chancellor of the University of Buea, Professor Vincent P. K. Titanji. In this "Memorandum on Issues in the University of Buea," SWELA wrote that while it "lauds the authorities of Higher Education for the opening of the department of Human Medicine in the University of Buea," it also "worried about the delay in the approval of the entrance examination into the said department." In the end, the association expressed its wish to see the government swiftly grant its "approval as soon as possible to enable the department [to] take off this academic year 2006/2007" (SWELA 2006c).

Remarkably, SWELA's privileged format for publicly communicating its interests and positions on those interests is memorandums and genres such as communiqués. Indeed, there is something about memorandums as a cultural form that is highly appealing to political communication in an authoritarian and vengeful political context such as Cameroon's. For one thing, memorandums are not written in the name of any single individual. Rather, they express collective political sentiments and positions. Political authorities who seek individual targets for political retribution must therefore ascertain who played what part in the memorandum. Of course, if authorities do embark on such detailed investigative work, they also run the risk of attracting retribution on themselves, because they would reveal themselves as vengeful. In this sense memorandums foster a politics of dissimulation. A collectively written memorandum affords elites a space to express themselves with less risk of retribution. They can hide in the numbers of the groups that take responsibility for the memorandum.

On another level, as I have shown above, memorandums can express both grievances and gratitude. And there is a long tradition of their use in Cameroon's political context. Their use can even be traced to the early moments of colonial sovereignty. Memorandums have therefore been one of the historical modes by which people in Cameroon have addressed colonial and postcolonial authority. As a cultural form memorandums can thus be assimilated to the broader colonial and postcolonial political aesthetics of petitioning and petition-writing, which not only are associated with democratic subjectivity, but also the pragmatics of a politics of identity and recognition in the struggles for decolonization (cf. Cody 2009). Direct petitioning, however, often carries a palpable sense of supplication. Its language is designed to attract sympathy or forgiveness from political authorities with the power to grant requests (see, e.g., Davis 1987). However, unlike petitions, memorandums do not often assume such supplicatory forms. Rather, as my discussion of SWELA's memorandums has shown, there is a strong current of entitlement, arrogance, and even outright challenge in the political communications addressed to political authorities with the power to grant claims. SWELA does not only express how "dissatisfied" or "dismayed" it is with various (in)actions of government that are damaging to its interests, it also explicitly "frowns" on them.

In addition, a central line of anthropological and historical inquiry on the politics of elite associations in Cameroon has been that such associations are mainly the instruments for promoting elite self-interest. This has been particularly the case in discussions relating to SWELA's political actions as a pressure group (Geschiere 2009; Nyamnjoh and Rowlands 1998; Nkwi 2006). As I have shown, the self-interest of elites who seek political appointments and lucrative contracts from the central government is a major motif of elite associations in Cameroon. Yet this emphasis on the "particularistic" aspects in elite demands must not obscure how we also understand their claims for broader, collective interests, however narrowly concerned with an ethnoregional community such as the South-West Region. As Abner Cohen (1981: xvi) has argued, elite organizations tend to have "functions and interests" that are "both universalistic and particularistic." Elites' pursuit of their corporate interests does not preclude their pursuit of society-wide interests. Of course, where the two are irreconcilable, they will privilege their own interests. In the case of SWELA, the memorandums demonstrate a concern with the dismal levels of government investments in public infrastructure for education, health care, transport, and so on. As Caven Nnoko Mbelle, its former secretary-general, remarked, SWELA constantly asks the government to provide good roads in the South-West Region because the poor state of the roads in many parts of the region explains the region's economic stagnation. New roads, he argued, will help "Southwesterners smile, live better, development will come and many other things will fall in place" (Sumelong 2006).

These memorandums also demonstrate that elites within SWELA worry about the low levels of representation of southwesterners (their community of origin and interest, to which they feel a moral and political responsibility) in the context of national struggles for resource redistribution and in the different spheres of political and economic life in the country. Yet, as I discuss below, such narrow, ethnic, or regionally based definitions of political communities and development interests evince a dramatic reversal of an earlier moment of Cameroon's political history. Development is now spoken about and pursued in largely ethno-regional frames, in contrast to the earlier phase, when development was envisioned within a framework of national development and nation-building. This dramatic reversal and the rise of elite associations must be situated both within the historical dynamics of the early postcolonial state under one-party leadership and within the broader context of political and economic liberalizations in the 1990s that spelled uncertainties for elites and the different regions.

CULTURAL POLITICS AND DEVELOPMENT AS ACCOUNTABILITY

In the years following Cameroon's democratization, SWELA's cultural politics of development through ethnicization and regionalization was hardly unique. The institutionalization of political liberalization in Cameroon in 1990 diminished the tight controls on freedoms of association and speech formerly exercised by the president under the one-party state. Elites exploited these freedoms to establish political platforms for promoting themselves on ethnic or regional bases, the most notable forms of which are elite associations. In addition, this divisive politics of belonging perfectly suited Biya's desire to survive the threat of regime change that democratization posed to his rule in the 1990s. Accordingly, democratization in Cameroon spurred the creation of a multiplicity of ethnic or regionally based political formations, including formal political parties and "elite associations."

Although SWELA was the first of these kinds of culturally defined political groups to emerge, others were created quickly thereafter. They include the Grand Sawa Movement (for the coastal communities around Douala and the Littoral Region), Essingang (for the Beti and Bulu communities in the Centre, South, and parts of the East Regions), Association des Élites du Grand Nord (for the northern regions), the Northwest Elite Association (for the other English-speaking region, the North-West), and the Laakam (for the Bamiléké communities in the West Region) (see Nkwi 2006; Nyamnjoh and Rowlands 1998). As I have shown for SWELA, each of these associations includes different ethnic communities within the same politically defined administrative boundaries, that is, a region.

But ethnic politics in Cameroon under Biya did not begin at the dawn of political liberalization in 1990. Rather, in the context of the unfolding process of democratization, it has been only part of Biya's political project to stay in power. Upon assuming power in 1982, Biya heralded his vision of governance under the sign of a break with his predecessor's authoritarianism and its degeneration of elite leadership (Bayart 1979; 1989). He promised bureaucratic "rigor" and the "moralization" of public life, a "New Deal" of zero tolerance for corruption, patronage, ethnic privileges, and nepotism, to Cameroonians who had been forced to bear these in silence under Ahidjo. In an ironic turn not lost on most Cameroonians, it is precisely these same "public bads" that Biya's stay in power has accentuated. Institutions and society in general have been hollowed out by corruption and the ethnicization of the state, particularly so by elites from his ethnic Beti-Bulu communities of the Centre, South, and East Regions. In contrast to these promises, Biya's leadership has been largely defined by the escalation of corruption and ethnicization of public life. Mbuagbo (2002: 432) has written that since the advent of Biya at the helm of the state in November 1982, "identity politics has been particularly intense" (see also Mbuagbo and Akoko 2004; Kofele-Kale 1986). In a similar vein, Peter Geschiere (2009) has remarked that the current explosive politics of identity and ethnic belonging under President Biya stands in stark contrast to the situation under his predecessor, Ahmadou Ahidjo.

Yet, as Richard Bjornson (1991: 108–46) illustrates, the intensification of ethnicization in the Cameroonian polity through a contradictory cultural politics of national unity discourses amid ethnic fragmentation did not even start with the arrival of Paul Biya at the helm in late 1982. Rather, from the onset, the trajectory of postcolonial statehood in Cameroon has been largely defined by this double reality: a public affirmation of unity and nationhood, on the one hand, and the desires for ethnic and or regional identity and privileges among elites and the national leadership, on the other. In a seminal volume edited by Paul Nkwi and Francis Nyamnjoh in 1997, entitled *Regional Balance and National Integration*, many contributors showed that ethnic and regional considerations have always been integral to the machinations of postcolonial sovereignty in Cameroon in one guise or another, especially in contradictory ways. Centrally, the political economy of redistribution and especially the political discourse on national development efforts have consistently woven the role of elites and ethnoregionalism together as dominant themes. Even so, students of Cameroonian politics and society recognize that there is a considerable difference between Cameroon's two autocratic leaders so far in the politics of belonging.

In both discourse and policy, Ahidjo vigorously pursued a nation-building project through an authoritarian developmentalism that relied on state planning, systematized in five-year development plans, spanning 1961 to 1987. To realize these plans despite "a good deal of discontent with his authoritarianism" (Bjornson 1991: 140), Ahidjo championed various public-only and public-private corporations aimed at public service-delivery. These included public utility companies, such as those for hydroelectric power supply, water, social housing, and urban development, among several others.

Though brutally repressive, Ahidjo's regime held steadfast to dreams of high modernism and the role of state intervention in redistributive politics. This was largely pursued through a national policy process. For example, based on central economic planning and direction by means of public corporate investment, his government provided support to agriculture and farmers in rural communities and small-scale enterprises in the towns and cities (Awung and Atanga 2002. Technocratic elites, with presumed expertise on need assessments and program management, were assigned a central role in such development planning. Frank Stark (1973) has shown in a seminal paper that the idea of development and particularly the technocratic rationality of planning in the way Ahidjo envisaged and operated with it, was deeply inscribed in a project of cultural and "symbolic politics." That is, at least officially, the idea of economic and development "planning" was central to Ahidjo's politics of national redistribution and its role in his political project for national unity. Development planning came to acquire a high political currency during his time as leader. Specifically, Ahidjo spoke of creating "un mystique du Plan" ("a mystique of Planning") (cited in Stark 1973: 8). Why this emphasis on development and planning from Cameroon's first autocratic leader?

Despite its contradictions, "planning" gave Ahidjo's redistributive politics anchorage in claims to rationality and fairness. Development planning, I argue, allowed Ahidjo to stake a claim to an ethics of accountability for his vision and project of political leadership for Cameroon. As he saw it, planning gestured toward political expectations for transparency, traceability, and social justice in both the logics and mechanics of government decision-making processes. More precisely, Ahidjo argued, planning opposed the opacity, "anarchy and social injustice" of the market or "classical capitalism" (cited in Stark 1973: 2). Ahidjo also believed that since development "appears to be a long term operation that requires considerable capital which an underdeveloped country such as ours, by definition, does not have," planning for economic development must be anchored in the political quest for national unity (cited Stark 1973: 7).

To a great extent, Stark argues, Ahidjo was obsessed with development and planning as objects of both technocratic efficiency and instruments of national unity. His success with these depended on a kind of "popularization" that responded to the realities of regional diversity in terms of socioeconomic endowments and infrastructural resources, in a manner that also sought participation from elites from these different regions. As Stark (1973: 18) writes, "The attempt to plan by regions seems to reflect both a desire to popularize the Plan and mobilize elites at different levels for its execution." In other words, Ahidjo hoped that centralized development planning would serve as a political device to ward off accusations of irrational, subjective, and politicized decision-making on what resources where to be allocated to what places.

To give material expression to this vision of authoritarian developmentalism based on planning, Ahidjo also institutionalized "regional balance" (Nkwi and Nyamnjoh 1997), a politically conscious and deliberately formulated—if somewhat incoherent and contradictory—public policy (Ngeve and Orock 2012). This provided the broad principles for the allocation of public resources in a manner that would recognize regions and communities that had historically been "late" to embrace the offerings of colonial modernity (education, health care facilities, etc.). For his political purposes, most of these historically late societies, it was argued, were located in his own northern regions, conveniently warranting greater resource allocations to them. Concomitantly, as Geschiere (2009: 39) explains—and also paradoxically given Ahidjo's emphasis on the role of elites in nation-building—Ahidjo discouraged elites from making collective demands or mobilizing on the basis of their ethnic or regional identities. Shortly after independence Ahidjo saw to it that the word "tribe" was excised from national identification papers (Banock 1992: 92) and on June 12, 1967, he "passed laws banning 'any association exhibiting an exclusively tribal or clan character'" (Azevedo 1995: 268). Elites who defied this tacit restriction in word or deed and brazenly played ethnic politics were often dealt with politically by Ahidjo (see Prouzet 1974: 55).

As I have shown, Biya's cultural politics of ethnic fragmentation runs contrary to Ahidjo's cultural political project of national unification through state-led national development plans and programs and the political restrictions on elite freedoms of ethnic association. From the onset of his leadership in late 1982, Paul Biya espoused ethnicization of the state as principle of governance in practice, even if he has maintained a platitudinous discourse of "national integration" over the last thirty-seven years. I have also evoked how, as elsewhere in sub-Saharan Africa, the onset of democratization in Cameroon worked a script opposing the affective politics of national unity and nation-building that had prevailed under the authoritarianisms of one-party rule. Rather, the politics of democratization in Cameroon has been driven by an affective politics of ethnic or regional solidarities as the ideological framework for political action.

All of these political developments following democratization mean that despite the turbulent onset of democratization in Cameroon, President Biya has retained a firm grip on the structures of the state, particularly with regards to the channels of revenue mobilization for the state, including a long-standing tradition of opacity in the management oil revenue that derives almost entirely from the South-West Region (see, e.g., Awung and Atanga 2011, 2002. Biya's predecessor, Ahmadou Ahidjo, had undoubtedly initiated such authoritarian management of the public wealth, allowing only loyal political supporters access to the prebends through political appointments. Yet under Paul Biya the intense desire for political loyalties over a commitment to national welfare has fueled elite corruption and looted the commonwealth by the caciques of the regime in Yaoundé. In reality, however, a considerable proportion of resources for national development are managed by elites from Biya's ethnoregional community in the South, Centre, and East Regions, and they exercise an outsized influence in the redistribution of these resources in favor of their own regions. Elites from the other seven regions in the country are locked in an ever-diminishing pool of resources, including political appointments and financial and material resources. These elites have established associations as a political instrument to engage in a political field where the logic of competition is largely shaped by ethnic and regional considerations.

CONCLUSION

This chapter set out to examine how development might serve as an idiom for an elite politics of accountability in Africa, a domain of political action where political identities and interests are specified and pursued vigorously through various forms of political mobilization. I approached this question by underlining that development is entangled with culture as a kind of aspiration for recognition and inclusion (see Appadurai 2007). In this Cameroonian case, I have explored the cultural politics of an elite association called SWELA, probing its modalities for operating political representation and accountability following the country's explosive return to multiparty politics in 1990. I have argued that while ethnic and regional identities serve as the primordial (as opposed to civic) basis for elite mobilizations in associations in Cameroon, demand for development and social improvement schemes is the central idiom of postcolonial claim-making.

In other words, the narrow and exclusionary cultural politics of ethnoregional associations serves as a primary vehicle for the articulation of expectations and demands for accountability in the distribution of public goods, which are by themselves inclusive and universally beneficial to users living within a defined ethnic or regional community. As Arjun Appadurai puts it, questions about the politics of recognition in our time cannot be separable from concerns about redistribution. And so in discussions about democratization and development anywhere (though especially in highly unequal postcolonial settings), we must remain attentive to the ambivalent workings of the cultural politics of identity and belonging. Specifically, the analysis of elite mobilizations based on such politics of belonging also underline how demands for "cultural recognition can be extended so as to enhance redistribution" (Appadurai 2007: 33).

NOTES

1. France was ceded two-thirds of the territory, first as a League of Nations Mandate and then as a United Nations Trusteeship. Under the same international obligations, Britain further divided its one-third territory into British Northern and British Southern Cameroons and administered these as parts of its Nigerian colonial administration. British Northern Cameroons was administered as part of the Northern Protectorate, and British Southern Cameroons was largely governed as part of the Eastern Region of Nigeria until 1957, when it attained regional autonomy and quasi self-government, in preparation for outright self-rule. Ever since the reunification of these two areas on January 1, 1961, a strong sense of marginalization has been felt among former Southern Cameroonians that has culminated in an "anglophone problem." Since October 2016 this problem has found expression in an evolving, violent political conflict over autonomist claims by Southern Cameroon activists, with a growing number of casualties for both government forces and autonomist groups, including civilians. On the "anglophone problem" see Konings and Nyamnjoh 1997, 2003; Ngoh 1999. On the ongoing violent confrontations in anglophone Cameroon, see Pommerolle and Heungoup 2017.

2. Interview with Caven Nnoko Mbelle. He is a prominent member of SWELA, also widely known as a former secretary-general of SWELA between 1993 and 2000 during the nascent and tumultuous years of elite political competition both within the South-West Region and across the country. He also served in a controversial political position as a presidentially appointed "native" government delegate to the Kumba City Council from 1996 to 2008. Across several major urban municipalities in the country these are people appointed by Biya, with powers above the elected mayors, who could be "strangers" to the area.

3. This is one of the major sources of resentment for anglophone Cameroonians and a major factor of the ongoing protests in since late 2016. These protests have morphed into an outright civil war that erupted in the two anglophone regions of the country in October 2017.

REFERENCES

Abrahamsen, Rita. 2000. *Disciplining Democracy: Development Discourse and Good Governance in Africa*. London: Zed Books.

Ahidjo, Ahmadou. 1965. *Contribution à la construction nationale*. Paris: Présence Africaine.

Albaugh, Ericka A. 2011. "An Autocrat's Toolkit: Adaptation and Manipulation in 'Democratic' Cameroon." *Democratization* 18, no. 2: 388–414.

Appadurai, Arjun. 2007. "The Capacity to Aspire: Culture and the Terms of Recognition." In David Held and Henrietta L. Moore, eds., *Cultural Politics in a Global Age: Uncertainty, Solidarity and Innovation*, 29–35. Oxford: Oneworld.

Awung, Wilfred, and Lucien M. Atanga. 2002. "Politics and Economic Policies in Cameroon." *Journal of Applied Social Sciences* 2, nos. 1–2: 25–40.

Azevedo, Mario. 1995. "Ethnicity and Democratization: Cameroon and Gabon." In Harvey Glickman, ed., *Ethnic Conflict and Democratization in Africa*, 255–67. Atlanta, GA: African Studies Association Press.

Banock, Michel. 1992. *Le Processus de la Democratisation en Afrique: Le Cas Camerounais*. Paris: L'Harmattan.

Bayart, Jean-François. 1979. *l'état au Cameroun*. Paris: Presses de la Fondation Nationale des Sciences Politiques.

Bayart, Jean-François. 1989. "Cameroon." In Donald B. C. O'Brien, John Dunn, and Richards Rathbone, eds., *Contemporary West African States*, 31–48. Cambridge: Cambridge University Press.

Bayart, Jean-François. 1993. *The State in Africa: The Politics of the Belly*. London: Longman.

Bensimon, Estela M., Robert Rueda, Alicia C. Dowd, and Frank Harris III. 2007. "Accountability, Equity, and Practitioner Learning and Change." *Metropolitan* 18, no. 3: 28–45.

Bjornson, Richard. 1991. *The African Quest for Freedom and Identity: Cameroonian Writing and the National Experience*. Bloomington: Indiana University Press.

Blundo, Giorgio, and Jean-Pierre Olivier de Sardan, eds. 2006. *Everyday Corruption and the State: Citizens and Public Officials in Africa*. London: Zed Books.

Bourdieu, Pierre. 1984. *Distinction: A Social Critique of the Judgement of Taste*. Translated by Richard Nice. Cambridge, MA: Harvard University Press.

Chabal, Patrick, ed. 1986. *Political Domination in Africa: Reflections on the Limits of Power*. Cambridge: Cambridge University Press.

Chabal, Patrick. 2009. *Africa: The Politics of Suffering and Smiling*. London: Zed Books.

Cody, Francis. 2009. "Inscribing Subjects to Citizenship: Petitions, Literacy Activism, and the Performativity of Signature in Rural Tamil India." *Cultural Anthropology* 24, no. 3: 347–80.

Cohen, Abner. 1981. *The Politics of Elite Culture: Explorations in the Dramaturgy of Power in a Modern African Society*. Berkeley: University of California Press.

Daloz, Jean-Pascal. 2009. *The Sociology of Elite Distinction: From Theoretical to Comparative Perspectives*. Basingstoke: Palgrave Macmillan.

Deutsche Welle. 2009. "African Elites Ignore Poverty Exacerbating the Continent's Problems." June 27. http://www.dw.de/african-elites-ignore-poverty-exacerbating-the-continents-problems/a-4434689

Dunn, John. 1986. "The Politics of Representation and Good Government in Postcolonial Africa." In Patrick Chabal, ed., *Political Domination in Africa: Reflections on the Limits of Power*, 158–74. Cambridge: Cambridge University Press.

Davis, Natalie Zemon. 1987. *Fiction in the Archives: Pardon Tales and Their Tellers in Sixteenth Century France*. Palo Alto, CA: Stanford University Press.

Ebrahim, Alnoor, and Edward Veisband, eds. 2007. *Global Accountabilities: Participation, Pluralism and Public Ethics*. Cambridge: Cambridge University Press.

Ekeh, Peter P. 1975. "Colonialism and the Two Publics in Africa: A Theoretical Statement." *Comparative Studies in Society and History* 17, no. 1, 91–112.

Englund, Harri, and Francis B. Nyamnjoh, eds. 2004. *Rights and the Politics of Recognition in Africa*. London: Zed Books.

Evans, Martins. 2010. "Primary Patriotism, Shifting Identity: Hometown Associations in Manyu Division, South-West Cameroon." *Africa* 80, no. 3: 397–425.

Geschiere, Peter. 2009. *The Perils of Belonging: Autochthony, Citizenship, and Exclusion in Europe and Africa*. Chicago: University of Chicago Press.

Geschiere, Peter, and Josef Gugler. 1998. "Introduction: The Urban-Rural Connection and Changing Issues of Belonging and Identification." *Africa* 68, no. 3: 309–19.

Gore, Charles, and David Pratten. 2003. "The Politics of Plunder: The Rhetorics of Order and Disorder in Southern Nigeria." *African Affairs* 102, no. 407: 211–40.

Huntington, Samuel P. 1991. *The Third Wave: Democratization in the Late Twentieth Century*. Norman: University of Oklahoma Press.

Joseph, Richard. 1987. *Democracy and Prebendal Politics in Nigeria: the Rise and Fall of the Second Republic*. Cambridge: Cambridge University Press.

Jua, Nantang. 1991. "Cameroon: Jump-Starting an Economic Crisis." *Africa Insight* 21, no. 1: 162–70.

Kapferer, Bruce. 2002. "Ethnicity, Nationalism and the Culture of the State." *Suomen Antropologi: Journal of the Finnish Anthropological Society* 2: 4–23.

Kelsall, Tim. 2003. "Rituals of Verification: Indigenous and Imported Accountability in Northern Tanzania." *Africa: Journal of the International African Institute* 73, no. 2: 174–213.

Kofele-Kale, Ndiva. 1986. "Ethnicity, Regionalism, and Political Power: A Postmortem of Ahidjo's Cameroon." In Michael G. Schatzberg and I. William Zartman, eds., *The Political Economy of Cameroon*, 53–82. New York: Praeger.

Konings, Piet, and Francis B. Nyamnjoh. 1997. "The Anglophone Problem in Cameroon." *Journal of Modern African Studies* 35 (2: 207–29.

Konings, Piet, and Francis B. Nyamnjoh. 2003. *Negotiating an Anglophone Identity: A Study of the Politics of Recognition and Representation in Cameroon*. Boston: Brill.

Lindberg, Steffan I. 2004. "The Democratic Qualities of Competitive Elections: Participation, Competition and Legitimacy in Africa." *Commonwealth and Comparative Politics* 42, no. 1: 61–105.

Lindberg, Steffan I. 2006. *Democracy and Elections in Africa*. Baltimore, MD: John Hopkins University Press.

Lindberg, Steffan I., Anna Lührmann, and Valeriya Mechkova. 2017. "From *De-jure* to *De-facto*: Mapping Dimensions and Sequences of Accountability." World Development Report Background Paper. Washington, DC: World Bank.

Lonsdale, John. 1986. "Political Accountability in African History." In Patrick Chabal, ed., Political Domination in Africa: Reflections on the Limits of Power, 126–57. Cambridge: Cambridge University Press.

Marcus, George. 1983. "'Elite' as a Concept, Theory and Research Tradition." In George Marcus, ed., *Elites: Ethnographic Issues*, 7–27. Albuquerque: University of New Mexico Press.

Mbembe, Achille. 2001. *On the Postcolony*. Berkeley: University of California Press.

Mbembe, Achille. 1992. "Provisional Notes on the Postcolony." *Africa: Journal of the International African Institute* 62, no. 1: 3–37.

Mbembe, Achille, and Janet Roitman. 1995. "Figures of the Subject in Times of Crisis." *Public Culture* 7, no. 2: 323–52.

Mbeki, Moeletsi. 2009. *Architects of Poverty: Why African Capitalism Needs Changing*. Johannesburg: Pan Macmillan South Africa.

Mbu, Ant. 1993. *Civil Disobedience in Cameroon*. Douala: Imprimerie Georges Frères.

Mbuagbo, Oben T. 2002. "Cameroon: Exploiting Anglophone Identity in State Deconstruction." *Social Identities* 8, no. 3: 1–10.

Mbuagbo, Oben T., and Robert M. Akoko. 2004. "Roll-Back: Democratization and Social Fragmentation in Cameroon." *Nordic Journal of African Studies* 13, no. 1: 1–12.

Mills, Charles W. 1956. *The Power Elite*. New York: Oxford University Press.

Mkandawire, Thandika. 2015. "Neopatrimonialism and the Political Economy of Economic Performance in Africa: Critical Reflections." *World Politics* 67, no. 3: 563–612.

Ngeve, Rebecca E., and Rogers Orock. 2012. "In the Name of Development: Ethnic Politics and Multicultural Public Policy in Cameroon." *International Journal of Sociology and Social Policy* 32, nos. 3–4: 214–32.

Ngoh, Victor J. 1999. "The Origin of the Marginalization of Former Southern Cameroonians (Anglophones), 1961–1966: An Historical Analysis." *Journal of Third World Studies* 16, no. 1: 165–85.

Nkwi, Paul N., and Francis B. Nyamnjoh, eds. 1997. *Regional Balance and National Integration in Cameroon: Lessons Learnt and the Uncertain Future*. Leiden: African Studies Centre; Yaoundé: International Centre for Applied Social Science and Training.

Nkwi, Walter G. 2006. "Elites, Ethno-regional Competition in Cameroon, and the Southwest Elites Association (SWELA), 1991–1997." *African Study Monographs* 27, no. 3: 123–43.

Nyamnjoh, Francis B. 2005. *Africa's Media, Democracy and the Politics of Belonging*. London: Zed Books.

Nyamnjoh, Francis B. 1999. "Cameroon: A Country united by Ethnic Ambition and Difference." *African Affairs* 98, no. 390: 101–18.

Nyamnjoh, Francis B., and Michael Rowlands. 1998. "Elite Associations and the Politics of Belonging in Cameroon." *Africa: Journal of the International Africa Institute* 68, no. 3: 321–37.

Okonta, Ike. 2014. "'Biafra of the Mind': MASSOB and the Mobilization of History." *Journal of Genocide Research* 2–3: 355–78.

Organized Crime and Corruption Reporting Project. 2018. "Paul Biya, Cameroon's Roaming President." February 18. https://www.occrp.org/en/28-ccwatch/cc-watch-indepth/7653-paul-biya-cameroon-s-roaming-president

Orock, Rogers. 2009. The State, Multi-party Politics and Ethno-regional Communities in Cameroon: The Strategic Discourses of South-West Elites. Unpublished M.Soc. Sc. thesis, Faculty of Social Sciences, University of Helsinki, Finland.

Orock, Rogers. 2014. "Welcoming the 'Fon of Fons': Anglophone Elites and the Politics of Hosting Cameroon's Head of State." *Africa: Journal of the International Africa Institute* 84, no. 2: 226–45.

Orock, Rogers. 2015. "SWELA, Ethnicity, and Democracy in Cameroon's Patrimonial State: An Anthropological Critique." *Critique of Anthropology* 34, no. 2: 204–33.

Parkin, David. 1978. *The Cultural Definition of Political Response: Lineal Destiny among the Luo*. San Francisco: Academic Press.

Piot, Charles. 2010. *Nostalgia for the Future: West Africa After the Cold War*. Chicago: University of Chicago Press.

Pommerolle, Marie-Emmanuelle and Hans de Maries Heungoup. 2017. "'The Anglophone Crisis': A Tale of the Cameroonian Postcolony." *African Affairs* 116, no. 464: 526–38.

Power, Michael. 1997. *The Audit Society: Rituals of Verification.* Oxford: Oxford University Press.

Prouzet, Michel. 1974. *Le Cameroun.* Paris: Librairie Générale de Droit et de jurisprudence.

Reno, William. 2016. "The Evolution of Insurgent Leadership in Africa." In Ebenezer Obadare and Wale Adebanwi, eds., *Governance and the Crisis of Rule in Contemporary Africa: Leadership in Transformation,* 197–210. New York: Palgrave Macmillan.

Röschenthaler, Ute. 2011. *Purchasing Culture. The Dissemination of Associations in the Cross River region of Cameroon and Nigeria.* Trenton, NJ: Africa World Press.

Ruel, Malcolm. 1969. *Leopards and Leaders: Constitutional Politics among a Cross River People.* London: Tavistock.

Schmitz, Gerald J. 1995. "Democratization and Demystification: Deconstructing 'Governance' as Development Paradigm." In David B. Moore and Gerald J. Schmitz, eds., *Debating Development Discourse: Institutional and Popular Perspectives,* 54–90. London: Macmillan.

Sen, Amartya. 1988. "The Concept of Development." In T. N. Srinivasan and Hollis Chenery, eds., *Handbook of Development Economics,* 1:2–23. New York: Elsevier Science Publishing.

Sen, Amartya. 1999. *Development as Freedom.* Oxford: Oxford University Press.

Smith, Daniel J. 2007. *A Culture of Corruption: Everyday Deception and Popular Discontent in Nigeria.* Princeton, NJ: Princeton University Press.

Smith, Daniel J. 2014. "Corruption Complaints, Inequality and Ethnic Grievances in Post-Biafra Nigeria." *Third World Quarterly* 35, no. 5: 787–802.

SWELA. 1992. Mundemba Declaration. *The Oracle,* May–June, 30–33.

SWELA. 2006a. "SWELA and the South-West Chiefs Conference: Two Faces of Same Coin." General Assembly of the South-west Chiefs Conference, Kumba, November 25, 2006.

SWELA. 2006b. Communique' on the recent government reshuffle.

SWELA. 2006c. Memorandum presented respectively to the Prime Minister Head of Government Chief Ephraim Inoni and Ministers Ngolle Ngolle Elvis, Achuo Hilman Egbe, and Dion Ngute, respectively, by the Secretary General of the South-West Elite Association (SWELA) Dr. Enow-Orock George, on the Occasion of Maiden Visits on Thursday 14 September 2006 to The General Secretariat.

Stark, Frank M.1973. "El Hadj Ahmadou Ahidjo's Use of Development as a Symbol of Political Unity Among Administrative and Political Elites in Cameroon." Paper presented at a joint conference of the School of International Affaris, Carlton University and the Canadian Association of African Studies, February 16.

Takougang, Joseph, and Milton Krieger. 1998. *African Politics in the 1990s: Cameroon's Political Crossroads.* Boulder, CO: Westview Press.

Taylor, Charles. 1994. "The Politics of Recognition." In Amy Gutmann, ed. *Multiculturalism and the Politics of Recognition,* 25–73. Princeton: Princeton University Press.

The Pilot. 1997. "After Biya's new gov't, who holds power?" December, 7–9.

Sumelong, Ernest. 2006. "Southwest MPs, mayors, chiefs say roads are priority," *The Post*, Thursday, 26 October. https://www.postnewsline.com/2006/10/southwest_mps_m.html

Urban, Greg. 2001. "How 'We' Moves through the World." *Suomen Antropologi: Journal of the Finnish Anthropological Society* 26, no. 4: 19–63.

Woods, Dwayne. 1989. "Ethno-regional Demands, Symbolic and Redistributive Politics: Sugar Complexes in the North of the Ivory Coast." *Ethnic and Racial Studies* 12, no. 4: 469–89.

Visible Hands: Taking Responsibility for Social Development. Geneva: UNRISD.

World Bank. 2003. *World Development Report 2004: Making Services Work for the Poor*. Washington, DC: World Bank.

Yenshu-Vubo, Emmanuel. 2006. "Management of Ethnic Diversity in Cameroon against the Backdrop of Social Crises." *Cahiers d'Etudes Africaines* 181: 135–56.

Zambo-Belinga, J. M. 1997. "Equilibre régional, replis identitaire et fragilisation croissante de l'intérêt national: Vers un effet 'boomerang' de la politique des quotas au Cameroun." In Paul N. Nkwi and Francis B. Nyamnjoh, eds., *Regional Balance and National Integration in Cameroon: Lessons Learnt and the Uncertain Future*. Leiden: African Studies Centre; Yaoundé: International Centre for Applied Social Science and Training.

CHAPTER 10

Elite Incorporation in Nigeria
The Case of Ohanaeze Ndi-Igbo

GODWIN ONUOHA

INTRODUCTION

Reminiscent of most multiethnic postcolonial states in Africa, Nigeria is confronted with the challenge of managing its ethnic diversity and forging a viable basis for national unity and integration. Virtually every ethnic group in Nigeria has a central ethnic organization committed to the advancement of its collective interests and aspirations. This tendency complicates interethnic relations and provides the context within which the uneasy relations among its 250 (or more) ethnic nationalities can be understood. Relations between Nigeria's ethnic groups have undergone processes of change and renewal over the decades. These sometimes have hinged on extant sociopolitical and economic contexts, the emergence of new actors and forces, and diverse forms of mobilizations and manifestations in the Nigerian public space. A remarkable feature of Nigeria's ethnic composition is that it provides the terrain in which major political issues are vigorously (and sometimes violently) contested along complex ethnic, religious and regional lines (Nnoli 1978; 1998; Osaghae 1998), and the elites of each of the groups occupy critical positions of influence and, invariably, determine the pitch, substance, and direction of these contestations.

This chapter critically examines the nature of post-civil war Igbo elite politics after the secessionist Republic of Biafra was defeated and reabsorbed into Nigeria under the banner of national unity in 1970. The chapter focuses on Ohanaeze Ndi-Igbo, the apex Igbo sociocultural group in Igboland, which was formed as a "bridge" to reintegrate the Igbo elite into mainstream Nigerian politics in the postwar era. The chapter is set against the backdrop of the existential crisis of the Igbo faction of the ruling elite, and how the Ohanaeze and its activities have shaped Igbo elite politics in Nigeria. Ohanaeze provides the terrain and context for elite Igbo mobilization in cultural, social, and political terms, and projects power and leverage in practical terms. This chapter does not simplify or reduce the Igbo elite to a monolith; rather it examines how Ohanaeze straddles the binary between its elitist origin and anchorage on the one hand, and its position as a group that speaks for, and on behalf of, the entire Igbo ethnic group on the other hand.

This chapter focuses on three broad phases in postwar Igbo elite politics in Nigeria. The first phase explores the role of Ohanaeze from its inception in 1976 to the end of the Second Republic in 1983, when the organization appeared to play the primordial role of an Igbo group that projects Igbo interests. The second phase examines the era of military rule, a period characterized by profound changes in the economic, social, and political landscape of the country. During this period, Ohanaeze and Aka Ikenga (its "intellectual wing") adopted a perspective that re-emphasized perceptions of Igbo marginalization and the need to carve out the Igbo share of the national patrimony. This unfolded in the context of the IMF- and World Bank–inspired structural adjustment programs (SAPs) that appeared to benefit elites from other ethnic groups who had access to power. The third and final phase, which spans the period of civilian rule from 1999 until the present, is perhaps the most turbulent in the organization's history. The authority and legitimacy of the group in Igboland was subjected to severe scrutiny and assault by several neo-Biafran groups that emerged with the opening of the political space in 1999.

This chapter draws on academic and popular literature, media sources, and interviews with both members of the Igbo elite and members of neo-Biafran groups who espouse a different brand of Igbo nationalism. The first section sets out the main aims and arguments of the chapter. The second section presents a conceptual framing of elite politics in Nigeria. It maps out the position of Igbo elites vis-à-vis elites from other ethnic groups, and the implication of this prevailing power configuration for the project of "incorporation." The third section examines Igbo elites in a historical and institutional context. This sets the stage for unpacking the three phases of Igbo elite politics. This involves the extent to which Ohanaeze (both as an actor and institution) embodies and accounts for the aspirations of its collective domestic constituency in Igboland, while at the same time maintaining its elitist anchorage, proclivities, relationships, and practices as a means of accessing power, privilege, and opportunity at the national level. The concluding section sums up the entire arguments of the chapter and the examines the emancipatory potentials of this form of elite politics in Igboland.

ELITE POLITICS AND THE PROJECT OF INCORPORATION

Scholars have advanced several definitions of elites (Lasswell 1961; Mills 1956; Hossain and Moore 2002; Chandra 2007), and these have generated competing explanations and conceptions about "who an elite is" in the day-to-day realities of politics in Africa (Chabal and Daloz 1998; Amundsen 2001; Lindberg 2003). A common thread that runs through the concepts and explanations is that there are those who are located at the apex of any society, and as a result determine the processes and outcomes in the political, economic, social, religious, and cultural spheres. To transcend the quagmire of the study of elites, attempts have been made to focus specifically on political elites (Quandt 1970; Zuckerman 1977). Following Higley and Burton's (2006: 7) functionalist definition, political elites are "persons who are able, by virtue of their authoritative positions in powerful organizations and movements of whatever kind, to affect national political outcomes regularly and substantially." But as Adebanwi (2014: 10) argues, the concentration on the political ignores the fact that elite status is so context-bound and spatially specific that the ability to "affect political outcomes regularly and substantially" need not be "national" to make powerful persons qualify as elites, and emphasizing "the social," rather than the "national political," might be a far more useful way to capture the elite. This chapter espouses Shore's (2002: 4) definition of elites as "those who occupy the most influential positions or roles in the important spheres of social life." This evokes tendencies like agency, exclusivity, power, influence, and dominance, as elites symbolize the conception of power in society and the ascription of control to persons (agents), rather than to impersonal processes, in the form of rules, institutions, and resources (Marcus 1983: 10).

In a context where loyalty to the ethnic group is stronger than loyalty to the state, this translates into the strengthening of elites and their ethnic centers of power, even though they paradoxically exploit their ethnic constituencies and state resources to sustain their own interests. The advent of colonialism and the introduction of the ethnic principle entrenched the divide and rule regime that sustained the colonial enterprise. But as Osaghae

(2006: 8) argues, "It took the interest-begotten efforts of the incipient elites, the new men of power, who exploited the infrastructure, for ethnic identities and claims as they exist today, to flourish." While colonialism provided the groundwork for ethnic divisions in contemporary Africa, the fundamental truism, as Nnoli (1978) argues, is that political elites and ruling classes were largely responsible for concretizing the so-called ethnic interests and in transforming the ethnic group "in-itself" into the ethnic group "for-itself." In the context of the prevailing power configuration in Nigeria, the study of elites, and by extension their politics, includes the "language and practices through which they represent themselves, and are represented, and the methods they adopt in legitimizing their positions" (Shore 2002: 13).

In the postwar reconfiguration of the Nigerian project, the Igbo faction of the ruling elite was effectively eliminated as a dominant power bloc. This perception was based on the fact that while the ruling elites of the other two dominant ethnic groups (the Yoruba and Hausa-Fulani) in the polity recognize the historical, political, social, and economic significance of the Igbo faction of the Nigerian ruling elite prior to 1967, they were also aware that the Igbo elite faction mobilized and formed the core of secessionist Biafra, which was defeated in 1970. Thus, the project of "incorporation" became an important means of entrenching accountability for two significant reasons. First, the "dominant" or "victorious" elites perceived incorporation as an optimal political strategy to accommodate the Igbo elites in an arrangement where Igbo elite access to power and privilege would depend largely on this prevailing power structure. Since the perceived benefits of incorporation outweighed its costs, this meant integrating them into organizations and structures that would guarantee their accountability to the dominant elites. The Igbo faction of the ruling elite was, thus, incorporated on the terms of the elites of the "dominant" ethnic groups, who consolidated their advantage in the "first circle" of power and privilege, while the "subordinated" elites were subjected to the "second circle." Second, for the "subordinate" Igbo elites, which had to defend their interests against rival elite factions backed by state power, the costs of incorporation were more acceptable than the alternative scenario of outright political and economic disenfranchisement. As the leader of the Igbo people, Ohanaeze perceived the quest for some form of elite incorporation as a form of elite accountability to Ndi-Igbo, so that the Igbo could access some of the material benefits of federal resources. The assault on their political and economic privileges made the subordinate Igbo elite accept incorporation as a survival strategy.

IGBO ELITES: THE HISTORICAL AND INSTITUTIONAL CONTEXT

The bulk of the literature on Igbo society points out differences in societal transformation in the precolonial and the colonial periods. Igbo societies were remarkably different from the monolithic kingdoms, hierarchical administrative systems, centralized political structures, and constitutional monarchies that existed among the Yoruba of western Nigeria and Hausa-Fulani emirates of northern Nigeria. Evidence suggests that precolonial Igbo societies were segmented in nature, stateless, acephalous, and individualistic (Green 1947; Forde and Jones 1950; S. Ottenberg 1959; Buchanan and Pugh 1962; P. Ottenberg 1965) and void of formalized, permanent, and hereditary leadership positions, or any definite seat of executive authority (Meek 1937; Hailey 1951, cited in Anber 1967; Uchendu 1965). But as the literature suggests, precolonial Igbo society also had slaves (*ohu*) and cult slaves (*osu*), and titled individuals (*ozo* and *obi*) who enjoyed a special degree of power and influence. Certain areas in Igboland had lineage heads, influential age-groups, and titled secret societies, and some of these positions were restricted to elders of certain lineages or based on personal achievements, status, or power (Harneit-Sievers 1998). While extant studies demonstrate widely held negative views about elites in other parts of the world (Khan 2012), there is evidence pointing to the existence of elites, in one form or the other, in precolonial Igboland, which are linked to popular movements and projects in the colonial and postcolonial period.

The study of elite power and influence in politics began to gain prominence in Africa from the late colonial period to the immediate independence era (Kuper 1965; Levine 1965). This, in many ways, was a period of monumental transformations, roughly coinciding with nationalist mobilizations for political independence and intense polarization of political developments as elites sought to position themselves for the eventual takeover of the reins of governance in most African countries. Igbo politics during this era coalesced around the influential and charismatic figure of Nnamdi Azikiwe, who had just returned from the United States with an impressive array of degrees. Popularly referred to as "Zik," he emerged as "the most important and celebrated nationalist leader" on the west coast of Africa, if not in all of tropical Africa (Coleman 1958: 220). With his provocative and combative brand of journalism, Azikiwe initiated a new era in the nationalist struggle and became the symbol and spokesman for the Igbo, who had largely remained at the periphery of the nationalist struggle, which was virtually dominated by their

Fig. 10.1. "Founding father": Dr. Nnamdi Azikiwe on Nigeria's five-hundred-naira note

southern rivals—the Yoruba (Coleman 1958: 224). Owing to the intense competition between the Igbo and Yoruba in Lagos, the hotbed of the nationalist struggle, Igbo elites were compelled to articulate their interests with the formation of an Igbo Union in Lagos in 1934. It was expanded in 1943 into a pan-Igbo union to include all Igbo unions countrywide and was called the Igbo Federal Union; and later in 1944, it became the Igbo State Union. While Azikiwe tapped into Igbo nationalism to mobilize the Igbo into a unified, cohesive, and political bloc in the colonial system, he also sought to assume the leadership role in the pan-Nigerian nationalist movement and its pan-African version as well.

Though these aspirations appeared to be contradictory in terms and mutually exclusive, Azikiwe did not perceive Igbo nationalism and Nigerian nationalism as conflicting, but as dual sources of inspiration in the struggle against colonialism. Matters were further complicated by his presidency of the Igbo State Union and his articulation of the "Manifest Destiny" of the Igbo in strikingly hegemonic terms (Crowder 1962: 228). These developments marked a watershed in ethnic relations in colonial Nigeria. It also lent the tripolar ethnic power struggle a much broader appeal by giving it the face of a zero-sum contest and brought into sharper focus the potential ethnonationalist rivalries that engulfed the country at independence.

After independence in 1960, Nigeria's federal experiment began to disintegrate, and eventually collapsed, ushering in a host of other crisis like the emergency rule in the Western Region in 1962, the census crisis of 1962–63, the election crisis of 1964–65, the intervention of the military in January 1966, a counter-coup six months later, and finally, the Nigeria-Biafra War, which started in 1967. There is a widespread view that the Biafran secession was an Igbo elite project, and its collapse effectively halted the Igbo elite challenge to the Nigerian project. This perspective gained prominence at a time when scholars began to substitute elite theories with various shades of class analysis (Sklar 1963; Shivji 1976). For Ikenna Nzimiro (1982), the shift to class analysis was particularly important in analyzing the singular most consequential event in Nigeria's history. Nzimiro argued that social classes existed in Nigeria, and that each class played significant economic and political roles in the First Republic in the buildup to the Nigeria-Biafra War. According to Nzimiro (1982: 10), the war reflected "hierarchies of power," where "those who controlled the upper structure of these hierarchies tried also to command the fundamental aspect of the structure." Nzimiro (1982: 10) disagrees with the analysis of "bourgeois social scientists" who interpret the Nigeria-Biafra War in ethnic terms, but emphasizes that the war broke out as "a class conflict within the ruling class," with a faction of that class (the Igbo elite class) leading Biafra's secessionist attempt.

"THE FRONT": OHANAEZE NDI-IGBO, EVOLUTION, AND SECOND REPUBLIC POLITICS (1976–1983)

In the immediate aftermath of the war, the Federal Military Government (FMG) launched the "Reconciliation, Rehabilitation and Reconstruction (3Rs)" program, which was aimed at reintegrating the Igbo into the Nigerian project. Its pronouncements were meant to guarantee the personal safety and security of the Igbo and their properties, secure the right to reside and work anywhere in Nigeria, ensure the reabsorption of public civil servants of Igbo ethnic extraction into the civil service and the military, and grant general amnesty to the Igbo (Theen and Wilson 1996: 500). But the reality of the situation was that the Nigeria-Biafra War had irreparably disrupted the prewar equilibrium between the three major ethnic groups, and shifted the balance of power in favor of the victorious elites, who subsequently increased their influence and pressed their advantage. Hence, the future of the Igbo in the post-civil war reconfiguration of Nigeria remained a concern, as the marginalization, alienation, and the distancing of the Igbo from mainstream national political and economic processes continued. The institutional and structural context of Igbo marginalization was reflected in a string of policies and fiscal decrees that disadvantaged the Igbo. These include the Banking Obligation (Eastern States) Decree of 1970, which did not recognize any deposits made into bank accounts within the former Eastern Region from May 30, 1967, up until January 12, 1970 (Achebe 1983: 46–55); the Nigerian Enterprises Promotion (Indigenization) Decree, which compelled foreign companies to sell part of their shares to Nigerians at a time when the Igbo had barely recovered from the effects of the war and were still economically emasculated (Achebe 1983: 46); and the FMG-instituted Abandoned Properties Implementation Committee, which presided over the sale of Igbo properties outside Igboland (Nwabueze 1985).

In the postwar era, the clamor, agitation, and struggle for greater access to and control over national resources by various factions of the ruling elite found expression in state creation, as "statehood" became a crucial factor in the allocation of a wide range of social opportunities in the Nigerian federation (Suberu 1991: 500; Alapiki 2005). Anticipating a new fiscal regime in which states would form the basis for revenue allocation, the 1976 state creation exercise created four Hausa-Fulani states, four Yoruba states, nine ethnic minority states, and only two Igbo states (Achebe 1983: 49). Discrimination against the Igbo in the 1976 exercise was condemned by Igbo elites, who argued that the creation of only two Igbo states had put them at a huge disadvantage in the competition for socioeconomic and political opportunities in the federation (Nwabueze 1983: 307). Against the backdrop of these developments, the dominant thinking within the Igbo ethnic group during this period was that there was an "unofficial policy" to punish the Igbo for their secessionist attempt, so as to forestall a recurrence from any section of the country (interview, Goddy Uwazurike, January 15, 2009). The outcome of these postwar settlements guaranteed a shift in the balance of power in favor of the other dominant ethnic nationalities in Nigeria. Chinua Achebe (1983: 45) would subsequently describe the Igbo as "a special thorn in the flesh of the Nigerian body-politic," the effect of which was the belief among the Igbo ethnic group that a great deal still had to be done to resolve the issues that led to the war.

Consequently, developments after the war compelled Igbo elites to embark on a brand of politics that demanded accommodation, incorporation, and (re)integration into the Nigerian project. This specific reading of postwar developments and their implications for Igbo fortunes was critical to the formation of Ohanaeze. The organization was founded in 1976 by a handful of postwar Igbo elite, including Chief Kingsley Mbadiwe, Justice Daddy Onyeama (late), Chief Jerome Udorji (late), Professor J. U. Agwu, Dr. Michael Opara (late), Dr. Pius Okigbo (late), and Professor Ben Nwabueze, partly as a response to post-civil war developments, and partly in the quest for centralized Igbo leadership in Nigeria. Ohanaeze was positioned to articulate and push the Igbo agenda just as its predecessor, the Igbo State Union, had done in the late colonial period up to 1966, when all ethnic organizations and associations were proscribed with the advent of the military (Irukwu 2007: 12). The term *Ohanaeze* is a conjoined word derived from *oha*, meaning "all" or "public," and *eze*, meaning "king" or "ruler." But as Ojukwu (2012: 129, cited in Ojukwu and Nwaorgu 2013: 109) points out, in the context of the organization, *oha* means the village or general assembly, an all-purpose body, while *eze* represents the Council of Elders (*Ndichie*). Nwankwo (1999: 3) argues that the shift of emphasis from *Ohabueze*, meaning "the village, public, or general assembly is king or ruler," which has depth and substance in Igboland, to *Ohanaeze*, which is only a mythical concept, is reminiscent of the imposition of monarchical and autocratic chieftaincy institutions by colonialists largely responsible for the political downturn and erosion of traditional authority in Igboland. Mainly driven and guided by the *ako-na-uche* (*ako* means idea; *uche* means reason) philosophy that is less confrontational and more subtle, tactful, and diplomatic, Ohanaeze has continued to flourish since its inception. Irukwu (2007: 66) points out that *ako-na-uche* calls for sound judgment in dealing with issues and situations, but more importantly, it "symbolises the value of approaching issues with the ancient wisdom of (Igbo) ancestors, dressed up with a lot of tact, diplomacy and respect for the interests and intelligence of others." This conciliatory tone has marked Ohanaeze's stance on Nigerian politics and shaped its dealings with the Nigerian state. The implication for politics is that members of an ethnic elite group like Ohanaeze relish their position and see themselves as "determinate hegemonic forces," with the ability to transform power and determine the position and privileges of their groups (Fontana 1993: 32). This tendency to position themselves as custodians of knowledge about what is good or bad for society has several consequences for the asymmetric social and power relations in Igboland.

It is imperative to state that what appeared to be a pan-Igbo ethnic organization, or an Igbo nationalist project led by Ohanaeze, was in part elite-based and in part sought accommodation with and recognition from elites in other ethnic groups. Consequently, Ohanaeze pursued several elite-led strategies, alliances, pacts, and coalitions across regional, ethnic, and generational divides to entrench its interests. As Irukwu (2007: 13) observes, in the process of Ohanaeze's evolution, issues began to emerge around its structure and management systems, and there were perceptions among Igbo at the grassroots level that the organization not only was immersed in partisan politics, but was nondemocratic and elitist in nature. These tendencies

Fig. 10.2. Dr. Azikiwe and Dr. Michael Okpara at NCNC rally in Urualla, present-day Imo state, Nigeria. Photograph by Eliot Elisofon, 1959. © Eliot Elisofon Photographic Archives, National Museum of African Art, Smithsonian Institution.

found expression in the opening of the political space in 1979, when Igbo expectations failed to materialize, primarily based on Ohanaeze's preference to align with the ruling hegemonic elites from other sections of the country. For strategic reasons, the leadership of Ohanaeze was inclined to the Shehu Shagari-led National Party of Nigeria (NPN) at the center and was largely recognized by many as the "Igbo wing" of the NPN. The leaders of Ohanaeze perceived the emergence of Dr. Alex Ekwueme (a fellow Igbo) as vice president under the Hausa-Fulani-led Shehu Shagari government, not only as a solution to the lack of leadership in Igboland, but as a means of reconnecting to mainstream politics at the national level, even if they had to assume a subordinate position in that arrangement. There was a rallying of Igbo elite positions behind Dr. Ekwueme, and Ohanaeze became strongly opposed to the Igbo- and Azikiwe-led Nigeria Peoples Party (NPP), arguing that Azikiwe and other Igbo in the NPP should accord recognition to Dr. Ekwueme as the highest elected official from Igboland. But the NPP promptly dismissed Dr. Ekwueme, Ohanaeze, and its leaders as stooges of the North.

Nevertheless, the political tendencies in Igboland became even more complicated with the arrival of the ex-Biafran leader, Chukwuemeka Odumegwu Ojukwu, from exile in 1982. Still intent on exploiting his place in Igbo politics, he was unwilling to accept the preeminence of Azikiwe in Igbo politics, the new leadership of Ekwueme in the ruling NPN, or the political agenda of Ohanaeze. In a bid to reenact his leadership, this time through the ballot box, Ojukwu launched the "Ikemba Front" in 1983 as a partisan political organization and tried to use his place in Igbo memory to garner election to the Senate, from where he would challenge Ekwueme's leadership. But the project met its Waterloo when his senatorial district in Nnewi, Anambra State, promptly rejected his candidacy. These emergent political tendencies created a tripartite division in Igbo politics, organized around Azikiwe, Ekwueme, and Ojukwu (Omoruyi 2003b). The following section examines how the nature and dynamics of this tripartite, elite-led vision directed the tone and tenor of Igbo politics beyond the Second Republic.

AN IMPASSE: MILITARY RULE, STRUCTURAL ADJUSTMENT, AND TRANSITION POLITICS (1986-1999)

The truncation of the Second Republic in December 1983 and the long-drawn military rule (1983-99) compounded economic conditions in the country. This led to the introduction of structural adjustment as a response to the economic crises, which inevitably widened the existing ethnonationalist cleavages as ethnic identities became more conflictual and competitive. As push came to shove with the SAP, diminishing resources and opportunities intensified the competition for jobs, contracts, and other benefits, and ethnic consciousness and ethnic connections became the hallmark of negotiation. The commercialization and privatization exercise attendant to the adjustment package reinforced factional struggles for resources and power at the elite level, thereby, fueling tension, mistrust, and conflict between the "winners" and the "losers" (Osaghae 1995). Aware of the growing concerns about marginalization, injustice, and underdevelopment in Igboland, and the dominance of the hegemonic group(s) that controlled federal power and oil resources, there was a push at the Igbo elite level to address the Igbo share of the national patrimony. Through various forums, Ohanaeze and Aka Ikenga (the intellectual wing of Ohanaeze) began to articulate the plight of the Igbo within the unfolding context, and the need to accommodate the Igbo in the national project. Aka Ikenga was formed in the throes of the adjustment program in 1980s as an Igbo think-tank comprising young, thriving Igbo professionals from several walks of life. Its main purpose was to act as a pressure group to agitate for the inclusion of the Igbo in mainstream politics as the hardship of the adjustment package unfolded under military dictatorship in Nigeria (interview, Goddy Uwazurike, January 15, 2009).

The convoluted democratic transition program initiated by the General Ibrahim Babangida administration (1985–93) introduced profound structural and contextual changes to the political system. As part of a grand design to transform himself into a civilian president and hang on to power, General Babangida contrived hiccups and manipulations in the transition process. This, inevitably, resulted in frequent disqualification of candidates and cancellation of presidential primaries and, ultimately, annulment of the June 12, 1993, presidential elections—which led to what was described in the press as a "democratic impasse." The Igbo did not produce any formidable presidential candidate but voted overwhelmingly for Alhaji Bashir Tofa, a northerner and opponent of Chief M. K. O. Abiola. Despite the broad-based acceptance of the June 1993 elections across the country, there were fundamental differences among political elites of Igbo extraction before and after the elections. On June 11, 1993, a day before the election, a veteran political mercenary and member of Ohanaeze, Chief Arthur Nzeribe, filed a suit at the Abuja High Court and obtained a ruling delivered at 21:15 p.m. by Justice Bassey Ikpeme restraining the National Electoral Commission (NEC) from conducting the presidential elections scheduled for the next day. The NEC went ahead with the elections based on the provisions of Decree 13 of 1993, which made it impossible for any court of law to stop the conduct of the elections, but the elections were eventually annulled. Some prominent Igbo elites played major roles in the annulment. These included the minister of justice, Clement Akpamgbo, who ordered the suspension of further release of election results; the minister for information, Uche Chukwumerije, who claimed that the election lacked legitimacy; the minister for education, Benjamin Nwabueze, who provided legal backing for the annulment as an act valid in law through his book *"Nigeria '93: The Political Crisis and Solutions"* (1994); and Ojukwu, who mobilized Igbo support for the annulment on the grounds that the Igbo were betrayed by the Yoruba during the Nigeria-Biafra War (Irukwu 2007; Chikendu and Kalu 1996).

However, some key members of the "progressive" wing of the Igbo elite, like Admiral Ndubuisi Kanu, Chief Sam Mbakwe, Dr. Chukwuemeka Ezeife, Chief Bobo Nwosisi, Chief Ralph Obioha, Dr. Pius Okigbo (late), and Ralph Uwechue (late), to name a few, in opposition to Ohanaeze, joined forces with pro-democracy groups to compel the military dictatorship in Nigeria to accede to the democratic will of the people by declaring Abiola winner of the elections (Omoruyi 2003a). But as events would prove, these "progressive" elements in Igbo politics were soon eclipsed, and what would emerge as antidemocratic forces in Igbo politics helped sustain the annulment and went on to play significant roles in the Abacha regime. The platform for a coherent Igbo agenda was quickly dissipated by another tendency that began to emerge in Igbo politics and was well nurtured by the military class at this time. Referred to as "new leaders" in Igboland, these included political appointees, contractors, commissioned agents, prominent Igbo citizens, and some prominent members of Ohanaeze. This group did not perceive Igbo politics from an Igbo standpoint, and they were unfavorably disposed to the idea of an Igbo presidency (Omoruyi 2003a). Rooted in the import-export trade, narcotics trade, and advance fee fraud (419), among others, Chinweizu (1998) characterized these emergent "monetized" Igbo elites as *Aku-Agwu* (hungry wealth). Through the military, they became sources of "hot money" and newfound political influence in Igboland (Nwankwo 1999).

The annulment of the elections and the struggle to validate the results led to the resurgence of ethnoregional conflicts and a national impasse that stretched the country to a breaking point. The perception that the Hausa-

Fulani had resolved to emasculate other ethnic nationalities in Nigeria was enhanced by the self-secession bid of General Sani Abacha, who assumed power in a bloodless military coup against the National Interim Government, headed by another Yoruba southerner, Ernest Shonekan, in November 1993. By the time General Abacha rolled out a new transition program after aborting General Babangida's unfinished transition, it became apparent that Nigeria had devolved into a new phase of military adventurism. The leadership of Ohanaeze, including Nwabueze, Ekwueme, Chukwuemeka Ezeife, and Edwin Ume Ezeoke, among others, participated actively in the 1994–95 National Constitutional Conference organized by General Abacha. Ekwueme articulated Ohanaeze's position on zoning and rotation of the office of the president as critical components of inclusive nationhood in a multiethnic and multilingual society. Emerging from this was a six-zone power structure, North-East, North-West, North-Central, South-South, South-East, and South-West, upon which post-transition politics was hinged (Onwudiwe 2004). The 1995 All Politicians Summit cochaired by Ekwueme and Chief Adekunle Ajasin was used as a springboard for establishing the Institute for Civil Society, from where the Group of 34 emerged and later the People's Democratic Party (PDP) (Ekwueme 2005). As it turned out, some members of Ohanaeze actively worked toward the realization of Abacha's self-secession bid. Remarkably, Arthur Nzeribe and Arthur Eze mobilized a coterie of Igbo political elites, most of whom were members of Ohanaeze, to ostensibly pay a "thank you" visit to General Abacha for the befitting state burial accorded to the late Azikiwe. The visit was particularly interesting as it provided these Igbo elites a veritable platform to call on Abacha to contest for the presidency to the displeasure of some Ohanaeze members who were present at the meeting (Ojukwu and Nwaorgu 2013: 112). The sudden demise of General Abacha ushered in a final transition to democracy and the birth of the Fourth Republic, but not after Abacha's five political parties, which were instrumental to his self-secession bid, were proscribed by the General Abdulsalam Abubakar regime, which assumed power on June 8, 1998.

Igbo political elites began to position themselves for the 1999 presidential elections once the Abubakar-led military regime rolled out its transition program. Shortly before the PDP primaries, many saw Ekwueme as a viable candidate with some impressive credentials, and the wave of public opinion in the South appeared to be overwhelmingly in his favor over General Olusegun Obasanjo, the retired military head of state (1976–79). The fact that he served as vice president under the Shagari-led NPN government in the aborted Second Republic made Ekwueme the highest Igbo political officeholder since 1966. The crucial role he played in the transition to democracy under the military, which led to the formation of the G-34, and eventually the PDP, endeared him to many Igbo as having a decent shot at the presidency. At the Jos Convention of the PDP, certain northern interests preferred Obasanjo's candidacy over that of Ekwueme, as the former was perceived by the North as the only acceptable face of the Southwest that needed to be "compensated" for the annulment of the 1993 elections won by another Yoruba. Ekwueme publicly accepted the results of the elections and called on his supporters to rally behind Obasanjo's candidacy. It is remarkable that Ekwueme's defeat was also engineered by fellow Igbo elites like Jim Nwobodo and Ojukwu, partly based on their political differences with him, and partly as a reflection of the tripartite divide that had come to dominate Igbo politics since the Second Republic. The only realistic route to an Igbo presidency eventually rested on the All People's Party (APP). But most Igbo elites were not happy about the process that led to the emergence of a relatively unknown presidential candidate in the person of Ogbonnaya Onu, a former governor of Abia State. After Ojukwu rejected Onu's candidacy and went as far as campaigning for Obansanjo against his own party, the APP, Onu was summarily dumped to accommodate a merger and adoption of the Alliance for Democracy candidate, Olu Falae, an outcome that shut the Igbo out of the 1999 presidential race. Though Nwabueze rallied the Igbo to vote against Obasanjo due to the PDP's rejection of Ekwueme, Ohanaeze and most Igbo elites pitched their tents with the PDP as the party swept the polls in national and state elections in the Southeast.

A WAKE-UP CALL FOR THE IGBO: DEMOCRACY, CRISIS, AND NEO-BIAFRAN POLITICS SINCE 1999

Since the end of the civil war, the "Igbo Presidency Project" has become central to Igbo politics, and a cardinal negotiating point of the Igbo quest for reinventing Nigeria. There is widespread feeling among the Igbo that they have been consistently denied the highest office of the land, and that Igbo reintegration in a post-civil war dispensation can only be complete when an Igbo attains the highest office of the land (interview, Goddy Uwazurike, January 15, 2009). This assumption formed the basis of the First Republic tripod theory, which holds that stability can only be achieved in the Nigerian federation when there is a balance of power among the three major ethnic groups. The demand for an Igbo presidency received renewed momentum in the Fourth Republic, and a faction of the Igbo elite renewed their push for the project. In a summit convened on January 9, 2001, in Enugu, under the aegis of Ohanaeze, 2003 was set as the year for the actualization of the Igbo Presidency Project. The summit was attended by virtually all prominent Igbo elites and politicians, and Orji Uzor Kalu, then governor of Abia state, delivered a well-publicized speech, entitled "A Wake-Up Call for the Igbo," where he argued that "if the Igbo fail to produce the president in 2003, we will be sentenced to the political wilderness for at least twenty years or more. It is obvious that 2003 is our date with destiny." According to Omoruyi (2003a) there were two basic questions in Igbo politics as of 2003 that Ohanaeze failed to resolve. The first had to do with a lack of consensus on the viability of the Igbo presidency project in 2003. It became apparent that this "Igbo appointment with destiny" which will culminate in the Igbo presidency in 2003 was not shared by many Igbo elites. There was confusion about the actual position of most attendees on the matter, and what the summit may have achieved. Remarkably, three weeks after the summit, Ohanaeze could still not produce a communiqué, but when it finally did, the group could only profess an unconvincing desire for the presidency in 2003. Ohanaeze's indecisiveness was described as a product of the "politics of intrigues and enlightened individual self-preservation of many Igbo politicians," who were being "careful not to externalize others who felt 2003 was not appropriate" (*This Day* February 18, 2001:1). Secondly, Ohanaeze's inability to articulate a coherent Igbo Presidency Project was demonstrated in its failure to advise Igbo political leaders whether to pursue their ambition within the ruling PDP or through another party. Hence, Ohanaeze failed to articulate a coherent Igbo Presidency Project when it could not advise Igbo political leaders whether to pursue their ambition within the ruling PDP or through another party. These, according to Omoruyi (2003a) were two basic questions of Igbo politics as of 2003 that Ohanaeze failed to resolve.

In the confusion that ensued, at least eight presidential aspirants of Igbo ethnic extraction emerged in the 2003 elections, with Ojukwu, the All Progressive Grand Alliance; Ike Nwachukwu, the National Democratic Party; and Jim Nwobodo, United National Independence Party, as the most prominent The Igbo candidates were perceived as unrealistic aspirants who were intent on fulfilling a "stalemate strategy." The only realistic chance for an Igbo presidency remained with Ekwueme, whose late entry into the race ended with a predictable defeat at the PDP National Convention. The presidential aspirations of Ojukwu, Nwobodo, and Ekwueme were to a considerable extent a reincarnation of the tripartite divide in Igbo politics dating back to the Second Republic. Even within the All Nigeria People's Party (ANPP), Ohanaeze and Igbo elites could not agree on a consensus candidate, and that was why the faction that sponsored the emergence of General Muhammadu Buhari in the ANPP quickly took advantage of their division. What appeared to be the ill-conceived nature of the Igbo Presidency Project within the ranks of Ohanaeze was justified by Nwabueze, who claimed that "it was not possible for Ohanaeze to produce only one candidate, and you cannot force Ndi Igbo to produce only one candidate, and Ohanaeze cannot persuade all political presidential aspirants to step down for one person" (Ojukwu and Nwaorgu 2013: 114). Ironically, Ohanaeze was even complicit in sabotaging its own self-proclaimed objective of electing an Igbo president in 2003, when its own appointed chairman of the committee to elect an Igbo president, Chief Emmanuel Iwuanyanwu, was alleged to have pulled all the strings and deployed the influence of Ohanaeze to campaign for the reelection of President Obasanjo in Igboland. This trend was replicated in the actions of the PDP Southeast governors, who, rather than fighting for a common cause and realizing the Igbo presidency dream, did the opposite by focusing on their own ambition to secure a second term, thus tying their political future to that of President Obasanjo. The crisis of 2003 demonstrated in vivid terms the weak underbelly and intricacies of Igbo elite politics as exemplified by Ohanaeze.

The contradiction between Ohanaeze's position and the realization of the Igbo presidency was further deepened at the inconclusive Constitutional Conference organized by the Obasanjo administration in 2006. Although the conference was largely a response to the demand for a Sovereign National Conference by different ethnic nationalities in Nigeria, the Obasanjo administration fashioned a heavily diluted version of the conference and attempted to use the review to ensure an amendment of the 1999 constitution that would grant him a third term in office. The third-term project finally collapsed at the National Assembly in May 2006. But the role of the leadership of Ohanaeze in this despicable project further discredited the entire organization and its leadership. At the Abakaliki Zonal hearing of the Constitutional Review Committee, the president of Ohanaeze, Professor Joe Irukwu, stated that it would endorse a three-term tenure for the presidency and other political offices. This was considered a tacit approval of the president's third-term agenda and a sellout by the Ohanaeze leadership on the Igbo Presidency Project for 2007.

Fig. 10.3. Chief Emmanuel Nwanyanwu kneeling down for blessings from Dr. Nnamdi Azikiwe while on a campaign to become the presidential flagbearer for the NRC in the early 1990s. Photo courtesy Nigerian Tribune Library.

Ohanaeze largely campaigned for the reelection of former president Goodluck Jonathan in 2011 and 2015 elections. While in the former it supported President Jonathan and rejected the calls for the North to complete the tenure of late president Yar' Adua (Jonathan's predecessor, who died in office in 2010), in the latter it campaigned against the candidacy of other Igbo candidates like Chief Chekwas Okorie of the United People's Party.

Given its already waning credibility, Ohanaeze was further undermined by a recurring leadership crisis. The immediate issue had to do with the tenure of office of the elected executives, which according to the Ohanaeze constitution is supposed to last for two years. The Professor Irukwu–led executive that assumed office in 2004 was supposed to hand over the affairs of the organization to a new executive by February 2006. But while in office Irukwu had cited the existence of a new Ohanaeze constitution which allegedly guarantees a four-year term for executives. The expiration of the tenure of the Irukwu-led executive in 2006 set the stage for a prolonged leadership crisis. The governors of the five southeastern states waded into the crisis by appointing a Care-Taker Committee led by Ndubuisi Kanu to conduct elections and hand power over to a new executive. Elections were conducted with the approval of the governors, and Chief Dozie Ikedife emerged as the president-general of the organization, while the Irukwu/Achuzia-led executive continued to carry on as the officials of the organization. Having lost face among the Igbo due to the third-term debacle that he tacitly supported, Irukwu became increasingly unpopular among the Igbo and resigned his position. He handed his office over to his deputy, Chief Ifeanyi Enechukwu, who also contemplated spending four years in office as president-general. The loss of the 2015 presidential elections by the PDP complicated the position of the organization, but the election of a new National Executive Committee (NEC) in 2017, led by Chief John Nnia Nwodo appears to have given the organization a breath of fresh air after several cycles of uncertainty and a protracted leadership crisis that effectively robbed the organization of its status in Igboland.

To compound the crisis within Ohanaeze, there emerged in Igboland a popular, grassroots, radical, and confrontational neo-Biafran movement with a strong adherence to Igbo self-determination. The Movement for the Actualization of the Sovereign State of Biafra (MASSOB) emerged in 1999, shortly after Nigeria's return to civilian rule. At its inception, Ohanaeze and, indeed, many prominent Igbo politicians, legislators, and governors from the southeast states quickly distanced themselves from the movement and were quick to remind Ralph Uwazuruike, the leader of MASSOB, that the dream of Biafra died in 1970 (Akinyele 2001: 633). While prominent elite Igbo groups like Ohanaeze and Aka Ikenga and the Igbo political class tacitly agree to the need to address the place of the Igbo in a post-civil war Nigeria, their opposition to MASSOB was predicated largely on disagreements on the best strategies for pursuing a collective Igbo agenda. The uneasy relationship between MASSOB and Ohanaeze is captured in the words of the former secretary-general of Ohanaeze, Chief Joe Achuzia, who made the following remarks about MASSOB:

> For me as an Ohanaeze chieftain, it [MASSOB] does not convey the type of meaning that should give me joy. . . . That the youths, because of the severe

hardship unleashed in the polity, now feel that they would rather pursue a separatist alternative should not give us joy, because we know the consequences of such a division. (Ejinkeonye 2005)

Ohanaeze's disinclination to MASSOB activities is confirmed by the position of Aka Ikenga, which disagrees with the neo-Biafra strategy and has called on the Igbo to move away from regurgitating the memories of the civil war and Igbo marginalization in Nigeria, to chart a new course for the future. Aka Ikenga organizes periodic lectures, seminars, and conferences and uses its contacts to influence decisions and engage the present crop of Igbo political leadership at the national, state, and local levels to make a difference in their offices. Reiterating the need for a different strategy, the vice president of the group, Chief Goddy Uwazurike, maintained that

> Ojukwu [the former Biafran secessionist leader] fought at 34, he will not fight at 54. Now in his 70s, he merely advises. The message of MASSOB sinks in within the youths in Igboland who did not witness the civil war. (Interview, Goddy Uwazurike, January 15, 2009)

The separatist alternative pursued by MASSOB contrasts with the moderate and conservative stance of Ohanaeze and Aka Ikenga. On several occasions, MASSOB openly accused both groups of complicity in the subversion of the Igbo agenda, describing them as a group of "elderly cowards" who have aided the marginalization of the Igbo (Akinyele 2001: 634). On that basis, possibilities for constructive engagement between these opposing views completely collapsed on many occasions and sometimes led to open threats of attack on prominent members of Ohanaeze by MASSOB members and several attempts to disrupt the Igbo Day celebrations (*The Nation*, September 30, 2008; *Daily Punch*, September 22, 2008). After Uwazuruike's arrest by state security forces, it took grassroots mobilization by Igbo youths in the East for Ohanaeze, Aka Ikenga, and the entire Igbo political class (comprising governors, senators, and members of the House of Representatives from the Southeast) to reluctantly call for Uwazuruike's release (interview with Chuks, January 26, 2009). The decision to release him took so long because the call for his release was not popular among the Igbo elites in general, and within Ohanaeze in particular, compared to the strong agitation for his release expressed by most Igbo youths (*Saturday Champion*, July 7, 2007: 14).

There is a generational dimension to the divide between the groups, and this is perceivable in the debate about who can best represent and defend Igbo

Fig. 10.4. Chief Odumegwu Ojukwu. Photo courtesy Nigerian Tribune Library.

interest in the Nigerian state. The leadership of Ohanaeze and other elite-led Igbo groups espouses pro-Nigerian sentiments and claims to speak the mind of the Igbo in a manner that would benefit the Igbo and all Nigerians at large. MASSOB has, however, demonstrated its ability to rally Igbo youths, artisans, and people at the grassroots level when it announced a sit-at-home order to commemorate "Biafra Day" in 2004, which was widely observed and adhered to. Ohanaeze and other Igbo elites were surprised by the success of the event. But more importantly, the possibility that the Ohanaeze's elitist agenda may be supplanted by youth power and enthusiasm led the organization to launch a less divisive and controversial annual "Igbo National Day" celebration that is intended to undermine and subvert the MASSOB's Biafra Day.

The activities of the neo-Biafra groups did not end with MASSOB. MASSOB began to decline amid allegations of corruption against Uwazuruike and his abdication of the Biafran project in support of President Jonathan's reelection bid in 2015.

Another group known as the Indigenous Peoples of Biafra (IPOB) soon emerged to articulate the Biafran project in Igboland. Though not necessarily new, IPOB's activities gained momentum shortly after the 2015 elections, as the movement became the latest in a string of post-civil war, second-generation, neo-Biafran movements to emerge in the Southeast. The situation was compounded by the advent of Radio Biafra, an unlicensed station dedicated to the neo-Biafran cause. The station dominated the airwaves in southeastern Nigeria and tapped into unresolved causes of the war to mobilize Igbo senses and sensibilities in the continued quest for Biafran independence. With a sharp male voice and unmistakable Igbo accent that frames the issues and minds of his listeners and audience, Nnamdi Kanu, the leader of IPOB and director of Radio Biafra, addressed the most painful chapter of Igbo history and evoked memories of Igbo defeat in the war. By October 2015, Radio Biafra had become a source of grave concern to the newly elected president, Muhammadu Buhari, and the Nigerian government, and Nnamdi Kanu was eventually arrested in Lagos as he was about to depart for London. After his arrest, the entire southeast region of Nigeria became engulfed in the "mother of all protests" as his supporters grounded commercial and vehicular activities in major cities of the region. Nnamdi Kanu was released in April 2017 but after repeated violation of his bail conditions, he was arrested by the Nigerian Army while on a purported routine military exercise in September 2017. IPOB was subsequently banned by the Nigerian government after a court ruling by a federal judge in Abuja, the nation's capital.

IPOB articulated the "Igbo condition" and based its agitation on the need for a referendum in the Southeast to ascertain the willingness of the people of the region to remain in the Nigerian federation. However, the tension between elite-led, top-down, and conservative approach of Ohanaeze versus IPOB's radical and separatist inclinations soon came to a head. In a statement credited to the president-general of the organization, Chief Nwodo, Ohanaeze expressed its support for the proscription of IPOB by the federal government and all the southeastern governors, maintaining that it would forestall any efforts by IPOB to drag the region into another civil war (*Daily Post*, December 15, 2017; *Vanguard*, October 11, 2017).

The search for the resolution of perceived Igbo marginalization in Nigeria continues in perpetuity. The neo-Biafran groups believe they are authentic representatives and defenders of Igbo interest in a federation perceived to be structured against Igbo. This notion informs their rejection of state-led processes and explains why the neo-Biafran groups latched onto ethnicity and a nationalist ideal to pursue the dream of a "New Biafra." Conversely, Ohanaeze's conciliatory stance with the state and its emphasis on devolution of power from the center to the periphery, true federalism, equal access to resources and power, a power shift to the east, and, ultimately, an Igbo presidency are yet to yield any substantial outcome. Given this scenario, there is a general perception that the Igbo are neither fully part of the Nigerian project nor citizens of another political and administrative arrangement (interview, Chuks, January 26, 2009). It is this dialectic between outright "independence" from the Nigerian state represented by the neo-Biafran radical groups, on the one hand, and Igbo elite accommodation within the Nigerian state championed by Ohanaeze and other moderate groups, on the other hand, that frames Igbo politics in contemporary Nigeria.

CONCLUSION

The chapter lays out the extenuating circumstances and context for understanding the existential crisis of Igbo elite politics and the tendencies that have shaped this brand of politics in contemporary Nigeria. Ohanaeze, the foremost pan-Igbo sociocultural organization in Nigeria, has struggled to mediate the divide between its elitist politics and anchorage vis-à-vis the necessity for popular representation of Igbo interests in Nigeria. The organization itself has undergone processes of renewal and change since its inception, and these have largely hinged on the prevailing sociopolitical and economic contexts; the advent of new actors, characters, and forces; and the possibility for various forms of mobilizations and tendencies to emerge in the Nigerian political space. The activities of Ohanaeze clearly demonstrate that elite politics is context bound, spatially specific, and consequently open to a range of possibilities that are largely dependent on the "position" of a specific elite group in relation to elites from other ethnic groups. Ohanaeze's demand for incorporation was not unusual. In fact, given the "zero-sum" and "winner takes all" nature of power configuration in Nigerian politics, where those excluded from state power were at the mercy of those in control, Ohanaeze perceived any form of incorporation into the prevailing power structure to be in its interest. Keen to address the displacement of the Igbo elite group in the post-civil war reconfiguration of Nigerian project, the idea of incorporation was not necessarily be a problem for Ohanaeze even when the terms of such processes were detrimental to Igbo interests at large.

From its inception in 1976, to the end of the Second Republic in 1983, to the post-1999 context, Ohanaeze, both as an actor and institution, has straddled a difficult divide. It started with positioning itself as the primordial articulator, defender, and bearer of Igbo interests during the era of military rule, a period characterized by profound changes in the economic, social, and political landscape of the country. In a bid to express their accountability to the Igbo ethnic group, Ohanaeze and Aka Ikenga (its "intellectual wing") condemned Igbo marginalization and echoed the need to carve out the Igbo share of the national patrimony. This was followed by a period popularly known for Ohanaeze's critical stance on national politics during the IMF- and World Bank–inspired SAP that appeared to benefit elites from other ethnic groups who had access to power. In the third and final context, the authority and legitimacy of Ohanaeze in Igboland has been subjected to severe scrutiny and assault by several neo-Biafran groups that emerged with the opening of the political space. This period has been characterized by Ohanaeze's quest to regain its credibility by adopting Igbo philosophy of *Ako na Uche*, which positions the group as one that is accommodating of the prevailing power structures in the country.

Despite its pervasive influence, the Igbo elite, like most elite groups in Nigeria, is not a monolith. But attempts to challenge or break away from the prevailing power configuration that undermines Igbo interests have been made virtually impossible by the organizational and institutional leverage of Ohanaeze. Some elements of the Igbo faction of the ruling elite are clearly disaffected with the status quo and the prevailing power configuration. Their clamor for an Igbo president is a way of re-admitting the Igbo elite into the arena of power (first circle) occupied by the two other ethnic groups. But some Igbo elites are openly expressing their reservations and outright opposition to the idea of an Igbo president, especially those benefitting directly or indirectly from the current dispensation who would like the Igbo to remain in a subordinate position (second circle) indefinitely. Ohanaeze's project of incorporation appears to align with the latter position and continues to shape interelite and interethnic relations between the Igbo and other ethnic groups in post–civil war Nigeria.

Ultimately, the project of incorporation is in part an invention of the Igbo faction of the ruling elite, and in part supported by elites from other ethnic groups who feel that the Igbo elite must equally remain accountable to them at the national level. Therefore, in critical terms, the project is not by any means emancipatory. This is because the Igbo elites, reminiscent of elites from other ethnic groups, have a very narrow social base of power and legitimacy, and do not enjoy the confidence of those whose interests they claim to represent, nor do they share in their common concerns and burdens of common citizenship. Ohanaeze justifies its project of incorporation on the grounds that it avoids a perpetual Igbo exclusion and alienation, and unnecessary conflict with other ethnic groups. The organization perceives its role to be akin to the Igbo philosophy and tradition of *Ako na Uche*, which is less confrontational and more subtle, tactful, and diplomatic. Indeed, the organization views the quest for Igbo inclusion in post-civil war Nigeria in the same manner, namely, that the need for inclusion is not just an Igbo concern; rather it is broad-based and affects virtually every ethnic group. Hence, the organization appears to be settled in its current position, where it plays second fiddle and remains a junior partner in the ruling elite coalition. While this position runs counter to radical and popular grassroots demands in Igboland, the strong tendency for elite incorporation holds sway and has become the major determinant of post-civil war Igbo politics in Nigeria.

REFERENCES

Achebe, Chinua. 1983. *The Trouble with Nigeria*. Enugu: Fourth Dimension.

Adebanwi, Wale. 2014. *Yoruba Elites and Ethnic Politics in Nigeria: Obafemi Awolowo and Corporate Agency*. New York: Cambridge University Press.

Akinyele, Rufus T. 2001. "Ethnic Militancy and National Stability in Nigeria: A Case of the Oodua People's Congress." *African Affairs* 100, no. 401: 623–40.

Alapiki, Henry E. 2005. "State Creation in Nigeria: Failed Approaches to National Integration and Local Autonomy." *African Studies Review* 48, no. 3: 49–65.

Amundsen, Inge. 2001. "The Limits of Clientelism: Multi-party Politics in Sub-Saharan Africa." *Forum for Development Studies* 28, no. 1: 43–57.

Anber, Paul. 1967. "Modernisation and Political Disintegration: Nigeria and the Ibos." *Journal of Modern African Studies* 5, no. 2: 163–79.

Buchanan, Keith M., and John C. Pugh. 1962. *Land and People in Nigeria: The Human Geography of Nigeria and Its Environmental Background*. London: University of London Press.

Chabal, Patrick, and Jean-Pascal Daloz. 1998. *Africa Works: Disorder as Political Instrument*. Oxford: James Currey; Bloomington: Indiana University Press.

Chandra, Kanchan. 2007. "Counting Heads: A Theory of Voter and Elite Behaviour in Patronage-Democracies." In Herbert Kitschelt and Steven Wilkinson, eds., *Patrons, Clients and Policies*, 84–109. Cambridge: Cambridge University Press.

Chikendu, Patrick, and Victor Kalu. 1996. *The Military Question: Path to a Pan-Nigerian Democratic Order*. Enugu: Mary Dan Publishers.

Chinweizu, Ibekwe. 1998. *Aku Agu Na Aku Mma: The Responsibilities of Wealth*. Lagos: Lenaus Advertising and Publishing.

Cohen, Phil. 1972. "Sub-cultural Conflict and Working-Class Community." Working Papers in Cultural Studies no. 2. Birmingham: University of Birmingham.

Coleman, James. 1958. *Nigeria: Background to Nationalism*. Berkeley: University of California Press.

Crowder, Michael. 1962. *The Story of Nigeria*. London: Faber and Faber.

Ejinkeonye, Ugochukwu. 2005. "Nigeria: A Meeting of the Minds." Conversation with Joe Achuzia. Chinua Achebe Foundation. http://magazine.biafranigeriaworld.com/chinua-achebe/2005nov28-chinua-achebe-foundation-col-joe-achuzia.html. Accessed June 11, 2018.

Ekwueme, Alex. 2005. "What Nigeria Lost by Abach's Untimely Death: Well-Thought Out Provisions of the 1995 Constitution." Dawodu.com. https://dawodu.com/ekwueme1.htm. Accessed June 11, 2018.

Fontana, Benedetto. 1993. *Hegemony and Power: On the Relation between Gramsci and Machiavelli*. Minneapolis: University of Minnesota Press.

Forde, Daryll, and Gwylim I. Jones. 1950. *The Ibo and Ibibio-Speaking Peoples of Southern Nigeria*. London: Oxford University Press.

Green, Margaret. M. 1947. *Ibo Village Affairs*. London: Sidgwick and Jackson.

Hailey, Lord. 1951. *Native Administration in the British African Territories*. London: Her Majesty's Stationery Office.

Harneit-Sievers, Axel. 1998. "Igbo Traditional Rulers: Chieftaincy and the State of Southeastern Nigeria." *Africa Spectrum*, 33, no. 1: 57–79.

Higley, John, and Michael Burton. 2006. *Elite Foundations of Liberal Democracy*. Lanham, MD: Rowman and Littlefield.

Hossain, Naomi, and Mick Moore. 2002. "Arguing for the Poor: Elites and Poverty in Developing Countries." IDS Working Paper no. 148. Brighton: Institute of Development Studies.

Irukwu, Joe. 2007. *Nation-Building and Ethnic Organization: The Case of Ohanaeze in Nigeria*. Ibadan: Spectrum Books.

Khan, Shamus R. 2012. "The Sociology of Elites." *Annual Review of Sociology* 38: 361–77.

Kuper, Leo. 1965. *An African Bourgeoisie: Race, Class and Politics in South Africa*. New Haven: Yale University Press.

Lasswell, Harold D. 1961. "Agenda for the Study of Political Elites." In Dwaine Marvick, ed., *Political Decision-Makers*, 264–87. Glencoe, IL: Free Press.

Levine, Donald N. 1965. *Wax and Gold: Tradition and Innovation in Ethiopian Culture*. Chicago: University of Chicago Press.

Lindberg, Staffan I. 2003. "'It's Our Time to "Chop"': Do Elections in Africa Feed Neopatrimonialism rather than Counter-Act It?" *Democratization* 10, no. 2: 121–40.

Marcus, George E. 1983. *Elites: Ethnographic Issue*. Albuquerque: University of New Mexico Press.

Meek, Charles. 1937. *Law and Authority in a Nigerian Tribe*. London: Oxford University Press.
Mills, C. Wright. 1956. *The Power Elite*. New York: Oxford University Press.
Nnoli, Okwudibia. 1978. *Ethnic Politics in Nigeria*. Enugu: Fourth Dimension Publishers.
Nnoli, Okwudibia, ed. 1998. *Ethnic Conflicts in Africa*. Dakar: CODESRIA.
Nwabueze, Benjamin O. 1983. *Federalism in Nigeria under the Presidential Constitution*. London: Sweet and Maxwell.
Nwabueze, Benjamin O. 1985. "The Igbos in the Context of Modern Politics and Government in Nigeria: A Call for Self-Examination and Self-Correction." Paper presented at the Ahiajoku Lecture Series.
Nwankwo, Uchenna. 1999. *Anatomy of Politics in Igboland*. Lagos: Centrist Productions.
Nzimiro, Ikenna. 1982. *Nigerian Civil War: A Study in Class Conflict*. Enugu: Frontline Publishing.
Ojukwu, Chris. 2012. "Ohanaeze Ndigbo and Political Transitions in Nigeria." PhD thesis, Department of Political Science, University of Ibadan.
Ojukwu, Chris, and Felix Nwaorgu. 2013. "Ethnic Elite Organization and Political Transitions in Nigeria: Ohanaeze Ndigbo in Perspective." *Canadian Social Science* 9, no. 1: 106–15.
Omoruyi, Omo. 2003a. "The Ndi-Igbo Question in Nigerian Politics Is Real (II): It Is Not for Obasanjo or Anybody, But Igbo Leaders to Handle—Part 2." Dawodu.com. https://dawodu.com/omoruyi8.htm. Accessed June 11, 2018.
Omoruyi, Omo. 2003b. "The Ndi-Igbo Question in Nigerian Politics Is Real (III): Solution: Igbo Should Return to PDP or ANPP." Dawodu.com. https://dawodu.com/omoruyi11.htm. Accessed June 11, 2018.
Onwudiwe, Ebere. 2004. "Geo-political Zones and the Consolidation of Democracy." In Adigun Agbaje, Larry Diamond, and Ebere Onwudiwe, eds., *Nigeria's Struggle for Democracy and Good Governance: A Festschrift for Oyeleye Oyediran*, 267–76. Ibadan: Ibadan University Press.
Osaghae, Eghosa. 1995. *Structural Adjustment and Ethnicity in Nigeria*. Research Report no. 98. Uppsala: Nordiska Afrikainstitutet.
Osaghae, Eghosa. 1998. *The Crippled Giant: Nigeria since Independence*. Bloomington: Indiana University Press.
Osaghae, Eghosa. 2006. "Ethnicity and the State in Africa." Working Paper Series no. 7. Kyoto: Afrasian Centre for Peace and Development Studies.
Ottenberg, Phoebe. 1965. "The Afikpo Ibo of Eastern Nigeria." In James L. Gibbs Jr., ed., *Peoples of Africa*, 3–39. New York: Holt, Rinehart and Winston.
Ottenberg, Simon. 1959. "Ibo Receptivity to Change." In William R. Bascom and Melville Herskovits, eds., *Continuity and Change in African Cultures*, 130–43. Chicago: University of Chicago Press.
Quandt, William B. 1970. *The Comparative Study of Political Elites*. Beverly Hills, CA: Sage.
Shivji, Issa. 1976. *Class Struggle in Tanzania*. New York: Monthly Review Press.

Shore, Cris. 2002. "Introduction: Towards an Anthropology of Elites." In Cris Shore and Stephen Nugent, eds., *Elite Cultures: Anthropological Perspectives*, 1–21. New York: Routledge.

Sklar, Richard. 1963. *Nigerian Political Parties: Power in an Emergent African Nation*. Princeton, NJ: Princeton University Press.

Suberu, Rotimi. 1991. "The Struggle for New States in Nigeria, 1976–1990." *African Affairs* 90, no. 361: 499–522.

Theen, Rolf H. W., and Frank L. Wilson. 1996. *Comparative Politics: An Introduction to Seven Countries*. 4th ed. Upper Saddle River, NJ: Prentice Hall.

Uchendu, Victor C. 1965. *The Igbo of Southeast Nigeria*. New York: Holt, Reinhart and Winston.

Zuckerman, Alan. 1977. "The Concept 'Political Elite': Lessons from Mosca and Pareto." *Journal of Politics* 39, no. 2: 324–44.

CHAPTER 11

Beyond Afro-Pessimism

Party-Monialism, Registers of Accountability, and the Politics of Corruption

WALE ADEBANWI

INTRODUCTION

Funding political parties has, historically, been one of the biggest challenges in democracies. This is particularly so in Africa, where the "pervasive impact of colonialism, abject poverty and political and cultural expediency" shaped the formation of political parties (Salih 2003: 1). Different models of funding have been devised in the modern era (IDEA 2003; Burnell 2017) to ensure the survival of political parties as crucial agencies of gaining legitimate power and running the state while also guaranteeing the transparency and competitiveness of the process of the attainment of power within multiparty democracies.

Financing political parties is more challenging in states and societies new to Western-style democracy, such as African states in the late colonial and early postcolonial periods, when politicians were confronted with a regulatory system of party financing that was difficult for many of them to adjust to. In the light of this, some studies have concluded that "practices of patronage, clientelism and corruption [constitute] part of the linkage between parties and the state, which are often seen as typical attributes of more recently established democracies, in particular those outside of Europe" (van Biezen and Kopecký 2007: 238). Dominant in such literature is the assumption that "parties penetrate and control the state and use public offices for their own advantage, as opposed to the general public good" (van Biezen and Kopecký

2007: 240; see also Müller 2000; Piattoni 2001; Roninger 2004). This has been described as "party clientelism." Indeed, historically, the discourse of party funding in Africa, to use the words of (Burnell 2017: 9), "seems to have been hijacked by a fascination with the phenomenon of corruption in its various guises." Burnell adds that "at times the accusations of corruption do not distinguish between illegality and impropriety" (9).

Against this backdrop, it is illuminating to reflect on (political) elite accountability in modern Africa by using Thandikha Mkandiwe's (2015) important essay about neopatrimonialism and economic performance in Africa in relation to his equally important article published more than a decade earlier on how to think about developmental states in Africa (Mkandawire 2001). In this chapter, I draw out—and then link—two of the most crucial arguments in the two essays to push a tentative argument about why what I call *party-monialism* can be a useful way to understand the building and consolidation of a dominant political party in the service of developmental agenda within a plural democracy. In the light of this, I argue that the building and consolidation of such a party in a plural democracy is fraught—as this chapter again emphasizes. I explore how party-monialism shapes the politics and economics of the constitution, elaboration, and consolidation of a dominant political party in a specific context, including the politics provoked by the unavoidable contestability of such dominance—or hegemony.

I draw a link between Mkandawire's two articles through the example of one of the most deliberate, most elaborate, and most successful, though less known, examples of a developmental state in late colonial and early postcolonial Africa. I use the example of Nigeria's Western Region government between 1954 and 1963 to complement and complicate Mkandawire's argument about the limitations or inadequacy of the neopatrimonial school in accounting for the complexity and multiplicity of the African experience. However, I argue that the experience of neopatrimonialism in tandem with the formation of a capitalist class does not depend as much on "socioeconomic conditions," as Mkandawire (2015) argues, as on the nature and ideology of the ruling political elite, particularly in relation to development. I also point to how the discourses and practices of "corruption" are deployed as part of intra- and inter-elite struggle for power—for or against developmental agendas in Africa.

What are the two crucial arguments in the two essays that I find useful to *think with*? I will demonstrate below that Mkandawire's arguments are useful not only in contesting prevailing Afro-pessimistic views about the political elite,[1] in particular, and leadership, in general, in Africa, but also in pointing to successful African practices of development—specific kinds of social thought that guided, mobilized, and elaborated the practices aimed at the generalization of human well-being.

Against the backdrop of strong evidence for dispelling "notions that African policies are singularly driven by the inexorable logic of neopatrimonialism," Mkandawire (2015: 601) argues that the framework is "too blunt and too formulaic an instrument for understanding the great variety of African experiences and the contradictory interests, ideologies, and motivations of social actors" (602). This is so because it often ends up rendering "monochromatic the many colourful and varied characters who have taken the African political stage over the last half century" (601), while impoverishing our "understanding of the complexities of the continent." In light of this—and this, for me, is Mkandawire's first crucial argument—he concludes that "in some places, *neopatrimonialism and the formation of a capitalist class have occurred simultaneously*, while in others it has not, depending on the socioeconomic conditions at the time," adding that the "management of [public resources] may be corrupt or clientelistic, but *neither corruption nor clientelism represent[s] their origins or raison d'être*" (578, 591, emphasis added).[2] This is illuminating because the incidence of corruption or clientelism is often used to dismiss examples of laudable management of public affairs and visionary governance in Africa, as if similar incidences do not appear in some of the most successful and much-praised governments in the contemporary history of the West.

The second critical argument is that nothing in Africa's history or practice "suffices to rule out the possibility of African 'developmental states' capable of playing a dynamic role than hitherto" (Mkandawire 2001: 289–90). However, to be able to usefully analyze this possibility, Mkandawire argues for "concrete analysis" of the character of the African state rather than the "pontifical and the teleological." In doing this, scholars will not throw the "proverbial baby out with the bath water" because they will be able to pay attention to possible lessons and capacities that have been ignored or wasted—through local agency and disruptive politics as well as through Afro-pessimistic views, policies, and actions.

Generally, in this chapter, I reflect on Mkandawire's conclusion that, even while it captures some aspects of the African crisis, the "attribution of all African ills to neopatrimonialism simply undermines internally driven change," because it does not exhaust the totality of the African experience and therefore fails, as it has been presented, as the single or most important explanatory model of African politics. I think that focusing on the politics of elite accountability is a very useful way to capture some of the complexities that are glossed over in the casual dismissal of the totality of politics of governance in Africa. Following Mkandawire, I focus on the example of a developmental state under regional self-rule in late colonial and early postcolonial Nigeria to argue against the "one-variable explanation" of neopatrimonialism and show how the politics of corruption can occlude, complicate, or even terminate an important conversation about the process of the mobilization of resources for the capture of power, a form of power that can subsequently be deployed by a progressive elite in the service of development and human well-being. Such an approach has been successfully explored by Richard Werbner (2004: back cover), who describes the Kalanga elite as "reasonable [elite] radicals," "a rare breed of powerful political elites who are not tyrants, torturers, or thieves."

My focus is on the elite of the ruling political party in Western Region of Nigeria, the Action Group, both as a corporate group and in relation to the government of the region (between 1954 and 1963), the federal government of Nigeria, and other political parties, particularly the ruling coalition at the center. The emphasis is on party politics determined by a progressive and developmental elite in a nascent African state and its important implications—and complications—for building a developmental state. The two key issues that I consider are (1) the complex question of how to fund and sustain a strong political party committed to building a developmental state without degenerating into what the neopatrimonial school has embraced as the dominant feature of African politics and the African state; (2) how to leverage the development agenda and programs of such a political party to reshape society and promote egalitarian rule. These are the twin questions that the Action Group—the ruling party in Western Nigeria, which was the opposition party at the federal center—and its preeminent leader, Obafemi Awolowo, and his colleagues confronted and answered in specific, though problematic, ways in late colonial Nigeria. As an elite group defined by "the control of specific resources by means of which it acquired political power" (Pina-Cabral 2000: 2), and one "embedded within wider socio-economic and political processes" (Shore 2002: 14), some of which were out of its control, the group also tried to sustain its political power by mobilizing this power to ensure material advantages that would strengthen the party.

One fundamental conclusion that the Action Group elite reached as they organized their political party was that political parties were the most critical instruments not only for gaining power, but also for aggregating visions of good governance and pressing it into reality when power was won through popular franchise. Thus, party supremacy was key for this elite. However, party supremacy in a nascent democracy in an agrarian society led as much to their success in government as to the problems encountered. I suggest that such was their fundamental attitude toward party supremacy and corporate agency that what the Action Group attempted to do could be described as *party-monialism*, which is distinct from (neo)patrimonialism. Party-monialism involves a certain attitude to the political economy of party politics based on the corporate agency of the party elite. For corporate agents who have the capacity for acting together strategically (not merely as the "summation of individuals' self-interest"), articulating shared interests, and organizing for collective action with specific outcomes (Archer 2000: 266), party-monialism necessitates the building by the (core) elite of a mechanism of access to state resources and support by members of the party elite and their allies through party-inspired business transactions in order to build the financial base of the party and secure its political operations so as to ensure and sustain the capture of power and the sustenance of party supremacy— and possibly hegemony. Party-monialism also involves the incorporation, combination, absorption, or merging of economic elites with political elites and the cross-cutting of the interests of these elites on the basis, primarily, of mutual ideological interests in the operation of the state. Such cross-cutting of interests in building and expanding the financial base of the party to ensure party supremacy while also promoting indigenous entrepreneurship was crucial for the Action Group in the context of (1) its relative weakness in relation to the ruling coalition (the Northern People's Congress and the National Convention of Nigerian Citizens) at the federal center, and (2) the need to build an "independent" resource base for the party and strengthen it in its developmental and welfarist agenda.

My argument about neo-party-monialism, though related to what I consider to be the core motivation for Tim Kelsall's (2011: 84) important argument that, under certain conditions, "neo-patrimonialism can be harnessed for developmental ends" (see also Crook 1989; Kelsall et al. 2010; Booth and Golooba-Mutebi 2012), it is different in that neo-party-monialism points to how African political elites can be driven by aspirations for development and general welfare through the strengthening of party dominance, and not individual enrichment.

PARTY-MONIALISM: FUNDING POLITICAL PARTIES IN AFRICA

Funding political parties, though an understudied area of scholarship on democracy in the past, now fosters debates for many years (Fisher and Eisenstadt, 2004: 620). "Competitive political parties," argue Fisher and Eisenstadt (620, following Paltiel 1981: 139), "require funds for three purposes: to run election campaigns, to maintain viable inter-election organizations and to provide research and other assistance to the leadership and representatives of the party. This leads us to the question of how the necessary funds for such operations are provided." Fisher and Eisenstadt conclude that where there are no genuine mass parties, political parties turn to groups and individuals for party financing.

Thus, globally, one of the fundamental issues in party politics that lead to corruption and often determine the nature of democratic governance is how to fund political parties and electioneering campaigns.[3] However, the literature on neopatrimonialism in Africa seems to take ethical challenges and corruption in party financing as an exceptional feature of African politics. Yet, the party-financing-corruption nexus, even in contemporary times, has been a feature of political scandals and worries in developed democracies all over the world, including in OECD countries (see Council of Europe 2003; Warner 2007; European Commission 2014).

The answers provided in the case of the ruling party in Nigeria's Western Region in the late 1950s and 1960s to the question of sustainable funding of a political party were both innovative and problematic. A brief background to this is important. First, it should be noted that this was at a point when there were few rules regarding political finance; thus, the regulation of the role of money in politics was not strong.

As Nigeria approached independence in the 1950s, there were three political parties largely defined around the three regions of the federation, the Eastern Region, the Northern Region, and the Western Region, dominated, respectively, by the three largest and rival ethnoregional groups, the Igbo, the Hausa-Fulani, and the Yoruba. The three dominant political parties were the National Council of Nigerian Citizens (NCNC), the oldest, initially the most nationalist and most radical of the three, led by Dr. Nnamdi Azikiwe; the Northern People's Congress (NPC), a conservative party, led by Sir Ahmadu Bello; and the Action Group (AG), a social-democratic party and the most methodical of the three, led by Chief Obafemi Awolowo. In the federal elec-

Fig. 11.1. Nigerian leaders: Awolowo, Azikiwe, Balewa, Endeley (leader of Southern Cameroon—which eventually voted to join Cameroon), and Bello. Photo courtesy Nigerian Tribune Library.

tions before independence under the Westminster parliamentary system, the NPC and the NCNC formed an alliance that took over power at the center with the NPC member of the Federal House, Abubakar Tafawa-Balewa, becoming the prime minister, while NCNC's Azikiwe became the ceremonial president (initially the governor general).

The Western Region, led by the AG, was the most educationally advanced region of colonial Nigeria. The region gained self-rule in 1956. Before then, in October 1955, AG's leader, Awolowo, became the premier of the region. He established arguably the most efficient, most effective, and most egalitarian government that Nigeria has ever had. It is no surprise that based primarily on what he achieved within five years (1954–59) as premier of the region, he was described as the "best president Nigeria never had" (for details see Adebanwi 2012). On the eve of the country's independence in October 1960, the AG became the opposition party at the (federal) center while it was in control of the government of the Western Region. Awolowo left as premier of the region to become the leader of opposition in the Federal House of Representatives in 1959, after failing to secure an alliance with the NCNC in the hope of becoming the prime minister of Nigeria.

In Nigeria, the Action Group was unique in its investment in elaborate planning, research, and debates on public policies. The party leadership provided "an intellectual program for political action" (Sklar 1966: 123). Awolowo was the most articulate in proposing concrete ideas and structures for the governance of a multicultural state such as Nigeria that was emerging from colonial rule. His book *Path to Nigerian Freedom* (1947) was the first to clearly articulate and defend the need for Nigeria to be organized as a federal state.

He was also a virulent critic of British colonial rule (Sklar 1966: 123). Thus, he was seen as a threat to British interests in colonial Nigeria and Britain's imperial interests after Nigeria's independence. Therefore, the Action Group was facing two strong adversaries: the British colonial/imperial state as well as the (federal) ruling coalition/federal government (see, among others, Sklar 1963; Diamond 1988).

Apart from this, the party, though formed primarily to gain power in the Western Region, also had ambition to spread its network around the country, including in the core Eastern and Northern Regions, where the party and its leader, Awolowo, were not so popular. The AG was convinced that it could overcome its unpopularity in the other two regions with the force of its ideology, party organization, and consistent and elaborate campaigns. To be able to establish itself not only in all the nooks and crannies of the Western Region (where it failed to achieve total hegemony, given the wide popularity of the regional opposition, the NCNC, particularly in the urban areas) but also in the Northern and Eastern Regions, the party adopted innovative ways of campaigning and funding of local parties (and allies) opposed to the dominant NPC and NCNC in their respective regions of greatest influence. This included dropping leaflets by helicopters and light aircraft in opposition areas—an innovative practice in 1950s Africa—traveling by road and air to all parts of the federation (unlike the leaders of the other parties, particularly the NPC, which operated only in the North), and massively funding local opposition and AG allies in the two other regions.

The AG also practiced party supremacy, as indicated earlier. All issues were deliberated upon by the party Federal Executive Committee and the party caucus (the superelite inner circle that acted as a consultative council), and the consensus was defended by party leaders, no matter their initial positions before consensus was reached (see also Sklar 1966: 126–27). However, this form of party organization and the wide network of campaigns—particularly in the face of strong antagonism presented by the two other parties and the colonial and postcolonial governments—created huge financial challenges. While the party was dominated by those who can be described in the ideal typology as *ideologically unified elite*, because of their close to total achievement of structural integration and value consensus (Burton, Gunther, and Higley 1992: 11),[4] the sustenance of this integration and consensus over the long term was doubtful without the party's financial muscle as well as autonomy. How was the party to be funded and how was it to sustain such funding, particularly in the light of deliberate efforts to castrate, if not obliterate, it?

Fig. 11.2. Awolowo (standing by the microphone) campaigning in the NPC stronghold in Sokoto for his party in 1959. Photograph by Eliot Elisofon, 1959. © Eliot Elisofon Photographic Archives, National Museum of African Art, Smithsonian Institution.

When the party was founded between 1951 and 1952 and immediately joined the campaign for the Western Region elections, it depended entirely on subscription by party members and donations from wealthy leaders of the party (Awolowo 1987: 383). In an agrarian society, it was obvious that subscriptions by party members and the beneficence of a few wealthy members would be grossly insufficient for the subsequent national elections that would demand massive resources.

The party caucus had several meetings to think about this. Some of the members of the party caucus (who were also wealthy and had made personal donations to the party), including Dr. Akinola Maja, Bayo Doherty, and Alhaji S. O. Gbadamosi, were also shareholders of the National Bank of Nigeria. Doherty and Gbadamosi—as the principal shareholders of the bank—informed the caucus that the bank was ready to help if the party would undertake to "cause the Government of the Western Region to use the bank as its principal banker" (Awolowo 1987: 383). Doubtless, this was a quid pro quo that ordinarily was contrary to the spirit of transparency and accountability. Also, if the government made a "substantial time-deposit with the bank," the directors promised, the bank would lend the party money "and work out ways and means of writing off the loans over a period." However, this agreement was defended by the leaders of the party as absolutely within the laws and the spirit of the government's development plans. According to one member of the party caucus, the caucus agreed with the request of the shareholders of the bank "since the undertaking sought by the bank was not at variance with party policy to encourage indigenous business to grow and flourish" (Awolowo 1987: 383).

In addition to the loan, the party was able to raise money through donations up to the tune of £100,000 (Awolowo 1987: 385) and thus was able to operate smoothly between 1952 and 1953. But in 1954, the party discovered that the bank had not fully kept its part of the bargain. Rather than give soft loans to the party or write off part of the loan, the bank imposed substantial interest on the loans while demanding more deposits from the government. Recalled Alfred Rewane, one of the leaders of the party, "The demands became endless[,] bordering on blackmail and everybody [in the party and government] became panicky.... Threats of [a] run on the bank by depositors withdrawing their money, and threats of probing and closure of the bank became a weekly occurrence" (Awolowo 1987: 385).

The party caucus therefore had to devise a new way of funding the party. One proposal, according to Rewane, was "negotiated agreement" with contractors who obtained contracts from government. However, Premier Awolowo was opposed to this, arguing that it "would be tantamount to taking money from the Government Treasury and using the contractors as conduit." Though he had no objections to contractors donating money to the party, he objected to making it a precondition for obtaining government contracts. The precondition, to him, would be corrupt, unethical, and indefensible.

Given the party's predilection for intellectual reflections on party and public challenges (see Sklar 1966: 123), it was resolved that two members of the caucus, Shonibare and Rewane, should conduct a study of how parties were funded in other democracies around the world. At the end of the study, the two-man study group reported that they found three useful models: The "British model," the "American model," and the "Israeli model." The team recommended the Israeli model as most "acceptable," particularly that of Histadrut (General Organization of Workers in the Land of Israel), a national trade union center representing the majority of the trade unions in Israel (see Tzahor 1996). Histadrut, which became a behemoth, was established in 1920 during the British Mandate of Palestine. As the backbone of the Labour Zionist movement, it took on a state-building role that was done mainly through its economic arm, Hevrat HaOvdim (Society of Workers), with investments in businesses and factories, through which it became the largest employer. Histadrut owned the country's largest industrial conglomerates, including the country's largest bank, Bank Hapoalim, and business enterprises such as Solel Boneh,[5] the largest engineering company in Israel and the thirteenth largest in the world at that time (the company has been doing business in Nigeria for many years), Koor Industries, and Kupat Holim Clalit. Thus, Histadrut became one of the most powerful institutions in Israel. Though it was not a political organization, it influenced elections in Israel. Interesting enough, the man who became the leader of Histadrut the year after it was founded, David Ben-Gurion, also became the primary founder of the State of Israel and its first prime minister. As Histadrut secretary-general, Ben-Gurion transformed Histadrut and centralized its leadership and operations. According to the report by the Shonibare-Rewane committee, Histadrut "engaged in intensive investment and business activities" and thus "was one of the two richest organisations in Israel, apart from the Government" (Awolowo 1987: 387). Histadrut did whatever the Labour Zionist movement wanted to do but could not do directly. It was the powerful instrument of political Zionism. The organization also had financial interests in El Al Airlines and Israeli Shipping Lines, with returns running into millions of pounds. "In short," according to the Action Group study team, "it had enormous resources and as such had

Fig. 11.3. Premier Akintola with Israeli prime minister Ben-Gurion during his official visit to Jerusalem in October 1961. The AG government in Nigeria's Western Region saw Israel as a model of successful state building in many ways. Wikimedia Commons.

no problem whatsoever funding anything it wished" (Awolowo 1987: 387). What the report overlooked was that the Histadrut was not founded on state support. Rather, it helped to build the state.

However, the party caucus decided on the Histadrut model and asked some members of the group to work out the details of starting a business outfit. I will like to describe this as a "corporation model" of party funding. This was a unique, even if problematic, model that was understandable in the context of an agrarian society in the capitalist periphery where opportunities for capitalist accumulation by indigenous businesses were severely limited.

Again, two of the directors of the National Bank, as members of the party caucus, were involved in the planning. It was decided that the company should go into property development. If the new company could obtain funds from the Western Region government or any of its agencies, the bank directors promised to surrender the bank's undeveloped properties in strategic areas of Lagos to the company for development. A committee of five (Maja, Doherty, Gbadamosi, Shonibare, and Rewane) was subsequently formed. The committee eventually proposed the formation of an investment company, the National Investment and Properties Company (NIPC), by the party. The NIPC was to have a relationship with the AG such as Histradut had with the Labour Zionist movement.

Members of the committee except Doherty, who were all ranking members of the ruling party in the region, subsequently became the directors of the company. The company approached the government of Western Region for a loan to develop some choice properties and was referred to a government agency, the Western Region Marketing Board (WNMB), which had substantial cash surplus invested overseas. Negotiations between the NIPC and the WNMB yielded loans on terms that the NIPC directors believed were more favorable to the government agency, the WNMB, than the latter could attract from its investments abroad. The properties to be developed were used as collateral for the loan. Also, the landed property was evaluated by an expert, with the value constituting a loan from the National Bank to the NIPC. Three years advance rents were to be collected from the developed property to do three things: pay back part of the (WNMB) capital loan plus interest in the period of the rent; repay part of the National Bank loan; and fund the Action Group party (Awolowo 1987: 389). One of the elements of the defense offered by the promoters of the NIPC and the party leaders was that supporting the company was part of the ways of realizing the government's ambition to promote indigenous entrepreneurs, thus "prevent[ing] the commercial areas in Western Nigeria from falling into the exclusive possession of expatriate investors," while "reduc[ing] the burden of the economic domination of the country by aliens" (Awolowo 1987: 107, 109).

It was also agreed that after the company had settled all the party's debt, the ownership of the company should revert to the trustees of the party, not as individuals but on behalf of the party, and as agents of the party. The four directors of the bank therefore signed undated share certificates transferring their shares to the trustees of the party.

Evidently, the NIPC model departed in important respects from the Histadrut model, but it was obviously constructed to fit the realities of the (Western) Nigerian context, which was markedly different from the experience in the mandate territory of Palestine in the early twentieth century.

Egalitarian Rule and Party-Monialism

In his 2015 essay, Mkandawire warns against the neopatrimonialism school's tendency to render "monochromatic the many colorful and varied characters who have taken the African political stage over the last half century (602)." One such character was Obafemi Awolowo. Through the agency of the Action Group, the leadership he offered in the Western Region involved the reconception and elaboration of the Enlightenment project such that by the time the party was proscribed in 1966 by the military, it had initiated one of the most successful modernist projects in Africa. In the light of this, he was described as "easily the most daring and enduring political thinker that Nigeria produced in the twentieth century" (Ofeimun 2006). As Odia Ofeimun, Nigeria's famous public intellectual, poet, and Awolowo's former private secretary, states, "In a very creative manner, [Awolowo] had domesticated the best in ideas that was being thought across the world about nation-building. He summarized for me an enlightenment tradition that went beyond what many of the original thinkers had thought. Compared to all his contemporaries, he was the master with whom it was most theoretically valuable to be in cahoots" (2006).

There are several accomplishments of the AG government that show that it was a developmental one—with massive investment in education, health, and social services—and not an example of the governments based on "elite clientelism" (van de Walle 2007: 3) that Afro-pessimism dismisses. When the party was formally announced in April 1951, the "basic principles" that brought the members together were summarized by the group's motto: "Freedom for All, Life More Abundant." These were elaborated to include "Freedom from British Rule; freedom from ignorance; freedom from disease; and freedom from want" (Awolowo 1960: 223). For the first time in Nigeria's history, a political party (the Action Group) took party politics and political consciousness to the rural areas and the peasantry (Awolowo 1960: 223). It published its policy papers and manifesto (forcing other political parties to do so later). When it came to power in the Western Region in 1951, it had "clear ideas as how to . . . achieve" its aims. The AG government instituted a free universal primary education and free medical treatment for all children up to the age of eighteen.[6] All of these programs strengthened the modernist advantages of the Western Region of Nigeria, with the states that were later created out of the region maintaining the highest scores in Nigeria on the human development index.

THE POLITICS OF CORRUPTION AND THE CHALLENGES OF DEVELOPING A LOCAL BOURGEOISIE

The role of the local or indigenous (national) bourgeoisie in building and consolidating social democracy or popular rule has been a subject of intense debate both in praxis and in the social science literature. As a formation, an indigenous bourgeoisie is one "whose economic activities and interests are seen as being different from and not dependent upon those of imperialism" (Gordon 1973: 192). However, within the radical tradition, the possibility of the national bourgeoisie working for social liberation has either been dismissed or understated, despite the fundamental interest of this class in developing the national economy against "internal feudal restrictions and imperialist domination" (Gordon 1973: 192). As early as the Second Congress of the Third International in 1920, Lenin stated that the national or industrial bourgeoisie were incapable of playing a leading role in national democratic revolution (Mahmoud 1983: 103). He dismissed them as often in cahoots with imperialist bourgeoisie after the success of national liberation, although he allowed that they might serve as ally in the struggle of workers and peasants against imperialism (Mahmoud 1983: 103). However, except in the case of India and later in Latin America, early analyses of the role of national bourgeoisie in colonial societies lacked familiarity with the concrete realities of these societies (Mahmoud 1983: 104) and the particularities that may place the local bourgeoisie in critical positions to facilitate social democracy and egalitarian rule. Though postcolonial analyses of the local bourgeoisie by radical scholars in the global South (such as Andre Frank, Samir Amin, and Hamza Alavi) have remedied this lack of familiarity with particularities, many of the analyses still place limited purchase on the viability of local bourgeoisie's efficacy in facilitating popular democracy.[7] The dominant trend in the literature "tended to minimize the power and independence of the local bourgeoisie," as they are often dismissed as "comprador bourgeoisie" who lack "the will and means to act as an independent entity" (Hewison 1981: 395).

While Mahmoud (1983: 106) has argued usefully in the context of the Sudan that "the way capital is accumulated and the conditions under which it operates . . . determine the independent nature or otherwise of the local bourgeoisie," it is important to note that the kind of model that the AG elite were trying to build, following the Histadrut model, attempted to subordinate capital and the local bourgeoisie who were leveraged to build and manage capital/wealth to the mission, vision, and purposes of a social democratic political party seeking for dominance/hegemony in a particular context of ideological struggle and party politics. In this context, the local bourgeoisie, particularly the type that the AG was hoping to develop and expand, constituted a leverage for a "national" political mission, with the power to insulate the party's social democratic project from the strictures and even the hostility of the dominant national ruling elite and their foreign backers, who were bent of stopping the party's brand of social democracy—which was regarded as a short-cut to "socialism" and eventually "communism."

When Awolowo decided to leave the Western Region as premier in 1959 and was elected to the Federal House of Representatives—in the hope that the AG, in alliance with one or more parties, would be able to form the government at the center so that he could be prime minister—he set the stage, unwittingly, for the crisis that engulfed Nigeria's First Republic and led to its collapse. After the AG lost the federal elections in 1959 with the NPC-NCNC alliance controlling the Federal House and the federal executive, a decision was taken to cripple the opposition party, AG, and its leader, Awolowo (see Sklar 1963, 1966; Diamond 1988). It was generally agreed among the leaders of the ruling coalition that the "gargantuan country-wide campaign" of the AG during the 1959 elections that tested the ruling coalition was aided by the financing of the party by the National Bank of Nigeria. The party had spent £1 million on the federal elections of 1959, which was more than the "combined expenditure of all the other parties" (Sklar 1966: 126). Akintola's biographer, Osuntokun (1984: 134) later argued that the AG and its business network constituted a "heavy drain" on the Marketing Board's resources (Diamond 1988: 95). Therefore, the ruling coalition decided to attack the source of funding so as to cripple the AG. This was the financial front of the two-pronged battle (the other being the political).

Indeed, the Western Region was relatively prosperous owing largely to a postwar boom in the world price of cocoa, the region's mail export crop (Sklar 1966: 126). Based on this, the AG government, as Sklar (1966: 126) notes, "fostered the creation of profitable opportunities for private enterprise. It used commercial patronage freely, including the allocation of loans, contracts, and trading licenses to secure the support of businessmen and guarantee a steady flow of funds into the party coffer." Thus, the AG was financially stronger than the other two major parties combined. To crush the operations of the party and the leaders of the party, if not the party itself, the federal government decided to set up a commission of inquiry into the activities of the National Bank.

Awolowo's successor—and later adversary—as premier of the Western Region, Chief S. L. A. Akintola, initially dismissed the "reprehensible" and "deplorable" decision of the federal government to conduct an inquiry into a bank that now belonged to the government of Western Region, a coequal federating unit, without consulting with the regional government. He concluded that the "decision has been taken by the Federal Government not in furtherance of the interest of the bank or of the Nigerian public but as a reprisal against the Government of Western Nigeria for no other reason than that it is controlled by the Action Group" (Sklar 1966: 50–51).

In the meantime, the managing director of the bank instituted a court action seeking the declaration of the action of the prime minister a "nullity" and an injunction restraining the commission of inquiry until the determination of the substantive issues of law raised by the suit at the Federal Supreme Court (FSC). The court ruled in his favor. But before the FSC could decide on this, the prime minister introduced two bills in the federal parliament. One was a bill for an act on the commission of inquiry to probe the transactions of the National Bank and another bill on a "Commission and Tribunal of Inquiry Act" of 1961 that gave the prime minister the power, not subject to judicial review, to institute commissions and tribunals of inquiry into any subject. Even though members of the AG opposed the bills, they were quickly passed by the majority the same day they were introduced. The next day, another commission of inquiry was appointed by the prime minister. However, two days later, the managing director of the National Bank again challenged the validity of the new commission and sought an interim injunction to restrain it from proceeding. The court again granted the injunction. The federal government's motion to the effect that the act precluded the court's jurisdiction was dismissed by the judge, who accused the federal government of "inquisitorial harassment of the citizen" (Sklar 1966: 53). But the judge referred two questions to the FSC: one, whether the federal parliament had the power to enact a law preventing any citizen from challenging in court the legality of a decision by the prime minister; and two, whether the federal parliament had the power to enact a law providing for the appointment by the prime minister of a commission of inquiry and thus, if the recently passed act was valid. On October 4, 1961, and October 27, 1961, the FSC ruled in the negative on both questions. This was a blow to the ruling coalition and the federal government.

However, a way was found around the Supreme Court's decision by the ruling coalition. On June 16, 1962, an official gazette, the "Emergency Powers (Statutory Corporations Inquiries) Regulations, 1962" was signed by the governor-general, Dr. Nnamdi Azikiwe. Thus, what was later described as the "Coker Commission," that is, the Commission of Inquiry into the Affairs of Certain Statutory Commissions in Western Nigeria, 1962, was established. It was a three-man commission headed by Justice George Ayoola Coker. The commission's work, as Robert L. Tignor (1993: 196) describes it, was "deeply rooted in Nigerian political infighting." By this time, Awolowo and some other leaders of the now fractionalized opposition party, AG, were either under restriction, house arrest, or in detention after the declaration of a state of emergency in the Western Region by the federal government. The commission was to do essentially the same thing that the Supreme Court had restrained the prime minister from accomplishing.

The Economist of London, to the irritation of the Coker Commission and the federal government, summed up the purpose of the commission in its July 28, 1962, edition entitled "Stop Thief in Lagos": "It could not happen elsewhere in West Africa. Admittedly, the whole enquiry is partly intended by the Federal Government to damage the Action Group which provides the Federal Opposition, but it may also impress at least some Nigerians with the dangers of corruption." On the contrary, the NCNC premier of the Eastern Region, Michael Okpara, attacked the AG as "a party of vandalism," while his party called for the disbandment of the AG "in the interest of the public good" (Diamond 1988: 108). However, Awolowo's teeming supporters in Yorubaland saw the inquiry as a politically motivated attempt to destroy the AG. In response to this and with an apparent intent to taunt the federal government and Awolowo's political adversaries who were investigating him for corruption, his supporters insisted in a popular folk song that Awolowo could "loot our Treasury" because the Treasury belonged to the people and Awolowo was a man of the people.[8] It was a rather ironic, if not damning, way of expressing popular trust in Awolowo and an indication of the existence of different registers of accountability. It is as if those singing this song took collective responsibility for what Awolowo's accusers saw as his financial "transgressions." However, beyond what may appear like an endorsement of corruption, Awolowo's supporters didn't actually believe that he stole money. In what might be described as the vernacular of Yoruba politics, "acknowledging" that Awolowo had "looted" the collective purse in this way was an expression of disdain for his accusers, rather than an admission of Awolowo's guilt. In the context of politics of accountability, it also can be argued that Awolowo's supporters were insisting that the most important mode of accountability that they cared about was his accomplishments as premier of the region, given the many programs of popular empowerment that he embarked upon. As Miranda Joseph (2014: x) has argued, accounting involves "complex performative representational practices" that can manifest in such folk songs as this popular response to accusations of corruption against a popular leader. Evidently, accountability, for the people was not only—and sometimes not necessarily, or not even—*financial* accountability. In such a context, accountability is fundamentally about a certain imagination of or attitude to *public good*, approached as the fulfilment of electoral promises in terms of social amenities and social programs. When this is the case, financial propriety, transparency, accusations of corruption, and so on are de-emphasized, if not largely dismissed, as the bases of measuring accountability among the political elite. This attitude, no doubt, constitutes a major impediment to transparent and accountable democratic governance.

Though he was glad that the majority of his people supported him, Awolowo did not embrace a trivialization of the accusation of corruption as evident in the folk song. The man who described the commission as "a cruel quasi-judicial machine deliberately constructed . . . for oppression, persecution, and total destruction of a political rival" (Awolowo 1987: 296–97) concluded that, given all the impediments placed in his way to defend himself at the commission (including not allowing him access to his documents), he was "fully convinced" that "the motive behind the Inquiry [was] to use the [it] as one of the instruments with which to discredit me, and destroy the Action Group" (Awolowo 1987: 295).

For Awolowo's loyalists in the AG, it was significant that in all its findings, the commission could not point to any concrete evidence of *personal* corrupt enrichment,[9] but the "diversion of large sums of money by both the National Bank of Nigeria Ltd. and the National Investment and Properties Co. Ltd. into the coffers of the Action Group" (Awolowo 1987: 302). Yet the directors of the NIPC, save the one who cooperated with the prosecution (and had switched over to support the federal ruling coalition), were recommended for prosecution for "stealing." The commission also concluded that the NIPC "was the backbone of the Action Group and that indeed [the] Action Group was the owner" of the NIPC (Awolowo 1987: 309) and that, based on this, "without doubt Chief Awolowo has failed to adhere to the standards of conduct which are required for persons holding such a post" (Awolowo 1987: 306). The charges were eventually withdrawn, with the accused discharged and acquitted by the federal judiciary for want of evidence.

Two of the directors of the NIPC had decided not to reveal to the commission that the company was formed by the party and owned indirectly by the party. The decision not to tell the commission the real purpose of the NIPC was taken on the advice of their lawyers, even though Awolowo objected. Two of the directors (Gbadamosi and Maja) eventually told the commission that the company was formed primarily to fund the party. Thus, the two who failed to disclose the purpose of the company perjured themselves before the commission, even though they were not formally accused of doing so.

One observer concluded that the commission's report was "so disgusting that any impartial observer cannot but come to the incontrovertible conclusion that the report is as politicised as the Corporation they were probing," adding that "the Commission was set up not primarily to expose corruption, but was an inquisition on the persons, character and activities of those who are politically opposed to the ruling powers in Lagos" (Awolowo 1987: 337).

Even though the executive council approved the loans totaling £4.2 million to NIPC during Awolowo's time as premier (1954–59)—the loans were all secured with landed property by the company—there were ethical issues that can be raised about loans granted by the government headed by the party leader to a company that was formed and practically owned by the party. But the party and Awolowo argued that it was not illegal. The loans were fully secured, while the interest rate was higher than the WRMB could secure abroad. Also, all the assets of the NIPC were mortgaged to the WRMB (Awolowo 1987: 108). Furthermore, though the commission found Awolowo's successor, Akintola, totally blameless in the relationship between the WNMB and NIPC, in fact, under his premiership, a further loan of £2 million, which had been opposed by Awolowo when he was in office, was granted to the NIPC by Premier Akintola without the approval of the executive council. This was yet another confirmation of the fact that the inquiry was about politics rather than corruption per se, as Akintola, by this time, had become an ally of the senior partner in the federal ruling coalition, the Northern People's Congress. More important, the building projects for which NIPC borrowed money from the WNMB had either been completed or were in the final process of completion by the time the commission of inquiry was instituted. It included some of what became the greatest evidence of economic growth and modernity in Western Nigeria, including the twenty-five-story skyscraper the Cocoa House, Ibadan—which was at this point and for many years the tallest building in Africa—and two other skyscrapers in Lagos, the twenty-floor Western House, then the tallest building in Lagos, and Investment House, Lagos. Therefore, even though the NIPC funded the Action Group, it did not "divert" the loan, as the commission claimed, nor did the directors "steal" the money. The total amount of money loaned to the NIPC was £6.2 million. The properties developed by the company were valued at £9 million. Even though the commission of inquiry rejected this as "over-valuation," eight months later, in the terms of settlement sanctioned by the court between the NIPC and the WRMB—in which the WRMB accepted only substantial, and not the entire, properties owned by the former—the latter took over the NIPC properties for over £10 million, £1 million more than the amount that the commission had dismissed as overvaluation. Thus, the NIPC was discharged from paying the £6.2 million loan due to the WRMB, while the latter also took over the loan of £3 million that the Anglo-Israeli Bank had given to the NIPC. Also, the WRMB undertook to complete all uncompleted building projects.

Indeed, before the inquiry was set up, the Akintola government had decided to acquire the properties developed by the NIPC to recover the debts to the WRMB and had valued the property at £8.9 million against the loan of £6.2 million. If the company was solvent enough to more than repay its loan to the bank, it was obvious that there was no need for the inquiry. Evidently, despite the ethical challenges that may be raised about the "substantial financial assistance" that the NIPC gave to the party, AG, its properties were still worth more than its liabilities and debts.

It can be argued that the AG derived undue advantage over other political parties in the region, particularly the NCNC (its chief rival in the region), due to this loan that the NIPC was able to get from the WRMB. It can even be assumed that if the NCNC had formed a similar company, the AG regional government would not have been eager to encourage or allow the WRMB to provide a loan to the party's company. However, though his party benefited from this transactions, Awolowo insisted in his memoir that there was nothing wrong with the relationship between the NIPC and the WRMB. He stated that he was prepared to tell the truth to the commission, despite the opposition by some of his other colleagues in the party caucus. "There was nothing corrupt or improper about [the relationship]," he argues. "The relationship between NIPC and WRMB was one of borrower and lender. And in this case, the NIPC, by all standards, was a good, viable, and at all times, solvent borrower. The acid test of a good borrower is the assured capacity to pay back the loan received. . . . No one with common sense . . . would ever regard the kind of transaction that had taken place between the NIPC and the WRMB as amounting to stealing" (Awolowo 1987: 381).

The story of the relationship between the NIPC and the WRMB and other agencies of the Western Region government is much more complex and elaborate than was allowed in the politics and discourses of corruption while the controversy lasted. However, the core issue raised was about the modes of accountability within a nascent democratic system in one of the new states in early 1960s Africa. While the AG elite saw its project as one devoted to the building of a strong and virile party—a party that could retain control of the region so as to continue its developmental agenda—through economic enterprises, the dominant elites at the federal center wanted to demobilize the party not only by destroying its access to funding and by accusing its leaders of lack of accountability and corruption, but also by destroying the party's legitimacy through pointing out to the electorate that the party and its leaders were unworthy of public trust and support.

It is, therefore, important to emphasize how this case illuminates Mkandawire's argument about the complexity of the reality in Africa, which the perspective of neopatrimonialism not only fails to capture but often simplifies. The NIPC was an attempt at capitalist accumulation and development aimed, primarily, at funding a political party to ensure the sustenance of the developmental agenda of a social-democratic party under pressure and threat of obliteration. However, while the whole process did not violate any law or lead to personal corrupt enrichment—as the courts and the process of the settlement confirmed—it nonetheless raised ethical questions about the means and process of party funding, particularly in the context of the struggle to ensure that the party was not held hostage to private business interests. These questions remain unresolved in present-day Africa, even though more ethically challenged, if not outright paralegal and illegal, "solutions" have been found by contemporary party elites in the continent—and elsewhere—to the problem of financing political parties.

CONCLUSION: ELITES, *PARTY-MONIALISM*, AND THE "DEVELOPMENTAL" STATE

Carol Greenhouse (1996: 12, emphasis added) has suggested that we seek for "dynamic and multifarious accounts of elites and their practices of accountability and *locally plausible* self-legitimation" in order to understand the complexity of the processes of negotiation and compromise that inform their actions. This does not necessarily translate to justifying the actions. But it means acknowledging the fact that such actions are fraught with contradictions, particularly in a context of ethnoregional struggles in the late colonial and immediate postcolonial era.

I follow Mkandawire here to argue that, though some developmental agendas in Africa may entail nepotism and ethical challenges, dismissing every such agenda as neopatrimonial and clientelistic and thus essentially corrupt overlooks some genuine, ideological commitments to the creation of developmental states by some progressive elites in specific contexts in Africa. As the example in this chapter shows, the challenge of funding a progressive opposition party, for instance, involves some compromises that may not be absolutely ethical and might even be corrupt, but this should not occlude our appreciation of the committed, even if fraught, attempts at resolving the question of party funding in late colonial and early postcolonial contexts and the accomplishments of some political elites, such as the leaders of the AG, in power.

Despite the fact that the AG can be accused of some measure of contradiction in trying to build democratic socialism through capitalist accumulation, there is no doubt that the practical developmental agenda of the party bore positive fruits and improved the lives of the people of Western Region of Nigeria. At any rate, paradoxes are at the heart of democratic politics. Against the background of AG's accomplishments, the argument by a strand of the neopatrimonial school that in Africa "the state lacks the capacity to provide social services" (Mkandawire 2015: 588) is demonstrably untrue in every instance. Similarly untrue in every case is the claim that "African governments will not spend much on education and health" (588–89), as the AG government invested heavily in these areas, thus helping to produce one of the highest rates of educated citizenry in the whole of Africa.

I will conclude by linking Mkandawire's two articles together, as hinted at the beginning of this chapter. Against the backdrop of Mkandawire's (2001: 290) analysis in the earlier article on developmental state, the Western Region under the AG was distinguishable as a developmental state through the *"ideology-structure nexus."* At the ideological level, as the party in power in the Western Region, the party elite conceived of the AG's mission in government as "that of ensuring economic development," including achieving a high rate of accumulation and kick-starting industrialization.[10] Such a developmental state "establishes as its principle of legitimacy its ability to promote sustained development" (Castells 1992: 55, cited in Mkandawire 2001: 290). The AG elite also attempted to establish "ideological hegemony" (Castells 1992: 55, cited in Mkandawire 2001: 290) so as to ensure that their project of development became "hegemonic" not just in the Western Region, but in the rest of Nigeria. At the structural level, the AG government mobilized the capacity for an astute and effective implementation of economic policies (Mkandawire 2001: 290). However, in the years in which the AG was in power in late colonial and early postcolonial Nigeria, the regional state failed to gain total *autonomy* from social forces, particularly the ruling political party and its elite, such that the government was, to some extent, encumbered by party interests (cf. Mkandawire 2001: 290). It is this reality that I capture as party-monialism. Yet when the overall context in which the party and its government operated is deeply analyzed, we can conclude that, despite this problem, Nigeria's Western Region remains a genuine developmental state, because, as Mkandawire (2001: 291) usefully argues, our definition of a developmental state must include "situations in which exogenous structural dynamic and unforeseen factors can torpedo genuine developmental commitments and efforts by the state."

Finally, Mkandawire (2015: 602) in his essay on neopatrimonialism cautions "against such generalizations and stereotypes" as lead to "notions that African politics are singularly driven by the inexorable logic of neopatrimonialism" (601) or that "neopatrimonialism of the bourgeoisie" is incompatible with capitalist accumulation (578). In the example I have related here, party-monialism was central to the new social contract that was created by the party elite in western Nigeria, which led to free education and other social welfare programs. In fact, I suggest that given the odds faced by the party and its core elite, the party's success in power was impossible without party-monialism. In the light of this example, it is evident that, as Mkandawire (2015: 598) argues, the neopatrimonial school overstates the existence of "a world without ideas and passion" in Africa. Although the Africanist literature is overwhelmed by analyses of many elite formations that turn "the state into an amoral market for profit from highest bidder or an extractive machine in the hands of a dominant class, beyond popular control" (Werbner 2004: 1; see Bayart 1993; Bayart, Ellis, and Hibou 1999; Chabal and Daloz 1999), there are, no doubt, some elite formations that are ideologically committed to the public good. Indeed, as this example shows, in Africa "policies are shaped not only by interests and structures but also by ideas" (Mkandawire 2015: 598), and the existence of contradictions and the politics of corruption evident in inter- and intraelite politics should not prevent the analysis of such examples, even if they were superseded or failed.

NOTES

1. For a robust defense of a particular strand of what is described as "Afro-pessimism" in a review of Werbner's *Reasonable Radicals and Citizenship in Botswana* (2004), see Chabal 2008. While he understands the position of scholars who are "fed up

with academic snobbishness against the study of African elites" (605), Chabal rejects the label of "Afro-pessimist," describing himself as an "an Afro-realist" (608).

2. For a useful critique of the neopatrimonial school, see Pitcher, Moran, and Johnston 2009. Pitcher et al., using the example of Botswana, point to the misreading of Weber in the analysis of the neopatrimonial school, while noting that the use of terms like *patrinomialism* and *neopatriminialism* "to explain contemporary strategies of governance in Africa has had three important consequences: (1) it has established and naturalized a supposedly characteristic form of leadership and governance to the continent as a whole; (2) it has attributed to this form of governance both the failure of African states to operate according to the principles of liberal democracy and the "passivity" of African citizens in demanding accountability; and (3) it has located the poor economic performance of postcolonial Africa in the political chaos caused by 'strong men' and 'weak states.' It thus makes historical, political, and economic claims about the continent as a whole, providing a neat and consistent explanation for violence, state collapse, petty to extreme corruption, irresponsible resource allocation, and a host of other ills" (149). Importantly, they add that patrimonialism "must be understood in context, evaluated for its positive as well as negative consequences, and not be used as a one-variable explanation for broad national outcomes" (149).

3. For some examples, see IDEA 2014, especially chapter 3, which focuses on Africa; Mathisen and Svåsand 2002.

4. Eventually, this gave way in the context of external intervention and personal ambitions.

5. The company, being one of the pioneer private road construction companies in late colonial western Nigeria, became a legend in Yorubaland. Given that the company constructed newer roads where drivers could speed, the name Solel Boneh was *vernacularized* by the Yoruba as Ṣ'ina bo'lẹ ("hit the gas"—that is, accelerate).

6. For other accomplishments, see Awolowo 1960: 262–93 and others such as Oyelaran et al. 2002; Oke et al. 2009; Ogunsanwo 2009; Adebanwi 2014.

7. For interesting perspectives, see Alavi 1975, 1972; Amin 1974; Frank 1969; Swainson 1977; Woddis 1977.

8. The popular song in this period was "Awolowo, Baba Layinka, maa kowo wa naa, igunnu lo ni Tapa, Tapa lo ni gunnu, maa kowo wa naa" ("Awolowo, Layinka's father, continue to loot our Treasury, the Igunnu masquerade belongs to the Nupe, and the Nupe belongs to the Igunnu masquerade, continue to loot our Treasury"). Sekoni 1997: 142.

9. Many commentators have failed to pay attention to the politics and the complexity of this case. An example of this is the Marxist scholar Segun Osoba (1996: 375, emphasis added), who, on the basis of the conclusions of the commission and without any evidence, describes "several ingenious and brazen devices by which Awolowo and his colleagues in the leadership of the Action Group Government of Western Nigeria *enriched themselves* and their party fabulously at the expense of the accumulated funds of the Cocoa Marketing Board, property of the whole people of Western Nigeria." One

of these "ingenious and brazen devices" that Osoba points to is "unsecured government loans"—which was certainly untrue in the case of NIPC. It is interesting that Osoba, when writing about the matter, neither bothered to read nor responded to Awolowo's 1987 account of what transpired and Awolowo's and others' critique of the reports of the Coker Commission.

10. For instance, the AG government started an industrial estate in Ikeja, Lagos.

REFERENCES

Adebanwi, Wale. 2012. *Authority Stealing: Anti-corruption War and Democratic Politics in Post-military Nigeria*. Durham, NC: Carolina Academic Press.

Adebanwi, Wale. 2014. *Yoruba Elites and Ethnic Politics in Nigeria: Obafemi Awolowo and Corporate Agency*. Cambridge: Cambridge University Press.

Alavi, Hamza. 1972. "The State in Post-colonial Societies: Pakistan and Bangladesh." *New Left Review* 1, no. 74: 59–81.

Alavi, Hamza. 1975. "India and the Colonial Mode of Production." In Ralph Miliband and John Saville, eds., *The Socialist Register 1975*. London: Merlin Press, 160–97.

Amin, Samir. 1974. "Accumulation and Development: A Theoretical Model." *Review of African Political Economy* 1, no. 1: 9–26.

Archer, Margaret S. 2000. *Being Human: The Problem of Agency*. Cambridge: Cambridge University Press.

Awolowo, Obafemi. 1947. *Path to Nigerian Freedom*. London: Faber.

Awolowo, Obafemi. 1960. *Awo: The Autobiography of Chief Obafemi Awolowo*. Cambridge: Cambridge University Press.

Awolowo, Obafemi. 1987. *Travails of Democracy and the Rule of Law*. Ibadan, Nigeria: Evans Brothers.

Bayart, Jean-François. 1993. *The State in Africa: The Politics of the Belly*. New York: Longman.

Bayart, Jean-François, Stephen Ellis, and Béatrice Hibou. 1999. *The Criminalization of the State in Africa*. Oxford: James Currey.

Booth, David, and Frederick Golooba-Mutebi. 2012. "Development Patrimonialism? The Case of Rwanda." *African Affairs* 111, no. 444: 379–403.

Burnell, Peter. 2017. "Introduction: Money and Politics in Emerging Democracies." In Peter Burnell and Alan Ware, eds., *Funding Democratization*. New York: Routledge.

Burton, Michael, Richard Gunther, and John Higley. 1992. "Introduction: Elite Transformations and Democratic Regimes." In John Higley and Richard Gunther, eds., *Elites and Democratic Consolidation in Latin America and Southern Europe*. Cambridge: Cambridge University Press, 1–37.

Chabal, Patrick. 2008. "On Reason and Afro-pessimism" (review article). *Africa* 78, no. 4: 603–10.

Chabal, Patrick, and Jean-Pascal Daloz. 1999. *Africa Works: Disorder as Political Instrument*. Oxford: James Currey.

Council of Europe. 2003. "Recommendations of the Council of Ministers to Member States on Common Rules against Corruption in the Funding of Political Parties and Electoral Campaigns." https://rm.coe.int/16806cc1f1 Accessed on May 28, 2018.

Crook, Richard C. 1989 "Patrimonialism, Administrative Effectiveness and Economic Development in Côte D'Ivoire." *African Affairs* 88: 205–28.

Diamond, Larry. 1988. *Class, Ethnicity and Democracy in Nigeria: The Failure of the First Republic*. Syracuse, NY: Syracuse University Press.

European Commission. 2014. *Special Eurobarometer: Corruption Report.*

Federal Government of Nigeria. 1962. *Report of Coker Commission of Inquiry into the Affairs of Certain Statutory Corporations in Western Nigeria*. Lagos: Federal Ministry of Information, Printing Division.

Fisher, Justin, and Todd A. Eisenstadt. 2004. "Introduction: Comparative Party Finance. What Is to Be Done?" *Party Politics* 10, no. 6: 619–26.

Frank, Andre Gunder. 1969. *Capitalism and Underdevelopment in Latin America*. New York: Monthly Review Press.

Gordon, Alec. 1973. "The Theory of the 'Progressive' National Bourgeoisie." *Journal of Contemporary Asia* 3, no. 2: 192–203.

Greenhouse, Carol J. 1996. *A Moment's Notice: Time Politics Across Cultures*. New York: Cornell University Press.

Hewison, Kevin J. 1981. "The Financial Bourgeoisie in Thailand." *Journal of Contemporary Asia* 11, no. 4: 395–412.

Institute for Democracy and International Assistance (IDEA). 2003. *Funding Political Parties and Election Campaigns*. Stockholm: Institute for Democracy and International Assistance.

Institute for Democracy and International Assistance (IDEA). 2014. *Funding of Political Parties and Election Campaigns: A Handbook on Political Finance*. Stockholm: International IDEA.

Joseph, Miranda. 2014. *Debt to Society: Accounting for Life under Capitalism*. Minneapolis: University of Minnesota Press.

Kelsall, Tim. 2011. "Rethinking the Relationship between Neo-patrimonialism and Economic Development in Africa." *IDS Bulletin* 42, no. 2: 76–87.

Kelsall, Tim, and David Booth, with Diana Cammack and Frederick Golooba-Mutebi. 2010. "Developmental Patrimonialism? Questioning the Orthodoxy on Political Governance and Economic Progress in Africa." Working Paper no. 9, July. London: Overseas Development Institute.

Mahmoud, F. M. 1983. "Indigenous Sudanese Capital: A National Bourgeoisie?" *Review of African Political Economy* 26: 103–19.

Mathisen, Harald, and Lars Svåsand. 2002. *Funding Political Parties in Emerging African Democracies: What Role for Norway?* Bergen, Norway: Chr. Michelsen Institute.

Mkandawire, Thandika. 2001. "Thinking about Developmental States in Africa." *Cambridge Journal of Economics* 25, no. 3: 289–313.

Mkandawire, Thandika. 2015. "Neopatrimonialism and the Political Economy of Economic Performance in Africa: Critical Reflections." *World Politics* 67, no. 3: 563–612.

Müller, Wolfgang C. 2000. "Patronage by National Governments." In Jean Blondel and Maurizio Cotta, eds., *The Nature of Party Government: A Comparative European Perspective*. Basingstoke: Palgrave, 141–60.

Ofeimun, Odia. 2006. "Awolowo and the Politics of the Next Stage." 2006 Obafemi Awolowo Memorial lecture organized by the Ogun State Governor's Office, Cultural Centre, Abeokuta, March 14.

Ogunsanwo, Olufemi. 2009. *Awo: Unfinished Greatness*. Lagos: Pace Books and Periodicals.

Oke, David O., Olatuji Dare, Adebayo Williams, and Femi Akinola, eds. 2009. *Awo: On the Trail of a Titan*. Lagos: Obafemi Awolowo Foundation.

Osoba, S. O. 1996. "Corruption in Nigeria: Historical Perspectives." *Review of African Political Economy* 23, no. 69: 371–86.

Osuntokun, Akinjide. 1984. *Chief S. Ladoke Akintola: His Life and Times*. London: Frank Cass.

Oyelaran, Olasope O., Toyin Falola, Mokwugo Okoye, and Adewale Thompson, eds. 2002. *Obafemu Awolowo: The End of an Era*. Ile-Ife: Obafemi Awolowo University Press.

Piattoni, Simona, ed. 2001. *Clientelism, Interests, and Democratic Representation: The European Experience in Historical and Comparative Perspective*. Cambridge: Cambridge University Press.

Pina-Cabral, João de. 2000. "Introduction." In João de Pina-Cabral and Antonia Pedroso de Lima, eds., *Elites: Choice, Leadership and Succession*. New York: Berg, 1–5.

Pitcher, Anne, Mary H. Moran, and Michael Johnston. 2009. "Rethinking Patrimonialism and Neopatrimonialism in Africa." *African Studies Review* 52, no. 1: 125–56.

Roninger, Luis. 2004. "Political Clientelism, Democracy and Market Economy." *Comparative Politics* 33: 353–75.

Salih, Mohamed M. A. 2003. "Introduction: The Evolution of African Political Parties." In Mohamed M. A. Salih, ed., *African Political Parties: Evolution, Institutionalism and Governance*. London: Pluto Press, 1–33.

Sekoni, Ropo. 1997. "Politics & Urban Folklore in Nigeria." In Karin Barber, ed., *Readings in African Popular Culture*. Oxford: James Currey, 142–46.

Shore, Cris. 2002. "Introduction: Towards an Anthropology of Elites." In Cris Shore and Stephen Nugent, eds., *Elite Cultures: Anthropological Perspectives*. New York: Routledge, 1–21.

Sklar, Richard. 1963. *Nigerian Political Parties: Power in an Emergent African Nation*. Princeton, NJ: Princeton University Press.

Sklar, Richard. 1966. "Nigerian Politics: The Ordeal of Chief Obafemi Awolowo, 1960–1965." In Gwendolen M. Carter, ed., *Politics in Africa: 7 Cases*. New York: Harcourt, Brace & World, 119–65.

Swainson, Nicola. 1977. "The Rise of the National Bourgeoisie in Kenya." *Review of African Political Economy* 4, no. 8: 39–55.

Tignor, Robert L. 1993. "Political Corruption in Nigeria before Independence." *Journal of Modern African Studies* 31, no. 2: 175–202.

Tzahor, Zeev. 1996. "The Histadrut." In Jehuda Reinhard and Anita Shapira, eds., *Essential Papers on Zionism*. New York: New York University Press, 473–508.

van Biezen, Ingrid, and Petr Kopecký. 2007. "The State and the Parties: Public Funding, Public Regulation and Rent-Seeking in Contemporary Democracies." *Party Politics* 13, no. 2: 235–54.

van de Walle, Nicholas. 2007. "The Path from Neopatrimonialism: Democracy and Clientelism in Africa Today." Working Paper Series no. 3-07, Mario Einaudi Center for International Studies. Ithaca NY: Cornell University.

Warner, Carolyn M. 2007. *The Best System Money Can Buy: Corruption in the European Union*. Ithaca, NY: Cornell University Press.

Werbner, Richard. 2004. *Reasonable Radical and Citizenship in Botswana: The Public Anthropology of Kalanga Elites*. Bloomington: Indiana University Press.Woddis, Jack. 1977. "Is There an African National Bourgeoisie?" In Peter C. W. Gutkind and Peter Waterman, *African Social Studies*. London: Heinemann, 267–78.

PART 4

Elites and Competitive Leverage in Violent Contexts

CHAPTER 12

Commanders, Classrooms, Cows, and Churches

Accountability and the Construction of a South Sudanese Elite

NAOMI PENDLE

THE MORAL AMBIGUITY OF A "THEFT"

He carefully showed me around his new, brick home. We walked between the series of brick-walled, newly plastered, unpainted rooms connected together into a small labyrinth and roofed with iron sheets. He named each empty room: "The lounge. The kitchen. The main bedroom. A smaller bedroom." His extended family members had already placed mattresses on the floor and hung clothes over lines of string as they made the new building their home. He said he would build a new latrine outside. He pointed to the open, window-shaped holes in the walls. "We will have metal frames made in Wau with shutters." As we talked, our dried-fish supper was cooked on the fire outside. All the surrounding homesteads were made from mudded walls and intricate thatched roofs. At the time, the only other visible brick buildings in the county of ninety thousand people were a couple of NGO-funded, local government buildings, NGO offices, and the classrooms of a diaspora-funded school and a church-funded school. All these had been built in the last three years. There were also a few remnants of older brick buildings dating back to the early twentieth century and the attempts by the Anglo-Egyptian government to administer this corner of Greater Bahr al-Ghazal (South Sudan). These brick-walled, iron-sheeted buildings were a clear symbol to distinguish power and wealth. That evening, I was grateful when the tour of the new house was over so that we could escape the heat of the iron-sheeted structure and sit outside to eat dinner.

My host was a senior South Sudanese lawyer and national political figure. He had played a seminal role in the Sudan People's Liberation Movement (SPLM) during the wars with the government of Sudan (GoS) in the 1980s and 1990s. He had supported the creation, in the 1990s, of a civil movement to compliment the Sudan People's Liberation Army (SPLA). In 2005, the SPLA and GoS signed the comprehensive peace agreement (CPA) to end their wars. This created the new government of South Sudan (GoSS) and cemented the SPLM as the dominant party in the GoSS and the SPLA as the legitimate army of the south. The CPA also provided a new flow of oil money to this new southern government elite. By the time I met this political figure in late 2010, he had already been a senior legal figure in the southern government.

This lawyer was one of the first of the SPLM government elites to build a brick home in this rural, home county. He had lived away from this rural homeland for decades as he gained his education, sought refuge in times of war, and then ascended in the legal and political hierarchy. He was one of the new elite from Bahr al-Ghazal who would dominate politics in South Sudan after the CPA and during the national, civil wars after December 2013. Others from the area held senior political and military positions and would build brick buildings in this home community over the following years. The brick walls were a clear indicator of superior power and wealth that set him apart from local leaders and the rest of his home community.

Despite the pride in his new home, this lawyer did not usually live in the village. He spent most of his time in the capital city of Juba or overseas. Therefore, while he funded the building of his new, brick-walled home, it was his brother who supervised its actual construction. His brother, who lived permanently in the village, dealt with the day-to-day procurement of materials and the contracting of laborers. The lawyer had even bought a tipper truck to assist with construction, and his brother managed this small business too.

It was not long into the house-building project that people drinking tea in the local market would commonly discuss the brother's slow "theft" of the money that he had been given to build the house. Lorries of bricks would trundle from Wau, but only half would be offloaded at this building project. Others would be carried further into the village and offloaded elsewhere. The additional bricks were apparently being sold for a profit for other aspirational house-building endeavors. The brother was allegedly pocketing the profit himself and not revealing it to the lawyer. The building work on the house made very slow progress.

What was striking was not the brother's alleged habitual theft. Instead, it was the way the story was told in marketplace conversations in that village. There was no condemnation of the brother's immorality but, instead, a tone of comedy about his daylight robbery. This was despite theft usually being a very shameful act, and the local chiefs' courts being very active in condemning and punishing other acts of theft in the community. The chiefs' courts regularly fined people hundreds of South Sudanese pounds or punished them with imprisonment or lashes for thefts of much smaller value, such as small goods from shops or for taking individual cattle. Yet there was little moral condemnation for the brother's deceptive acquisition of wealth. Despite the lawyer's superior wealth and money, it appeared that he was struggling to establish his moral authority and even his right for legal protection at home.[1]

His brother's alleged theft was possible because this lawyer had no sight and knowledge of the daily economic and political dealings of the village. His distance from the village was intimately entangled with his very identity and distinctiveness as part of the South Sudanese elite. However, this deprived him of a local knowledge that was needed to empower him at home. As people joked about the theft, they found a small comedy and consolation in the possibility that local knowledge could occasionally trump the power even of national elites. His brother's story turned on its head the prevailing discourses and experiences of South Sudanese in which elites and their militarized and economic power were often both superior and brutal.

There was no case brought to court against the brother. However, I asked the chiefs of the chiefs' courts what they would do if such a case had been brought before them and if the brother had been found guilty. They asserted that the customary law would still apply even if the lawyer was an elite and usually found living at a distance from the home community. He was theoretically still part of the legal and moral community despite his elite status. Yet they presented an interpretation of the law that questioned whether his brother's actions were theft, and that left the brother unpunished. They turned on its head the lawyer's assertion of power. As the national lawyer built his new, brick home on family-owned land, it was unclear if the house (and the materials to build it) belonged to him individually or to the family collectively. Therefore, the brother arguably had customary legal rights to spend the money as he wished, without fully consulting the brother. If the brother needed to take the money, maybe it was simply because the lawyer was failing to fulfill his family obligations. By spending money in his home village and building on land that he claimed as his own through the customary rights of his family, the elite lawyer subjected himself to the logic of authority of the chiefs' courts and to different registers of accountability that could be actively reinterpreted to challenge the powers of the new South Sudanese elites. Local interpretations of property could entangle elites in different and new moral and legal communities over which they sometimes had little power or knowledge. If a key part of the lawyer's claim to be distinct and elite was his access to wealth, the chiefs and community more widely appeared to be challenging the very notions of property upon which this wealth made him individually distinct.

ELITES, ACCOUNTABILITY, AND CONFLICT IN SOUTH SUDAN

This opening example illustrates the complex local realities in which elites negotiate their authority even in political contexts that are assumed to be elite-centered. Recent international discussion and investigations into South Sudanese elites have promoted their representation as archetypal African elites characterized by corruption, oil wealth, and armed conflict (Enough 2017). In contrast, the example of this alleged theft highlights the complexity of the construction of elites' distinctiveness and the relationships between elites, their families, and their home communities.

This chapter will explore these more complex understandings of the relationship between elites and their home communities by exploring how elites establish themselves as "distinct" in Bourdieu's sense (1984). Not only political and economic factors help elites establish themselves as distinct, but elites draw upon various cultural, political, economic, and social resources to establish their distinction (Abbink and Salverda 2013; Shore and Nugent 2002). The cultures that they draw on are themselves unstable and are constantly remade, including by the elites themselves (Adebanwi 2014). The chapter will chart examples of the cultural dynamics and repertoires that elites use to perpetuate their rule, dominance, and acceptance, and place this within the wider historical and social context (Abbink and Salverda 2013; Cooper 2002; Shore and Nugent 2002). It will analyse the language and practice through which elites represent themselves and the techniques they use to legitimise their position (Daloz 2002: 13), and will explore the symbols of superiority and distinction that have been used (Bourdieu 1984). At the same time, the examples discussed highlight that different elites, even when trying to create distinctiveness among the same cultural, legal, and moral communities, deploy significantly varied strategies.

As elites draw upon cultural dynamics, repertoires, and institutions, they entangle themselves in multiple registers of accountability. Elite attempts may be contested using the very moral and cultural universes that they hoped to draw upon to assert their legitimate distinctiveness. The chapter will consider the consequences of their engagement with these cultural repertoires and moral universes for the public's ability to hold them accountable. It will highlight how even militarized elites, in their attempts to make themselves locally plausibly self-legitimate (Greenhouse 1996: 2), make themselves subject to logics and registers of accountability that are not based on the force of the gun alone or on patronage networks funded by immense oil wealth. These registers of accountability are often embedded in mentalities of rule based on specific historic contingencies and contexts. However, elites themselves contest and remake these local registers, reshaping social obligations in ways that bring both accountability and conflict.

By focusing on elites in South Sudan, this chapter also provides an example of elites in the context of war and armed violence. Among policymakers and in the literature on complex emergencies and political settlements, there has been a growing focus on the pivotal role that elites and their political contestations play in shaping the trajectories of violent conflict and development (DFID 2010; World Bank 2017). More nuanced literature does not just discuss elites as "evil" or focus on their "greed" as if it were a personal characteristic. Instead, the focus shifts to the institutional configurations that constitute elites, concentrate power in their hands, and incentivize them to use violence to redress grievances or to seek money or power. De Waal's recent political marketplace analysis based on elite ethnography has highlighted how, when institutions are weak, elites use violence as a means of bargaining to redress grievances and gain material goods or power (De Waal 2014, 2015). However, this literature has largely focused on national elites and international interventions, and interelite bargaining at a national level. Yet to understand elites, we need to understand how they operate between the global and the local (Abbink and Salverda 2013). There is little ethnographic work that has explored the relationship between elites, their publics, and the elites' home communities in these contexts of armed conflict.

This chapter focuses on the question of how national elites in post-CPA South Sudan have reconstructed their relationships with the home communities and how local communities are also reinterpreting these moral communities to deal with new elites. To do this, the chapter focuses on how national politico-military elites from the politically powerful region of Bahr al-Ghazal have used various strategies and resources to constitute themselves as elites in their home communities. The chapter highlights how they have drawn upon preexisting mentalities of rule, institutions of governance, and moral and cultural ideas of power among their own home communities. It also highlights how they become entangled with and subject to the logics of such rule.

The rest of this chapter is divided into two parts. First, the chapter highlights the importance of home communities to South Sudanese elites. This also provides a background to the histories of current ideas of what it is to be an "elite" in South Sudan. Second, the chapter discusses three methods used by elites from Bahr al-Ghazal to develop relationships with their home communities. These three methods are cattle purchase, classroom construction, and church building. As these elite interventions are described, the chapter also discusses how each of these activities has subjected these elites to local repertoires of accountability that, in the end, elites find hard to control.

THE IMPORTANCE OF THE HOME COMMUNITIES TO SOUTH SUDANESE ELITES

Over the last hundred years and through the SPLA wars of the 1980s and 1990s, many national elites consistently gained their distinctiveness by living and working at a spatial distance from their home communities. Elites built their power through service in national armies or rebel armies that often involved them in fighting wars and commanding forces far from their homelands. Some also received education in schools, universities, and military academies around Sudan and the world. The limited number of schools in South Sudan throughout most of the twentieth century meant that distance from rural or home areas was almost a necessary precondition of education. From the 1980s, leadership of the Sudan People's Liberation Army/Movement during the wars between the SPLA and GoS was a clear source of legitimacy for the new, post-CPA elite (De Waal 2014; Johnson 2012; Pinaud 2014; Rolandsen 2005). This leadership of the SPLA often took elites away from rural home constituencies and meant that they needed to rely less on home community support.

For South Sudanese, this spatial distance is also associated with a social distance. Leonardi has highlighted that South Sudanese often make a distinction between the moral spheres of the *home* and *government* (Leonardi 2007, 2013). The *home* sphere is associated with the villages, families, and authority of the elders. The *government* sphere is associated with towns, travel, education, the government itself, and also formal, armed rebel forces. This is visible in the use of the term *beny hakuma* in this part of Bahr al-Ghazal to describe those who have otherwise been called "elites." *Beny* conveys a general idea of leadership that is also used to describe local leaders such as chiefs or divine authorities. *Hakuma* refers to the social sphere of government. This conflation in language also encourages people to see elites as morally synonymous with government and subject to the same moral standards, expectations, and excuses.

These *beny hakuma* drew distinction not only from their connection to the government, but also through their international connections and their control of access to international aid and finance. This limited the need for popular support among the public and their home communities. In the early years of the SPLA war, elites such as SPLA leader John Garang brokered political alliances with Ethiopia and the Soviet powers to supply arms and resources. After the end of the Cold War, he was also able to forge alliances with Western powers. At the same time, the UN and aid organizations arranged some of the world's largest aid operations in SPLA territory, and the SPLA acted as a form of gatekeeper (Karim et al. 1996; Maxwell, Santschi, and Gordon 2014). Some SPLA leaders gained wealth through their management and theft of aid and trade (De Waal 1997; Duffield 2001; Keen 2008). During the 1990s, the new effort in the SPLA to develop a civilian, political wing encouraged a new cohort of elites whose power was built on their political skills and formal education alongside their support of the SPLA/M.

Since the 2005 CPA, the distinguishing features of the South Sudanese elite have shifted. The CPA made the government oil rich. Pinaud argues that this made a new "aristocracy" of oil-rich elites in South Sudan (Pinaud 2014). Since the nineteen century in Europe, "elite" has been used in relation to modern ideas of class and power (Shore and Nugent 2002: 10). These new aristocrats could be considered as "elites" in this European sense. Their wealth was the new marker of distinction.

Shortly after the CPA, the SPLA leader, John Garang, was killed in a helicopter crash and Salva Kiir took over leadership of the SPLA and southern government. Kiir used the oil revenues to buy loyalty of the militarily powerful and to incorporate them into the SPLA and his government (De Waal 2014). Kiir reconfigured the hierarchy among the elites at the national level. In this

Fig. 12.1. John Garang's image on South Sudan's one-pound note

interpretation, contemporary power and access to oil wealth were more necessary conditions of being an elite than long-term loyalty to the SPLA. This oil wealth created further distinction, but also distance, between the national elite and the broader South Sudanese public and home communities.

From the CPA, GoSS also became an independent state government in waiting. The CPA had promised a referendum on southern independence and, in July 2011, South Sudan became a new, internationally recognized state. The national elites in South Sudan could also now use the symbolic resources that they were constructing for the state to establish their legitimate power. This was a radically new context, after the war years, upon which to establish oneself at the apex of society.

Since the CPA, the national capital has been in Juba, at a spatial distance from the home communities of many of the national elite. With the gift of government jobs, many of the elite were concentrated in Juba at a distance from their home communities. Many South Sudanese will never themselves go to Juba. Even visiting Juba makes you part of another class of people with a unique knowledge and power.

In the early post-CPA years, national elites found it relatively easy to reestablish themselves as exclusive gatekeepers to the international community and to finance as international policymakers after the CPA opted (at least in public and in policy) for a positive perception of the elites and the new government. International interventions after the CPA focused on state building and economic development. Among policymakers and international diplomats, ongoing armed conflict in South Sudan was often presented as a result of the inexperience and lack of capacity in this new South Sudanese state and the weakness of its emerging institutions. During the twenty-two years of war, elite politicians in the United States, United Kingdom, and other European nations had come to know the SPLA leadership on a personal basis. These countries had also diplomatically and financially invested in the CPA and were eager for it to work (Young 2012). The 2010 elections and the 2012 conflicts in Jonglei State started to rock the faith of these donor governments in the government of South Sudan, but support continued, even if cautiously.

In response to this pro-government agenda of international policymakers, academic research argued that continued violent conflict was not just a result of a lack of capacity, and that elites in government were also causing much of this violence. Academic research usually highlighted how, in general terms, government elites used the post-CPA era to loot the nascent southern state (De Waal 2014: 367; Jok 2017). Elites were described as leasing large stretches of land to international investors for personal gain (Deng 2011) and using ethnic identity as a strategy to make claims over land (Justin and De Vries 2017; Hutchinson and Pendle 2015). Elites also transformed small-scale contestations over natural resources into violent political conflicts (Gore 2014). The nature of politics in South Sudan also meant that contending elites used force or the threat of force as a means of bargaining for rents from the government's national, oil-rich budgets (De Waal 2014: 348). De Waal describes the 2006 Juba Declaration between Salva Kiir and Paulino Matiep as an "implicit promise of honour among thieves"—thieves who together would steal money from the government's oil (De Waal 2014: 355). In this framework, much of the violence could be explained by "the naked greed of the political marketplace" (De Waal 2014: 365).

In December 2013, armed conflict erupted in Juba. In the wars that followed, power has shifted between factions in government, and it has also remade elites' dependence on their home constituencies. In the wars of the 1990s, Garang had built his own elite cabal on internationally funded education and military training that often separated the elites from reliance on their home communities. These elites became known as "Garangists" and relied heavily on Garang's patronage. However, Garang's death and their declining authority over the following decade highlighted the problems with detaching themselves from a home constituency. One story of the wars since December 2013 is the decline in power and wealth of the Garangists and their replacement by those who have strong home constituencies.

Many leaders from Greater Bahr al-Ghazal, such as General Alor Kor and President Salva Kiir himself, have gained power. Paul Malong was the governor of Northern Bahr al-Ghazal State (a state in the Bahr al-Ghazal region) and had built his authority in his home area over decades of commanding in this region. In 2012, during armed conflict with Sudan over an oil-rich border area, Malong with the support of Salva Kiir mobilized a force from among his home community known as the Mathiang Anyoor to defend South Sudan's interests (Pendle 2015). However, in 2013, the SPLA high command (dominated by Garangists) refused to integrate this force into the SPLA and did not allow its soldiers to be paid government salaries (Pendle 2015). In the wars since December 2013, Malong moved to the center of the government and became the chief of staff of the SPLA. His *Mathiang Anyoor* proved crucial for the defense of Kiir's government. In 2017, internal Bahr al-Ghazal politics removed Malong from power. Malong's mobilizations during the war had also lost him much support at home. Yet this pattern continued to highlight the rise of the power of the elites who had strong home constituency support.

Furthermore, elites in South Sudan also have to preserve their elite distinction and authority in times of financial hardship. Oil shutdowns and the wars since December 2013 have restricted the financial capacity of elites. This is especially the case for elites who have fought in the armed opposition and, therefore, have not had access to government oil revenues. Despite this, elites have still been more easily able to marry, assert authority, and access the international. This prompts questions about the alternative sources for this power and distinction.

After December 2013, De Waal's (2014) description of the kleptocratic nature of politics in South Sudan quickly gained resonance. However, there has been little empirical research that has explored the relationship between elites and the public. De Waal has highlighted the use of government payrolls as a way for elites to buy loyalty and create patronage networks (De Waal 2014: 361). Pinaud has discussed commanders' gifts of bride wealth and wives to their subordinates in order to build followers and cement their own status as a dominant class (Pinaud 2014). However, such research often leaves the perception that non-elites are naively accepting or victims of their powerful, elite masters.

Alternatively, the chapter will highlight how elite reliance on home constituencies creates space for elite accountability, however small. The chapter explores the ways in which people at the most local level and during daily realities try to scratch back accountability for even the highest elites. Elite strategies forge legitimacy not just through the power of the gun, the authority of the "state," or immediate gifts of patronage. In addition, they draw on other registers of legitimacy to build a longer-term authority in their home communities, and this leaves them accountable within these moral frameworks.

In exploring the construction of distinctiveness among the home communities of Bahr al-Ghazal, this chapter will document and discuss different examples of elites in one specific county of Bahr al-Ghazal and how they have become embroiled in different registers of legitimacy and accountability. These examples are not comprehensive and do not include all elite investments and interactions even in the post-CPA period. For example, even in this same period in this one county in Bahr al-Ghazal, other elites used a variety of different strategies to assert their elite distinction. Some invested in fenced, large farms, others bought guns and ammunition for armed young men, and some held large rallies before the national elections. However, these examples highlight some of the less-visible elite investments in their home communities and provide examples of how elites attempt to engage in and are challenged by the moral, legal, and cultural universes of the home.

This chapter is based on ethnographic research between 2009 and 2013, as well as qualitative research in Bahr al-Ghazal and South Sudan from 2013 to 2017. Various life histories have also informed this chapter. Qualitative interviews have dominantly been with non-elites and local residents, elders, and chiefs in villages in Bahr al-Ghazal. These have been supplemented by occasional conversations with elites and observations of their rural investments. During this ethnographic research, I taught at an elite-funded school. As an educated foreigner with the finances to fly in and out of South Sudan, I also embodied another form of elite living and working in Bahr al-Ghazal at the time.

The following section goes on to outline three strategies used by elites to construct their distinction and support in Bahr al-Ghazal.

INVESTING IN CATTLE

Beny hakuma have used their oil monies to purchase large numbers of cattle that are kept in their home communities. Through their investment in cattle, these *beny hakuma* are reproducing in the present moment long-held ideas about leadership. Ownership of cattle has not just demonstrated material wealth but is also synonymous with authority and distinction.[2]

For many people in Bahr al-Ghazal, cattle ownership is the dominant display of the wealth of the *beny hakuma*. It was often striking in conversations how invisible to people in Bahr al-Ghazal was the *beny hakuma* wealth and lifestyles in Juba. Few could see their opulent lifestyles or grasp the costs of their V8 Landcruisers or even the brick buildings that were built in Juba and Wau, or occasionally in the villages. However, when elites purchased cattle, they visibly displayed their wealth to these rural populations in property whose value was commonly known.

Among the Dinka, cattle ownership has also long been entwined with notions of what it means to be a *beny* (Lienhardt 1961). Through their herds and the ability to gift cattle, *beny hakuma* can make themselves powerful in local marriage arrangements and in local political contests between *beny baai (leaders of the home)*. They can also reshape the meaning of legal and moral concepts, such as the power and consequences of compensation and revenge (Pendle 2018).

Over the past hundred years in South Sudan, the relationship between cattle and authority has radically developed and adapted to new global markets, new forms of war and government, and the use of money (Hutchinson 1996). For example, cattle owners have engaged in the billion-dollar East African cattle commerce to build up their own wealth and herds. The Dinka have not hesitated to purchase cattle to add to their herds.[3] During the wars of the 1980s and 1990s, armed raiders depleted cattle herds in Bahr al-Ghazal. However, in parts of Bahr al-Ghazal, a large, swampy grazing land allowed many cattle to be hidden out of harm's way (Cormack 2014. This allowed people to preserve larger herds in comparison to other areas, such as Aweil. In addition, this risky acquisition and defense of cattle only entrenched further their material and political value.

Various actors, including government, have actively maintained the cattle-authority link. In the early twentieth century, the government saw cattle as crucial for social order among the Dinka (and other southern pastoralists). Plus, the government, through the chiefs' courts, has preserved the link between cattle, wealth, and power in the Western Dinka. In this area of Bahr al-Ghazal, the chiefs' courts have permitted the cattle to be used for bride wealth and compensation. Therefore, people could meet their legal and social obligations through large herds and assert social control through the cattle they could offer in negotiations. Even the few people who worked for government still had obligations in terms of cattle. From the creation of the chiefs' courts in the early twentieth century, the government has been eager to entrench institutions that would maintain home communities' control over those southerners who were involved in government and living in the towns. Therefore, chiefs' courts could still demand cattle payments from those who were educated, worked in the government, and lived at a spatial distance from the home communities. Officials in the Anglo-Egyptian government passed laws to make sure that southern Sudanese who were part of the *hakuma* did not escape the obligations of the moral and legal community of the home.

In contrast, in recent years, the *beny hakuma*'s link to the laws of the home has not just tethered the *beny hakuma* to the legal order of the home but provided opportunity for the *beny hakuma* to shape the home. With their new wealth after 2005, *beny hakuma* have used their belonging to these moral worlds and their ability to buy cattle with government oil money to reshape local power to their advantage. Researchers have argued that elites have used cattle wealth to build patronage networks (Gebreyes, Lemma, Deng and Abdullahi 2016 Pinaud 2014). Some have suggested that gifts of bride wealth to supporters have allowed politicians to build an uncritical support base of nepotistic and clientelistic networks (Pinaud 2014). Rising bride prices have, according to some observers, made men more susceptible to elite patronage, where cattle protection and military loyalty are exchanged for gifts from elites of guns and ammunition (Sommers and Schwartz 2011).

Plus, individual elite ownership of large herds has been used to challenge and reshape deeply held social norms and the meanings of legal sanctions. The radical redistributions of cattle wealth and the acquisition of large herds by the *beny hakuma* have changed the meaning of compensation. Some *beny hakuma* have been able to devalue the power of the chiefs' courts through their excessive cattle wealth and the ease with which they can pay compensation without it causing them pain (Pendle 2018). In these cases, compensation is no longer able to redress the social and spiritual dangers that arise from killing. Therefore, compensation is often not enough to cool people's hearts and deter revenge (Pendle 2018). Moreover, the promise of easy compensation payments makes it easier for the *beny hakuma* to mobilize supporters to violence.

However, *beny hakuma* investments in cattle have empowered opportunities for support accountability among their home communities because cattle entangle the *beny hakuma* in the moral order of the home communities.

Elites' use of their herds to comply with social and legal obligations is not always voluntary. Their herds are governed by rulings of the chiefs' courts, which often have more immediate access to the herds than the *beny hakuma* themselves. It is not uncommon for elites and their cattle to be discussed in the rural chiefs' courts. Cattle can be taken from a herd on the chiefs' orders before the *beny hakuma* even know of the ruling. The cattle may be order from a *beny hakuma*'s herd as punishment for his own actions or to fulfill social and legal obligations of his families and clans.

To avoid this, *beny hakuma* will sometimes seek to hide their cattle from sight. *Weŋ aca mai ran de* is a Dinka phrase used to describe cattle that are entrusted to another person's herd. People entrust cattle to other herds to keep the cattle safe from raiding or while the owner is away. It has also become used to denote cattle that are given to another to conceal the true owner's identity in order to protect the owner from the usual social obligations. Less wealthy *beny hakuma*, with fewer cattle, often try to do this. However, this highlights their recognition of their legal and social obligations in the communities and their recognition of the authority of the local courts over them.

Investments in cattle also necessitate that *beny hakuma* rely on local cattle guards and elders for the care of their herds. Cattle owners based in Juba are at a spatial distance from their herds, which have material demands, including space, waters, and grasses to graze. The very highest *beny hakuma* have fenced ranches in proximity to Juba in order to have more control over their cattle. However, most *beny hakuma* in Bahr al-Ghazal keep their cattle in the grazing lands of their home communities.

Some *beny hakuma* have kept their personal cattle segregated and have not integrated them into their family's and clan's cattle camps. In order to do this, they have had to find trusted cattle guards who are able to care for the welfare of the cattle and protect them from raiding. As these cattle guards are not their family members, they would not usually be expected to look after the elite person's herd. As the elites cannot draw on preexisting social obligations to demand the support of these cattle guards, they have had to reward their labor. Elites have used various rewards beyond just payment in milk. These cattle guards occasionally receive a minimal monetary wage. They also have the promise of health care provision if they are unwell or injured. This starts to shift the sociopolitical and economic relationships between the cattle guards and older members of the community.

However, to the extent that these large cattle herds have been kept in their home grazing lands, they have been visible to the local community and subject to local expectations and obligations over the cattle. Therefore, although *beny hakuma* may have segregated the herds for the purposes of grazing and guarding, they have failed to socially separate them. Chiefs still see them as cattle for the purposes of the customary laws.

FUNDING CLASSROOMS

Bourdieu highlighted that schools in Europe have played a critical role in the reproduction of the distribution of power among elites (1984: 5). He documented how elite schooling was playing a socially reproductive role in advanced societies. In her work in Nigeria, Lloyd (1966) had previously documented how children of the educated elite in Nigeria made a new, distinct social group. At the same time, formal education in South Sudan has a distinct history, cultural meaning, and implications for distinction.

Formal education and literacy in South Sudan have long been associated with governmental power and the *beny hakuma*. During the early years of the Anglo-Egyptian Condominium, the Sudan government's investment in formal education was limited. Yet by 1920, although pupil numbers across the whole of southern Sudan were as small as four hundred, "The irreversible establishment of Western-style education as a factor in the life of southern Sudanese had taken place" (Sanderson 1980: 163). These small numbers meant that having a formal education necessarily made people distinct and provided access to claims of being elite. This was reinforced by the link between formal education and government work; from the 1920s, the purpose of education for the government shifted toward the provision of a junior cadre of administrative assistants for government service (Sanderson 1980). This was crucial for the development and the creation of a southern Sudanese beny *hakuma*. In the 1930s, the government even stringently limited the growth of intermediate education to make sure the supply of educated southerners did not exceed the number of government jobs (Sanderson 1980: 166). By the 1950s, the educated were being treated with deference by other southern Sudanese (Sanderson 1980: 168). They had become distinct and often powerful. This association between education and becoming a *beny hakuma* was then reinforced as those with a formal education ascended into government positions in Khartoum and later in the SPLA. However, being a *beny hakuma* was not necessarily more sought after than being a *beny baai*.

At its inception in 1983, the SPLA championed a developmentalist approach that promised an eventual economic liberation to South Sudanese (Thomas 2015). This economic liberation would include increased access to education, health care, and other government services. This SPLA discourse allowed its broad appeal across South Sudan and in peripheral areas of Sudan itself (Thomas 2015). During the war years, the SPLA provided formal education to its child soldiers in the training camps in Ethiopia. Many who fled

South Sudan also received a formal education in the refugee camps of East Africa. Through these experiences of war and displacement, basic education became available to a much broader range of southern Sudanese. Education was not a marker of elite distinction in itself.

However, *beny hakuma* did use formal education to entrench distinction. In the 1980s and 1990s, John Garang (then leader of the SPLA) used sponsorship of higher levels of education to build his tight, loyal network of Garangists. Plus, during the 1980s and 1990s, the large aid operations also emphasized that people were more likely to be interlocutors between the local communities and international aid if they had a basic, formal education.

By the post-CPA era, schooling had become associated both with wealth and with access to government power. Civil service jobs often required at least a minimal level of education. NGO employment demanded a higher level of education. In periods of government austerity, NGOs became the dominant actors capable of providing valuable salaries. At the same time, education also carried access to power and symbols of distinction. The languages of government and its written documents required formal education to be accessed. Home communities saw its value as they sought to deal with government, whether to work with it or resist it (Epstein 2012).

After the CPA and the formation of the southern government, formal legislation made basic, formal education free and compulsory in South Sudan (the General Education Act of 2012). It was not to be the preserve of the elite. However, many children had no access to education and the education that was available was often limited to the first years of primary school. International donors and UN agencies did invest in primary education in South Sudan. However, access to formal education of quality was still limited. For example, the World Food Programme provided food for schools. However, WFP would provide food for schools only if they met basic standards such as having a kitchen, a secure store, and proximity to clean water. This excluded 75 percent of schools in one area of Bahr al-Ghazal (Epstein 2012: 229).

Therefore, in the post-CPA era, to achieve a valuable formal education, South Sudanese usually needed to attend private schools, the best of which were in Juba or abroad. Support from *beny hakuma* could make this possible. The *beny hakuma* could also use this provision to ensure the next generation was distinct.

Families and communities would often request from the *beny hakuma* fees for school and university. Through these requests, families were reconstituting intrafamily social obligations and the normative codes of the *home*. In

Bahr al-Ghazal, there had long been social obligations to provide for those in the family and clan who were in need. In the post-CPA era, chiefs' courts were still enforcing the sharing of animals and food by relatives who had resources and who were neglecting their neighbours. Redistribution of resources was a legally enforced obligation.

Increasingly, families were also demanding fees for their children's education. It was now seen as crucial to future material and political security. Even when in Juba, *beny hakuma* would frequently receive such requests by phone. Elites joked about avoiding visits to their home villages unless they could afford these inevitable requests. This demand for education would often alienate less wealthy members of the diaspora, who were often assumed to be elite-like in the villages, and would often stop them from visiting their home communities.

In Bahr al-Ghazal in the post-CPA era, *beny hakuma* have been far from homogenous in their response to requests. Some have refused. Others have invested in the education of their communities in different ways. Some have invested tens of thousands of US dollars in the education of individual sons or nephews. They hope that such education will gain their nephews high-level government positions and access to government revenues that will support their families in the future. They are using education to reproduce their own elite status and access to power and wealth. For the nephews, education is exchanged for heavy future social obligations.

Other *beny hakuma* have instead sought to educate a broader section of their communities and enact the developmentalist vision of wider access to education. In this developmentalist vision, South Sudan would develop through having its own educated elite. A marker of elite distinction would be education. This initial vision suggested the active role of the state government. However, as they personally embody notions of government, some *beny hakuma* have extended their personal responsibility to see these policies enacted through their own resources. Elites have not necessarily undermined development, as has been the case elsewhere (Adebanwi 2014). In research in Rundu (Nambia), Fumanti (2016) discovered the liberation elites' investment in education represented not just a strategy but also strong moral and emotional values and a sense of civility. Some *beny hakuma* in South Sudan have also seen the building of schools as an enactment of the reasons for their sacrificial liberation struggle and as part of developing South Sudan.

In the county I studied in the post-CPA era, by 2013 two *beny hakuma* had funded large schools (Epstein 2012: 223). One school received funding from a senior military figure. A public intellectual and well-known member of the diaspora opened the other. He had long experienced strong social obligations to fund his many siblings' education. He sponsored many family members who lived and were educated far from home in Uganda. As the CPA was signed, demands extended to a large group in the community. In the new peacetime context, this educated *beny hakuma* decided it was a more efficient use of resources to build a local school for his family members to attend. Therefore, he founded a school near his father's home. In his home community, this *beny hakuma* was able to establish his distinctiveness through the school's visible display of his ability to mobilize support through international networks. He recruited foreign teachers and found the financial resources to build brick buildings and to pay more to the best local teachers.

The school's founder had been away from his home community for over a decade during the years of the war. He had completed the later years of his education in various international universities. He had also supported international aid operations in the 1990s and served in the national government in Juba since 2005. The school remade his belonging in the community, but also established his significance and distinctiveness in these rural parts.

He built the school on his father's land, and, therefore, his own family had the easiest access to this school. Yet he did not limit access to the school to his own relatives. Pupils from a neighboring, competitive clan dominated many classes in the school. Pupils walked up to two hours each day each way to access the school. Therefore, the founder widened the range of those to whom he had a social obligation and rebuilt a broader sense of community.

In founding the school, this *beny hakuma* also enacted a civility that he hoped the government itself would one day mimic. In the post-CPA years, this public intellectual became increasing critical of the South Sudanese government, its mismanagement of its resources, and its failure to implement the vision of economic liberation that southerners had been told they were fighting for. His ability to fund and run the school was itself almost a protest against the government, as it was a constant reminder of the government's failings. He constantly asked the government to pay his teachers' salaries. However, any government support was never enough for him to stop paying funds himself.

This intellectual *beny hakuma* performed many actions to distinguish himself as a *beny hakuma* but also to distinguish himself from the government itself, which he increasing perceived as corrupt. For example, most *beny hakuma* traveled to their homes in the village in their own cars. These journeys by car were themselves displays of wealth that set them apart (Pinaud 2014). However, this school's founder always traveled by public transport and then on foot. He wanted to make himself available to the people of the *baai* to distinguish himself from the amoral, exclusive nature of the government.

At the same time, by providing this school for his community and setting himself up in a quasi-governmental role, the founder subjected himself to accountability akin to that of the local government. Therefore, the community held him accountable for the flows of money to and from the school. They demanded salaries from him. During community meetings with this *beny hakuma*, community members were often vocal in their criticism. Local politics would often prompt people to try to force the founder into recruiting certain teachers or cooks. Land disputes that arose when the school expanded still had to be settled by local elders. There seemed little hesitation to push back against the founder for the way he ran the school. While the school did allow him to build a sense of local legitimacy, this projection of authority was accompanied by a tight sense of accountability to the promises that he had made and the notions of civility he promoted.

REMAKING OBLIGATIONS THROUGH THE LOCAL CHURCH

In one village in Bahr al-Ghazal, the current most visible display of elite wealth has been the erection of a large church building funded by one *beny hakuma*. For years, the church had met under a large tree near the market and the home of the paramount chief. The church was accepted as having authority in the *baai* and did not challenge the authority of *beny baai*. The Catholic church was run by a catechist and was rarely visited by a priest or other leader in the Catholic church. The teachings of the church did not exclude the cosmological logics of many of the other local *beny baai*. For example, many church attenders also sacrificed cattle in order to petition their ancestors in times of need. The catechist himself was polygamous.

The Juba-based politician had many other homes than just in the rural villages. He had lived in Australia and London. As a child he had been taken to school in Juba. However, for political and economic reasons he was eager to reestablish his connections to his home communities.

He first promised to build the large, brick church building after the CPA was signed. He promised to raise funds among the *beny hakuma* of Juba in order to build this church back home. After years of promises, he eventually produced the initial funding for a fence to demarcate the land. Then, by November 2015, the church itself was erected. The politician had managed to raise funds for cement and iron sheets. The members of the church also gave their labor and time to make and fire the bricks that would be used for its walls. This politician had managed to make it a joint exercise and include himself as a partner in the building of this local church, a large brick building. This materially displayed his distinct power and access to wealth.

The church was massive, with twenty large, arched windows per side, and roofed with green iron sheets. After its construction, one friend commented, "Now our village is a city." The church's size and red bricks invoked images of the Catholic Cathedral in Wau—an old mission center and the center of the diocese. Wau was just a couple of hours drive from this rural church.

Therefore, by building the church, the *beny hakuma* was not just displaying his material wealth and distinction. He was also drawing on symbols of power, modernity, and government to remake his distinction and the role of the *beny hakuma* in the *baai*. The church was a way for this *beny hakuma* to demonstrate his power to bring the symbols of the town and the government to the space and sphere of the *home* itself. By building a church that resembled the Wau cathedral, he was claiming a power to make his home community into a town and a center of government in which his government authority would itself powerfully resonate.

By building a church, the *beny hakuma* was also drawing on notions of divine power and development to establish his authority. He was reshaping the discourses of power. Churches had established their ability to hold authority as both a local and an international institution. By associating himself with the church, this *beny hakuma* drew on an established repertoire to show how he could have authority both at home and in the government.

At the same time, in these villages, as in much of South Sudan, the church was closely associated with the sphere of the *government* and the aspirations of development. In the war years of the 1990s, churches had been considered an essential foundation for the social development (as evidenced by material from Eisei 2005 17; Nikkel 1994). The presence of a church became a sign of the development of a village, alongside the presence of a school, a market, and a clinic. Churches were also associated with education. For much of the twentieth century, missionaries had run the schools across South Sudan (Sanderson 1980). In the post-CPA era, the best schools were still church run. Therefore, as this *beny hakuma* supported the building of the church he also engaged with notions of civility and the promises of a government that would work for development in the rural areas. The church was not so much about challenging the cosmologies of the *home* as showing that the *hakuma* could be part of this *home* sphere and that the rural areas did not need to be excluded from development.

However, his building of this large church itself challenged the authority of the state and international church. The church was not built in the administrative headquarters of either the government or the church. Instead, it was built within a few minutes' walk of this *beny hakuma*'s rural home, in an area where his clan held the chiefdom. He was remaking this home village as a significant center without the explicit consent of the national government or international church.

In this church, the church-*hakuma* link was maintained. Most who attended the church in the village were also people who went to school or considered themselves to have had a formal education. Attending church was a way to situate yourself as a member of the local, educated class—a class that bridged the notions of the *baai* and the *hakuma*. In addition, the church was also often a local forum for announcements about the politics of the government. For example, before the January 2011 referendum on southern succession, the church notices each week included extensive speeches about the need to vote for independence.

However, the church links people to a specific moral authority and the international notions of authority and political powers of the global Catholic Church. It presents alternative cosmologies that may undermine the political theories or practices of the *hakuma*. This association with the international church comes with a register of legitimacy over which the *beny hakuma* of South Sudan cannot be sure of control. The government of South Sudan had had a cooperative relationship with a range of church denominations. From the 1990s, the church became part of Garang's discourse against the Khartoum government. In the post-CPA era, the church was celebrated for its contribution to the liberation struggle. For years, President Salva Kiir personally attended a Catholic church in Juba on a Sunday morning. Political elites would even attend church to lobby him and have a chance to talk to him.

However, in the context of the civil war that began December 2013 and especially as conflict spread to the Equatoria region, some church leaders became increasingly critical of government and they used their churches and this public space as a way to challenge the government. Their international connections did not make them safe but did give them a broader audience. For example, Catholic bishop Santo Loku Pio Doggale has explicitly stated that "the government is the orchestrator of the war, and the people are suffering as a result" (Herlinger 2017). Such comments prompted the government to accuse the church of being antigovernment and in favor of the rebels.

The *beny hakuma* who invested in this large, rural church in Bahr al-Ghazal hoped to both establish his authority in the *baai* as well as impress those in government. He had close ties to the president at the time. However, the increasingly critical nature of the church in South Sudan challenged the elite's assumptions and forced further accountability.

CONCLUSION

In the post-CPA era, elites in South Sudan have had access to incredible militarized power and immense wealth from government oil-revenues. This power and wealth have made them distinct and reconstituted what it means to be a *beny hakuma* in the post-CPA South Sudan. At a national level, these powers appear to have allowed these elites to operate without any restraint and with a total absence of accountability. The few, weak institutions that there are at a national level appear to be easily subsumed beneath the logics of a political marketplace. In this political marketplace, elites bargain for wealth and power through displays of violence that have killed hundreds of thousands. However, elites' national power has increasingly relied on their having support from their home communities.

In their struggle for distinction and support at home, elites have not been able to assume that they are also seen as distinct and carry legitimate power in their home communities. Instead, *beny hakuma* in Bahr al-Ghazal have actively engaged in constituting their elite authority in their home communities through a variety of strategies. To establish themselves as distinct, *beny hakuma* have used their economic and political power, often to invest in cultural patterns and moral worlds to build their social and cultural distinction. These have included investments in cattle, classrooms, and churches. Yet through these investments, the *beny hakuma* have become entangled in alternative, local logics of accountability and opportunities for auditing. They may try to reshape them or wrestle away from them. However, they still provide opportunities to hold these *beny hakuma* to account.

International research on elites has usefully turned debates away from a focus on state failure and assumptions that solutions will be found through technical, state-building expertise. At the same time there is a danger that this elite focus reduces the causes of war to the greedy nature of individual leaders in the government and armed opposition, blaming the war on personal agendas of wealth and power seeking (Enough 2017). The United States' and EU's issuing of individual sanctions on elites appear to be driven by these assumptions of individual elite culpability. As journalist Simon Allison stated for *The Guardian* in November 2017 "It's clear there are no good guys leading this war—only the rich and powerful trying to get richer and more powerful, casually risking the lives and futures of South Sudan's people to do so" (Foltyn 2017). The elites are perceived as out of control and without restraint.

At the same time, international policymakers who seek positive social change in South Sudan through making elites more accountable need to pay careful attention to the hidden opportunities for the auditing of elites at the most local level. They also need to think about the South Sudanese registers of accountability that have the most traction in the current context. Currently in South Sudan, internationally familiar methods of accountability, such as national elections, may be easily captured by elites. Other registers of accountability are likely to be more powerful.

NOTES

1. Peter P. Ekeh's (1975) work described the creation of two publics during the colonial period in Africa. The two publics have different moral foundations, and only one has linkages to the private realm.

2. Since the work of Lienhardt (1961) and Evans-Pritchard (1940), a wealth of anthropological literature has highlighted the political role of cattle for the Dinka (Deng 1984; Hutchinson 1996).

3. WND 64 B.1., c. 1933, "Assistant District Commissioner to Governor," as quoted by Hutchinson 1996: 64.

REFERENCES

Abbink, Jon, and Tijo Salverda. 2013. *The Anthropology of Elites: Power, Culture, and the Complexities of Distinction*. New York: Palgrave Macmillan.

Adebanwi, Wale. 2014. *Yoruba Elites and Ethnic Politics in Nigeria: Obafemi Awolowo and Corporate Agency*. New York: Cambridge University Press.

Bourdieu, Pierre. 1984. *Distinction: A Social Critique of the Judgment of Taste*. Translated by Richard Nice. London: Routledge and Kegan Paul.

Cooper, Frederick. 2002. *Africa since 1940: The Past of the Present*. Cambridge: Cambridge University Press.

Cormack, Zoe. 2014. *The Making and Remaking of Gogrial: Landscape, history and memory in South Sudan*. PhD diss., Durham University.

Daloz, Jean-Pascal. 2002. Elites et représentations politiques: la culture de l'échange inégal au Nigeria. Pessac: Presses Universitaires de Bordeaux.

Deng, David K. 2011. *The New Frontier: A Baseline Survey of Large-Scale Land-Based Investment in Southern Sudan*. Report 1/11, Norwegian People's Aid, March.

Deng, Francis. 1984. *The Dinka of the Sudan*. Prospect Heights, IL: Waveland Press.

De Waal, Alex. 1997. *Food and Power in Sudan: A Critique of Humanitarianism*. London: African Rights.

De Waal, Alex. 2014. "When Kleptocracy Becomes Insolvent: Brute Causes of the Civil War in South Sudan." *African Affairs* 113, no. 452: 347–69.

De Waal, Alex. 2015. *The Real Politics of the Horn of Africa: Money, War and the Business of Power*. Cambridge: Polity Press.

Duffield, Mark. 2001. *Global Governance and the New Wars: The Merging of Development and Security*. London: Zed Books.

Department for International Development (DFID). 2010. *The Politics of Poverty: Elites, Citizens and States Findings from Ten Years of DFID-Funded Research on Governance and Fragile States, 2001–2010: A Synthesis Paper*. London: DFID and OECD.

Kurimoto, Eisei. 2005. *A Report of the Evaluation Survey on Peace-Building Programmes in the East Bank, Equatoria Region, South Sudan*. Utrecht and Osaka: Pax Christi and Osaka University.

Ekeh, Peter P. 1975. "Colonialism and the Two Publics in Africa: A Theoretical Statement." *Comparative Studies in Society and History* 17, no. 1: 91–112.

Epstein, Andrew. 2012. "Maps of Desire: Refugee Children, Schooling, and Contemporary Dinka Pastoralism in South Sudan." PhD diss., University of Wisconsin–Madison.

Enough. 2017. *Weapons of Mass Corruption: How Corruption in South Sudan's Military Undermines the World's Newest Country*. Washington, DC: Enough.

Evans-Pritchard, E. E. 1940. *The Nuer*. New York: Oxford University Press.

Foltyn, Simona. 2017. "EXCLUSIVE: Leaked audit report shows how family and friends of top government officials benefited from letters of credit scam," *Mail & Guardian*, 3rd November 2017.

Fumanti, Mattia. 2016. *The politics of distinction: African elites from colonialism to liberation in a Namibian frontier town*. Herefordshire: Sean Kingston Publishing.

Gebreyes, Yacob, Lemma, Gezu Bekele, Deng, Luka Biong and Abdullahi, Shaif. 2016. *Impact of Conflict on the Livestock Sector in South Sudan*.

Greenhouse, Carol J. 1996. *A Moment's Notice: Time Politics across Cultures*. Ithaca, NY: Cornell University Press.

Gore, Paul Wani. 2014. "The overlooked role of elites in African grassroots conflicts: A case study of the Dinka-Mundari-Bari conflict in Southern Sudan," *CMI Sudan Working Paper*, WP2014:3, Bergen: Chr. Michelsen Institute.

Herlinger, Chris. 2017. "South Sudan Church Balances Prophetic Role, Practical Challenges," National Catholic Reporter, August 21.

Human Rights Watch. 2014. *South Sudan's New War: Abuses by Government and Opposition Forces*. August 7.

Hutchinson, Sharon. 1996. *Nuer Dilemmas: Coping with Money, War, and the State*. Berkeley: University of California Press.

Hutchinson, Sharon, and Naomi Pendle. 2015. "Violence, Legitimacy and Prophecy: Nuer Struggles with Uncertainty in South Sudan." *American Ethnologist* 42, no. 3: 425–30.

Johnson, Douglas. 2012. *The Root Causes of Sudan's Civil Wars: Peace or Truce*. Oxford: James Currey.

Jok, Jok Madut. 2017. *Breaking Sudan: The Search for Peace*. London: Oneworld.

Jok, Jok Madut, and Sharon Hutchinson. 1999. "Militarism, Gender and Reproductive Suffering: The Case of Abortion in Western Dinka." *Africa* 69, no. 2: 194–212.

Justin, Peter Hakim, and Lotje De Vries. 2017. "Governing Unclear Lines: Local Boundaries as a (Re)source of Conflict in South Sudan." *Journal of Borderland Studies* 34, no. 1: 31–46.

Karim, Ataul, Mark Duffield, Susanne Jaspars, Aldo Benini, Joanna Macrae, Mark Bradbury, Douglas Johnson, George Larbi, and Barbara Hendrie. 1996. *Operation Lifeline Sudan—A Review*. July. Nairobi: United Nations.

Keen, David. 2008. *The Benefits of Famine: A Political Economy of Famine and Relief in Southeastern Sudan, 1983–1989*. 2nd ed. Oxford: James Currey.

Leonardi, Cherry. 2007. "'Liberation' or Capture: Youth in between '*Hakuma*' and 'Home' during Civil War and Its Aftermath in Southern Sudan." *African Affairs* 106, no. 242: 391–412.

Leonardi, Cherry. 2013. *Dealing with Government in South Sudan: History of Chiefship, Community and State*. Woodbridge: James Currey.

Lewis, Bazett A. 1972. *The Murle: Red Chiefs and Black Commoners*. Oxford: Clarendon Press.

Lienhardt, Godfrey. 1961. *Divinity and Experience: The Religion of the Dinka*. Oxford: Clarendon Press.

Lloyd, Barbara. 1966. "Education and Family Life in the Development of Class Identification among the Yoruba." In P. C. Lloyd, ed., *The New Elites of Tropical Africa*. Oxford: Oxford University Press, 163–83.

Nikkel, Marc. 1994. "God Has Not Thrown You Away . . . God Has Not Deserted You." Pastoral Letter no. 3. Church Missionary Society.

Pendle, Naomi. 2015. "'They Are Now Community Police': Negotiating the Boundaries and Nature of Government in South Sudan through the Identity of Militarized Cattle-Keepers." *International Journal on Minority and Group Rights* 22: 410–34.

Pendle, Naomi. 2018. "'The Dead Are Just to Drink From': Recycling Ideas of Revenge among the Western Dinka, South Sudan." *Africa* 88, *no.1: 99–121*.

Pinaud, Clemence. 2014. "South Sudan: Civil War, Predation and the Making of Military Aristocracy." *African Affairs* 113, no. 451: 192–221.

Rolandsen, Øystein H. 2005. *Guerrilla Government: Political Changes in the Southern Sudan during the 1990s*. Uppsala: Nordic Africa Institute.

Sanderson, Lilian Passmore. 1980. "Education in the Southern Sudan: The Impact of

Government-Missionary–Southern Sudanese Relations upon the Development of Education during the Condominium Period, 1898–1956." *African Affairs 79, no.313:* 157–69.

Shore, Cris, and Stephen Nugent. 2002. *Elite Cultures: Anthropological Perspectives.* London: Routledge.

Sommers, Marc, and Stephanie Schwartz. 2011. "Dowry and Division: Youth and State Building in South Sudan." USIP Special Report no. 295. Washington, DC: United States Institute of Peace.

Thomas, Edward. 2015. *South Sudan: A Slow Liberation.* London: Zed Books.

Tvedt, Torbjorn. 1983. "Colonial Technicians: The Sudan Veterinary Service 1898–1956." PhD thesis, University of Bergen, Norway.

Maxwell, Daniel, Martina Santschi, and Rachel Gordon. 2014. "Looking Back to Look Ahead? Reviewing Key Lessons from Operation Lifeline Sudan and Past Humanitarian Operations in South Sudan." Working Paper no. 24, Feinstein International Center. London: Secure Livelihoods Research Consortium.

World Bank. 2017. *World Development Report 2017: Governance and the Law.* Washington, DC: World Bank.

Young, John. 2012. *The Fate of Sudan: The Origins and Consequences of a Flawed Peace Process.* London: Zed Books.

CHAPTER 13

Sudanese Elites

Riverain Arabs, Political Dominance, and the Sudanese State

JENNIFER PEKKINEN

When South Sudan seceded from Sudan in 2011, Sudan gained a new identity as an Islamic, Arab country. No longer did a substantial portion of the population identify as ethnically African or Christian. However, how the country is ruled and who it is ruled by changed little, continuing to disenfranchise those who do not identify as the regime's brand of Muslim or who are not ethnically Arab.

Nile riverain Arab tribes—particularly the Ja'aliyiin, Shaygiyya, and the Dangala—have dominated Sudan's political, economic, and security sectors since precolonial days. The dominance of these tribes has come at the expense of peace as the Sudanese elites progressively imposed their version of Arab-Islamic "Sudanese" identity on the country through their manner of governance. The elites undermined the purported autonomous nature of state institutions by injecting their Arab-Islamic principles. More importantly, the imposition of this Arab-Islamic identity alienated non-Arabs and non-Muslims and weakened their connection to the Sudanese state, leading to conflict, particularly in the periphery of the country.[1] The northern Arabs asserted this identity primarily to maintain and reinforce their hegemony as a minority government but also in part because of their own identity struggle as an African state that wishes to be an Arab state. The rest of the Arab world looks down upon Sudan as an African, not an Arab, country, something the Sudanese elite deeply resent.

This chapter aims to add to the scholarship about how elites manipulate identity and use it to co-opt power structures. It looks to expand on the ways this identity manipulation weakens the state and leads to conflict, using Sudan as a case study. In particular, this chapter explores how the riverain Arabs achieved ascendancy despite being minorities, and how their dominance has impacted the Sudanese state. It looks at various theories regarding identity formation and consolidation and how these apply to Sudan. This chapter also examines the history of Sudan and how, particularly in the postcolonial period, the Sudanese elite constructed a Sudanese identity based on a narrow Arab-Islamic definition, alienating those who did not fit. Construction of a new Sudanese identity not based on this narrow vision may be the only way to mitigate future conflict in Sudan.

This chapter was completed prior to the events of April 2019, when large-scale protests sparked by economic grievances forced out President Omar al-Bashir. It is too soon to tell if and how the fundamental structures of governance will change, but questions of identity have already emerged as the Sudanese grapple with how to move forward after a thirty-year dictatorship. Hopefully this chapter provides a useful context to those trying to understand the entrenched power structures in Sudan and the challenges the population faces in attempting to remake a system of governance decades in the making.

ETHNICITY IN IDENTITY FORMATION AND NATIONALISM

There are several theories about identity formation and the role of ethnicity and nationality in identity formation in Africa. Many scholars dismiss Clifford Geertz's view that primordial attachment to kin, family group, or tribe is a critical element of human behavior (Hyden 2006: 186–87). Rather, they argue that ethnicity in Africa is a colonial construct, in that the Europeans rigidly defined groups whose identities previously were fluid. Bruce Berman, Dickson Eyoh, and Will Kymlicka note that colonial bureaucracies played a key role in the construction of "tribal" identities out of kinship groups and political units, building upon indigenous power relations to facilitate indirect rule (Berman, Eyoh, and Kymlicka 2004: 5). These tribal identities are the products of contests over wealth and power, particularly access to state resources (Berman, Eyoh, and Kymlicka 2004: 317). Some scholars argue that while ethnicity, or rather ethnic identity, may have been a product of the colonial era, its major stimulus comes from competitive politics (Welsh 1944:

485). In other words, ethnic identity has been used as a political resource. In Sudan, identity has become a means to achieve power and resources. People identify with an ethnic group that can bring them economic and political benefits. Frances Deng, a prominent South Sudanese diplomat and scholar, notes that in Sudan, such factors have moved from the realm of benign self-perception to the politically contested stage of national symbolism with the implications of shaping and sharing power, wealth, and other national values (Deng 1995: 4).

Those in power often use narratives to justify their authority. M. A. Mohamed Salih defines narratives as modern or traditional discursive forms employed by authors to explain, justify, or subvert a system of authority or dominance. According to Salih, the prevailing discourse magnifies the political role of the dominant ethnic group and its relation to the state. This group thus uses narratives to maintain the status quo and reinforce its dominance. This also can contribute to the marginalization of minority groups, who can be seen as a threat to the nation-building project (Salih 1998a: 5–6). This chapter will examine the use of narratives by the northern Arab Sudanese elite to justify and to maintain their monopoly on power.

Promoting nationalism is another way to strengthen and preserve identity. Ann Mosley Lesch describes Sudan's north-south civil war as a clash between two divergent views of nationalism. The northern elite favored the ethnic nationalist approach in which the state corresponds with one self-defined ethnic group, the riverain Arabs. On the other hand, the south favored the territorial model, which is based on the idea that residents in a particular territory have a common allegiance to the state, regardless of ethnicity (Lesch 1998: 6–7). Donald Rothchild and Alexander Groth (1995: 70–71) maintain that ethnonationalistic groups promote their identity through the exclusiveness of the national group's definition based upon particular criteria, and through the maintenance, internal cohesion, and loyalty to the group based on perceived outside threats. These are classic strategies employed by the northern Sudanese elite. The conflict between these two theories of nationality can help explain the Sudanese civil war.

Sudan has more than fifty ethnic groups, and the largest (self-defined) groups are Arabs, Fur, Beja, Nuba, and Fallata.[2] Sudanese identity remains a complicated issue. Broadly speaking, modern-day Sudanese identity is divided into Arab versus African, Muslim versus Christian, northerner versus southerner, to name a few. Focusing on the northern center will enable the reader to understand the ruling riverain tribes and how they maintain power in Sudan. Arabs comprise roughly 70 percent of the population in Sudan following the 2011 secession of South Sudan; prior to 2011, Arabs made up only 40 percent of the population, with the riverain Arab tribes an even smaller percentage.[3] The riverain tribes, as defined by R. S. O'Fahey, refer to the inhabitants of the Nile Valley between Aswan and Khartoum as well as those living in Gezeira, between the branches of the Nile River and to the east and west in the savannahs. O'Fahey describes them as "overwhelmingly Arabic-speaking, wholly Muslim, and to a greater or lesser degree identify themselves genealogically or culturally as Arab" (1996: 259).

Sudanese Arabs share ethnic and religious identities. While many Arab tribes claim genealogical lines dating back to the prophet Muhammad, several northern "Arab" groups are Arabized Africans. They adopted Arab language, culture, and Islam over centuries of contact with Arab traders and merchants as well as Arab holy men (Deng 1995: 400–401). The Ja'aliyiin and the Dangala claim to be "pure" Arabs, descendants of the Ismailite tribes in northern Arabia. Non-Arab groups such as the Nubians, Beja, Nuba, and Fur have adopted Arab customs and the Arabic language and converted to Islam (Wai 1981: 20–23). As a result, over time it has become difficult, if not impossible, to look at someone and declare that person "Arab" or "African."

The religious identity of Sudanese Arabs is generally based on Sufism, a largely peaceful religious tradition. Sudanese Arabs also are overwhelmingly Sunni Muslims. There are several religious fraternities known as *tariqas*, each centered around the personality and teachings of a particular saint, sheikh, or master. The *tariqas* exist within Sunni and Shia Islam, not as separate sects (Al-Rahim 1970: 239). Religion and politics are intertwined in Muslim societies, and this has resulted in rivalries between the various *tariqas*, particularly the Mahdiyya and Khatmiyya traditions. The Mahdi tradition (Mahdiyya) advocated a purist form of Islam and rejected Sufism and the *tariqas*. The prominent Mirghani family in Sudan embraced the Khatmiyya tradition of Sufism, a more moderate tradition closely associated with Egypt (Al-Rahim 1970: 239–41). The northern educated elite tend to be tied to one of the *tariqas*. However, most Sudanese outside Khartoum follow a more mystical, Africanized form of Islam based on the Sufi tradition. While many are devout Muslims, they do not follow the strict interpretations of Islam practiced by the northern riverain Arabs. The numerous Sudanese ethnic groups have an identity based on language, religion, and racial and ideological identification with Arabs from North Africa and the Middle East that has helped unify them (Wai 1981: 23).

HISTORICAL BACKGROUND

From 1500 to roughly 1800, most of what is now present-day Sudan was considered the Funj Sultanate of Sinnar. The Funj, an Arabized and Islamicized group, overthrew the Christian Kingdom of Nubia in 1504 and institutionalized Islam as the national religion (Idris 2005: 26). The Sinnar sultanate and its sister sultanate in Darfur were well-known slave-raiding kingdoms, and the Muslim slave-raiders of Sinnar and Darfur became a dominant regional force. Islam and Arabism were seen as the carriers of civilization, as Amir Idris calls it, and those who were not Arab or Muslim were subject to subordination, exploitation, and enslavement. At the time, agricultural and other "menial" labor was considered socially humiliating. Thus non-Muslim and non-Arab slaves, who did much of that work, were looked down upon, and the Arabic-speaking riverain Muslims came to see themselves as culturally superior (Idris 2005: 18, 27).

This situation continued with the 1821 Turco-Egyptian conquest of Sudan, which helped make it a more centralized state. Prior to the Turco-Egyptian invasions, what is now South Sudan had virtually no contact with the north. Geographical barriers such as swamps formed by the Nile River and the wet tropical climate ensured that Arab influence did not penetrate the south in any appreciable way until the Turks and the Egyptians increased their slave raids into the region. Arab settlers moved in and exploited existing conflicts between the African groups over resources such as land and cattle (Wai 1981: 27–28). The Turco-Egyptian regime ended with the arrival of Muhammad Ahmad, who claimed to be the Mahdi ("Rightly Guided One," or a prophet). The Madhi movement was a politico-religious movement based on the idea that the Mahdi would guide believers into power and return society to the practice of the purest forms of Islam (Lesch 1998: 28). In 1883, Ahmad and his troops defeated the Turks and the Egyptians in a final battle at El-Obeid (in what is now North Kordofan) and established a Mahdist state based on Islamic principles (Smith 2007).

THE COLONIAL PERIOD

In 1898, a joint Anglo-Egyptian military force ousted the Mahdi regime and established the Anglo-Egyptian Condominium in what is now present-day Sudan (excluding the independent Sultanate of Darfur, which would not be incorporated into the Condominium until 1916). In the beginning, the British tolerated slavery by working with powerful Muslim slave traders to consolidate the state (Idris 2005: 33). The British saw the slave traders, the precolonial elites, as their largest threat. To avoid anticolonial resistance, they gave them a stake in the system. The British favored the self-defined "Arabs," whom they viewed as "civilized," for education and administrative jobs, while those of "slave descent" (blacks) had more menial jobs or joined the army. Gordon College in Khartoum, one of the few institutions of higher education, did not admit southerners until 1944 (Sharkey 2007: 21, 29). At the same time, Arab merchants and local government officials spread the riverain Arab-Islamic identity (meaning speaking Arabic, the riverain manner of dress, and restrictions on women) to the east, west, and south (O'Fahey 1996: 261). A specific Arab-Islamic identity based on the riverain Arabs' practice of Islam already had begun to spread throughout Sudan.

Socioeconomic development during colonial times largely was concentrated around Khartoum and in the Northern Province, particularly with regard to commercial investments, social services, and education. Elfatih A. A/Salam notes that this resulted in the emergence of a national middle class that monopolized power over the economic, administrative, and political activities in the center of the country. It also meant that ethnic groups not part of that middle class had difficulty challenging those in power, in political and economic terms (A/Salam 2008: 118–19). While A/Salam refers to it as a "national" middle class, there was no country-wide middle class. Rather, there was a small middle class who came from the northern riverain areas and dominated the administrative, political, and economic apparatus in central Sudan, where power was held. Historically, the center controlled political and economic power at the expense of the periphery.

The British looked at Sudan as having an Arab north and an African south, and they ruled the country as such. By governing the south separately, it was imagined the south would one day either be its own independent region or be integrated into British East Africa (now Kenya). In the south, the British discouraged the use of Arabic, banned Islamic religious practices, replaced Arab administrators with indigenous ones, and instituted a policy of using the local language in primary schools (Wai 1981: 35; Burton 1991: 512). In 1922, the British introduced the Closed District Ordinance, which prohibited people from traveling to the south or the west without permits. Idris believes this policy sought to eradicate Arab-Islamic influences and maintain the African identity in the south. He argues that while Arabism was a product of enslavement, Africanism was a product of colonial indirect rule, in that colonial rulers reinforced the indigenous "African" system instead of imposing their own. Peter Kok describes the legacy of British colonialism as the consolidation of an Arab-Islamic hegemonic bloc in north-central Sudan and the conservation of underdevelopment and tribal peculiarities in the south (1996: 556). While the north viewed itself as a single, homogenous, cultural identity superior to the rest of the country, the British fostered a separate southern identity, cementing existing differences and exacerbating the divide between the two regions.

The politicizing of identities began during the colonial period in the early 1900s. Jay O'Brien discusses how ethnic labels were used in reference to lifestyle. For example, "Arabs" were nomadic pastoralists, and "Baggara" were cattle herders (1998: 66). The colonial state institutionalized the racial identities of "Arab" and "African" through indirect rule and their policy of ruling north and south separately.[4] Idris argues that "Arab" and "African" thus were transformed from flexible cultural identities to rigid political identities because of state policies. He notes that colonial rule institutionalized ethnic and racial entitlements, rights, and privileges and consequently created unequal forms of citizenship. This resulted in political tension and violence as groups became marginalized and faced discrimination (Idris 2005: 10–11, 20).

At independence, the British shocked the southerners and decided the south and the north should gain independence as one country. The British and northern elites made this decision without southern input (Sharkey 2003: 92). The northerners resented separate rule for the south, believing the south eventually would have become Arabized and Islamicized (Lesch 1998: 33). The decision put the southerners at a distinct disadvantage, as they were ill-placed to gain meaningful roles in the political and economic life of a newly independent, united Sudan. In 1955, the first southern war began when the south rebelled against northern domination (Deng 1995: 177). The southerners viewed the northern government as a colonizer and believed their identity would be ignored in the newly independent state (Wai 1981: 8).

SUDANESE NATIONALISM

What it meant to be "Sudanese" evolved over time, particularly during the colonial period. The term "Sudan" was first found in the writings of early Muslim geographers who referred to the area south of the Sahara Desert as

Bilad al-Sudan, or "Land of the Blacks." Through the slave trade and the fact that the vast majority of slaves were black, the term "Sudanese" came to take on connotations of servitude. Until at least 1900, northerners used the term "Sudanese" to refer to people from the non-Muslim, non-Arab areas that were the historical targets of slave raids. During the 1920s and 1930s, the northern elites started using "Sudanese" to refer to a national concept. Heather Sharkey argues that by favoring the self-defined Arabs at the expense of all other groups, the British cultivated a group of men who had the educational and political capabilities to develop nationalist ideologies (2007: 29–30; 2003: 17–18, 23–24). It is significant that the majority of educated Sudanese belonged to the northern riverain groups. During the 1930s and 1940s, when nationalism became a dominant force in Sudan, the educated elite defined the terms of the political discourse.

Idris describes Sudanese nationalism as being less about fighting the British than about competing political claims for the identity of the postcolonial state (2005: 44). The northern riverain Arabs viewed themselves as the natural successors to the British and began to craft a "Sudanese" identity based on their own identity. Sharkey describes a notion that arose in the 1940s, articulated by future prime minister Muhammad Ahmad Majub, in which Sudan was defined by its hybridism of Arab and African identity, while its cultural superiority was attributed to the "Arabs" (2007: 33). History was constructed to portray the northern elite's view of the past, placing themselves at the center of the Sudanese historical narrative. The discourse they used was an expansion of the ideology about the historical right of Arabized Islamic peoples to rule over non-Muslim and non-Arab groups (Idris 2005: 17). Writings and speeches at this time were filled with language denoting Arabic and Islam as the pillars of the nation (Sharkey 2003: 11). The northern elite used this narrative to justify and legitimize their hold on power (Idris 2005: 15). They also used their Arab-Islamic identity to attempt to unite several disparate ethnic groups under the guise of nationalism. That the vision was meant to be a unifying one was of little consolation to those who did not fit in that narrow category, particularly those living in southern Sudan and Darfur.

In the 1940s and 1950s as Sudanese nationalists grew more vocal, the British attempted to appease them by increasing the number of Sudanese in government, a policy that was known as "Sudanization" (Sharkey 2003: 73). This policy allowed the educated northern elite to dominate the country's administrative structure, with few other Sudanese groups gaining entry. Thus, when Sudan gained independence, the northern elite already were entrenched in government.

Citizenship also was a tool for the northern elite to construct its Sudanese identity. The 1948 Nationality Act defined citizenship in terms of membership in ethnic groups living within the territorial boundaries established by Anglo-Egyptian rule in 1898. Being born in Sudan, even to parents born in Sudan, did not necessarily entitle someone to Sudanese citizenship (Idris 2005: 95). In practice, someone who belonged to an Arab tribe was granted citizenship, whereas being a member (or being suspected of being a member) of a tribe that had West African origins could disqualify that person from Sudanese citizenship, even if his or her family had been there long before the British came (O'Brien 1998: 67).

THE IDENTITY OF INDEPENDENT SUDAN

Once Sudan gained independence in 1956, the northern elite began a policy of Arabization to unify the country following the divisive British rule. General Ibrahim Abboud, in power from 1958 to 1964, championed Arabic and Islam and promoted religious and cultural homogeneity without regard for the differences in the south and elsewhere in Sudan (A/Salam 2008: 120). He Arabized southern administrative and educational institutions, expelled all foreign missionaries, and introduced Arabic as the main language in Sudan (Sharkey 2007: 33-34). Nationalism and national integration was equated with Arabization and Islamization, something that would be true in subsequent administrations (Wai 1981: 85). However, Sharkey notes that while proving successful in terms of a cultural process spreading the Arab identity, Arabization failed in its original intent to unify the country and provoked hostility and resentment in the south (2007: 22, 37). Deng observes that the northerners generally assumed that their identity was the national model, and what prevailed in the south was a distorted image that the colonialists had imposed to divide the country. The northerners believed that Arabization and Islamization eventually would help reintegrate the country (Deng 1995: 148).

In 1964, a popular uprising against Abboud led to his downfall.[5] Sadiq al-Mahdi, great-grandson of the Mahdi who overthrew the Turco-Egyptian forces in 1883, became prime minister in 1966. Lesch quotes remarks that al-Mahdi made after he became prime minister to foreshadow what his policies would be: "The dominant feature of our nation is an Islamic one and its overpowering expression is Arab, and this nation will not have . . . its prestige and pride preserved except under an Islamic revival" (1998: 42). Around the same time, Hassan al-Turabi, an Islamist with strong ties to the Egyptian-based Islamic movement called the Muslim Brotherhood, returned to Sudan from studying overseas and began uniting the Sudan branch of the Muslim Brotherhood with other like-minded groups. Al-Turabi viewed the old forms of Islam—Mahdiyya and Khatmiyya among others—as outdated. He believed in a modernized version of Islam, based on ideology rather than traditional historical family ties. Al-Turabi formed the Islamic Charter Front, the precursor to the National Islamic Front (NIF).[6] Al-Mahdi and al-Turabi drafted a constitution that established Islam as the state religion and Arabic as the state language. Islamic law was the main source of legislation (Warburg 1995: 232–33). The constitution was never passed, though, as al-Mahdi was overthrown by Ja'afar Nimeiri in 1969.

Nimeiri was inspired by Egypt's Gamal Abdel Nassar and saw himself as secular, socialist, and pan-Arab (Lesch 1998: 45). He is credited with ending the 1955–72 north-south civil war by signing the 1972 Addis Ababa Agreement. The document enshrined in the constitution the idea of a dual Arab and African identity for Sudan and respect for Islam, Christianity, and traditional religions. However, Nimeiri lacked support for his government and faced several coup attempts, including one by al-Mahdi and al-Turabi in 1976.[7] To mitigate the situation, Nimeiri embraced national reconciliation, which meant opening up talks with al-Mahdi and al-Turabi. He brought them back into government, thereby allowing the emergence of a hard-line Islamic group that increasingly gained clout (ICG 2002: 12).

Following al-Mahdi's and al-Turabi's return to government, Nimeiri faced increasing pressure to withdraw his support for the Addis Ababa Agreement and implement an Islamic constitution. In 1983, Nimeiri unilaterally abrogated the agreement, instituted sharia (Islamic) law, and divided the south into three regions. Particularly disturbing for non-Muslims and southerners was that *hudud* punishments (harsh punishments for offenses such as drinking alcohol, adultery, or theft) were introduced and applied equally to Muslims and non-Muslims. By following an Islamization policy, Nimeiri believed he could enhance his legitimacy among the Muslim population (Lesch 1998: 47, 52–55). However, his policies alienated both secular Muslims and non-Muslims. Idris argues that the imposition of sharia law on Sudan relegated southern Sudanese (as non-Muslims) to subjects rather than citizens. He notes that state-enforced discrimination had the unintended consequence of violence between those who ruled by exclusion and those who wanted inclusion in the state (Idris 2005: 11–12). The abrogation of the Addis Ababa Agreement and the ensuing Islamist policies led to the resurgence of war in 1983.

By 1985, Nimeiri had alienated most northerners and southerners because he failed to honor his promise to facilitate ethnic pluralism and was unwilling to abandon his authoritarian ways. The economy was in a free fall and the country faced a growing famine that Nimeiri refused to address. He was ousted in a bloodless coup while in the United States in April 1985. A transitional government ruled until 1986, when Sadiq al-Mahdi was reelected prime minister, twenty years after his first term. While al-Mahdi supported the Arabization and Islamization of the south, he believed that the Islamic laws implemented by Nimeiri were un-Islamic and should not infringe on the rights of non-Muslims (Warburg 1995: 224). Al-Mahdi promised to suspend the Islamic laws and negotiate with the southern rebels. However, he failed to honor these commitments and was overthrown by the NIF in 1989 (Lesch 1998: 86).

THE REIGN OF THE NIF

Successive postindependence governments have undermined non-Muslims' and non-Arabs' connection to the Sudanese state through their Islamist polices, although perhaps none more so than the NIF. When Lieutenant-General Omar al-Bashir, Sudan's longest-running president, and al-Turabi toppled al-Mahdi in 1989, the NIF began implementing its Arabization and Islamization policies in earnest, institutionalizing the political, economic, and social foundation of an Islamic state (Idris 2005: 54). Lesch describes the monolithic view that the NIF had of Sudan: a country in which Arab and Islam reigned supreme in all facets of life, where minorities could be merged into the majority (1998: 113). Al-Turabi, who played a key role in the implementation of sharia law as attorney general under Nimeiri, was widely regarded as the architect of the NIF's Islamization project. He reportedly asserted that without the forced separation of the north and south by the British, southern ethnic groups would have disappeared through intermarriage and the gradual diffusion of Arabic and Islam (Lesch 1998: 33).

The NIF used rhetoric to pursue Islamization, such as referring to the war against the southern rebels as jihad. By defining the conflict in religious terms, the Islamic elite highlighted their superiority complex and reinforced the idea that southerners, by not sharing their Arab-Islamic identity, are not truly "Sudanese." The NIF also turned ostensibly autonomous government institutions into institutions staffed by those who shared its vision. The NIF purged approximately twenty thousand people from the government, civil service, judiciary, professional associations, and trade unions and replaced them with NIF cadres and supporters in the year following the coup (Lesch 1998: 113; Warburg 1995: 230). Alex de Waal discusses efforts at the height of the 1990s by the NIF Islamists to turn local government into a source through which Islam was spread and put local services in the hands of Islamic organizations (2007: 14–15). Lesch once again succinctly summarizes the NIF's reach: "Islamist associations monopolized the political, economic, and social areas, and NIF cadres dominated the civil service, schools, and diplomatic corps. They controlled the security and military apparatuses and operated parallel intelligence, police, and paramilitary forces" (1998: 146–47).

The NIF government pushed the introduction of sharia law that Nimeiri had started in 1983 and pursued a puritanical version of Islam with strict dress codes and rules regarding separation of the sexes (Salih 1998b: 77). The NIF also introduced *hudud* punishments based on sharia law in 1991. The terms the NIF used for administrators and administrative units were terms from Islamic history (Manger 2004: 111–12). The NIF nationalized Christian schools in 1992, Arabizing and Islamizing curriculums, and also purged the Ministry of Education, replacing administrators and teachers in schools all over the country with NIF supporters. Arabic became the language of instruction at all public universities, making it difficult for southerners to gain access (Lesch 1998: 140, 143–44).

The NIF also was willing to establish an Islamic state by force (Warburg 1995: 234). The government officially established the Popular Defense Forces (PDF) in 1989, recruiting primarily from members of the Muslim Brotherhood (Salih 1998b: 76; Natsios 2006: 31–32; Burr and Collins 2008: 285). The PDF had a distinctly Islamic agenda and was seen as a force whose primary job was to defend Islam, particularly the cultural and religious purity of the north (Lesch 1998: 135). The Bashir government saw the PDF as a replacement to the army, despite its inferior military capabilities, and by 1996 the PDF outnumbered the army (80,000 regular army troops to 150,000 PDF troops) and was a major fighting force in southern Sudan (Salih 1998b: 77; Salmon 2007: 18–19).

The PDF was not the only Arab paramilitary force the government used to advance its cause. The government used Arab militias, known as *janjaweed*, to fight against largely non-Arab rebels in Darfur. These forces—low-cost alternatives to trained military professionals—had poor military capabilities and a distinct Arab-Islamic philosophy and agenda. The government's reliance on these paramilitary forces reinforced the notion the government valued Arab lives over non-Arab lives, particularly given the massive human rights abuses these Arab militias committed against non-Arab civilians (ICID 2005).

The NIF (now known as the National Congress Party—NCP) toned down its Islamization and Arabization campaign toward the end of the 1990s, particularly after al-Turabi was sidelined after a falling out with President Bashir in 1999–2000.[8] The regime appeared to eschew its overtly Islamist agenda, particularly in foreign policy, and adopt a more pragmatic approach to governance and foreign relations. Throughout the 2000s, Bashir sidelined a number of prominent Islamists in a bid to consolidate power and cultivated relations with Gulf countries that ostracized Sudan during its hardline Islamist days (ICG 2016: 5–6, 12). Bashir adeptly redefined the regime's identity in the eyes of the international community from an extremist Islamist regime to a more moderate Islamic state. However, many non-Arabs and moderate Muslim citizens do not believe the regime shed its NIF roots.

THE END OF THE NORTH-SOUTH WAR

As discussed earlier, a major impetus for the Sudanese civil war was competing views of nationalism. The NIF/NCP had an ethnonationalistic view of the Sudanese state, believing it should revolve around its Arab-Islamic identity. In the ethnic nationalist approach, the leaders of the dominant ethnic group seek a homogeneity that represses differences and glosses over other ethnicities (Lesch 1998: 7). The southern rebels, the Sudan People's Liberation Movement (SPLM), on the other hand, had a territorialistic view of identity. John Garang, leader of the SPLM before he died in a helicopter crash in 2005, advocated a vision of a "New Sudan." This was his attempt at rewriting Sudanese nationalism based on territorial nationality, which would include all the peoples of Sudan. Garang's "New Sudan" was based on the principle of a voluntary unity of the country with a fundamental change in the country's governance. The territorial model advocated by Garang would have provided southern Sudanese and northern groups that are excluded from the elite with an attachment to the state.

Prior to Garang's death, the Sudanese government and southern rebels had reached a military stalemate after decades of war and had recognized that they needed to move forward with a resolution to the conflict. Peace talks eventually led to the signing of the Comprehensive Peace Agreement (CPA) in 2005, which provided for an autonomous southern government and incorporated southerners into central government leadership positions before a referendum on the south's status, including possible independence, in 2011. During that same interim period, sharia law would remain in the north.

With the CPA, the north preserved its ethnonationalist approach in that it viewed the north (e.g., greater Khartoum) as the center of Sudan and thus maintained its Islamic identity. While the north compromised some positions in the central government, the real power remained with the northerners. Southerners, on the other hand, rejected Garang's vision of a "New Sudan" by voting overwhelmingly in 2011 for independence. Many southerners believed the NCP would never give up power and would never recognize southerners as full citizens of Sudan. They saw themselves as having an identity that was incompatible with the Sudanese state as it was defined. They had no attachment to it, and in fact, the northern elite made clear that the southerners did not fit into what they viewed as the true Sudanese identity. In 2010, President Bashir vowed to change the constitution if southern Sudan seceded to reflect that Sudan was an Arab, Islamic republic. Indeed, after South Sudan's independence, the government changed the nationality law to essentially strip Southerners, including those living in Sudan, of their Sudanese citizenship. Their citizenship was finally reinstated in June 2018 (*Sudan Tribune* 2018). Unfortunately, independence has not brought peace to South Sudan, which is embroiled in its own civil war in part over the domination of institutions by one ethnic group.

DARFUR

The southerners were not the only ones adversely affected by the ethnonationalist view held by the riverain elite. The longtime discrimination against and marginalization of the overwhelmingly Muslim region of Darfur sparked conflict multiple times throughout Sudan's history. Darfur's geography can be broken down into roughly three zones: northern Darfur includes Arabs and non-Arabs, such as the Zaghawa, who are mainly camel-herding nomads; central Darfur is primarily non-Arab sedentary groups, such as the Fur and Masalit; and southern Darfur is mostly cattle-herding Arabs, such as the Baggara (Rizeygat) (Mahmoud 2004: 3). While the Darfurians are overwhelmingly Muslim, most do not subscribe to strict Islamic practices. In the mid-1980s, the Sudanese government reached a deal with Libya to supply arms to Khartoum for its fight against the SPLM. In return, the government turned a blind eye while Libya used Darfur as a rear base for its wars in Chad. The thousands of Libyan Islamic Legion soldiers, many with strong Arab supremacy beliefs, and Chadian Arabs that flooded into Darfur helped spark the 1987–89 Arab-Fur war in Darfur (Flint and De Waal 2005: 24–25). During this time, the *janjaweed* were first organized. The original *janjaweed* were Chadian Arab militias that befriended and armed their Sudanese Arab militia allies. The Arab supremacist ideology espoused by many *janjaweed* was exported to Sudan via Chad through these militant Arabs, supported by Libya (Haggar 2007: 121, 125). These *janjaweed* became the government's primary tool to fight rebel groups in Darfur.

After the NCP seized power in 1989, it reoriented the system of local governance in Darfur (known as native administration) to conform to Islamic practices and in 1995 redefined the roles of a native administrator to be one of a religious leader who should prepare the youth to fight a holy war in the Christian south (Abdul-Jalil, Mohammed, and Yousuf 2007: 51). It also attempted to "Arabize" Darfur. The traditional power base in the region was the non-Arab, sedentary tribes such as the Fur and Masalit. However, the government rewarded the Arab groups that fought on its behalf by creating new local government administrative units that provided them with power (ICG 2003: 11). For example, in 1995, the local government of West Darfur was divided into thirteen emirates, with six being allocated to Arabs mainly from Chad. This sparked a war between the Masalit, who historically ruled this area under an independent sultanate, and the Arabs. The government frequently has interfered with the power structure in Darfur to give more power to its Arab allies.

In 2000, *The Black Book: Imbalance of Power and Wealth in Sudan* was published. The *Black Book* was a revolutionary tract that for the first time documented the systematic control exercised by three riverain Arabs tribes of the vast majority of the country's economic and political power, including the military hierarchy, civil and provincial administrations, the judiciary, and the presidency and ministries (Flint and De Waal 2005: 18). The book also emphasized the marginalization of the other regions of Sudan. In 2001, the Justice and Equality Movement (JEM), one of Darfur's primary rebel groups, claimed authorship of the *Black Book*. Two years later, the JEM and the Sudan

Liberation Army launched their first major attacks against the government, and the government responded by unleashing the *janjaweed*. The Darfur war, referred to as a genocide in 2004 by the US government, resulted in non-Arabs being driven off their land, the displacement of at least 2.7 million people, and up to three hundred thousand civilian deaths (BBC 2009). A 2017 UN report indicates that as of October 2016, 2.6 million people remained internally displaced, and some were unable to return home because of Arab occupation of their land, despite the overall reduction of armed conflict throughout Darfur (OHCHR and UNAMID 2017: 3, 22).

The balance of power since the publication of the *Black Book* has changed little. If anything, the prolonged conflict has weakened many Darfurians' attachment to the state. As long as the attacks against non-Arab citizens continue and the Darfur people are reminded that they do not have what the elite consider a true Sudanese identity, the more tenuous their attachment to the Sudanese state will become and the longer the conflict will persist.

CONSEQUENCES FOR THE SUDANESE STATE

Goran Hyden identified three general problems with the state in Africa. First, he argued that the state lacks the autonomy from society that makes it an instrument of collective action. It tends to respond to community pressures that undermine its authority as a public institution. Second, state officials do not adhere to the formal rules that constitute public authority. They do not distinguish between what is public and what is private. Finally, individuals appointed to public office rarely subordinate their personalities to the definitions of the roles they are supposed to perform (Hyden 2006: 65). How the northern riverain elites, particularly the Bashir government, have run the Sudanese state exemplifies the problems identified by Hyden. The Sudanese elites used the state to line their pockets and promote their narrow political and economic agendas at the expense of the rest of the population. The state has not been autonomous from a small group who sought to use it to impose a narrow identity on the entire country, instead of serving as an independent institution responsive to the population's needs. State institutions dictate public and private rules of behavior based on the NCP's interpretation of Islam, through sharia law, rules regarding dress, and other private actions. Those running these institutions, the NCP cadres and supporters, do not view themselves as agents of autonomous state institutions. Rather, they view their positions as a means to promote the NCP's agenda. The NCP has used the state and its institutions to realize an Arab-Islamic state, which has fundamentally weakened state institutions, as well as the connection to the state felt by groups not fitting the Arab-Islamic identity that the NCP has deemed "Sudanese."

The colonial state made no effort to establish a distinction between state and regime, allowing the northern elite to monopolize and define the state. This will consistently lead to conflict unless the state no longer is associated strictly with the regime. The Darfur war and conflict in the so-called Two Areas (South Kordofan and Blue Nile) show an alienation from the Sudanese state. That the Darfur rebel groups have not called for secession or independence for Darfur, however, indicates they still have some attachment to the Sudanese state. Capitalizing on that attachment will be necessary to build an identity based on a broader definition of what it means to be Sudanese. This may be one way to mitigate conflict in Sudan in the future.

Sudan's history cannot be written solely from the point of view of the northern riverain elite. It must reflect the totality of the Sudanese experience: its various groups, religions, and ethnicities. Sudan is far from monolithic and even discussions of the "northern Sudanese" and the "southern Sudanese" implicitly exclude many ethnic groups, such as the Misseriya Arabs and the Nuba, that do not identify with the dominant groups that have come to define the north and the south. As long as Sudan is associated with the narrow vision of the riverain elite, there will always be alienated groups and, given Sudan's violent history, the potential for violence.

One aspect that has not yet been addressed is why the northern elites are so focused on Arabizing the country. Their primary reason is to extend and maintain their hegemony as a minority group. By imposing their identity on others, they define the terms of what being "Sudanese" is and place themselves in an authoritative position. But there is another factor. The northern elite view Sudan as an Arab country, not a black African country. That this view has some traction is evidenced by the fact that Ghana is frequently referred to as the first African country to gain independence, rather than Sudan, which gained independence nearly a year before Ghana. To live up to the notion that Sudan is an Arab country, it is imperative that the rest of the country be assimilated into Arab culture. Deng comments that Arab identity in Sudan is a much stronger aspiration than it is within the Arab world, meaning that Sudanese Arabs are desperate to belong to the Arab world, while the Arab world is less preoccupied with them. He describes incidents of racist treatment of Sudanese laborers in Gulf states because of their black skin color (Deng 1995: 380). The difficulty in distinguishing between a Sudanese "Arab" and a Sudanese "African" based on his or her appearance has led to the mistreatment of Sudanese Arabs in the Middle East, where they are viewed as black Africans, regardless of the fact they are Muslim and speak Arabic. The government seems to ignore the irony that its favored citizens are treated abroad much the way non-Arabs and non-Muslims are treated at home.

CONCLUSION

The northern riverain elites, who are both Arab and Muslim, have dominated Sudan since precolonial times, using history to justify their hegemony and their narrative as the foundation of what it means to be "Sudanese." They did this in part because of the narrative they constructed of the civilizing effect that Arab-Muslims had and through their dominance as slave raiders. The British colonizers also viewed the Arab-Muslims as superior to non-Arabs or "blacks" in southern Sudan and reinforced this difference through separate forms of rule. The northern elites thus were able to impose their vision of Sudan on the rest of the country.

In a sense, Sudan has been the victim of two identity hijackings.[9] First, the British allowed the commandeering of Sudanese identity by allowing the northern Arabs to redefine "Sudan" as synonymous with themselves. As previously discussed, the name *Bilad al-Sudan* referred to land of the blacks. The northern Arabs redefined this identity in their terms, denying the original meaning and those who were represented by it. The second was the Muslim fundamentalist usurpation of the more moderate Sufi traditions that were historically present in Sudan. Islam has become far more radicalized by postindependence regimes. The first identity hijacking set a precedent for the second one, as the northern Arab elites gained confidence in their ability to manipulate the identity of the Sudanese state.

The secession of South Sudan in 2011 meant Sudan's population became more homogenous, but that population remains diverse. The northern elite's manipulation of Sudanese identity has damaged the attachments of other groups to the state, as is evidenced by the continued conflict on the periphery. Those marginalized groups—particularly rebels from non-Arabs groups in Darfur, South Kordofan, and Blue Nile—continue to equate the regime with discrimination. In early July 2018, the leader of one Darfur rebel group expressed a desire to rebuild Sudan based on citizenship without discrimination, something he argued could not be done under the ruling party ("International Efforts" 2018). The viability of the Sudanese state is at stake as long as it remains defined as the riverain elite would like to define it. A new definition of what it means to be "Sudanese" is needed.

NOTES

The views expressed are the author's own and do not necessarily represent those of the US government.

1. Namely the 1955–72 north-south civil war, the 1983–2005 north-south civil war, the low-intensity conflict in the east from 1996 to 2006, and the ongoing Darfur war.

2. CIA World Factbook, https://www.cia.gov/library/publications/the-world-factbook/geos/su.html, accessed June 18, 2018.

3. Library of Congress, "Country Profile: Sudan," December 2004, https://www.loc.gov/rr/frd/cs/profiles/Sudan-new.pdf; CIA World Factbook, accessed June 18, 2018.

4. Darfur was not incorporated into the Anglo-Egyptian Condominium until 1916 and then was ruled as part of the north, although with even more colonial neglect.

5. A combination of civil war in the south, a declining economic situation, and a repressive political environment led to demonstrations in October 1964 calling for Abboud to step down. He did, in favor of a civilian government, and elections were held in 1965.

6. The NIF was the political party that would take power in a 1989 coup, led by Lt. General Omar al-Bashir and al-Turabi. The NIF was later renamed the National Congress Party (NCP).

7. Nimeiri faced coup attempts in 1971, 1973, 1974, 1976, and 1985.

8. Bashir was at odds with al-Turabi, often touted as the real power behind the regime, over his support of Islamic fundamentalism. Al-Turabi overreached in 1999 when he introduced a bill to limit the president's powers. Bashir then dissolved parliament, declared a state of emergency, and later had Turabi arrested.

9. This idea was given to me by Dr. John Harbeson. I expanded on it slightly for the purpose of this chapter.

REFERENCES

A/Salam, Elfatih, A. 2008. "The Politicization of Ethnic Sentiments in the Sudan: Implications for Nation-Building." *Journal of Third World Studies* 25, no. 1 (Spring), 118–20.

Al-Rahim, Muddathir 'Abd. 1970. "Arabism, Africanism, and Self-Identification in the Sudan." *Journal of Modern African Studies* 8, no. 2 (July), 239–41.

BBC News. 2009. "Q&A: Sudan's Conflict." March 5. http://news.bbc.co.uk/2/hi/africa/3496731.stm

Berman, Bruce, Dickson Eyoh, and Will Kymlicka, eds. 2004. *Ethnicity and Democracy in Africa*. Athens: Ohio University Press.

Burr, J. Millard, and Robert O. Collins. 2008. *Darfur: The Long Road to Disaster*. Princeton, NJ: Marcus Wiener Publishers.

Burton, John W. 1991. "Development and Cultural Genocide in the Sudan." *Journal of Modern African Studies* 29, no. 3 (September), pg. 512.

De Waal, Alex, ed. 2007. *War in Darfur and the Search for Peace*. Global Equity Initiative, Harvard University.

Deng, Francis M. 1995. *War of Visions: Conflict of Identities in the Sudan*. Washington, DC: Brookings Institution.

Flint, Julie, and Alex De Waal. 2005. *Darfur: A Short History of a Long War*. London: Zed Books.

Hyden, Goran. 2006. *African Politics in Comparative Perspective*. Cambridge: Cambridge University Press.

Idris, Amir H. 2005. *Conflict and Politics of Identity in Sudan*. New York: Palgrave Macmillan.

International Commission of Inquiry on Darfur (ICID). 2005. *Report of the International Commission of Inquiry on Darfur to the United Nations Secretary-General*. January. http://www.un.org/news/dh/sudan/com_inq_darfur.pdf

International Crisis Group (ICG). 2002. *God, Oil and Country: Changing the Logic of War in Sudan*. Africa Report no. 39, January. Brussels: International Crisis Group.

International Crisis Group (ICG). 2003. *Sudan's Other Wars*. Africa Briefing, June. Khartoum/Brussels: International Crisis Group.

International Crisis Group (ICG). 2016. *Sudan's Islamists: From Salvation to Survival*. Africa Briefing no. 119, March 21. Nairobi. International Crisis Group.

"International Efforts to Solve Sudan Peace Talks Impasse." 2018. *Radio Dabanga*, July 1. https://www.dabangasudan.org/en/all-news/article/international-efforts-to-solve-sudan-peace-talks-impasse

Kok, Peter. 1996. "Between Radically Restructuring and Deconstruction of State Systems." *Review of African Political Economy* 23, no. 70 (December), pg. 556.

Kron, Josh. 2010. "Islamic Sudan Envisioned If South Secedes." *New York Times*, December 9. https://www.nytimes.com/2010/12/20/world/africa/20sudan.html

Lesch, Ann Mosley. 1998. *The Sudan-Contested National Identities*. Bloomington: Indiana University Press.

Mahmoud, Mahgoub El-Tigani. 2004. "Inside Darfur: Ethnic Genocide by a Governance Crisis." *Comparative Studies of South Asia, Africa, and the Middle East* 24, no. 2, pg. 3.

Manger, Leif. 2004. "Reflections on War and State and the Sudan." *Social Analysis* 48, no. 1 (Spring), 111–12.

Natsios, Andrew S. 2006. "Moving Beyond the Sense of Alarm." In Samuel Totten and Eric Markusen, eds., *Genocide in Darfur: Investigating the Atrocities in the Sudan*, 25–42. New York: Routledge.

O'Fahey, R. S. 1996. "Islam and Ethnicity in Sudan." *Journal of Religion in Africa* 26, no. 3 (August), pgs 259, 261.

Office of the United Nations High Commissioner for Human Rights (OHCHR) and the African Union–United Nations Hybrid Operations in Darfur (UNAMID). 2017. "The Human Rights Situation of Internally Displaced Persons in Darfur 2014–2016." November. https://reliefweb.int/sites/reliefweb.int/files/resources/UNAMID_OHCHR_situation_Darfur2017.pdf

Rothchild, Donald, and Alexander J. Growth. 1995. "Pathological Dimensions of Domestic and International Identity." *Political Science Quarterly* 110, no. 1 (Spring), pgs 70-71.

Salih, M. A. Mohamed. 1998a. "Other Identities: Politics of Sudanese Discursive Narratives." *Identities* 5, no. 1, pgs 5-6.

Salih, M. A. Mohamed. 1998b. "Political Narratives and Identity Formation in post-1989 Sudan."

Salih, M. A. Mohamed, and John Markakis, eds. 1998. *Ethnicity and the State in Eastern Africa*. Uppsala: Nordiska Afrikainstitutet.

Salmon, Jago. 2007. "A Paramilitary Revolution: The Popular Defence Forces." Small Arms Survey HSBA Working Paper no. 10, December. http://www.smallarmssurveysudan.org/fileadmin/docs/working-papers/HSBA-WP-10-Paramilitary-Revolution.pdf

Sharkey, Heather J. 2003. *Living with Colonialism: Nationalism and Culture in the Anglo-Egyptian Sudan*. Berkeley: University of California Press.

Sharkey, Heather J. 2007. "Arab Identity and Ideology in Sudan: The Politics of Language, Ethnicity, and Race." *African Affairs* 107, no. 426 (December), 21–22, 29–30, 33–34, 37.

Smith, Stephen. 2007. "Sudan's History in Regional Context: A Timeline." October. Unpublished.

Wai, Dunstan M. 1981. *The African-Arab Conflict in the Sudan*. New York: Africana Publishing.

Warburg, Gabriel. 1995. "Mahdism and Islamism in Sudan." *International Journal of Middle East Studies* 27, no. 2 (May), pgs. 224, 230, 232-234.

Welsh, David. 1996. "Ethnicity in Sub-Saharan Africa." *International Affairs* 72, no. 3 (July), pg. 485.

CONTRIBUTORS

Wale Adebanwi is the Rhodes Professor of Race Relations, Director of the African Studies Centre, and fellow of St Antony's College, University of Oxford, United Kingdom. He is the author of *Yoruba Elites and Ethnic Politics in Nigeria: Obáfémi Awólówò and Corporate Agency* (2014) and editor or coeditor of six books, including *The Political Economy of Everyday Life in Africa: Beyond the Margins* (2017). He is also a coeditor of *Africa: Journal of the International African Institute*.

Yasmine Berriane is a tenured researcher at the Centre Maurice Halbwachs, *Centre national de la recherche scientifique*, in Paris. She has previously been a senior researcher and lecturer at the University of Zurich (2013–2017) and a researcher at the Leibniz-Zentrum Moderner Orient in Berlin (2011–2013). Trained in political science and Middle Eastern studies in Germany, the United Kingdom, and France, she is mainly interested in political and social transformations in Middle Eastern and North African states, particularly in contexts where neoliberal reforms and norms are introduced. She is the author of *Femmes, associations et politique à Casablanca* (2013) and of numerous articles.

Alex K. D. Frempong is a Senior Lecturer at the Department of Political Science, University of Ghana. He teaches Electoral Politics in Ghana at the undergraduate level and Governance and Democracy at the graduate level. He has to his credit several published articles and books on elections and governance in Ghana and Africa. He was an African Presidential Scholar at the University of Michigan in 2008–9. He has attended and presented papers at conference across the globe.

Timothy Gibbs is a Lecturer in African history at University College London and is author of *Mandela's Kinsmen: Nationalist Elites and Apartheid's First Bantustan* (2014).

Danny Hoffman is a Professor of anthropology and the Bartley-Dobb Professor for the Study and Prevention of Violence at the Jackson School of International Studies at the University of Washington. He is the author of two books on West Africa's Mano River region, *The War Machines: Young Men and Violence in Sierra Leone and Liberia* (2011, Duke University Press), and *Monrovia Modern: Urban Form and Political Imagination in Liberia* (2017, Duke University Press).

Roukaya Kasenally is a democracy scholar, CEO of the African Media Initiative (AMI), and Senior Lecturer on Media and Political Systems at the University of Mauritius. Since July 2015, she has been a board director for the Electoral Institute for Sustainable Democracy in Africa. She has been a Regan Fascell Democracy Fellow at the National Endowment for Democracy (Washington, DC) (2011–12) and a Draper Hills Democracy Fellow at Stanford University (2015). Kasenally has published widely on media and democratic systems.

Michael C. Lambert is an Associate Professor in the African, African American and Diaspora Studies and Adjunct Associate Professor, Anthropology, at the University of North Carolina at Chapel Hill. His research has principally been in francophone West Africa with a primary focus on issues related to migration. His first book, *Longing for Exile: Migration and the Making of a Translocal Community in Senegal*, explores the social history of urban migration in a Senegalese community. In addition, he has published on francophone intellectual history, gender, youth politics, and political conflict. He also works in the field of American Indian studies, and his most recent book, *Up from These Hills: Memories of Cherokee Boyhood* (coauthored) explores the American Indian experience in the mid-twentieth century.

Godwin Onuoha is a Lecturer in the Department of Anthropology and Program in African Studies at Princeton University. He was previously the African Humanities Post-Doctoral Research Associate at Princeton University, where he co-convened the African Humanities Colloquium. Prior to that he was an African Research Fellow at the Human Sciences Research Council, South Africa. He is a political anthropologist with interdisciplinary research interests that broadly intersect identity politics, resource governance, and development in Africa. He is the author of *Challenging the State in Africa: MASSOB and the Crisis of Self-Determination in Nigeria* (LIT Verlag, 2011), and his articles have appeared in *Nationalism and Ethnic Politics, African Studies, Ethnic and Racial Studies, Review of African Political Economy, Current Sociology*, and *National Identities*. He is on the editorial board of *Democratic Theory: An Interdisciplinary Journal*.

Rogers Orock is a Lecturer in the Department of Social Anthropology, University of the Witwatersrand, Johannesburg, South Africa. His work on elites and accountability focuses on development, governance, and struggles for democratic participation. Rogers's work on these themes has appeared in peer-reviewed journals such as *Africa, Cultural Dynamics, Critique of Anthropology, Anthropological Quarterly*, and others.

Anja Osei is a Senior Research Fellow and Lecturer at the Chair of International Politics and Conflict Management, University of Konstanz, Germany. She holds an MA and PhD in African studies from the University of Leipzig. Her current main research interest is in democracy and autocracy in sub-Saharan Africa. She is focusing on power structures, elite networks, and political institutions such as parliaments across various regime types. Anja's work has appeared in such journals as *African Affairs, Party Politics*, and *Democratization*.

Jennifer Pekkinen has worked on Africa at the Department of State for over fifteen years and is currently an analyst focused on Sudan and South Sudan. She spent two years as the Deputy National Intelligence Officer covering Central Africa and the Sudans at the Directorate of National Intelligence. Pekkinen has a MA in international affairs with a focus on African studies from Johns Hopkins–School of Advanced International Studies and an MA in international affairs from American University.

Naomi Pendle is a postdoctoral researcher in the Firoz Lalji Centre for Africa, London School of Economics. Her research primarily focuses on conflict, violence, law, displacement, public authority, and humanitarian aid, principally in Africa. Her research in South Sudan since 2009 has included extended periods of ethnographic research in the western Nuer and Dinka, as well as the use of other creative methods. Her work has been published in various journals including *Africa, American Ethnologist*, and the *Journal of Eastern African Studies*. Her ongoing research includes projects on patterns of violence and restraint in South Sudan's wars; the moral dynamics of money in politics in Africa; the politics of return in South Sudan; and the role of religion in peacemaking.

Ramola Ramtohul is Senior Lecturer in sociology and gender studies at the University of Mauritius. She has published on gender and politics, citizenship, higher education, and elite migration in Mauritius. Ramtohul has received research awards from the University of Cape Town, American Association of University Women, University of Cambridge, and University of Pretoria and is currently coeditor of *Journal of Contemporary African Studies*.

Emmanuel K. Siaw is a Doctoral Researcher at the Department of Politics and International Relations, Royal Holloway University of London. His research interests include understanding Africa's international relations through ideologies, African agency in international relations, and elections and democracy in Africa.

Roger Southall is an Emeritus Professor in sociology at the University of the Witwatersrand and Professorial Research Associate, SOAS, University of London.. He has written extensively on African and South African politics and society. His books include *Imperialism or Solidarity? International Labour and South African Trade Unions* (1995), *Liberation Movements in Power: Party and State in Southern Africa* (2013), and *The New Black Middle Class in South Africa* (2016). He is presently embarking on a new book project on whites and democracy in South Africa.

INDEX

Abacha, Sani, 293
Abboud, Ibrahim, 373
Abdullah, Ibrahim, 47
Abel, Richard, 208
Abiola, M. K. O., 291, 292
Abubakar, Abdulsalam, 293
academic elites, 230
accountability, defined, 3, 8–13, 19–20, 218, 249; democratic accountability, 2, 19, 132, 240; horizontal accountability, 220, 227–229, 233–237; local accountability, 341–342, 343, 344, 349–351, 357, 360; social accountability, 9, 12, 17, 220, 227, 228–229, 237–239; vertical accountability, 220, 227–229, 231–233. *See also* democratic government establishment and operations; elites, defined; nonaccountability (Mauritius); political accountability
accounts (narratives), 12
Acheampong regime (Ghana), 117
Achebe, Chinua, 287
Achu, Simon Achidi, 262–263
Achuzia, Joe, 298–299
Action Group (AG, Nigeria), 311–331; accomplishments of, 321, 330; Coker Commission on, 323–329; corporation (Histadrut) funding model, 318–320, 322; funding proposals and study findings, 317–320; goals of, 311–312, 314–315, 320, 321; indigenous entrepreneurship and, 312, 320; National Bank of Nigeria funding, 317, 319, 320, 323–326; operations of, 315; party-monialism and, 309, 312, 320–321, 331; property development investment by, 319–320, 322, 327–328; public policy work by, 314

activism. *See* protests; Senegalese politics, student activism in; South Africa, rights debates chronology; universities, as political activism path
Addis Ababa Agreement (1972), 374–375
Addo, Nana Akufo, 121
Adebanwi, Wale, 7, 282
Adua, Yar', 297
aesthetics of accountability, 20
AFRA (Association for Rural Advancement, South Africa), 200–201, 203
African elites. *See under* elites
African governments, broad discussions and comparisons, 1, 19, 62, 208, 284; education availability, 137–139, 142, 152, 330; electoral representation in, 15, 85–90, 92–93, 103–106, 254; elite-citizen linkages, 90–91, 249, 253; generational divide, 41; historical scholarship since decolonization, 4–8, 10; indigenous self-rule, 17, 371; neopatrimonialism, 33, 309, 310–311, 313, 329–331; party politics, 10–11, 91, 145, 308–309, 310; political funding, 308–309, 313; postcolonial administrative and technical employment gap, 138–140, 143–144, 152; postcolonial power consolidation, 145; "public" and "private" spheres, 16, 260, 261; strength/weakness, 14, 228–229; structural adjustment programs, 142; warlord politics and big-man era, 44–45, 49, 53; women in, 87, 89. *See also* democratic government establishment and operations; parliament (Ghana and Togo); specific country

391

African identity, 368, 370–371
Africanist scholarship, 18, 86, 89–90, 331
African National Congress (ANC, South Africa): corruption reputation, 171, 172, 173, 174–175, 179, 181–183; Dlamini-Zuma and, 172–173, 175, 177–179; EFF opposition, 174–175; elite transition and, 160–162; land rights issues and, 192; Malema and, 173–175; as power elite, 164, 166–167; Ramaphosa and, 173, 175, 177, 178–179, 182–183; white monopoly capital and, 167, 168; Zuma-Gupta brothers association and, 2, 18, 170–173, 175–176, 182. *See also* South Africa; Zuma, Jacob
African nationalism, 207, 285, 366–368
Africa Works (Chabal and Daloz), 86
Afrobarometer data, 92, 94, 97, 98, 132, 232, 233
Afro-Creoles (Mauritius), 18, 222, 226–227
Afro-pessimism, 310, 321
age: generation gap in Igbo politics, 299–300; generation gap in Sierra Leone, 34–35, 39–42; representation issues in Ghana and Togo, 89, 94, 96, 97, 103–104. *See also* Senegalese politics, student activism in
agency, 259
Agwu, J. U., 287
Ahidjo, Ahmadou, 269, 270–271
Ajasin, Adekunle, 293
Aka Ikenga ("intellectual wing" of Ohanaeze), 281, 291, 298, 299, 303
Akan (ethnic group), 98, 99, 104, 130
Akintola, S. L. A., 319, 323–324, 327, 328
Akoto, Baffuor Osei, 117
Akpamgbo, Clement, 292
Akposso (ethnic group), 98, 99
Akudibillah, Joseph, 126
Akufo Addo, Nana, 121, 128, 129
Akufo regime (Ghana), 117
Ala Adjetey, Peter, 125, 127
al-Bashir, Omar, 366, 375, 376
Alder, Simeon, 114

Algiers, 137
Alliance for Change (AFC, Ghana), 121
Alliance pour la république (Senegal), 151
Allison, Simon, 361
All Nigeria People's Party (ANPP), 296
All People's Congress (APC) party (Sierra Leone), 36, 39, 47
All People's Party (Ghana), 118
All People's Party (APP, Nigeria), 294
al-Mahdi, Sadiq, 373–374, 375
al-Turabi, Hassan, 374, 375, 377
Amin, Samir, 6
Amin Dada, Idi, 49–50, 52
Amponsah, R. R., 117
Angola, 137
Ankrah, J. A., 117
anticolonialism, 138–139, 266–267, 285, 315, 370
anticorruption efforts (Mauritius), 220, 227, 228, 233–239. *See also* corruption
Antoh, S. G., 117
Apaloo, M. K., 117, 118
apartheid, 160–161, 189. *See also* chiefdom, traditional (South Africa); South Africa
apolitical elites (Morocco), 74–77, 80, 81
Appadurai, Arjun, 253, 273
Appiah, Joe, 117
Arab-Fur war (1987-89), 379
Arab-Islamic "Sudanese" identity, 365, 366, 370, 371, 372, 373; NIF/NCP and, 375–376, 377, 381. *See also* Sudanese identity construction
Arab Spring protests, 150
Arab Sudanese elites. *See* Sudanese identity construction
Arc-en-ciel (Togo), 96
Arkaah, Kow Nkensen, 121–122
Armed Forces Revolutionary Council (Ghana), 117
Arriola, Leonardo R., 89, 104
A/Salam, Elfatih A., 370
Asamoah, Obed, 127
associational sphere, legitimacy claims

(Morocco), 60, 62, 63–68; associations' functions, 64–65, 71, 81; clientelism and, 63, 66–67; increased number of associations, 63–64, 65, 68, 72, 81; infrastructure development for, 65; lines of argumentation, 18, 62, 68–70, 80; monarchy involvement, 75, 77–80, 81; participation in, 60, 62, 63–64, 67, 71, 77, 80; training programs, 71–72; volunteering/professionalization split, 73–74. *See also* local elites (Morocco); National Initiative for Human Development (INDH, Morocco)
Association for Rural Advancement (AFRA, South Africa), 200–201, 203
Atta, William Ofori, 118
audit culture, 9
authoritarianism. *See* democratic government establishment and operations; parliament (Ghana and Togo); representation theory
autochthony to represented locale, 68–70, 72, 80
Awolowo, Obafemi, 7, 311, 313–318, 320–321, 323, 325–328
Azikiwe, Nnamdi ("Zik"), 284–285, 289, 290, 297, 313–314, 324

Baah, Moses Dani, 126
Babangida, Ibrahim, 291
Bah, Abu Bakkar, 39
Bahr al-Ghazal, South Sudan. *See* home communities of South Sudanese elites; South Sudanese elites
Bam, Fikile, 199–200, 202, 209–210
Bantu Authorities Act (South Africa, 1952), 191
Bantu Self-Government Act (1959), 191
Bantustans (South Africa), 188–189, 191, 193–194, 196–199, 202–204, 206–207. *See also* Native Reserves (South Africa)
Barro, Fadel, 150
Bawa, Rashid, 126
Bayart, Jean-François, 15, 41
Bello, Ahmadu, 313–314

belongingness, 18; politics of belonging, 259–261, 268, 269–270. *See also* ethnic groups; Sudanese identity construction
Ben (Moba, ethnic group), 98, 99
Ben-Gurion, David, 318, 319
Benin, 137, 143
Bennani-Chraïbi, Mounia, 61
beny hakuma (South Sudanese elites), term defined, 345. *See also* South Sudanese elites *(beny hakuma)*
Bérenger, Paul, 225
Berman, Bruce, 366
Berriane, Yasmine, 18
Best, Heinrich, 87
best-loser system (Mauritius), 219
Biafra, 283, 285–286; neo-Biafra groups, 281, 298–302, 303
Biko, Steve, 198
Bilad al-Sudan, 372, 382. *See also* Sudan
Bio, Julius Maada, 34
Biya, Paul, 252–253, 257, 258, 262–264, 269, 271–272
Bjarngard, Elin, 89
Bjornson, Richard, 269
Black Book, The: Imbalance of Power and Wealth in Sudan (JEM), 379–380
Black Community Programmes (South Africa), 198, 199, 209
Black Consciousness Movement, 188, 199–200, 208
black economic empowerment policy (BEE, South Africa), 162, 167, 175, 176
Black Lawyers Association (South Africa), 202
Black Skin, White Masks (Fanon), 138
Blay, Freddie, 126
Blundo, Giorgio, 9, 17
Boahen, Adu, 122
Bond, Patrick, 45, 161
Bono, Irene, 62
Bophuthatswana (Bantustan), 197
Boudet, Catherine, 223
"Boul Falé" (Positive Black Soul), 150
Bourdieu, Pierre, 342, 353
de La Bourdonnais, Mahe, 221

bourgeoisie: local and indigenous formations, 321–322; in Mauritius, 223; in Morocco, 60–61; in South Africa, 160. *See also* elites, defined
Bratton, Michael, 60
Brechenmacher, Saskia, 240
Brown, Peter, 194, 200, 201
Budlender, Geoff, 200–201, 202, 204, 205, 206
Buhari, Muhammadu, 2, 296, 301
Burnell, Peter, 309
Burton, Michael, 2, 282
Busia, K. A., 118
business elites, 19; corporate elites in South Africa, 165–167, 180–181. *See also* economic elites
Butler, Judith, 8–9

Cabral, Amilcar, 6
Cameroon, 19, 249–273; constitution of, 258; elections in, 257–258, 263; geography of, 261; liberalization and democratization history, 252, 258, 259–263, 268–269, 272; medical schools in, 265–266; multiparty politics transition in, 257, 258, 268, 273; politics of belonging, 269–270; redistributive politics under Ahidjo, 270–271; reunification anniversary celebrations, 252–253; student protests, 143. *See also* development discourse (Cameroon); South West Elite Association (SWELA, Cameroon)
Cameroon People's Democratic Movement (CPDM), 257, 262
Canca, Richard, 193, 194, 199
capitalism, 43–44, 161–163, 165–166, 309. *See also* neoliberalism
Carothers, Thomas, 240
Carvalho, Jean-Paul, 114
Casablanca, Morocco, 67–68
cattle, as wealth and status marker, 344, 349–352, 360
Center for Democratic Governance (Ghana), 93

Centre de Recherche et de Sondage d'Opinions (Togo), 93
Cerveaux, Roger, 227
Chabal, Patrick, 12–13, 14–16, 86, 90, 91
Chad, 379
Chambras, Mohammed Ibn Chambras, 126
Cheikh Anta Diop University. *See* University of Dakar (Cheikh Anta Diop University, Senegal)
chiefdom, traditional, 16, 36–37, 115
chiefdom, traditional (South Africa): apartheid-state backed, 189, 190, 191, 193, 194, 197, 203–205, 208; CONTRALSEA and, 190, 205–206, 208–209; post-apartheid power, 205–207, 208–209. *See also* South Africa, land rights in
Chinweizu, Ibekwe, 292
Christian humanitarianism (South Africa), 190, 195
Christians, representation issues, 99
Christian schools (Sudan), 376
Chukwumerije, Uche, 292
Church Agricultural Project (CAP), 201
church funding (South Sudan), 344, 357–360
Ciskei (Bantustan), 197
citizenship (Sudan), 373
civic public, 16, 260
civil conflict theory, 114
civil servants: in Cameroon, 265; in Ghana, 118; in Mauritius, 228, 230, 234, 239; in Morocco, 61–62, 67, 71; in Nigeria, 286
civil society: scholarship on, 14, 19, 62; social accountability through, 228, 237, 238, 239
civil society organizations (CSOs, Cameroon), 259
civil society organizations and associations (Morocco), 65
Claassens, Annika, 207
claim-making politics, 249–250, 251, 253, 273; SWELA and, 255, 256, 261, 265,

267, 270. *See also* South Africa, land rights in

class: debates on elites' status, 5; middle class in Sudan, 370; power and privilege and, 18; social mobility and, 91, 223. *See also* ethnicity and class interests of elites (Mauritius); South Africa

classrooms. *See* education

clientelism: associational, in Morocco, 63, 66–67; in Ghana, 90, 92; in Mauritius, 226; party clientelism, 309; in representation theory, 86, 90, 91, 92–93, 94; SWELA and, 262–263. *See also* corruption

Cohen, Abner, 40, 267

Cohen, Robin, 5

Coker, George Ayoola, 324–325

Coker Commission (Nigeria), 323–329

Cole, Femi Claudius, 54–55

Collectif Sauvons le Togo (CST), 96

colleges. *See* universities

colonialism: anticolonial theorists and revolutionaries, 138–139, 266–267, 285, 315, 370; in Cameroon, 261, 266; ethnic principle and ethnicity defined during, 282–283, 366, 371, 382; in Ghana, 115–117; Igbo politics during, 284–286, 288; legitimacy claims through experience of, 40; in Mauritius, 219; missionary school of modernity, 10; in Nigeria, 284–286, 288, 314; scholarship on bourgeoisie of, 322; in South Africa, 189; in Sudan, 369–371, 373, 381, 382. *See also* independence

colonialism, power transfer after: in Cameroon, 255, 268, 269; development's importance in, 308, 309, 311; education's importance in, 138–139, 152; ethnoregional struggles during, 329; historical scholarship since decolonization, 4–8, 10; in Mauritius, 219, 221–227, 229; in Nigeria, 7, 284, 314–315; party politics, 10–11, 308, 315; postcolonial governance characteristics, 16, 32–33, 38, 53, 260–261; scholarship on, 4–6; in Sierra Leone, 40, 41. *See also* education; party politics

colored elite (Mauritius), 223

Comaroff, Jean, 9–10

Comaroff, John, 9–10

Communist Party (South Africa), 195

compensation. *See* financial compensation; income; wealth

Competition Commission (2008, Mauritius), 235

comprehensive peace agreement (CPA, South Sudan), 340, 345–346, 378

Congress of South African Trade Unions (COSATU), 162, 166, 169, 175, 181

Congress of Traditional Leaders (CONTRALESA, South Africa), 190, 205–206, 208–209

consociationalism, 114, 223

Convention People's Party (CPP, Ghana), 112, 115–117, 126

corporate elites (South Africa), 165–167, 180–181. *See also* economic elites

corruption: ANC reputation, 171, 172, 173, 174–175, 179, 181–183; anticorruption efforts, in Mauritius, 220, 227, 228, 233–239; in Cameroon, 269; cattle investment and, 351; by chiefs in Bantustans, 203; Coker Commission claims (Nigeria), 323–329; by ethnic elites, during colonialism, 282–283; funding political parties and, 309, 311; in Mauritius, 220, 226, 227, 228, 229, 231, 233–239; in Morocco, 76; protests against, 2, 3; in South Sudan, 340–341, 347; in Sudan, 380; Zuma reputation, 2, 167–168, 171–172, 175. *See also* Action Group (AG, Nigeria); clientelism; funding political parties

Corruption Perceptions Index (Transparency International report), 229

Côte d'Ivoire, 49

Cotta, Maurizio, 87

Credit Suisse, 159

cultural politics, 7, 19, 253, 268–273. *See also under* ethnic groups

Curé, Maurice, 223
currency, 19–20

Dalindyebo, Sabata, 194, 197, 207
Daloz, Jean-Pascal, 7–8, 16–17, 86, 90, 91
Dangala (Arab tribe), 365, 368
Danquah, J. B., 117
Dapaah, Albert Kan, 129
Darfur region (Sudan), 378–380, 382–383
Darga, L. Amadee, 232
de Boeck, Filip, 33, 47, 48
Deleuze, Gilles, 52
democracies, components of, 1, 240; media, 228, 237–239. *See also* accountability, defined; corruption; elections; parliament; representation theory
Democracy Compromised (Ntsebeza), 209
democratic accountability, 2, 19, 132, 240. *See also* accountability, defined
democratic government establishment and operations: in Cameroon, 252, 258, 262–263, 268–269, 272; in Ghana, 95; in Mauritius, 219, 229, 239–240; in Nigeria, 291, 293–294, 312, 328–329; in Senegal, 142, 145; in Sierra Leone, 37, 42, 48–49; in South Africa, 161, 163, 167, 168–169, 176, 204; success metrics, 231–232, 240, 254. *See also* accountability, defined; colonialism; elections; funding political parties; Ghana, elite conflict and consensus in; parliament; party politics; representation theory; South Africa, rights debates chronology
Democratic People's Party (Ghana), 122
Democratic Republic of Congo, 143
democratic reversals and stability (Ghana): emerging issues, 130–131; during Fourth Republic, 119–132; independence gained, 112–113; postindependence era, 117–118, 130; preindependence era, 115–117, 130; safeguarding, 112, 131–132. *See also* elections (Ghana); Ghana, elite conflict and consensus in; power transfers
Democratic Socialist Party (Senegal), 152

Deng, Frances, 367, 373, 381–382
Department of Land Affairs (South Africa), 204–205
descriptive representation, analysis of Ghana and Togo parliament, 86, 96–99, 103–104, 105, 106; research methods, 93, 94
descriptive representation scholarship, 87–88, 89, 91, 93, 96
developmental states, 308, 309, 310–311, 329–331. *See also* Action Group (Nigeria)
development discourse (Cameroon), 250; accountability through, 268–272; in Mundemba Declaration, 255–258; redistribution politics in, 256–257, 267–271; reunification anniversary celebrations, 253; in SWELA constitution, 259, 260; through memorandums, 267–268. *See also* Cameroon
De Waal, Alex, 343, 348, 376
diasporas, 18
Didiza, Thoko, 205, 206
"Diogoufi" ("Nothing Has Changed," Keur Gui Crew), 151
Diop, Cheikh Anta, 138. *See also* University of Dakar (Cheikh Anta Diop University, Senegal)
Diop, Samba, 6
Diouf, Abdou, 145–146, 147
Dippel, Christian, 114
distinction, elites' establishment of, 342
Dlamini-Zuma, Nkosazana, 172–173, 175, 177–179
Doctor, Manilal, 222–223
Dogan, Mattei, 93
Doggale, Santo Loku Pio, 359–360
Doherty, Bayo, 317, 320
Dryzek, John S., 87
DuBois, W. E. B., 139
Dubow, Saul, 190
Dunn, John, 255

Eastern Region government (Nigeria), 313–314

Economic Crimes Office (ECO, Mauritius), 234
economic crisis (1980s), 11
economic elites: party-monialism and, 312; in South Africa, 160, 166, 168; in SWELA, 251, 252
economic elites (Mauritius), 220, 221, 240; Corporate Governance accountability efforts, 233, 236; horizontal accountability for, 235–237; national unity and power-sharing among, 223–224; neoliberalism and, 226; social accountability for, 238–239
Economic Freedom Fighters (EFF), 173–175
Economist, The (magazine), 325
economy, national: economic growth in South Africa, 168–169; in Mauritius, 219–220; national wealth management, in Cameroon, 272; oil wealth in South Sudan, 345–346, 351. *See also* African governments, broad discussions and comparisons; development; South Africa
education, 5; academic elites, 230; of African citizens in 1960s, 139; African governments' focus on, 137–139, 142, 152, 330; audit culture and, 9; economic prospects and, across Africa, 139–140, 142–143, 144, 152; economic prospects and, in Senegal, 138, 142–143, 144, 146–147, 150–151, 152; elite alumni associations, 260; of legal elite in South Africa, 193–194; in Mauritius, 223; medical schools in Cameroon, 265–266; MPs' level of, 94, 97–98, 104; in Nigeria, 321, 353; in South Sudan, 344, 353–357, 360; SWELA members' level of, 251–252; training programs for association leaders, in Morocco, 71–72. *See also* Senegalese politics, student activism in; universities
Egbe, Emmanuel Tabi, 252
Egypt: Al-Azhar University founded, 137; Anglo-Egyptian rule in Sudan, 339, 351, 353, 369, 373, 374; Muslim Brotherhood, 374; Sufism in, 368; Turco-Egyptian invasions of Sudan, 369, 373
Eisenstadt, Todd A., 313
Ekeh, Peter, 16, 260–261
Ekpe (Ekpo) societies, 260
Ekwueme, Alex, 290, 293–294, 295–296
elections: in Cameroon, 257–258, 263; as component of democratic accountability, 15, 85, 87, 114, 229, 254; electoral representation, adoption across Africa, 15, 85–90, 92–93, 103–106, 254; funding political parties and, 313; in Liberia and Kenya, 34, 49; in Mauritius, 223, 224, 225, 229, 231–233, 236–237; in Morocco, 61–62, 63, 67, 76; in Senegal, 145–151; in South Africa, 161, 165, 172–174, 178–179, 181–182 , 204; in South Sudan, 347; in Sudan, 349, 361, 375; in Togo, 96; in United States and France, 34, 43; vertical accountability and, 228, 229, 231–233; women as elected elites, 18, 61, 67. *See also* parliament; representation theory; Tarawalley, Mohammed, Jr. (MT), presidential campaign (Sierra Leone)
elections (Ghana), 105, 112–113, 116, 117, 119–132; 1992, 95, 119–120, 123–124; 1996, 95, 121, 122–124; 2000, 123, 124–127; 2004, 127; 2008, 95, 128; 2012, 95, 128–129; 2016, 129; electoral reforms, 120–121, 129
elections (Nigeria), 285, 290, 291–294, 295–298, 300–301, 314; AG and, 317, 323
Electoral Commission (EC, Ghana), 120–121, 130
elite capture, 218, 226, 241
elite conflict and consensus. *See* Ghana, elite conflict and consensus in
elite lawyers. *See* legal elites
elites, collusion among (Mauritius), 220, 230, 235, 239, 240–241

elites, defined, 2, 220–221, 230, 240, 249; exclusivity and agency attributes, 259, 260, 261; nomenclature debates, 5–6; power elite (South Africa), 160, 163–167; research deficit, 13–14; scholarly research and theory, 4–8, 13–14, 88–89, 113–115, 282–284. *See also* accountability, defined; bourgeoisie; economic elites; legal elites; local elites; political elites; South Sudanese elites *(beny hakuma)*; South West Elite Association (SWELA, Cameroon); women, elite formation of

elites, educating new elite class (Senegal). *See* universities

elites-masses interaction, 2–3, 19, 20, 90–91, 249, 253

elite transition (South Africa), 160–162, 164, 180–181. *See also* power transfers

Elvis, Ngolle Ngolle, 264

Enaw, A. T, 252

Endeley, E. M. L., 314

Enechukwu, Ifeanyi, 298

equal, nondiscriminatory treatment, 219, 371

equality, income: income inequality, 7, 149, 159, 180, 183, 220. *See also* wealth

Equal Opportunities Commission (Mauritius), 233

Eriksen, Thomas Hylland, 222

Esaiasson, Peter, 94

Eskom, 170, 176

Ethiopia, 143, 345, 353

ethnic groups: in Cameroon, 258, 261, 264, 268; ethnic principle and ethnicity defined during colonialism, 282–283, 366, 371, 382; ethnoregional elites, 258, 268, 271–272, 329; indigenous self-rule, 17, 371; Sudanese identity construction and, 366–368. *See also* Igbo (ethnic group); South West Elite Association (SWELA, Cameroon); Sudanese identity construction; specific group

ethnic groups (Ghana): electoral issues, 130; representation issues, 90–91, 94, 95, 96, 98–99, 104

ethnic identity construction theory, 366–367. *See also* Sudanese identity construction

ethnicity and class interests of elites (Mauritius), 219; collusion in, 220, 230, 235, 239, 240–241; Franco-Mauritians, 18, 221, 222, 223–224, 235; Hindu hegemony, 223, 226; Indo-Mauritius, 18, 222–223; national unity and power-sharing, 223–224; neoliberalism and, 226–227; phases of establishment, 221–227; religious groups and, 230, 236–237

ethnic politics and political elite (Nigeria), 280; First Republic tripod theory, 294–295; Hausa-Fulani, 283, 284, 287, 292–293, 313; Yoruba, 7, 283, 284, 287, 313. *See also* Action Group (AG, Nigeria); Igbo (ethnic group); Ohanaeze Ndi-Igbo (Igbo sociocultural group, Nigeria)

Everyday Corruption and the State (Blundo and Olivier de Sardan), 9

eviction and forced land removals (South Africa), 190, 191, 195, 197, 200, 203, 205

Ewe (ethnic group), 98, 99, 104

exclusivity, 259, 260–261

Eyadema, Gnassingbe, 50

Eyadema, Gnassingbé, 95–96

Eyoh, Dickson, 366

Eze, Arthur, 293

Ezeife, Chukwuemeka, 292, 293

Ezeoke, Edwin Ume, 293

Falae, Olu, 294

Fanon, Frantz, 6, 138, 151

Federal Military Government (FMG, Nigeria), 286–287

Fifth Parliament of Ghana, 95

financial compensation: cattle used for, in South Sudan, 351–352; wage legitimization for local elites, in Morocco, 72–74, 81. *See also* income; wealth

Fisher, Justin, 313

Fomenky, Chief, 252

formal representation, 87

Fou Malade, 150
France, 34, 42, 43
Franco-Mauritians, 18, 221, 222, 223–224, 235
Freetown, Sierra Leone, 35–36
Freire, Paulo, 198
Front de patriotes pour le Démocratie (FPD, Togo), 96
Fumanti, Mattia, 355
funding political parties, 308–309, 313, 317–331; Coker Commission (Nigeria) and, 323–329; corporation (Histadrut) model, 318–320, 322; donations and bank loans, 317; party-monialism, 309, 312, 320–321, 331. *See also* Action Group (AG, Nigeria); party politics

Gandhi, Mahatma, 222–223
Garang, John, 345–346, 347, 354, 359, 377–378
Garangists, 347–348, 354
Gasa, Nomboniso, 207
Gbadamosi, Alhaji S. O., 317
Geertz, Clifford, 366
gender, elite formation and, 18; MT and, 51–52, 54–56; SWELA membership and, 251. *See also* women, elite formation of
gender, representation issues, 94, 97, 105. *See also* women, representation issues
General Idi Amin Dada: A Self-Portrait (documentary), 49
generation gap: in Igbo politics, 299–300; in Sierra Leone, 34–35, 39–42
George Enonchong, Enow-Orock, 252, 265
Geschiere, Peter, 14, 269, 271
Ghana: clientelism in, 90, 92; independence gained, 112–113; multiparty politics in, 95, 116–118, 119–120; University of Ghana founded, 137. *See also* elections (Ghana); parliament (Ghana and Togo)
Ghana, elite conflict and consensus in, 112–132; emerging issues, 130–131; during Fourth Republic, 119–132; institutionalization for accountability, 113–114, 117, 131; postindependence era, 117–118, 130; preindependence era, 115–117, 130; research context, 113–115; VAT issue, 121. *See also* democratic reversals and stability (Ghana); elections (Ghana); National Democratic Congress (NDC, Ghana)
Gibbs, Timothy, 18
Gigaba, Malusi, 167, 172
global elites, 113
Gnassingbé, Faure, 96
Gnassingbé dynasty (Togo), 95–96
Goetz, Anne Marie, 218, 241
good governance concept, 218, 234, 236
Gordhan, Pravin, 167, 168, 171–172, 173
Gore, Charles, 17, 250–251
government elites. *See* political elites
government of South Sudan (GoSS), 340, 346–347, 354
government of Sudan (GoS), 340
government sphere (South Sudan), 345, 358–359. *See also* home communities of South Sudanese elites
government types. *See* African governments, broad discussions and comparisons; colonialism; democratic government establishment and operations; power transfers
Grant, Ruth W., 9
grassroots organizations, 63, 64, 78
Great Alliance (Ghana), 122, 124
Greenhouse, Carol, 329
Groth, Alexander, 367
Growth, Employment and Redistribution (GEAR) program (South Africa), 161–162, 169
Guardian, The, 361
Guattari, Félix, 52
Gumede, Archie, 195
Gupta, Ajay, 171
Gupta, Atul, 171

Gupta brothers, 2, 18, 170–173, 175–176, 182
Gurib-Fakim, Ameenah, 231

Hanekom, Derek, 203, 204, 205
Hausa-Fulani (ethnic group), 283, 284, 287, 292–293, 313. *See also* Igbo (ethnic group)
Hayatou, Sadou, 258
health care (Ghana), 126
higher education. *See* education; universities
Higley, John, 2, 282
Hindu elites (Mauritius), 223, 226
hip-hop music and student activism (Senegal), 150–151
Histadrut trade union (Israel), 318–319
Holomisa, Pathekile, 206, 207
home communities of South Sudanese elites, 339–361; cattle importance in, 349–352; church construction in, 357–360; education in, 354; elites' distance from, 341–342; home sphere, term, 345, 358–359; importance of, 344–349; school construction in, 344, 353–357, 360. *See also* South Sudanese elites (*beny hakuma*)
horizontal accountability, 220, 227–229, 233–237
House of Bondage (Mqotsi), 193
Hughes, Begyina, 127
human rights organizations: in Mauritius, 233; South African rights debates and, 189, 190, 200–201, 202–204
Huntington, Samuel P., 113, 132
Hyden, Goran, 380

identity politics: in Cameroon, 269; ethnic identity construction theory, 366–367; politics of belonging, 259–261, 268, 269–270. *See also* nationalism; Sudanese identity construction
Idris, Amir, 369, 370–371, 372, 374
Igbo (ethnic group), 280–304, 313; colonial-era politics and, 284–286, 288; generation gap and, 299–300; Igbo nationalism, 281, 285; Igbo Presidency Project, 295–296; Igbo unions, 285, 288; marginalization of, 286–287, 299; postwar perception of, 283, 286; precolonial society of, 284; state creation for, 287; tripartite political division, 290, 296. *See also* Ohanaeze Ndi-Igbo (Igbo sociocultural group, Nigeria)
Ikedife, Dozie, 298
Ikpeme, Bassey, 291–292
income: salary of university graduates, 138, 143; wage legitimization for local elites (Morocco), 72–74, 81. *See also* wealth
income inequality, 7, 149, 159, 180, 183, 220. *See also* South Africa
incorporation (political strategy), 283, 302, 303–304
independence: elites' role in achieving, 221; era of, across Africa, 284; Ghana gains, 112–113; Mauritius gains, 219, 223; Nigeria gains, 285; north/south unification in Sudan, 371–373, 382; universities founded to fill administrative positions after, 138, 139, 152. *See also* colonialism
Independent Commission Against Corruption (ICAC, Mauritius), 233, 234–235
INDH. *See* National Initiative for Human Development (INDH, Morocco)
Indian South Africans, 18
indigenous bourgeoisie, 321–322
indigenous entrepreneurship, 312, 320
indigenous groups. *See* ethnic groups
Indigenous Peoples of Biafra (IPOB), 301
Indo-Mauritians, 18, 222–223
Inoni, Ephraim, 252, 264
intellectual/professional elites, 19
International Monetary Fund (IMF), 9, 11, 143, 161
Inter-Party Advisory Committee (IPAC), 121, 122
Irukwu, Joe, 288, 296, 297–298
Islamic Sudanese elites. *See* Arab-Islamic

"Sudanese" identity; Sudanese identity construction
Israel, 318
Iyok, David, 252

Ja'aliyiin (Arab tribe), 365, 368
janjaweed militia, 376–377, 379, 380
Jara, Mazibuko, 207
Jenkins, Rob, 218, 241
Johnson, Martha C., 89
Johnson-Sirleaf, Ellen, 51–52
Joint Transition Team (Ghana), 125
Jonas, Mcebisi, 171–172
Jonathan, Goodluck, 297, 300
Joseph, Miranda, 325
Joseph, Richard, 52
Joshi, Devon K., 89
journalism and media, 33, 228, 237–239
Juana, Abubakar, 55
judicial elites (Mauritius), 240. *See also* legal elites
Justice and Equality Movement (JEM), 379–380

Kabye (ethnic group), 95, 98, 99, 104
Kagame, Paul, 42, 43
Kalu, Orji Uzor, 295
Kanu, Ndubuisi, 292, 298
Kanu, Nnamdi, 301
Kapuwa, Patrick, 47
Karefa-Smart, John, 40
Kasenally, Roukaya, 18
Kathrada, Ahmed, 173
Keen, David, 39
Kelsall, Tim, 17, 250, 312
Kenya, 34, 49, 138, 143
Kenyatta, Jomo, 138
Keohane, Robert O., 9
Keur Gui Crew, 150, 151
Khobe, Maxwell, 38
Khrouz, Driss, 64–65
Kiir, Salva, 345–346, 347–348, 359
Kinshasa, Democratic Republic of the Congo, 47–48
Kitschelt, Herbert, 93

kleptocracy (South Sudan), 348
Kok, Peter, 371
Kor, Alor, 347
Kufuor, John, 122, 123, 124, 125, 127, 128
Kyeremanten, Alan, 128
Kymlicka, Will, 366

land ownership: of elites in Mauritius, 221, 222; of elites in South Sudan, 339–342. *See also* South Africa, land rights in
Langa, Pius, 198
Lawyers for Human Rights (South Africa), 189, 202, 204, 209
legal activism, history in South Africa. *See* South Africa, rights debates chronology
legal elites (judicial elites, Mauritius), 240
legal elites (South Africa): Black lawyers as, 192, 193–194, 197–200, 202; struggle lawyers, 188, 190, 192–193, 196, 198–199, 206, 208. *See also* South Africa, land rights in
Legal Resources Centre (South Africa), 189, 201, 202–203, 206, 209
legitimacy claims, 51, 218, 349, 359; through experience of colonialism, 40; through military service, 344. *See also* associational sphere, legitimacy claims (Morocco)
Lenin, Vladimir, 322
Leonardi, Cherry, 345
Lesch, Ann Mosley, 367, 373, 375
Liberal Party (South Africa), 188, 192, 194–195, 200, 208
Liberia, 50–51, 51–52; elections in, 34, 49; MT and, 37, 38; war in, 37, 43
Libya, 379
Limann, Hilla, 117–118
Lindberg, Staffan I., 86, 90, 92, 104
Lloyd, Barbara, 353
Lloyd, P. C., 139, 140
local accountability (South Sudan), 341–342, 343, 344, 349–351, 357, 360. *See also* South Sudanese elites *(beny hakuma)*

local elites (Morocco), 7, 60–81; apoliticism and virtue of, 74–77, 80, 81; "associational elite" qualification, 63–68; autochthony and proximity of, 68–70, 72, 80; existing research on, 60–62; in grassroots organizations, 63, 64; intermediary functioning by, 66, 72, 81; monarchy and, 75, 77–80, 81; in municipal elections, 67, 76–77; oversight of public centers by, 65; professionalization of, 70–74, 80–81; social and economic background of, 65–66, 68–70, 80; volunteer work of, 71, 73–74; women as, 18, 61, 67, 70, 73. *See also* associational sphere, legitimacy claims (Morocco); National Initiative for Human Development (INDH, Morocco)

Lonsdale, John, 189, 254

Macron, Emmanuel, 42, 43
Mahama, Aliu, 128
Mahama, Edward, 123
Mahama, John, 128–129
Mahmoud, Mahgoub El-Tigani, 322
Maigari, Bello Bouba, 257
Maja, Akinola, 317
Majub, Muhammad Ahmad, 372
Makgoba, Thabo, 209–210
"Malaise Creole," 227
Malawi, 7, 137
Malema, Julius, 173–174
Malema Chiefdom, Sierra Leone, 35–36
Malena, Carmen, 228
Mali, 143
Malikane, Chris, 167–168
Malong, Paul, 347–348
Mamdani, Mamood, 189
Mancotywa, Sonwabile, 206–207
Mandela, Nelson, 192, 195, 196
Mangope, Lucas, 197, 203
Mansbridge, Jane, 87
Manson, Andrew, 197
Mantanzima, Kaiser, 194
Marcus, George, 11, 259
Margai, Milton, 40

Marixsm, 5, 6, 145, 225
Matanzima, Kaiser, 191, 193, 196, 199
Matiep, Paulino, 347
Mauritius, 7, 218–241; constitution, 219, 221, 222, 234; corruption in, 220, 226, 227, 228, 229, 231, 233–239; corruption score, 229; democratic strength of, 219, 229, 239; economic history, 219–220; elections in, 223, 224, 225, 229, 231–233, 236–237; elites, collusion among, 220, 230, 235, 239, 240–241; Franco-Mauritians (historical elites), 18, 221, 222, 223–224, 235; geography and history, 218–219; independence gained, 219, 223; Indo-Mauritians, 18, 222–223; media in, 237–238; national unity through power-sharing in, 223–224; phases of elites' establishment and roles in, 221–227; as sugar colony, 219, 220, 221–222, 224. *See also* nonaccountability (Mauritius)

Mauritius Labor Party (MLP), 223, 225
Mauritius Police Force, 239
Mbadiwe, Kingsley, 287
Mbakwe, Sam, 292
Mbeki, Govan, 193
Mbeki, Moeletsi, 162, 169, 173–174, 181, 182
Mbeki, Thabo, 162
Mbelle, Caven Nnoko, 267
Mbembe, Achille, 15, 32–33, 38, 49, 53, 250
Mbenga, Bernard, 197
Mbuagbo, Oben T., 269
Mda Mda, 193, 194
media, 33, 228, 237–239
members of parliament (MPs). *See* parliament (Ghana and Togo); representation theory
memorandum format, 266–267
men, elite formation of, 18. *See also* gender, elite formation and
Mensah, J. H., 128
middle class (Sudan), 370. *See also* class
Middle East, 18
military elites, 19, 117, 163, 164, 343, 344, 347–348

millenarianism, of MT's vision, 34, 39, 40, 43, 44, 53, 54
Mills, C. W., 163, 164, 165
Mills, John Atta, 122, 124, 125, 128
minority groups, representation issues, 87–88, 89; ethnic groups, 90–91, 94, 95, 96, 98–99, 104; in Mauritius, 219. *See also* ethnic groups; women, representation issues
Mirghani family (Sudan), 368
Mkandawire, Thandika, 13, 90, 309–311, 313, 320, 329–331
Mngadi, Elliot, 195, 201
modernity, markers of, 10
Mogoeng Mogoeng, 204
Mohammed VI, king of Morocco, 64, 77–80
Moki, Mbella, 253
Mole-Dagbani (ethnic group), 98, 99
monarchical rule (Morocco), 60, 75, 77–80, 81
Moran, Mary, 51
Morocco, 137; elections in, 61–62, 63, 67, 76. *See also* associational sphere; legitimacy claims (Morocco); local elites (Morocco); National Initiative for Human Development (INDH, Morocco)
Morrison, Minion K. C., 90
Mouvement du 23 juin (Movement June 23), 150
Mouvement Militant Mauricien (MMM), 224–225
Movement for Freedom and Justice (MFJ, Ghana), 119
Movement for the Actualization of the Sovereign State of Biafra (MASSOB), 298–300
Moyn, Samuel, 190
Mozambique, 137
Mpati, Lex, 202
Mqotsi, Livingstone, 193, 196
Msimang, Selby, 195
MT. *See* Tarawalley, Mohammed, Jr. (MT), presidential campaign (Sierra Leone)

multiparty politics, 10–11, 91; in Cameroon, 257, 258, 268, 273; in Ghana, 95, 116–118, 119–120; in Senegal, 145. *See also* party politics
Mundemba Declaration (SWELA), 255–258, 263, 264
Muslim Brotherhood, 374
Muslims, representation issues, 99, 104
Muslim Sudanese elites. *See* Sudanese identity construction
Musonge, Peter Mafany, 263–264

Nambia, 355
narratives, dominant groups' use of, 12, 367
Nassar, Gamal Abdel, 374
National Association of Democratic Lawyers (South Africa), 203
National Audit Office (NAO, Mauritius), 233, 234
National Bank of Nigeria, 317, 319, 320, 323–326. *See also* Action Group (AG, Nigeria)
National Congress Party (NCP, Ghana), 121–122, 123
National Congress Party (NCP, South Sudan), 378, 379, 380–381; as NIF, 374, 375–377
National Council of Nigerian Citizens (NCNC), 313–314, 315, 323, 325, 328
National Democratic Congress (NDC, Ghana), 118–129, 131, 132; contested issues involving, 121–122, 123, 126; elections, 1992, 95, 119; elections, 1996, 95, 124; elections, 2000, 124–125; elections, 2004, 127; elections, 2008, 95, 128; elections, 2012, 95, 128–129; elections, 2016, 129; parliamentary representation by, 95, 96, 97, 98, 99, 104. *See also* Ghana, elite conflict and consensus in
National Electoral Commission (NEC, Nigeria), 292
National Executive Committee (NEC, South Africa), 181

National Human Rights Commission (Mauritius), 233

National Initiative for Human Development (INDH, Morocco), 78, 79; implementation logistics and operations of, 65, 66, 69, 71; local associations increase after formation of, 64, 68, 72; misappropriated funds, 74. *See also* local elites (Morocco)

National Investment and Properties Company (NIPC, Nigeria), 320, 326–329

National Islamic Front (NIF), 374, 375–377; as NCP, 377, 378, 379, 380–381

nationalism: African, 207, 285, 366–368; Igbo, 281, 285; Nigerian, 285; Sudanese, 366–368, 371–373, 377–378. *See also* identity politics

National Liberation Council (Ghana), 117

National Liberation Movement (NLM, Ghana), 116–117

National Party (NP, South Africa), 160–161, 164, 194

National Party of Nigeria (NPN), 290

National Reconciliation Commission (Ghana), 126

National Reform Party (Ghana), 124

National Union for Democracy and Progress (Cameroon), 257

National Union of South African Students (NUSAS), 201

Native Authorities Act (South Africa, 1927), 196

Native Reserves (South Africa), 188, 189, 191, 192, 194–197, 205–206. *See also* Bantustans (South Africa)

Navsa, Mohammed, 202

Ndi, John Fru, 262

Ndondo, Bathandwa, 198–199

Nene, Nhanhla, 170–171

neoliberalism, 6, 9–10, 159; in Mauritius, 226–227; in South Africa, 160, 161–162, 166, 169, 181

neopatrimonialism, 33, 49–50, 53; Mkandawire on, 90, 309, 310–311, 313, 320, 329–330, 331; party-monialism as distinct from, 312

New Elites of Tropical Africa, The (Lloyd), 139

New Patriotic Party (NPP, Ghana), 131, 132; contested issues involving, 125–126; elections, 2000, 95, 124–125; elections, 2004, 95, 127; elections, 2008, 128; elections, 2012, 128–129; elections, 2016, 129; elite conflict and consensus and, 122–129; in Great Alliance, 122, 124; parliamentary representation by, 95, 96, 97, 98, 104

new public management (NPM) reform, 9

Ngcobo, Sandile, 198, 202

Ngubane, Sizani Jean, 201, 207

Ngute, Dion, 264

Niemeyer, Simon, 87

Nietzsche, Friedrich, 8

NIF. *See* National Islamic Front (NIF)

Nigeria, 19, 280–304, 308–331; Coker Commission in, 323–329; democratization of, 291, 293–294, 312, 328–329; educated elite in, 321, 353; geography of, 261; Ghana trade agreements, 126; independence gained, 285; nationalism in, 285; neo-Biafra groups in, 281, 298–302, 303; Nigeria-Biafra War, 285–286, 292; #OurMumudondo protests, 2, 3; statehood creation and resource allocation, 287; structural adjustment programs in, 281, 290–291; student protests, 143; University of Ibadan founded, 137. *See also* Action Group (Nigeria); funding political parties; Igbo (ethnic group); Ohanaeze Ndi-Igbo (Igbo sociocultural group, Nigeria)

Nigeria '93: The Political Crisis and Solutions (Nwabueze), 292

Nigeria Peoples Party (NPP), 290

Nimeiri, Ja'afar, 374–375, 376

Nketia, Asiedu, 128

Nkongho, Victor Arrey, 264

Nkrumah, Kwame, 113, 116, 117, 138, 141
Nkwi, Paul, 269
Nnoli, Okwudibia, 283
nonaccountability (Mauritius), 218, 224, 231–241; horizontal accountability and, 233–237; social accountability and, 237–239; vertical accountability and, 231–233. *See also* ethnicity and class interests of elites (Mauritius); Mauritius
non-European Unity Movement (NEUM, South Africa), 188, 192–194, 196, 199–200, 202, 208–209
nongovernmental organizations (NGOs), 230, 258, 354
Nonkonyana, Mwelo, 206, 207
Norman, Hinga, 38
North Africa, 18
Northern People's Congress (NPC, Nigeria), 313–314, 315, 323, 327
Northern Region government (Nigeria), 313–314
North/South Sudan conflict. *See* Sudan, north/south conflict and civil war
Nouveau type de Sénégalais (New Type of Senegalese), 150
Ntsebeza, Dumisa, 196, 198–199, 203
Ntsebeza, Lungisile, 189, 199, 209
Nwabueze, Benjamin, 287, 292, 293, 294, 296
Nwachukwu, Ike, 295
Nwankwo, Uchenna, 288
Nwanyanwu, Emmanuel, 297
Nwobodo, Jim, 295–296
Nwodo, John Nnia, 298, 301
Nwosisi, Bobo, 292
Nwuanyanwu, Emmanuel, 296
Nyamnjoh, Francis, 269
Nzeribe, Arthur, 291, 293
Nzimiro, Ikenna, 286

Obasanjo, Olusegun, 293, 294, 296
Obioha, Ralph, 292
ocular politics, 33–34, 48, 53–54
O'Fahey, R. S., 368
Ofeimun, Odia, 321

Ohanaeze Ndi-Igbo (Igbo sociocultural group, Nigeria), 280–304; Aka Ikenga in, 281, 291, 298, 299, 303; from civilian-rule era to present, 281, 294–300, 302, 303; during era of military rule, 281, 290–294, 303; formation and early phase of, 281, 287–290, 303; historical context preceding, 284–287; neo-Biafra groups' scrutiny of and assault on, 281, 298–302, 303; project of incorporation by, 283, 302, 303–304. *See also* Igbo (ethnic group)
oil wealth, 345–346, 351
Ojukwu, Chukwuemeka Odumegwu, 288, 290, 295–296
Okigbo, Pius, 287, 292
Okorie, Chekwas, 297
Okpara, Michael, 287, 289
Olivier de Sardan, Jean-Pierre, 9
Omoruyi, Omo, 295
On the Genealogy of Morals (Nietzsche), 8
Onu, Ogbonnaya, 294
Onyeama, Daddy, 287
Oomen, Barbara, 207, 209
Oracle, The (magazine), 256
Osaghae, Eghosa, 282–283
Osei, Anja, 114–115
Osuntokun, Akinjide, 323
#OurMumudondo protests (Nigeria), 2, 3
Oxfam, 159

Padmore, George, 139
Parekh, Jagdish, 171
parliament (Ghana and Togo), 92, 93–106, 114–115; descriptive representation analysis, 86, 93, 94, 96–99, 103–104, 105, 106; national assemblies' composition, categorization of, 95–99, 103–104; research methods for study, 93–95; substantive representation analysis, 100–103, 104–106. *See also* elections (Ghana); representation theory
parliament (Mauritius), 219, 225, 232
participation, 19. *See also* democratic government establishment and operations

participation (Morocco), 68; in associational sphere, 60, 62, 63–64, 67, 71, 77, 80; in leftist movements, 75–76; proximity and, 69–70. See also associational sphere, legitimacy claims (Morocco); local elites (Morocco)
participation, in elections. See elections
participation, of citizens. See social accountability
Parti démocratique sénégalais (Senegalese Democratic Party), 145
party-monialism, 309, 312, 320–321, 331. See also neopatrimonialism
party politics, 14, 232, 315; in Africa broadly, 10–11, 91, 145, 308–309, 310. See also Action Group (AG, Nigeria); funding political parties; multiparty politics; individual political party
Path to Nigerian Freedom (Awolowo), 314–315
Paton, Alan, 194
patronage. See clientelism; corruption
Peasants Revolt, The (Mbeki), 193
Pedagogy of the Oppressed (Freire), 198
Pekkinen, Jennifer, 19
Pélassy, Dominique, 93
Pendle, Naomi, 19
People's Convention Party (PCP, Ghana), 122–123, 125, 126
People's Democratic Party (PDP, Nigeria), 293–294, 295–296, 298
People's National Convention (PNC, Ghana), 96, 123
People's National Party (PNP, Ghana), 117–118
People's Party (Sierra Leone), 34, 35, 36, 39, 47
performance of elitism, 49–50
Peters, Krijn, 39
petitions, 267
Phosa, Matthews, 198
Piketty, Thomas, 159
Pinaud, Clemence, 345, 348
Piot, Charles, 50
Pitkin, Hanna Fenichel, 86, 87, 96

plural democracies, 1, 309
political accountability: in African developmental states, 309; in Cameroon, 250, 253, 254, 255; in Ghana, 115, 117, 131; in Mauritius, 231; in Nigeria, 325–326; scholarship on, 16, 91, 106, 228. See also accountability, defined; elections; nonaccountability (Mauritius)
political activism. See Senegalese politics, student activism in; universities, as political activism path
political aesthetics, 19, 33, 34, 49, 53, 266
Political Domination in Africa: Reflections on the Limits of Power (Chabal), 14–15
political elites, 18–19, 282, 340; in Cameroon, 251, 252, 262–265; horizontal accountability by and for, 227–229, 233–235; social accountability for, 228–229; in South Africa, 164–165, 166–167; vertical accountability for, 228–229. See also elites, defined; local elites (Morocco); South Sudanese elites
political elites (Mauritius), 223, 226, 230; horizontal accountability for, 233–235, 236–237; nomination processes for, 235, 237, 240; social accountability for, 237–239; vertical accountability for, 231–233
political finance. See funding political parties
political liberalizations, 253–254. See also democratic government establishment and operations
political parties, funding. See funding political parties
politics of belonging, 259–261, 268, 269–270
politics of recognition, 253, 261, 267, 272–273
politics of redistribution, 256–257, 267–271, 273. See also development discourse (Cameroon)
Popular Defense Forces (PDF, Sudan), 376
Popular Patriotic Reformation Movement (PPRM), 31, 42, 53, 54–56

populism, 31, 42–43
Positive Black Soul, 150
Posner, Robert D., 91
postcolonial governance characteristics: Ekeh on, 16, 260–261; Mbembe on, 32–33, 38, 53. *See also* colonialism; democratic government establishment and operations; power transfers
poverty, in South Africa. *See* South Africa
power elite (South Africa), 160, 163–167
power transfers: Huntington's two-turnover test, 113, 132; peaceful, in Ghana, 113; postcolonial power consolidation, 145; in Sierra Leone, 40, 41; in South Africa, 161, 163, 167, 168–169, 176. *See also* democratic reversals and stability (Ghana); elections
Pratten, David, 17, 250–251
presidential campaigns. *See* elections; Tarawalley, Mohammed, Jr. (MT), presidential campaign (Sierra Leone); individual candidate
Prevention of Corruption Act (2002, Mauritius), 234
primordial public, 16, 261, 273
Prisoner Welfare Education Programmes (South Africa), 198
Pritchett, Lant, 12
private sector elites (Mauritius), 230, 235, 238. *See also* economic elites
professional elites (Cameroon), 251, 252
protests, 2, 3; in Cameroon, 143; in Ghana, 120, 121; in Mauritius, 224–225; in South Sudan, 366. *See also* Senegalese politics, student activism in; universities, as political activism path
Provisional National Defense Council (PNDC, Ghana), 118, 119
proximity to represented locale, 68–70, 72, 80
Public Accounts Committee (PAC, Mauritius), 233, 234
public and private spheres, Ekeh's "two publics" distinction, 16, 260, 261
public servants. *See* civil servants

race, accountability and, 18
racialization, challenging, 19
racialized wealth distribution. *See* South Africa; wealth
"radical economic transformation" program (South Africa), 166, 168, 173–175, 177–179
radicalism: Bantustan era, South Africa, 196–202; of MT, 31, 41–42, 44, 54–55; neo-Biafran groups, 298, 301, 302; in Nigeria, 298, 301, 302, 311; North-West Cameroon, 263; in Sudan, 322, 382; Unity Movement, 194, 200
Radio Biafra, 301
Ramaphosa, Cyril, 173, 175, 177, 178–179, 182–183
Ramgoolam, Navin, 226
Ramgoolam, Seewoosagur, 223, 224
Ramphele, Mamphela, 198–199
Ramtohul, Ramola, 18
Rawlings, Jerry, 118, 119, 122, 123, 124, 125, 127
Rawlings, Nana Konadu Agyeman, 128
Redistribution and Development Programme (RDP, South Africa), 161
redistribution politics (Cameroon), 256–257, 267–271
Reform Movement (NDC faction, Ghana), 124
regime types. *See* African governments, broad discussions and comparisons; colonialism; democratic government establishment and operations; power transfers
Regional Balance and National Integration (Nkwi and Nyamnjoh), 269
regional elites. *See* local elites (Morocco); South West Elite Association (SWELA, Cameroon)
religion, representation issues, 94, 96, 99, 104. *See also* minority groups, representation issues
religious groups (Mauritius), 219, 230, 236–237. *See also* ethnic groups

religious identity (Sudan). *See* Sudanese identity construction
Reno, William, 44
Reporters Without Borders report, 237
representation issues, 19; age, 89, 94, 96, 97, 103–104; ethnic groups, 90–91, 94, 95, 96, 98–99, 104; gender, 94, 97, 105; material measures of, 254–255; religion, 94, 96, 99, 104; in SWELA's interests, 253; women, 87–88, 89, 96, 97, 101–102, 103–104, 105. *See also* parliament (Ghana and Togo)
representation theory, 85–93; clientelism issue, 86, 90, 91, 92–93, 94; ethnic groups issues, 90–91; issues and debates in, 90–93; research deficit, 86; theory overview, 87–90. *See also* descriptive representation; parliament (Ghana and Togo); substantive representation
reproduction and disruption, 19, 140, 144–145, 153
Republic of the Congo, 137
Revolutionary United Front (RUF), 36, 42, 55
Rewane, Alfred, 317–318
Richards, Paul, 39, 42
rights debates. *See* South Africa, rights debates chronology
riverain Arab tribes. *See* Arab-Islamic "Sudanese" identity; Sudanese identity construction
Roitman, Janet, 38
Rosatom, 170
Rothchild, Donald, 367
Ruedin, Didier, 89
Rural Betterment directives (South Africa), 191, 197
rural communities, South African land rights issues for. *See* South Africa, rights debates chronology
rural elites, 36, 61. *See also* home communities of South Sudanese elites; local elites (Mauritius)
Rwanda, 42, 43, 114

Saddique, Boniface, 126
Salih, M. A. Mohamed, 367
Sall, Macky, 151
Sallah, M. K., 118
Salverda, Tijo, 7, 223
Sane, Aliou, 151
Sangoni, Themba, 198
Sartwell, Crispin, 33
Schroeder, Barbet, 49
Seko, Mobuto Sese, 143
Senegal: elections in, 145–151; University of Dakar founded, 137, 141. *See also* universities; University of Dakar (Cheikh Anta Diop University, Senegal)
Senegalese politics, student activism in, 140–151; political reforms in 1970s, 140, 142; protests in 1968, 140, 141–142; protests in 1987–88, 140, 146–148, 150; Senegalese Democratic Party, 148–151; Socialist Party opposition, 140, 145–148, 152; structural adjustment programs' impacts, 140, 143–144, 146, 150, 152; Wade presidency opposition, 141, 148–151; Wade presidency support, 146–148, 151
Senghor, Leopold, 142, 145–146
sharia law, 374, 376, 378
Sharkey, Heather, 372, 373
Shehu Shagari government (Nigeria), 290
Shia Muslims, 368. *See also* Arab-Islamic "Sudanese" identity; Sudanese identity construction
Shonekan, Ernest, 293
Shonibare, S. O., 318
Shore, Chris, 67, 282
Sierra Leone: Fourah Bay College founded, 137; generation gap in, 34–35, 39–42; PPRM in, 31; 42, 53, 54–56; war history of, 37–38, 39–40. *See also* Tarawalley, Mohammed, Jr. (MT), presidential campaign (Sierra Leone)
Sierra Leone People's Party (SLPP), 34, 35, 36, 39, 47
Siham (Moroccam local elite), 77–79
Sino-Mauritians, 224

Sithole, Owen, 202
Sklar, Richard, 323
slavery, history in Sudan, 369, 372
Sobrinho, Alvaro, 231
social accountability, 9, 12, 17, 220, 227, 228–229, 237–239. *See also* nonaccountability (Mauritius)
social class. *See* class
Social Democratic Front (Cameroon), 262
Socialist Party (Senegal), student opposition to, 140, 145–148, 152
social media, 33, 239
social mobility, 91, 223. *See also* class
Sommers, Marc, 39
South Africa, 19, 45, 159–183; as democracy, 161, 163, 167, 168–169, 176, 204; economic growth in, 168–169; elections in, 161, 165, 172–174, 178–179, 181–182, 204; elite transition stages of, 160–162, 164, 180–181; neoliberalism in, 160, 161–162, 166, 169, 181; party factionalism in, 164, 170, 172–173, 177–178, 181, 182, 195; power elite in, 160, 163–167; Treasury control in, 161, 168, 170–171, 173, 176; University of Cape Town founded, 137; white monopoly capital in, 160, 166, 167–168, 175, 176–180. *See also* African National Congress (ANC, South Africa); Zuma, Jacob
South Africa, land rights in, 188–210; AFRA and, 200–201, 203; Bantustans and, 188–189, 191, 193–194, 196–199, 202–204, 206–207; Black Consciousness Movement and, 188, 199–200, 208; Christian humanitarianism and, 190, 195; communal shift in, 204–208; current policy issues, 190; defining rights and freedoms, 190, 198, 205–208; forced removals, 190, 191, 195, 197, 200, 203, 205; human rights organizations and, 189, 190, 200–201, 202–204; land restitution processes, 189, 190, 201, 205; legal elites' relationship with clients, 190, 191, 192, 193–194; Liberal Party and, 194–195, 200, 208; peasants' rights in, 191, 193, 198, 208; postcolonial "legal pluralism" and, 189; rural revolts issues, 191; struggle lawyers and, 188, 190, 192–193, 196, 198–199, 206, 208; student activism on, 200–201; Unity Movement and, 188, 192–194, 196, 199–200, 202, 208–209. *See also* chiefdom, traditional (South Africa)
South Africa, rights debates chronology, 188–210; in mid-twentieth century, 188, 191–196, 208; in 1970s Bantustans, 188, 196–202, 208–209; in apartheid's final decade, 189, 202–204, 209; postapartheid era, 189, 204–208, 209
South African Communist Party (SACP), 162, 169, 175, 181
Southall, Roger, 18
South Sudan. *See* Sudan, north/south conflict and civil war
South Sudanese elites *(beny hakuma)*, 19, 342–361; *beny hakuma* term, 345; cattle investment, 344, 349–352, 360; church building, 344, 357–360; education and, 344, 353–357, 360; financial capacity in preserving elite status, 348; home communities' importance, 344–349; legitimacy and, 349, 359; local accountability, 341–342, 343, 344, 349–351, 357, 360; military elites, 343, 344, 347–348; physical distance issues, 341–342, 344, 346; social distance issues, 344–345; violence and, 343, 346–347, 360. *See also* home communities of South Sudanese elites
South West Elite Association (SWELA, Cameroon), 251–268, 273; claim-making politics and, 255, 256, 261, 265, 267, 270; form and mission of, 259–262; "Mega Forum" event, 252–253; membership criteria and operations of, 251–252, 259, 260; memorandums by, 262–268; Mundemba Declaration, 255–258, 263, 264. *See also* Cameroon
spectacle, 49–50

Stark, Frank, 270, 271
state, formation of. *See* African governments, broad discussions and comparisons; colonialism; democratic government establishment and operations; power transfers
state capture, 2, 19, 168–171, 173, 179, 182
Stevens, Siaka, 36, 40
structural adjustment programs, 11, 142; in Morocco, 64; in Nigeria, 281, 290–291; in Senegal, 140, 143–144, 146, 150, 152
struggle lawyers, 188, 190, 192–193, 196, 198–199, 206, 208
student activism, 143; land rights in South Africa and, 200–201. *See also* Senegalese politics, student activism in; universities, as political activism path
substantive representation, 86, 91–95, 100–103, 104–106; defined, 87, 88. *See also* parliament (Ghana and Togo); representation theory
Sudan, 19, 322; Anglo-Egyptian rule in, 339, 351, 353, 369, 373, 374; *Bilad al-Sudan* name, 372, 382; elections in, 349, 361, 375; Turco-Egyptian invasions, 369, 373
Sudan, north/south conflict and civil war, 343, 344–348, 359–361; Addis Ababa Agreement and, 374–375; Arabization policies, 373, 375–377, 381; British unification declaration, 371–373, 382; CPA and, 340, 345–346, 378; Darfur region and, 378–380, 382–383; Islamization policies, 374–377; military forces in, 376–377, 379; nationalism and, 367, 371–373, 377–378; "New Sudan" vision, 377–378; northern elites, 367, 371–373, 378, 381–382; southern elites, 340, 345–346, 350–351, 353–354; southern exclusion, 370–371, 378, 382
Sudanese identity construction, 365–383; after independence, 373–380; citizenship in, 373; during colonial era, 369–371, 373, 381, 382; consequences on Sudanese state, 380–382; in Darfur, 378–380, 382–383; divisions outlined, 367–368; end of civil war and, 377–378; ethnicity in, 366–368; historical background, 369–380; Islamization policies' effects on, 374–375; nationalism and, 366–368, 371–373; NIF/NCP importance in, 375–377, 380–381; north/south divisions, 365, 367, 370–371, 373; slavery and, 369, 372. *See also* Arab-Islamic "Sudanese" identity
Sudan People's Liberation Army (SPLA), 340, 344, 348, 379–380
Sudan People's Liberation Movement (SPLM), 340, 377–378
Sufism, 368, 382
sugar colony, Mauritius as, 219, 220, 221–222, 224
Sunni Muslims, 368. *See also* Arab-Islamic "Sudanese" identity; Sudanese identity construction
Sursaut National (Togo), 96
Swidler, Annand, 7
symbolic representation, 87

Tafawa-Balewa, Abubakar, 314
Taiwo, Olufemi, 10
Tambo, Oliver, 192
Tarawalley, Lamine, 41
Tarawalley, Mohammed, Jr. (MT), presidential campaign (Sierra Leone), 31–56; "bush paths" in, 34, 35–39; generation gap in Sierra Leone and, 34–35, 39–42; outsider positioning, 31–32; performance of state subversion in, 35, 42–52; personal history of MT, 36–38; political aesthetics and, 33, 34, 49, 53; PPRM and, 31, 42, 53, 54–56; violence and security and, 49–52; wartime activity of MT, 37–38. *See also* Sierra Leone
tariqas (Muslim religious fraternities), 368
task definition, of parliamentary representatives, 94–95, 100–103
Taylor, Charles, 43, 50–51, 52, 253
Terreblanche, Sampie, 161

Thiat (Keur Gui Crew member), 151
Tignor, Robert L., 324–325
Titanji, Vincent P. K., 266
Tlakula, Pansy, 204
Tofa, Alhaji Bashir, 291
Togo, 50. *See also* parliament (Ghana and Togo)
Toulabor, Comi, 15
Tozy, Mohamed, 61
traditional rulers. *See* chiefdom, traditional; ethnic groups
Transkei Territories (first South African Bantustan), 191, 192–193, 194, 197
Transnet, 170
Transparency International, 229
Traore, Moussa, 143
Trump, Donald, 43
Tsotsi, Wycliffe, 193, 196

Udorji, Jerome, 287
Uganda, 16, 49, 137, 356
Umkhonto we Sizwe (MK), 164
Union démocratique des etudiants sénégalaise (Democratic Union of Senegalese Students), 141
Union des Forces de Changement (UFC, Togo), 96
Union nationale des travailleurs du Sénégal (National Union of Senegalese Workers), 141
Union pour la Republique (UNIR, Togo), 96, 97, 99, 104
Union progressiste sénégalaise (political party), 145
United Gold Coast Convention (UGCC, Ghana), 112, 115, 116
United National Convention (Ghana), 118
United Nations (UN), 9
United Nations Convention Against Corruption (2003), 233
United Party (UP, Ghana), 117
United States: elections in, 34, 43; rise in capitalist power, 1950s, 163
Unity Movement (South Africa), 188, 192–194, 196, 199–200, 202, 208–209

Unity Party (Sierra Leone), 54–56
universities, 137–153; as elite formation path, 138–140, 143–144, 152–153; founded in Africa, historical overview, 137–140. *See also* education
universities, as political activism path, 138–153; colonialism opposition fomented in, 138–139; in Europe, 139; postcolonial power opposition fomented in, 139; revolutionary leaders' educations, 138–139. *See also* Senegalese politics, student activism in
University of Benin, 137, 143
University of Dakar (Cheikh Anta Diop University, Senegal): academic year 1987-88 cancelled, 150; as activism nexus, 147–148, 150–151, 152; admissions and size of student body, 141, 148–149; demographic history of, 141; founding of, 137, 141, 152; government raid in 1988, 147. *See also* Senegalese politics, student activism in
University of Zimbabwe, 137, 143
Uwazurike, Goddy, 299, 300
Uwazuruike, Ralph, 298
Uwechue, Ralph, 292

value-added tax (VAT) system (Ghana), 121
van de Walle, Nicolas, 90
van Rooyen, Desmond, 170–171, 176
van Vliet, Martin, 86, 92, 104
Venda (Bantustan), 197
vertical accountability, 220, 227–229, 231–233
violence, 19; following Islamization policies in Sudan, 374–375; MT and security in Sierra Leone, 49–52; in South Sudan, 343, 346–347, 360. *See also* war
voting. *See* elections; representation
vulgar aesthetics, 32, 49, 50, 53

Wade, Abdoulaye, 145, 146–151; students' opposition to, 141, 148–151; students' support for, 146–148, 151

Wade, Karim, 149
wages. *See* financial compensation; income
Wahman, Michael, 104
Walker, Cherryl, 200–201, 205
Wang, Yikai, 114
war, 19; in Liberia, 37, 43; Nigeria-Biafra War, 285–286, 292; in Sierra Leone, 37–38, 39–40. *See also* Sudan, north/south conflict and civil war
warlord politics and big-man era, 43, 44–45, 49, 52, 53, 163, 164
Watkins, Susan C., 7
waves of political liberalizations, 10, 19
Weah, George, 51
wealth, 50; cattle in South Sudan and, 349–352; income inequality, 7, 149, 159, 180, 183, 220; MT's goals, 43–44; national wealth management, in Cameroon, 272; oil wealth of South Sudan government, 345–346, 351; white monopoly capital (South Africa), 160, 166, 167–168, 175, 176–180. *See also* financial compensation; income; South Africa
wealth, racialized distribution of (South Africa). *See* South Africa
Werbner, Richard, 8, 249, 311
Western Region government (Nigeria), 309, 311, 313, 314. *See also* Action Group (Nigeria)
Western Region Marketing Board (WRMB, Nigeria), 320, 327–328
white elites (Mauritius), 224, 226
white monopoly capital (South Africa), 160, 166, 167–168, 175, 176–180
whiteness, income and social inequality and, 7

white South Africans, 18
women, elite formation of: Dlamini-Zuma, in South Africa, 172–173, 175, 177–179; in Morocco, 18, 61, 67, 70, 73; South African land rights activism and, 201; in SWELA, 251. *See also* gender, elite formation and
women, representation issues, 87–88; in democratic *vs.* authoritarian regimes, 89, 96, 97, 101–102, 103–104, 105
World Bank, 9, 11, 143, 148, 161
World Food Programme, 354
Wretched of the Earth, The (Fanon), 138

Y'en a marre (I'm Fed Up, or Enough Is Enough), 150, 151
Yoon, Mi Yung, 87, 89
Yoruba (ethnic group), 7, 283, 284, 287, 313. *See also* Igbo (ethnic group)
Young, Daniel J., 90
youth. *See* age
Yugoslavia, 114

Zaire, 143
Zeilig, Leo, 139, 143
Zimbabwe, 137, 143
Zuma, Duduzane, 171
Zuma, Jacob, 164, 167, 168–177, 179, 181–182; Gupta brothers association with, 2, 18, 170–173, 175–176, 182; patronage and corruption reputation, 2, 169–170, 171–172, 175; "radical economic transformation," 168, 173–174, 175, 177. *See also* African National Congress (ANC, South Africa)
Zuma Must Fall campaign (South Africa), 2, 3